Humphrey Llwyd

CRONICA WALLIAE

Humphrey Llwyd

CRONICA WALLIAE

Edited with Introduction and Notes

by IEUAN M. WILLIAMS

and J. BEVERLEY SMITH

UNIVERSITY OF WALES PRESS
CARDIFF

© *Cronica Walliae* University of Wales Press, 2016

© Introduction, Estate of Ieuan M. Williams 2016

The present volume was prepared for publication by J. Beverley Smith

First published in 2002 (hardback)

www.uwp.co.uk

British Library Cataloguing-in-Publication Data
A catalogue record for this book is available from the British Library.

ISBN 9781783169481

Printed and bound by CPI Group (UK) Ltd, Croydon, CR0 4YY

CONTENTS

PREFACE

The presentation in this volume of the text of the 'Cronica Walliae' marks the first appearance in published form of the history of Wales written by the humanist scholar Humphrey Llwyd in 1559. The edition is the result of studies pursued by the late Professor Ieuan M. Williams over several years, work which was virtually completed when he died on 20 January 2000. Professor Williams had returned to the study of the sixteenth-century historians of Wales, a subject on which he had been engaged many years earlier, upon his retirement from the chair of Adult Education at the University of Wales, Swansea, in 1983, concentrating his efforts upon the preparation of a critical edition of Llwyd's main historical work. Humphrey Llwyd's 'Cronica Walliae' was the first account of the history of Wales to be written in English but, although manuscripts of his work became known among contemporary scholars, it was never published. His work then formed the basis of David Powel's *History of Cambria*, published in 1584, but the precise nature of Llwyd's contribution has never been fully recognized. The appearance of this edition, prepared by a scholar who greatly respected Humphrey Llwyd's erudition, and who was moved by the cultured patriotism that inspired his work, will ensure that Llwyd's contribution to the foundation of modern Welsh historiography will be better appreciated than it has been hitherto.

In preparing the volume for the press care has been taken to adhere to the editorial method that Professor Williams adopted. His main concern was to establish from the surviving manuscripts, not one of which is in the author's hand, a text that approximates as closely as possible to Llwyd's work. In the introduction to the volume Professor Williams provides a detailed examination of the author's use of his source materials. By doing so he has been able to identify the historical texts to which Llwyd had access during the preparation of the history and to consider his method of working, and he thereby provides an invaluable discussion of the composition of both the introductory Description of Wales and the narrative of the history of Wales which forms the main part of the work. This in turn enables him to bring out the underlying themes that mark Humphrey Llwyd's distinctive and immensely influential contribution to Welsh historical studies. If ill health had not hindered his efforts Professor Williams might have added an assessment of Llwyd's work, but he was pleased that he had been able to complete the discussion that he regarded as the essential complement to the presentation of a definitive text of the history. Matters noticed in the introduction are often elaborated, along with the elucidation of textual problems, in the notes which follow the text. In both introduction and notes some added reference is made to writings, and especially recent contributions, that have a direct bearing upon the discussion, but no attempt has been made to extend the editorial discussion to any significant extent.

The progress of Professor Williams's editorial work and the completion of what remained was eased considerably by the kindness of several scholars and their help is gratefully acknowledged. Particular thanks are due to Michael Borrie and Claire Bray at the British Library, Timothy Hobbes at Trinity College, Cambridge, and Daniel Huws and Alwyn Roberts at the National Library of Wales. Andrew Boyle kindly provided the benefit of his close acquaintance with the archives at Arundel Castle. During the preparation of the volume for publication the text was checked against the original manuscript that Professor Williams chose as the basic text, NLW Llanstephan MS 177, by Nia Henson and Karen Andrews, who were engaged to do so by the Board of Celtic Studies of the University of Wales, and who completed the work with meticulous attention to detail. Our gratitude is also due to Susan J. Davies who offered valuable guidance during the course of the work. The texts of the Latin verse in the 'Cronica Walliae' present some difficulty, and we are grateful to Telfryn Pritchard whose careful reading made it possible to eliminate obvious scribal errors without attempting to establish a substantially revised text. A particular debt of gratitude is owed to Professor Geraint Gruffydd who, over many years and especially during the later stages of the work, drew on his knowledge of Humphrey Llwyd and his contemporaries to provide most valuable guidance. Daniel Huws was also able to provide advice on matters that arose during the final revision of the text. The considerable labour of preparing a word-processed text was largely borne by Jean Matthews, to whom our warmest thanks are due. Janet Davies undertook the formidable task of preparing the index and it is a pleasure to record her most helpful contribution. At the University of Wales Press, who undertook publication on behalf of the Board of Celtic Studies, thanks are due to the Director, Susan Jenkins, and to Ceinwen Jones and her colleagues who completed the production of the volume with exemplary care and unfailing courtesy.

Professor Williams would, most of all, wish to express his deepest gratitude to his wife, Gwen, his loving companion for over fifty years, for her selfless devotion, her constant care and her innumerable acts of practical assistance. Ieuan and Gwen together would also wish to record their great debt of gratitude to their daughter, Nia, and her husband, Eric Roderick, for their love and solicitude over the years. Sustained by the support of his family, Professor Williams, showing exceptional fortitude in his determined pursuit of his studies during years of failing health, was able to complete a task that had brought him much joy and fulfilment during his retirement.

J. Beverley Smith
Aberystwyth, May 2002

ABBREVIATIONS

AC	*Annales Cambriae*
ASCh	*Anglo-Saxon Chronicle*
ArchCamb	*Archaeologia Cambrensis*
BBB	The Black Book of Basingwerk (NLW MS 7006)
BBCS	*Bulletin of the Board of Celtic Studies*
BL	British Library
Brut	*Brut y Tywysogyon*
BS	*Brenhinedd y Saesson or The Kings of the Saxons*, ed. T. Jones (Cardiff, 1971)
BT	*Brut y Tywysogyon*
C	BL, Cotton Caligula MS Avi
CPR	*Calendar of Patent Rolls*
CM	*Mathaei Paris Chronica Majora*, ed. H. R. Luard, 7 vols. (London, Rolls Series, 1872–84)
CW	'"Cronica de Wallia" and other documents from Exeter Cathedral Library MS 3514', ed. T. Jones, *BBCS*, 12 (1946–8), 27–44
Descr. Kambriae	*Descriptio Kambriae, Giraldi Cambrensis Opera*, vi, ed. J. F. Dimock (London, Rolls Series, 1868)
DWB	*Dictionary of Welsh Biography to 1940* (London, 1959)
EHR	*English Historical Review*
Giraldus Cambrensis, Opera	*Giraldi Cambrensis Opera*, ed. J. S. Brewer, J. F. Dimock and G. F. Warner, 8 vols. (London, Rolls Series, 1861–91)
HC (1584)	*The Historie of Cambria now called Wales . . . Written in the British Language . . . translated into English by H. Lhoyd Gentlemen, corrected, augmented and continued by David Powel* (London 1584; reprinted Amsterdam and New York, 1969)
HC (1811)	*The Historie of Cambria now called Wales . . . Written in the British Language . . . translated into English by H. Lhoyd, corrected by David Powel* (London, 1811).
HH	Henry, Archdeacon of Huntingdon, *Historia Anglorum. The History of the English People*, ed. and trans., D. Greenway (Oxford, 1996)
HistAng	*Matthaei Paris Historia Minor, 1067–1253*, ed. F. Madden, 3 vols. (London, Rolls Series, 1866–9)

HW	J. E. Lloyd, *A History of Wales from the Earliest Times to the Edwardian Conquest* (London, 1911)
Itin. Kambriae	*Itinerarium Kambriae, Giraldi Cambrensis Opera*, vi, ed. J. F. Dimock (London, Rolls Series, 1868)
Ll	NLW, Llanstephan MS 177
MA	*The Myvyrian Archaiology of Wales*, ed. O. Jones, E. Williams and O. Pughe (Denbigh, 1870)
N	NLW MS 23202B
NLW	National Library of Wales
NT	*Nicholai Triveti, Annales*, ed. T. Hog (London, English Historical Society, 1845)
OP	*The Description of Penbrokeshire, by George Owen of Henllys*, ed. H. Owen, 4 vols. (London, 1902–36)
PBA	*Proceedings of the British Academy*
Pen20	*Brut y Tywysogyon Peniarth MS 20*, ed. T. Jones (Cardiff, 1941)
Pen20Tr	*Brut y Tywysogyon, or the Chronicle of the Princes, Peniarth MS 20 Version, Translation and Notes*, ed. T. Jones (Cardiff, 1952)
RBH	*Brut y Tywysogyon, or the Chronicle of the Princes, Red Book of Hergest Version*, ed. T. Jones (Cardiff, 1955)
RCAHMW	Royal Commission on the Ancient and Historical Monuments of Wales
RW	*Roger of Wendover, Flores Historiarum*, ed. H. G. Hewlett, 3 vols. (London, Rolls Series, 1896–9)
THSC	*Transactions of the Honourable Society of Cymmrodorion*
TYP	*Trioedd Ynys Prydein*, ed. R. Bromwich (Cardiff, 1961)
WHR	*Welsh History Review*

INTRODUCTION

The basic biography of Humphrey Llwyd was compiled by Anthony Wood in his *Athenae Oxoniensis* of 1691–2. More recent accounts of Llwyd's brief life, *c.*1527–68, make extensive repetition here unnecessary and a summary account will suffice.[1] Humphrey Llwyd was born in Denbigh about 1527, the only child of Robert Llwyd of Denbigh and his wife Joan Piggott. He was admitted at Oxford, graduating BA in 1547/8 and MA (from Brasenose College) in 1551. Two years later he entered the service of Henry Fitzalan, earl of Arundel (d. 1580),[2] and, although his exact functions in the household are unclear, his presence among those who served the earl is well attested among documents in the Arundel Castle archives and in other sources.[3] His main duties may be uncertain but it is known that he spent much of his time helping to bring together Arundel's splendid library at Nonsuch.[4] He served as Member of Parliament for East Grinstead in 1559, and as the Member for the Denbigh Boroughs in 1563. He was probably by then residing

[1] *DWB*, 594; Ieuan M. Williams, 'Ysgolheictod hanesyddol yn yr unfed ganrif ar bymtheg', *Llên Cymru*, 2 (1952–3), 111–24, 209–23; R. Geraint Gruffydd, 'Humphrey Llwyd of Denbigh: some documents and a catalogue', *Transactions of the Denbighshire Historical Society*, 17 (1968), 54–107; 18 (1969), 178–9.

[2] For a discussion of the reasons for accepting 1553 as the date at which he joined Arundel's household, see Williams, 'Ysgolheictod hanesyddol', 111. There appears to be no evidence to sustain the date of 1558 indicated in S. Jayne and F. R. Johnson, *The Lumley Library: The Catalogue of 1609* (London, 1956), 6. Llwyd's connection with Arundel is noticed in M. McKisack, *Medieval History in the Tudor Age* (Oxford, 1971), 54.

[3] Andrew Boyle, research scholar at Lincoln College, Oxford, presently engaged on a study of Henry Fitzalan, earl of Arundel (d. 1580), who was consulted at the kind suggestion of Dr J. M. Robinson, archivist and librarian to His Grace the Earl of Norfolk, in a very generous reply to an inquiry has confirmed that there are no household records at Arundel Castle for the period of Humphrey Llwyd's service, but that his presence is indicated in several records. Llwyd and David Gogh were appointed the earl's attorneys to deliver seisin of Arundel Place in the Strand to Sir Thomas Palmer and William St Alban for the use of the earl and countess on 8 September 1556 (Arundel Castle Archives MX/50); on 1 April 1559 Arundel granted a lease of the manor of Hayling, Hampshire, to Lord Lumley, who leased it to Llwyd and Thomas Stoughton, and in 1562 they granted a lease to Ralph Henslowe (Arundel Castle Archives MD 495, ff. 1–32; GE/6, A 252 and Sandbeck Park EMA 1/5); Llwyd and Stoughton were also the earl's feoffees in transactions concerning manors in Sussex in 1564–5 (*CPR, 1563–65*, 138, 309). Mr Boyle's kindness in supplying these references, which provide firm evidence of Llwyd's service in the period 1556–65, including the period in which he wrote the 'Cronica Walliae', is greatly appreciated. For Llwyd's service see further, below, p. 2.

[4] The association of Llwyd and Lord Lumley in the development of the library at Nonsuch, Surrey, is discussed in Jayne and Johnson, *Lumley Library*, 6; Williams, 'Ysgolheictod hanesyddol', 112, 116–17.

mainly at Denbigh and was married to Barbara, sister of Lord Lumley, who was Arundel's son-in-law, and he was addressed as 'Humphrey Llwyd of Denbigh' in a eulogy by Gruffudd Hiraethog in 1563.[5] He is credited, while Member for Denbigh, with facilitating the passage of the Bill for the translating of the Bible and the Book of Common Prayer into Welsh.[6] In 1566–7 he attended Arundel on a continental tour, visiting Italy, Germany and the Netherlands. In the Netherlands he made the acquaintance of Abraham Ortelius, the Antwerp geographer, and upon his return prepared two maps, one a map of Wales, for inclusion in Ortelius's *Theatrum Orbis Terrarum*.[7] Llwyd died at Denbigh on 21 August 1568 and was buried in the north aisle of the parish church, Llanfarchell or Eglwys Wen (Whitchurch), where a memorial was erected in his memory.[8]

Professor Geraint Gruffydd has argued convincingly to dispel the view, generally held since Wood's biography, that Llwyd had studied medicine at Oxford, had translated into English two Latin medical works, and had joined the household of Henry Fitzalan, earl of Arundel, as medical adviser.[9] Of the works safely attributable to Llwyd, two are no longer extant. The first, 'An Almanacke and Kalender, conteynynge the daye houre, and mynute of the change of the Moone for ever . . .', Llwyd's earliest work, is known only from a description of it in a letter by Robert Davies of Llannerch near St Asaph. The second, 'Augustine Nyphus auguries, or divinations, translated into English by Humfrey Flood, manuscript, Gallice', described thus in the 1609 catalogue of the Lumley Library, was a translation by Llwyd from Augustino Nifo's *De Auguriis libri duo*, possibly working from the French version published at

---

[5] P. W. Hasler, *The History of Parliament: The House of Commons 1558–1603*, 3 vols (London, 1981), II, 481–2; below, p. 8. For the eulogy, *Gwaith Gruffudd Hiraethog*, ed. D. J. Bowen (Cardiff, 1990), no. 28.

[6] Gruffydd, 'Humphrey Llwyd', 54; Peter R. Roberts, 'Tudor legislation and the political status of "the British tongue"', in G. H. Jenkins (ed.), *The Welsh Language before the Industrial Revolution* (Cardiff, 1997), 145, quoting Gruffudd Hiraethog.

[7] For Llwyd's maps see F. J. North, 'Humphrey Llwyd's maps of England and Wales', *ArchCamb*, XCII (1937), 11–63.

[8] Llwyd's letter to Ortelius of 23 August 1568, his will, dated two days later, and his epitaph are published in Gruffydd, 'Humphrey Llwyd', 99–104. For the portrait of Llwyd, 1561, which appears as the frontispiece to this volume, his memorial in the church of Llanfarchell, and his map of Wales, see Peter Lord, *Imagining the Nation*, The Visual Culture of Wales (Cardiff, 2000), 26–7, 37–8 (nos. 29, 30, 50).

[9] Ibid., 56–7. Professor Gruffydd argues that the translation of the medical works should be attributed to Humphrey Lloyd of Leighton, co. Montgomery, who was in the service of Henry Stafford, first Baron Stafford (d. 1563), to whom one of the works is dedicated.

Lyons in 1546.[10] Another five works can be attributed to Llwyd, four of
which were published. All four are mainly chorographical and include
the two maps Llwyd prepared for his friend Abraham Ortelius:
'Cambriae typus', a pioneer map of Wales, and 'Angliae regni
florentissimi nova descriptio', a map of England and Wales. Both were
sent to Ortelius on 3 August 1568, together with Llwyd's *Commentarioli
Britannicae Descriptionis Fragmentum*, a brief historical and geographical
account of England, Scotland and Wales. This was published in Cologne
in 1572 and translated by Thomas Twyne as *The Breuiary of Britayne* in
1573. At Ortelius's request, Llwyd had also sent to him on 5 April 1568
a letter, 'De Mona druidum insula . . . Epistola', dealing mainly with the
name and antiquities of Anglesey. This was published in Ortelius's atlas,
Theatrum Orbis Terrarum (Antwerp, 1570), and also by Richard Prise,
after the death of his father Sir John Prise, in his edition of his father's
work, *Historiae Brytannicae Defensio* (London, 1573).[11] Llwyd's earliest
and by far his largest extant work, however, which he completed in
1559, is a translation into English of what he describes as an account of
the lives and acts of the kings and princes of Wales from Cadwaladr to
Llywelyn ap Gruffudd, the last native Welsh prince. This is his sole
surviving work written in English and his only mainly historical work.
Its writing clearly helped to stimulate his interest in place-names and
natural features, and he introduced at the beginning (f. 2) the 'perfecte
discription of the Countrey as hit was in olde tyme and as hit is at thees
dayes' so that the reader could better understand the historical account
which followed. This work was the basis for David Powel's *Historie of
Cambria* published in 1584, a quarter of a century after Llwyd's death,
but it has not otherwise been published except as a revision or reprint of
Powel's work.[12] Powel explains his editorial process in his preface, but it
is shown later in these pages that many of the changes he made cannot in
fact be identified without direct comparison with Llwyd's own work,
and that the uncritical acceptance hitherto of Powel's rendering has
given rise to much misrepresentation, in some instances possibly quite
serious, of Llwyd's work.

[10] Ibid., 55–6.
[11] *Commentarioli Britannicae Descriptionis Fragmentum* (Cologne, 1572); this work, along
with 'De Mona druidum insula . . . epistola', was republished by Moses Williams as H.
Llwyd, *Britannicae Descriptionis Commentariolium necnon De Mona Insula et Britannica Arce*
(London, 1731). For the translation of the *Commentarioli . . . Fragmentum*, T. Twyne, *The
Breuiary of Britayne* (London, 1573).
[12] Below nn.40–1.

I Manuscripts of the 'Cronica Walliae'

Five manuscript copies of this work are known to exist, none of them in Llwyd's handwriting.[13] These can be described briefly as follows:

MS 1 BL, Cotton Caligula MS Avi (MS C in this edition)
This was the best known to earlier writers on Llwyd. The text is preceded by a colophon in the hand of Sir Robert Cotton, 'Cronica Walliae a Rege Cadwalader ad an(num) 1294 Humfredo Floid authore', giving rise to the name 'Cronica Walliae' by which Llwyd's text is nowadays commonly known. Another colophon at the end of the text (f. 221), 'At London 1559 by Humphrey Lloyd', is also in the hand of Sir Robert Cotton. It seems likely that the manuscript came into the possession of Dr John Dee in 1575. The numerous marginal annotations are mostly in his hand and so is the latter part of the text itself, ff. 192–22lv.[14] Folio 42, containing verses beginning 'Tri mab oedd y Rodri mewn tremyn y kaid', has been added to the manuscript, again probably by Dee; a note alongside the English translation of the verse reads: 'Morice Kyphin did thus trans[late] them 1578 Feb. 12 after my cosen Thomas Griffith had geven me . . .'.[15] Another insertion, f. 218, contains a translation into English of the verse beginning 'Dowed i wyr Gwynedd galon galed' which has been added in the margin of f. 217v.[16] The numbering of folios has been altered more than once to incorporate these additions and other changes;[17] and at ff. 89–96v there has been a serious misplacing of folios including some duplication of textual matter.[18] The final numbering throughout is in a more modern script.

---

[13] Others, notably Trinity College Cambridge MS 0.10.18, bear some resemblance to the MSS described, but are not reproduced from Llwyd.

[14] There are noticeably fewer annotations in this section and instances occur of improvement or modernization of the spelling of Welsh place-names, for example Ll, f. 198 Oswestreye, Cardiff, Blaenllynfi, Llandilo Vawr. Dee's original for this section implies the existence of another copy of Llwyd's MS, which might or might not be the one received from Sir Henry Sidney. For Dee's possession of the MS, see MS 2.

[15] See n.19 below; see also note f. 36v; notes in this form refer to the textual notes printed at the end of the text.

[16] See note f. 223.

[17] After an ambiguous beginning, ff. 2–40 are deleted and altered to 3–41; ff. 43–7 have a difference of two to incorporate the additional f. 2. The next two, numbered in the same sequence, have been crossed through as a deletion because the text is then repeated, though the folio numbering remains unbroken, but with a difference of four, changing for no apparent reason to a difference of five, ff. 54–80, reverting to a difference of four, ff. 81–8, after which occurs the misplacing of ff. 89–96v.

[18] See note ff. 80v–85v.

MS 2 Bodleian Library, Ashmole MS, 847
The manuscript was copied by Robert Glover, Somerset Herald, from
MS 1, sometime after 1578. A note on the title page, 'This booke was
gyven to Mr J. D[ee] of Mortlake by his cousyn Mr Olyver Lloyd of the
Welsh Pole 1575', obviously written after 1578, must refer to Glover's
original, BL Cotton Caligula MS Avi (MS 1). Dee's marginal notes and
inserts in the Cotton Caligula MS have been copied by Glover. Powel
saw the Ashmole 847 manuscript.[19]

MS 3 BL MS 48090 (Yelverton MS 99), ff. 4–105v
This is a copy of MS 2.

MS 4 NLW, Llanstephan MS 177 (MS Ll in this edition)[20]
Llwyd's text (ff. 1–227v) bears no title, but will continue to be referred
to as 'Cronica Walliae'. It is preceded by a copy of 'Kyfrinach y Beirdd',
a grammatical treatise, which follows a folio bearing two verses
attributed to Iolo Goch, then the words 'John ap D'd ap R'c toke
possetion upon theyrsdaye beyng the XXjth of Majj the XV yere of the
Rayng of our quene Elizabeth 1573 in the hande of Ieuan ap Dav' ap
Jankyn[21] thys beyng wyttenessed Gryffythe mechen, John ap Owen,
Gryffyth ap holl, Robart ap John Rondell, thomas Hirllayd . . .'. The
reference on f. 228v to 'Richard Middleton de Castro Chircko', who
died in 1575, could be taken to strengthen an assumption that the
manuscript as it stands was put together before Dee received either his
incomplete copy in 1575 or Glover's transcript in 1578. As a copy of the
'Cronica Walliae' this manuscript is complete with the exception of the
Latin verse epitaph to Alfred (though the space left blank in f. 40
indicates the intention to include it) and, on f. 165, of the original Welsh

[19] Dee's marginal note in BL, Cott. Cal. MS Avi, f. 42 is rendered by Robert Glover as
'Morice Kyphin did thus translate them 12 Februarii 1578 after Thomas Griffith had geven
them to Mr J. Dee of Mortlake his cousyn' (Williams, 'Ysgolheictod hanesyddol', 113);
HC (1584), [v–vi]; 1811, xiii.
[20] This manuscript and MS 5 (NLW 2302B) are described in W. Marx, *The Index of
Middle English Prose. Handlist XIV: Manuscripts of the National Library of Wales* (Cambridge,
1999), 69, with references to earlier notices.
[21] The suggestion in *Pen20Tr*, l, n.2 that this was the son of Dafydd ap Jenkin
Amrhedydd (not Ieuan ap Dafydd ap Jenkin as given in the note, which has been suitably
amended in *RBH*, xii, n.1) who transcribed NLW, Mostyn MS 159, is possible but
unlikely, not only because the father's copy was made twenty-eight years later than 1559,
in 1587, but also in view of the likelihood that the copyist of NLW, Llanstephan MS 177
(as of BL, Cott. Cal. MS Avi) was unfamiliar with the Welsh tongue (below, p. 8). In any
case the list of witnesses suggests that the quoted declaration would relate more
appropriately to another MS, perhaps a law MS, than to Llanstephan 177.

of the verses which in Cotton Caligula MS Avi begin 'Gwae'r offeriad byd', though again the blank space on the lower section of the folio points to the intention to place it immediately before the English translation on the following page.[22] The folio numbering throughout is remarkably clear and straightforward; signs of later interference are few in the manuscript as a whole. The text in the present edition is based on this manuscript.

MS 5 NLW 23202 B (MS N in this edition)
This manuscript came to light comparatively recently and was purchased by the National Library of Wales from the Thomas Fairfax Collection in December 1993. The copy of Llwyd's Chronicle that it contains, well written in the same hand throughout, occupies ff. 1–165. It is preceded first by a folio containing an intricate signature with a colophon attached in a hand later than the text, 'by Powell the original Autograph . . . see his name at end', then by several folios of the names of rulers from Cadwaladr to Madog ap Llywelyn, who was sent to 'perpetuall prison' following his revolt in 1294–5; and it ends with the name 'Tho. Powell'. The fewer folio numbers as compared with MSS 1 and 4 reflect a text much reduced by an extraordinary number of omissions ranging from single words to several folios in extent, and clearly omitted deliberately by the copyist. This discarded material relates in the main to events outside Wales, also to Church affairs and especially to matters concerned with the papacy. Anecdotes of various kinds are omitted, as are explanations of Welsh personal and place-names, sections of the longer elegiac eulogies, the attacks on Polydore Vergil and many of Llwyd's frequent elaborations on the Welsh links of the Arundel line. Other kinds of interference involve textual changes, many as corrections of obvious minor errors but others, such as adjustments to patronymic prefixes, the spelling of place-names and the titles attached to Welsh regional rulers, are clearly intended as more positively considered 'improvements'. Although this manuscript has several interesting features of its own, the nature and extent of such interference removes or distorts much textual evidence that has a bearing on issues such as Llwyd's motives and methods as well as his use of sources, not only of those by English chroniclers but occasionally of the basic *Brut y Tywysogyon* source itself. It also, of course, makes it unreliable as a touchstone for what Llwyd actually wrote.

[22] See note f. 165. This and other evidence of the transcriber's apparent lack of familiarity with the Welsh language is discussed below, p. 8.

Although occasional reference will be made to NLW MS 23202 B (MS 5), in the notes to the text and the footnotes below (abbreviated as N), it is clear that the important base manuscripts are BL, Cotton Caligula MS Avi (MS 1 referred to henceforth as C) and NLW, Llanstephan MS 177 (MS 4 referred to henceforth as Ll). As already indicated the text is based on Ll, with variant readings from C. There is no significant difference in content between them: both begin with the ending of the rule of the Britons over the whole of Britain following Cadwaladr's exile in Brittany and death in Rome. There follows immediately (in Ll, f. 2; C, f. 3) the description of Wales with no heading, simply Llwyd's reason for its inclusion, a reason he repeats when it ends (Ll, f. 24v; C, f. 29).

The 'historie following' then proceeds in unbroken sequence of rulers under their appropriate headings from Ifor the son of Alan to Llywelyn ap Gruffudd. Under the year 1270 (Ll, ff. 216v–217v; C, f. 212–212v), having described the division of the territories of Gruffudd ap Madog, lord of Bromfield, between his four sons, Llwyd goes on to say:

And at this place leaveth myne author,[23] and writeth no further of the ende of this Prince, but leaveth him at the hiest and most honorable staye that any Prince of Wales was in of many yeres before, beinge abashed peradventure . . . to declare the utter fall and ruine of his countrey . . . But I entendinge to fynishe that worke which I have taken in hande, and promised to accomplish at the beginninge of this boke,[24] have sought out in other cronicles, written in the Latyne tonge, especially in the cronicle of Nicholas Treuet . . . and suche other, as muche as I colde finde touchinge my matter . . .

Llwyd ends his account in the year 1295,[25] following the capture and imprisonment of Madog ap Llywelyn after the battle of Cefn Digoll, with the words: 'After this there was nothinge done in Wales worthy memory, but that is to bee redde in the Englishe Cronicle.'

Although these two key manuscripts, Ll and C, largely agree in content, there are numerous differences in transcription. The nature of these differences makes it clear that neither is Llwyd's original copy, the most obvious of many being the incomplete state of both: in C (MS 1 above) a lengthy missing section was copied in by John Dee after 1575 and Ll (MS 4 above) lacks the Welsh and Latin sections. Again, though

[23] HC (1584), 327; (1811), 231, 'the Brytish booke'; no version of *Brut y Tywysogyon* ending at this point is known to exist (see *Pen20Tr*, xiv–xvi; below pp. 16–19).
[24] HC (1584), 327; (1811), 237, 'intending to finish the historie during the gouernment of the Brytaines'.
[25] Not, as assumed in *Pen20Tr*, xv, in 1282; see below, pp. 18–19; for 1295, below, p. 59.

neither can be the actual copy used by Powel,[26] some of the variant
readings tend to show that C is closer to that copy.[27] On the other hand,
a good deal of such evidence suggests that Ll is closer to Llwyd's own
original account.[28] It is obvious also that Llwyd wrote the 'Cronica
Walliae' while in England: that is the clear implication of his comment
that the Welsh tongue was commonly spoken in his day 'on this side' of
Wales's boundary with England, instancing Herefordshire, Gloucester-
shire and a great part of Shropshire.[29] In 1559 Llwyd was still engaged by
the earl of Arundel and represented East Grinstead in the Parliament of
that year.[30] Although here and there errors due to a lack of familiarity
with place-names in southern Wales can possibly be attributed to Llwyd
himself,[31] most of the misspellings and misunderstandings found in both
manuscripts must reflect ignorance of the language on the part of the
copyists. There can be no other explanation for rendering 'the land of
Môn' as 'the lande of the mone', or for slurring the diphthong 'wy' in
Dryslwyn to make it 'Drosolan'; numerous other such errors can be
found in the text and some of these are identified in the notes to the
text.[32] Further evidence is provided, of course, by the omission of the
Welsh versions of the verses in Ll and their inclusion in C in a different
hand, and probably in such details as the frequent confusion of 'ap' with
the ampersand.[33]

However, errors occurring in both manuscripts which may argue a
common source, some of them possibly attributable to Llwyd himself, are
by no means confined to personal names and place-names. There are
several examples of identical omissions and at least one of careless misdating

[26] Powel received his copy from Sir Henry Sidney; there is no evidence that either Ll
or C had been in Sidney's or Powel's possession. Powel himself relates that he had
belatedly received Glover's copy (MS 2 above). Also there are differences in the readings
in HC as compared with both MSS (in addition to Powel's own editorial changes) which
cannot reflect misreadings; for example HC (1584), 31; (1811), 26: Thracians, for Ll, f. 34v
Troianes; C, f. 39 Territories.

[27] Many are indicated in the notes to the text, for example (indicated by folio nos),
notes ff. 7, 31v–32, 34, 44v, 45, 139.

[28] For example, notes ff. 3v, 29v, 33, 136v, 176.

[29] See note f. 5v.

[30] East Grinstead borough was part of the Duchy of Lancaster estate in Sussex of which
Arundel was made steward in 1549 (R. Somerville, History of the Duchy of Lancaster, I
(London, 1953), 617); above n.5.

[31] Below, p. 14.

[32] See note f. 7; other examples are referred to inter alia in notes ff. 20, 21, 35, 120,
174v.

[33] For example, notes ff. 15–15v, 165. Similar evidence points, of course, to the scribes'
lack of familiarity with Latin, especially the treatment of the Latin epitaph to Alfred, and
the failure to recognize conventional terms such as olim (notes ff. 21, 40).

in both manuscripts.[34] The inclusion in the text of 'a holy man' as a gloss on 'anchorite' and of an unclear reference to the chronicler Marianus Scotus seem to combine an initial oversight with a lack of understanding by a copyist; and copyists' inclusion of an identical marginal reminder to confirm a text reference has its own significance in this respect.[35] Such occurrences arose, one suspects, from the haste in which the work was written and may help to explain Llwyd's apparently sincere intention to revise what he manifestly saw as a hurried first draft 'which I shall desire the readers not enviousley to smatter at but gentlye to admonish me of the errors which by ther advise and helpe shalbe amended'.[36]

Llwyd's tragically early death before these intentions could be fulfilled doubtless encouraged the subsequent enthusiastic re-editing and 'improvement' of his work. That this process had begun before the publication of David Powel's *Historie of Cambria* in 1584 is demonstrated by the incorporation of Dee's amendments and additions to MS C as part of the text in the copy prepared for him in 1578 by Robert Glover (MS 2). Some of those amendments suggest that Dee might have seen another (unknown) manuscript copy of Llwyd's work, while others were clearly added after he had seen Powel's edition.[37] This 'editorial' process was continued during the following century, first by Robert Vaughan of Hengwrt[38] and then by William Maurice of Cefn-y-braich,

[34] See, for omissions, notes 15v, 38, 158v, 169v and 186v; for misdating, note f. 156v.

[35] Notes ff. 54, 69, 150.

[36] Ll, f. 24. Llwyd's sensitivity in this respect is expressed elsewhere in the 'Cronica', as when, Ll, f. 8, he undertakes to provide further arguments in his quarrel with Polydore Vergil over the naming of Anglesey when 'I have more leasure and occasion to write of this matter'; and nine years later he refers to authorities *quas pro historia Britannica edenda paratas habeo* (whiche I have readie in stoare foare a British Hystorie) (*Descriptionis Commentariolum* (1731), 12; *Breuiary of Britayne*, 8b–9a). He declares his intention *hanc materiam . . . luculenta oratione et eleganti stylo fusius tractare* (to handle the same matter more at large, in fayre discourse, and finer stile) (*Descriptionis Commentariolum*, 120; *Breuiary of Britayne*, 94b).

[37] See, for example, above n.26; and notes ff. 7v–8, 8v, 13, 71. Some entries in N suggest familiarity with *HC* or more probably with *HC*'s MS source, more especially *Quo Warrante*, *bonp y don*, Ll, 222; N, 162.

[38] See *Pen20Tr*, xix; it is stated ibid., n.1, that William Jones, by stating that the *Historie of Cambria* was reprinted in 1663 by William Hall 'with the valuable notes of Robert Vaughan of Hengwrt Esqr.', had confused a new edition of Sir John Prise's *Description of Wales* (below, n.52) with a new edition of the *Historie of Cambria*; this is not correct for it fails to take account of Vaughan's preparation of an edition of the *Historie* which was partly printed by William Hall in 1663 but never published. A copy of the *Historie* of 1663, containing 128 pages of text, with no title page but with a preface by William Hall, and with the respective contributions of Llwyd, Powel and Vaughan identified by Hall's typesetting practice, is at the National Library of Wales, shelfmark W.s. 198, and is discussed in J. Beverley Smith, 'Gruffudd Llwyd and the Celtic alliance, 1315–18', *BBCS*, 26 (1974–6), 469 and n.6.

whose annotated copy of Powel's book may have been intended as preparation for a new edition.[39] Such a new edition, entitled *The History of Wales*, 'newly augmented and improved' by William Wynne, appeared in 1697 and was reprinted in 1702, 1774 and 1812, and was published in a German translation by P. G. Hubner in 1725.[40] Wynne's edition was further revised and augmented by Richard Lloyd (Shrewsbury, 1872). A very useful reprint of Powel's original edition was issued by John Harding in 1811 and another in 1969.[41]

The expressed purpose of all these publications, with the exception of the last two named, was to improve on Powel's edition of Llwyd's translation of the Welsh chronicles and none of them was concerned to identify what Llwyd had actually written. It has been shown elsewhere that Powel introduced many unacknowledged changes and additions and by doing so he has given rise to some confusion. On the one hand, subsequent writers have mistakenly referred to Powel as a source and, on the other, they have wrongly taken Llwyd to task when criticism should have been levelled at Powel.[42] Therefore the temptation to produce yet another 'edited' version of the text has been resisted; and it is felt that the aim of approaching, as closely as is possible in the circumstances, to what Llwyd actually wrote can be best achieved by reproducing

[39] NLW MS 4760. Llwyd comes in for Maurice's criticism, for example, p. 257, for a biased translation of the *BT* original when referring to Llewelyn ap Iorwerth as the acknowledged supreme lord of Wales. Maurice had more than one copy of the Welsh chronicle at his elbow: he refers on p. 20 to *RBH* and gives, p. 85, the *RBH* version of the proverb rather than that of *Pen20* and *BS*; and his correction 'Brut 1140' for 1142 as the date of the murder of Hywel ap Maredudd ap Bleddyn is sustained only in *RBH* (for Maurice's familiarity with *RBH* see *Pen20Tr*, xxi–xxii). The entries added by him after 1270, pp. 376–9, are clearly based on a *BS* version. His note on Powel's assertion, *HC*, that the 'Brytish booke' ended at 1270 states firmly: 'this is not true for we have many membranes extant continuing thees Annals for many yeres after ye death of this Prince Llywelyn.' Similarly in NLW, Llanstephen MS 63, a transcript of *RBH*, Moses Williams notes: 'NB. here endeth the copy H[umphrey] Ll[wyd] and D[avid] P[owel] perused. Ergo they did not see Ll[yfr] Coch Hergest.' See *Pen20Tr*, xxiv.

[40] *The History of Wales . . . from Cadwalader the last King, to Lhewelyn the Last Prince, of British Blood. Written originally in British by Caradoc of Lhancarvan; and formerly published in English by Dr. Powel. Now newly augmented and improved by W. Wynne* (London, 1697). Wynne's work was reprinted 1702 and 1774 (London), and 1812 (Merthyr Tydfil). For the German translation see P. G. Hubner, *Die Historie van Walles* (Coburg, 1725).

[41] *The Historie of Cambria now called Wales . . . written in the Brytish Language . . . translated into English by H. Lhoyd, corrected by David Powel* [1584] (London, 1811); Caradoc of Llancarvan, *The Historie of Cambria London 1584*, Number 163 The English Experience (Amsterdam and New York, 1969).

[42] Williams, 'Ysgolheictod hanesyddol', 215–16, 219–20; among instances quoted later see, for example, notes ff. 129v (Bryn y Pina), 222 (Bonp y don); see also the statement in *Pen20Tr* xv that Llwyd's account ended in 1282 (made to appear so by Powel) rather than 1294–5 (above, n.25).

faithfully one of the existing manuscript copies of his work. It has already been said that the text in Ll is probably nearer to Llwyd's original account, despite its obvious errors and omissions, which in any case occur far more frequently in C.[43] As a manuscript it is certainly the more complete and ostensibly the more correct; it bears very few marks of interference and is therefore a cleaner copy and less difficult to reproduce accurately; the folio numbering is straightforward, in contrast with C, and as no copy is known to exist the manuscript is unique. The Llanstephan 177 manuscript – Ll – has therefore been adopted as the text on which this edition of the 'Cronica Walliae' is based, and variant readings in the C text are given at the foot of each page. In order to reproduce Humphrey Llwyd's text as far as it is possible to do so, obvious scribal errors, and especially minor omissions, in the Ll text that can be supplied from better readings in the C text are corrected, each emendation noted as a variant reading. Similarly, errors which can be identified from the reading in the *Historie of Cambria* are corrected and these, comparatively few in number, are identified in square brackets.[44] The punctuation supplied by the scribe of the Ll text is erratic and, for ease of reading, a measured use of conventional punctuation has been adopted. In doing so, as in supplying paragraph indents within the headed sections of the text, account has been taken of the practice adopted by David Powel in preparing his manuscript for publication as the *Historie of Cambria*. In transcription there is no interference with orthography and normal editorial conventions are respected.[45] Both

[43] The footnote variants show the extent of the omissions, and the notes to the text also refer to instances in both MSS. In Ll, apart from the omitted Latin and Welsh verses, see, for example, the notes to ff. 38v, 109v, 139; and for C, notes ff. 7, 33, 35, 38, 44v, 45, 65, 85, 115–115v, 126 and others. For examples of errors in Ll, see notes ff. 47v, 59v, 60v; and in C, notes ff. 34, 71, 85, 136v, 186v etc.

[44] Variant readings normally cite the forms in C, with occasional reference to N. With the Latin text of the eulogy to Rhys ap Gruffudd (Ll, ff. 160–1) readings from the *Pen20* text are given as variants. References to the textual notes that follow the text in this edition are given in the form: 'note f. 5v'.

[45] In transcription the conventions used are primarily those recommended in R. F. Hunnisett, *Editing Records for Publication* (British Records Association, 1977). Modern capitalization has been used, but with exceptions that respect the conventions of the MS and, especially, the form of place-names and personal names, in which cases the exact forms used by the scribe (for example, Northwales, Southwales) are retained. A personal name that may often be abbreviated but may on occasion be extended is consistently given in its extended form (for example, Griff' which is sometimes given in the MS as Griffith, appears as Griffith throughout). Spelling used in the MS is retained, the word endings -*tion* and -*cioun* being transcribed as they appear, and the letter forms *u* and *v*, and *i* and *j*, where the distinction is uncertain, are transcribed so as to indicate the sound of the spoken word. The contractions *wth* and *wch* have been extended as *with* or *which*. The thorn (þ) occurs occasionally but has been transcribed as *th* in all cases, and the ampersand (&) as *and*.

manuscripts number folios on the recto side only but, in transcribing, verso numbering has been added for easier reference; the numbers appear in the text within brackets thus: [1], [1v]. Dates quoted from the *Brut* are given throughout in uncorrected chronicler's form to facilitate direct comparison with Llwyd's. Quotations are generally in translated (English) form.

II The Text

1 *The Description of Wales*
Llwyd begins his 'Cronica Walliae' with a very brief outline of the traditional version of the end of the rule of the Britons over the whole island of Britain. He then declares his own purpose, which was to write the lives and acts of the kings and princes of Wales from that point to the reign of Llywelyn ap Gruffudd, the last native prince. Before doing so, however, he thought it necessary (f. 2) to describe the country of Wales 'as hit was in olde tyme and as hit is at thees dayes that therby the readere may the more playnely and easely understande the woorke following'.[46] When he wrote those words Llwyd had been attached to Arundel's household and involved in the development of his library for some six years[47] and would have known of Giraldus Cambrensis's *Descriptio Kambriae*, of the descriptions of Britain later written by Ranulph Higden and others, and also of various works of a like nature written in the vernacular as well as in Latin by authors on the continent.[48] His opening statement, together with his declaration at the end of the Description (f. 24) that 'I was the first . . . to put thees thinges into the Englishe tonge. For that I wolde not have the inhabitantes of

---

[46] The Description appears in Ll, ff. 2–24v.

[47] Above, p. 1.

[48] These books, among numerous others bearing Llwyd's signature as well as those of Arundel and Lumley, are listed in Jayne and Johnson, *Lumley Library*, and are described in Williams, 'Ysgolheictod hanesyddol', 112, 116–18; Gruffydd, 'Humphrey Llwyd', 86–91. They include, for example, no. 1302: Leandro Alberti, *Descrittione di tutta Italia* (Venice, 1553); no. 1161: Guillaume Postel, *De Hitruriae Originibus . . . Commentatio* (Florence, 1551), a gift to Llwyd from Henry Maltravers, Arundel's son, in 1556 (see T. M. Chotzen, 'Some sidelights on Cambro-Dutch relations', *THSC*, 1937, 136); and no. 2507: Pope Pius II, *Cosmographia I Asiae Europae elegans descriptio* (Paris, 1509). See also below, n.130. Andrew Boyle is able to add one title to the list of those known to have been seen by Llwyd: Jacobus Philippus Foresti, *Supplementum Chronicorum* (Paris, 1535), BL, C. 75.g.5, no. 1459 in Jayne and Johnson, *Lumley Library*, his name being discerned on the top left of the title page of a volume that bears the ownership marks of Archbishop Cranmer, Arundel and Lumley.

this Ile ignorant of the histories and cronicles of the same', reveal even at this early stage Llwyd's concurrence with the contemporary view of the significance of the relationship between history and topography and of the status of vernacular tongues. They also make it plain that his underlying purpose was to present what he regarded as the true history of Wales to readers outside its borders.[49] Accordingly the Description begins with a brief reference to the traditional account of the division of Britain between the three sons of Brutus before proceeding to a description of Wales. The Description is constructed about a framework of its cantrefs and commotes arranged according to the division by Rhodri Mawr into what Llwyd terms (f. 5ᵛ) 'three territories which they called kingedomes'.[50] This he does because the 'hystorie' treats of wars between the princes of these three territories as well as between them and the Saxons, Normans and Flemings. Llwyd, as was the wont also of so many writers of his time, names very few sources other than distant, mostly classical, authors; and the references to those few are usually concerned with particular, often incidental matters.[51] Nowhere does he give a source either for the framework nor for the body of the Description itself. The view generally accepted after Llwyd's day that it was in the first instance the work of Sir John Prise of Brecon seems to derive mainly, if not indeed entirely, from the wording of the title in Powel, that it was 'Drawne first by Sir Iohn Prise Knight, and afterward augmented and made perfect by Humfrey Lhoyd, Gentleman'.[52] In his

[49] *HC* obscures these quite clear purposes by separating the Description from the rest of the text and by 'silently' abbreviating and rewriting the opening sentences; Powel omits entirely Llwyd's remarks at the end of the Description. By attributing unequivocally the original authorship to Sir John Prise he has tended to diminish the full measure of Llwyd's accomplishment.

[50] Nowhere in this work does Llwyd employ the traditional phrase 'Y Tair Talaith', nor does he at this stage show any awareness of the different accounts of the apportionment between Rhodri's sons; see notes ff. 13, 36v.

[51] Thus he refers to Giraldus Cambrensis in relation to the name 'Wales' (f. 3), the boundary between England and Wales (f. 5v), the extent and status of Dinefwr (f. 17v) and the beavers in the river Teifi (f. 22v); but makes no mention of him in respect of the division of Britain and Wales (ff. 2, 5v–6, 36–36v) nor for the framework of cantrefs and commotes, where in both instances their accounts differ.

[52] Others who followed give different accounts of Llwyd's part. In an edition of the Description printed in separate form in 1663, Sir John Prise *A Description of Wales* (Oxford 1663), it is said that Llwyd merely 'perused' Prise's original. See, for example, Egerton Phillimore, *Y Cymmrodor*, xi, 54, n.5; *Pen20Tr*, xix, n.1. F. J. North, *DWB*, 594, refers to it as an enlarged version of a 'tract' by Prise, written in Latin according to E. D. Jones, *DWB*, 786. N. R. Ker, 'Sir John Prise of Brecon', *The Library*, 5th ser., 10 (1955), 1–24, surmises that 'in the end Prise worked up his notes on Wales into an historical description' expanded and altered by Llwyd, and adds, strangely in view of the main thrust of Prise's *Defensio*, that probably 'the abuse of Polydore Vergil which it contains is Llwyd's contribution'.

introductory address 'To the Reader', however, Powel admits that in
the description 'I haue taken the lesse paines, looking dailie for the
comming foorth of the painefull and studious trauel of some other, who
hath labored in that behalfe', and Camden's *Britannia* appeared two years
later in 1586. For his part Llwyd names John Prise once only, in what is
a clear reference to his *Historiae Brytannicae Defensio*.[53]

As to the framework of the Description, four lists of cantrefs and
commotes are to be found in manuscripts which existed before Llwyd
wrote his 'Cronica': BL, Cotton Domitian MS Aviii, ff. 119–20b
(printed in Leland's *Itinerary in Wales*), in the Red Book of Hergest
(Jesus College, 111), cols. 377–80, in NLW Peniarth MS 50 ('Y Cwtta
Cyfarwydd'), ff. 133–8, and in NLW Peniarth MS 163, ff. 57–60 (by
Gruffudd Hiraethog in 1543). Llwyd's listing can be shown to be
different in a number of respects from the first three but is almost
identical with the last named list transcribed by Gruffudd Hiraethog,
even to the errors which, among other characteristics, distinguish both
from the other three 'ancient' lists.[54] Virtually all these errors relate to
parts of south Wales, and several, notably Ystrad Tywi, Cantref Bychan
and Gorfynydd abut Sir John Prise's native Brecknockshire. The
corrections in his hand to the list in Cotton Domitian MS Aviii, often
adduced as examples of his informed interest, are in fact very few and,
strangely, refer wholly to the area of Snowdon in north Wales.[55]

---

[53] 'Remittinge the reader to the apologie of the British historie . . . writen by Sir John
Price Knight' (f. 4). Llwyd could only, of course, have known it in its MS form as it was
not published until 1573, when it appeared as Sir John Prise, *Historiae Brytannicae Defensio*
(London, 1573). A copy of that edition bearing the signatures of Arundel and Lumley is
listed in Jayne and Johnson, *Lumley Library*, no. 1241. Llwyd makes no reference to Prise at
all in his later works, the *Commentarioli . . . Fragmentum* and 'De Mona druidum insula
. . . Epistola', noted above, p. 3.

[54] They are the only texts that name clearly the divisions into Llwyd's 'three territories',
and give the correct locations for Uwch and Is Rhaeadr. More significantly, these two
alone commit the errors of naming Ystrad Tywi as Carmarthenshire; confusing Cantref
Mawr and Cantref Bychan and naming the latter Cantref Ffiniog; naming several non-
existent commotes such as Pennal in Meirionnydd, Haverne in Powys Wenwynwyn, and
Trefdraeth in Dyfed (Ll, ff. 9,12v, 18v); and corrupting Gorfynydd in Glamorgan as
Croneth. The main differences between Llwyd's list and Gruffudd Hiraethog's are that
Llwyd inexplicably places Brycheiniog at the end, after Gwent, whereas Gruffudd
Hiraethog, in common with the other lists, places it next to Ystrad Tywi. Llwyd,
however, places Dyfed correctly within Dinefwr between Ceredigion and Carmarthen
(i.e. Ystrad Tywi) whereas Gruffudd Hiraethog places it after Gwent; see note f. 21; also
HW, I, 280, *OP*, III, 215–19, 230–1. Gruffudd Hiraethog's list is printed in *MA*, 735–7;
J. G. Evans, *Reports on Manuscripts in the Welsh Language*, 2 vols (London, 1898–1910), I,
952–4.

[55] That is Llŷn, Penllyn, Arfon, Nanconwy and Gwyrfai. See *The Itinerary in Wales of
John Leland*, ed. L. Toulmin Smith (London, 1906), 5–9. Balliol College MS 353, a

Altogether, therefore, it is difficult to perceive evidence of Prise's influence in Llwyd's listing of cantrefs and commotes which, in the pattern both of its defects and rectitudes, seems to bear the mark of a north Wales hand. However that may be, it is manifestly as part of Llwyd's own declared intention to bring his account up to date that he adds to his tripartite division into the historical territories the information that what was 'in the olde tyme' called Gwynedd and Powys was 'at thees dayes' the six shires of north Wales; and that the six shires subject to the territory of Dinefwr (with Radnorshire) were 'nowe commenly called South Wales'.[56] The actual description of the regions begins in north Wales with Gwynedd and ends after Brycheiniog with a brief reference to some of the features of south Wales. There is a marked imbalance in the space given to the accounts respectively of north and south Wales, two-thirds being devoted to the former and the description of Llwyd's home town of Denbigh enjoying more space than that of the whole of Prise's native Brycheiniog.[57]

However one views the part played by Prise in compiling the Description, Llwyd certainly, as we have seen, came under the influence of his *Historiae Brytannicae Defensio*. It was an influence that, no doubt, at least helped to sharpen Llwyd's antagonism to Polydore Vergil's views on Britain's distant past, to sustain his own estimation of the antiquity and quality of the Welsh linguistic and literary tradition, and to bring together a formidable array of quotable authorities both native and classical. Gruffudd Hiraethog, one of the redoubtable company of scholars and *literati* who were his neighbours in his native town of Denbigh, would have exercised a deeper and more direct influence on the younger Humphrey Llwyd. Tangible evidence of both connections is, however, regrettably tenuous, limited as it is to the one and only reference in the 'Cronica Walliae' to the *Defensio* and to Gruffudd Hiraethog's eulogy to Llwyd and the pedigree of Foulk Lloyd taken by Gruffudd from a copy in Llwyd's hand.[58]

'commonplace book' in the hand of Sir John Prise, lists, f. 164b, the names of the cantrefs of Wales out of the Red Book of the Exchequer; Phillimore describes the list as 'both defective and corrupt' (*Cambrian Journal*, 1857, 39–47; *OP*, IV, 605).

[56] Ll, ff. 17v, 22.

[57] The north Wales section occupies ff. 6v–17v, south Wales ff. 18–23v.

[58] NLW, Llanstephan MS 145, f. 41; for the elegy, NLW, Peniarth MS 134, f. 370; see Gruffydd, 'Humphrey Llwyd', 93–4; Bowen, *Gwaith Gruffudd Hiraethog*, no. 28; for the pedigree, Gruffydd; 'Humphrey Llwyd', 67; D. J. Bowen, *Gruffudd Hiraethog a'i Oes* (Cardiff, 1958), 23 (facing). For others in the neighbourhood of Denbigh who would probably have influenced him, Williams, 'Ysgolheictod hanesyddol', 114.

2 The main text and its relationship to Brut y Tywysogyon

(a) Material relating to Wales

As with the Description, Llwyd is less than helpful in the matter of indicating the sources for his historical material. He does, it is true, name a number of ancient authors, both classical and British, essentially to establish the antiquity and therefore the authority of the traditional account of his nation's past. In relation to certain matters he names Giraldus Cambrensis and Matthew Paris several times, and others, such as the laws of Hywel Dda and the chronicle of Henry of Huntingdon, more sparingly. He tells us that, when his Welsh base copy ended in the year 1270, he sought out his material in the chronicle of Nicholas Trevet and other chronicles written in Latin to enable him to complete the work he had promised to accomplish.[59] On several occasions before that, however, when Trevet was also apparently the source, he makes no such acknowledgement; indeed, nowhere does he acknowledge any specific source, apart from those few already indicated, for the frequent and often quite extensive references to English affairs before the year 1270.

As to his main Welsh base copy, his own references to it tell us little more than its ending date. He does not give it a name,[60] but he does in some instances seem to indicate a single author source by such terms as 'the Welsh Cronicler', 'my Welshe author', and 'myne author'.[61] Otherwise he refers to his source, always in the singular, as 'the Britishe Cronicle', 'the Welsh historie', 'the Welsh booke', or, 'the British booke'.[62] David Powel sought to give a clearer definition to Llwyd's vague references by relating the main Welsh source to the chronicle, supposedly compiled by Caradog of Llancarfan up to the year 1156 and then continued 'in either of the Abbeis of Conwey and Stratflur . . .

---

[59] Ll, f. 216v–217; below, p. 42.

[60] Below, n.64

[61] Ll, ff. 160, 209v, 216v.

[62] Ll, ff. 14, 23v, 37v, 74, 81, 117, 127v. Such expressions could possibly echo the tradition stemming from Geoffrey of Monmouth of the 'Welsh booke' translated from Latin by Walter Archdeacon of Oxford. On the rare occasions when Llwyd uses the plural form the reference is more general, as when he explains the need for an English translation 'for that I wolde not have the inhabitantes of this Ile ignorant of the histories and cronicles of the same' (f. 24); *Pen20Tr*, xiv, n.3, is misleading in this respect. Llwyd's reference, almost a decade later, to 'hystories written in the British tongue, which of late so far as I suppose were by me first translated into English' (*Commentarioli . . . Fragmentum*, pp. 9–10, quoted from *Breuiary of Britayne*, 7) is ambiguous, and in any case comes after a period of considerable additional study and of close contact with Welsh scholars around his home in Denbigh.

untill the yeare 1270 . . . a little before the death of the last Lhewelyn',[63] which ultimately became generally known as *Brut y Tywysogyon*.[64] Powel goes on to say that these 'collections were copied by diuers' so that there were in his day at least a hundred copies, and that it was 'this booke' that Humphrey Llwyd translated into English. The apparent implication that these one hundred copies, and also Powel's 'two ancient copies' of the 'Brytish booke' which he consulted,[65] ended in 1270 was accepted literally by the late Professor Thomas Jones and, as none of the surviving copies of the *Brut* ends at this point, he concluded that 'the family of MSS to which Llwyd's and Powel's copies belonged has died out'.[66] Earlier J. E. Lloyd had remarked more cautiously that 'the whole family, if such there was, has died out',[67] and later Thomas Jones, too, seemed to have modified his view saying that 'this figure [of one hundred], which was obviously meant to be only approximate, must have included copies of the two versions of the *Brut* proper and of *Brenhinedd y Saesson*'.[68] Dee compared his copy of Llwyd's manuscript with Powel's edition and with a manuscript of the *Brut*; and examination of those surviving manuscripts of the *Brut* which were available to other sixteenth- and early seventeenth-century antiquaries demonstrates that they were aware of differences due to lacunae in the text and varying ending dates, caused by loss or damage.[69] They were also aware of, and often involved in, the practice of completing and correcting defective manuscripts by comparison with others.[70] Llwyd himself makes clear his view that the early ending by his 'author' was deliberate,[71] which makes

[63] *HC* (1584), [i]; (1811), ix. Powel of course prepared his edition twenty-five years after Llwyd's death, between September 1583, when he received his copy from Sir Henry Sidney, and March 1584, when he wrote his dedicatory letter to Sir Philip Sidney.

[64] A title was not used by sixteenth- or early seventeenth-century antiquaries such as John Dee, George William Griffith of Pembrokeshire or Robert Vaughan, nor later by Bishop Humphrey Humphreys of Bangor and others. That it was gaining currency is shown, however, by the title, dated '17th cent', attached to a short series of *RBH* excerpts contained in NLW, Llanstephan MS 100, 'Llyma Fryt y Tywysogion'; also in 'The correct Annales of Brittaine . . . gathered out of severall Authors, but most especially out of Brut y Tywysogion', compiled in an English text in 1688 by Thomas Sebastian Price of Llanfyllin (NLW MS 1599); the Welsh text in the same MS contains a note by William Maurice of Cefn-y-braich referring to 'nostrae Brut y Tywys[ogion]'; see *Pen20Tr*, liii–iv; *RBH*, xxxv.

[65] *HC* (1584), [v]; (1811), xiii.
[66] *Pen20Tr*, xiv–xvi.
[67] J. E. Lloyd, *The Welsh Chronicles*, *PBA*, xiv (1928), 85.
[68] *RBH*, xx–xxi.
[69] For example, above, n.64.
[70] Ibid., and examples in *Pen20Tr*, xlix–lv; *RBH*, xxi–xxxi; *BS*, xviii–xix.
[71] Ll, f. 216 v.

it even more strange that none of these near contemporaries was moved
to comment on the existence of a 'family' of manuscripts ending at that
date. William Maurice of Cefn-y-braich rejected firmly Powel's assertion that the 'Brytish book' ended in 1270, and also concluded pointedly
that neither Llwyd nor Powel could have seen the Red Book of Hergest
version of *Brut y Tywysogyon*.[72]

That Powel himself may well have found it difficult to reconcile his
view of the 'collections' as Llwyd's source with Llwyd's apparent
indication of single authorship may possibly account for some of his
unacknowledged changes. These include, for instance, replacing Llwyd's
'Welsh Chronicler' and 'myne author' with 'the Brytish book' and
omitting entirely the passage containing the phrase 'my Welsh author'.[73]
He seems also to have deemed it necessary to diminish the apparent
discrepancy between Llwyd's stated purpose of ending his account with
the death of Llywelyn ap Gruffudd and, on the one hand, claiming the
abrupt ending of his source copy in 1270 and, on the other, following
his account through to 1295.[74] There seems to be no other reason for
changes such as replacing Llwyd's words at the 1270 ending, 'I
entendinge to fynishe that worke, which I have taken in hande and
promised to accomplish at the beginninge of this boke' with 'intending
to finish the historie during the government of the Brytaines', marking
this date (1270) with his own note on the preceding paragraph: 'Here
endeth the Brytishe copie. That which foloweth vnto the death of this
Prince was collected by Humfrey Lhoyd, Gentleman.'[75] Then at the year
1282, following Llwyd's account of the death of Llywelyn ap Gruffudd
and the imprisonment of Rhys Fychan, Powel again adds his own note,
'Thus endeth the Historie of the Brytish Princes.'[76] Finally, though
Llwyd's relation of events between 1282 and 1295 is incorporated in
Powel's account, he does not acknowledge it as being Llwyd's.[77] In
brief, therefore, it can be argued that these various changes by Powel
confirmed more satisfactorily the link he had made in his preface
between the 'collections' by several compilers and 'this book' which
Llwyd translated; and, by distinguishing between Llwyd's 'British copy'

---

[72] For Maurice, above, n.39.
[73] *HC* (1584), 249, 327, 324–5; (1811), 181, 237, 234–5.
[74] Ll, ff. 2, 216v, 227v; above, p. 7.
[75] Ll, f. 216v; *HC* (1584), 327; (1811), 237.
[76] Ll, f. 225v; *HC* (1584), 375; (1811), 274.
[77] Cf. *HC* (1584), 378–82; (1811), 277–80 with Ll, ff. 225v–227v. Powel's only
mention of Llwyd (marginal note *HC* (1584), 378; (1811), 277) harks back to a reference
in the Description, Ll, f. 10v; *HC* (1584), Description x; (1811), xxv.

ending in 1270 and the 'History of the British princes' ending in 1282, he blurs the anomaly in ending dates and together with his masking of Llwyd's subsequent account gives a misleading impression of the actual ending date of Llwyd's text.[78]

Llwyd himself, however, compounds the difficulty of identification by occasionally quoting specifically the authority of his main source in a way which suggests that it could not have been any known version of the *Brut*. The clearest example is his proposal (f. 14) to tell the reader 'what the Britishe Cronicle saithe of Northwales, which affirmeth that three tymes hit came by enheritannce to women', and after which he gives a detailed account of this tradition, which finds no place in any of the *Brut* versions.[79] On another occasion he names the first of the twelve knights who, according to a tradition again not mentioned in the *Brut*, helped Robert Fitzhamon to conquer Glamorgan, as 'Londres or London as the Welshe booke nameth him'.[80] Although at this point the 'Welsh booke' is the authority for the name only, features of the passage as a whole could point to its being the source for the entire tale.[81] Elsewhere Llwyd explains that Owain Gwynedd, after the death of his father Gruffudd ap Cynan in 1137, was crowned prince of North Wales 'for the name of kinge is no further used in the British Booke'.[82] Yet very shortly afterwards, in 1148 and 1149, *Brenhinedd y Saesson (BS)* and *RBH* each refer to 'Owain King of Gwynedd', and all three versions to Madog ap Maredudd as 'King of Powys'. Llwyd has 'prince' in each instance and his customary care for matters of this kind would seem to make it unlikely that such a discrepancy, if it existed, would have been allowed to go unnoticed.[83]

In fact, therefore, very few of Llwyd's direct references to his main Welsh source tally satisfactorily with any known versions of *BT* or *BS*.[84] The same difficulty occurs on those occasions when Llwyd makes no clear reference to a particular source, but when it seems safe to assume

[78] See *Pen20Tr*, xv, and Thomas Jones's comment (ibid., xvi) on the need to print Llwyd's text as distinct from Powel's edition of it.

[79] See note f. 14.

[80] Ll, f. 81; for the conquest of Glamorgan see below, pp. 25–6.

[81] Ll, ff. 79v–81; see note f. 81.

[82] Ll, f. 117.

[83] Ll, f. 124v. Powel, *HC* (1584), 6; (1811), 5 comments on the use of 'king', 'prince', by 'this author'. Dates quoted from *BT* and *BS* are given throughout in uncorrected chronicler's form to facilitate direct comparison with Llwyd's dates.

[84] A rare instance is when he explains 'the Black Normanes' by adding 'for so the Britishe booke calleth the Danes' (Ll, f. 37v *s.a.* 890: *BS* 'Y Nordmannieit Duon', *RBH* 'Y Normanyeit Duon', *Pen 20* 'ynormanyeid duon'. For a similar example see Ll, f. 74 and *BT*, *BS s.a.* 1070.

that he has his base copy in mind. He will sometimes denote the
beginning and end of passages interposed in the text by him, as when he
proposes to explain the division of Powys. He signals the digression with
'And here youe shall understande howe Powis lande came to be devided
in many partes', and ends 'But to my matter',[85] presumably to indicate a
return to his Welsh source copy. Then follows the account, given
incorrectly as in *BS*, that 'the same yere was Cadwalhon ap Madoc ap
Idnerth taken by . . . Enyon Clud',[86] and then that he was to be
imprisoned in Winchester.[87] After referring to two English matters not
given in the *Brut*, Llwyd notes the death of Meurig bishop of Bangor,[88]
then two more English events again not mentioned in the *Brut* before
relating, as in the Peniarth MS 20 (*Pen20*) version of the *Brut* and *BS*,
the loss of the castle of 'Walwern',[89] a loss which grieved Owain
(Gwynedd) so much 'that nothinge colde make him mery'.[90] Owain
followed his adversary 'to Seavarn'.[91] The following year 'Owen, sonne
to Griffith ap Meredith . . . and Owen sonne to Madoc ap Meredith'
seized the castle of Carreg Hofa.[92] In this brief passage (Ll, ff. 133v–134,
RBH, s.a. 1158–61, *BS, Pen20, s.a.* 1159–62) Llwyd's account seems to
derive in succession from the particular events, described differently in
the several versions, given in *BS*, *Pen20*, then *BS* and *RBH*, *BS* and
Pen20, *BS* (or possibly NLW, Peniarth MS 213, NLW, Mostyn MS
143), *Pen20* and *RBH*, Peniarth MS 213.

Examples of such apparent diversity of *Brut* source versions are to be
found throughout Llwyd's account. An early instance, after an interpolation concerning the date of Easter, begins with the crowning of
Offa and Brihtric (Brichtrich) as kings of Mercia and the West Saxons,[93]
followed by an incorrect account of two Welsh incursions into Mercia.
These and Offa's Dyke are described in this way only in *BS*. Llwyd adds
detail to his account of Offa's Dyke which is found only in the Black
Book of Basingwerk (BBB) version while his dates differ from those of

---

[85] Ll, ff. 133–133v.

[86] *Pen20* and *RBH*, correctly, state that Cadwallon seized Einion Clud; see *BS*, 163,
14–17nn.

[87] Winchester is named only in *Pen20*.

[88] Correctly as in *RBH*, *BS*; *Pen20*, 'Maredudd'.

[89] *RBH*, 'Castell Dafolwern'. For nn.87–9, see *Pen20Tr*, 62.5–6nn.; .10n.; .12n.; .22n.

[90] As in *Pen20*, *RBH*; in *BS* the death of his mother caused him grief.

[91] *BS* 'Gorddwr Hafren' (also Peniarth MS 213, Mostyn MSS 143, 159), *Pen20*
'Llanidloes'.

[92] This arrangement of personal names occurs only in Peniarth MS 213. See note
f. 77v.

[93] Ll, f. 29; these accounts occur only in *BS* (*s.a.* 773).

BS and *BT*.[94] Immediately afterwards, however, although the events described are much the same as those in the *Brut*, there are differences in detail.[95] One more such illustrative excerpt out of many must suffice: after relating the tale of Madog's discovery of America, Llwyd returns 'to my hystorie'[96] by recording the marriage of Princess Eleanor to Alphonse, king of Castile, an event not given in the *Brut*. Then follows the departure for Ireland of Richard Strongbow, 'Earle of Strigill', a description not in the *Brut* but given in the *Annales Cambriae* (*AC*).[97] Llwyd's account of Strongbow's marriage is similar to the *Brut,* but none of the versions mentions the resulting seizure of his lands in England or his later reconciliation to the king. Llwyd, like *BS*, but unlike *Pen20* and *RBH*, makes no mention of the Forest of Dean as the place where Rhys ap Gruffudd met the king; but Llwyd's '14 pledges' given by Rhys and the king's seizure of Caerllion-on-Usk accords with *BS* and *Pen20* as against *RBH*, while his 'Yngharad' agrees with *RBH* as against 'Dyddgu' in *BS* and *Pen20*.[98] Then again, according to Llwyd, the king gave Rhys the lands of Cardigan, Ystrad Tywi, Arwystli and Elfael, whereas the last two are named more correctly in *Pen20* and *RBH* as Ystlwyf and Efelffre.[99] Finally Rhys is said by Llwyd to have taken Cardigan from the earl of Gloucester, not the earl of Clare as in *RBH, Pen20*; *BS* refers only to the capture of Robert FitzStephen.

So much then for the few extracts chosen from among those sections of his account where Llwyd himself makes it clear that he is translating his main Welsh source copy.[100] Taken together, at the very least they give added substance to doubts, already implied in relation to Llwyd's ending-date, as to whether he was in fact translating directly a version or versions of the *Brut*.[101] Any further testing of that view clearly cannot be sustained without a detailed scrutiny of the work as a whole in its relationship to

[94] In *Pen20* and *RBH*, Offa harried 'the men of the south' and the 'Britons'. Llwyd's description of Offa's Dyke here, and in the Description (Ll, ff. 5–5v), is much the same as BBB in *BS*, ll. 8–20nn. Llwyd does not, strangely, add the details in BBB concerning Ffyrnfael the son of Idwal. Llwyd's date of 763 is ten years behind *BT* and *BS*, and that of the second incursion seven years behind *BS*. For BBB, the Black Book of Basingwerk (NLW MS 7006), see *Pen20Tr*, xviii–xx.

[95] See note f. 29v.

[96] Ll, ff. 142–3.

[97] *AC* s.a. 1171 'comes de Striguil'; see *Pen20Tr*, 65.34n.

[98] Ll, ff. 142v–143v; see *RBH*, 155, 1–3n.; *Pen20Tr*, 66.31n.; 66.37n.

[99] *BS*, 173.32n.

[100] Examples, in addition to those detailed above, are referred to in notes ff. 26v, 29v, 33, 36, 77v, 198, 203. Some of the many others that occur in the text can be found in ff. 32, 35, 38, 51, 151.

[101] Above p. 19 and note f. 81.

the *Brut* and with an eye also to any material extraneous to the *Brut* which Llwyd may have introduced. Some reference to the latter has already been made and other instances are discussed below.[102] In a much earlier study of the 'Cronica Walliae' in relation to the *Brut* I concluded that broadly, and with some notable exceptions, *BS* in its BL, Cotton Cleopatra MS Bv version was a significant source until it ended in 1197, and the *Pen20* version afterwards up to 1270 when Llwyd's main Welsh source (his so-called 'myne author') ended.[103] The more precise yet much more expansive examination made possible by the publication since then of Thomas Jones's definitive editions of the *Brut* texts, while confirming that broad pattern, has also exposed many more departures from it than could until then confidently be identified. These in turn have multiplied the recognizable instances of source material unique to *Pen20* and occasionally *RBH* versions occurring in the earlier period up to 1197 (that is, the end of the Cotton Cleopatra MS Bv version of *BS*).[104] The examples of a seeming *BS* source in the later period, after the end of Cotton Cleopatra Bv, though few,[105] gather interest when set alongside other occasions when the BBB version of *BS* could well be assumed to have been the source for Llwyd's material.[106] These two circumstances add strength to the foregoing evidence that chronicles relating to Wales other than the main *Brut* versions underlie parts of the 'Cronica Walliae'.[107] It can be added, too, that some of the features of Llwyd's version of the verse epitaph and elegiac verses on the death of the Lord Rhys (ff. 160–1) regarded in conjunction with those in *Pen20* and *CW* could well imply yet another different chronicle source.[108]

Some of these examples adduced to illustrate the apparent diversity of Welsh chronicle sources also show Llwyd's account to be wrong because it follows a faulty version of the *Brut*. This is not, of course, surprising in view of the various and frequently conflicting accounts in the source

---

[102] Below, pp. 24–31.

[103] Williams, 'Ysgolheictod hanesyddol', 118–19.

[104] For example, Ll, ff. 47v, 60v (see note), 62v, 68v, 69v, 115, 117, 129, 146, 146v.

[105] They include references Ll, f. 166 to Madog 'sonne to Gruffith Bromfelde'; f. 190 to Henry Pigot, 'Lorde of Evas'; also the descriptions, unique to *BS* (BBB text) f. 196v, of Joan, wife of Llywelyn ap Iorwerth as 'princesse of Wales', and, f. 204, of Wales as a 'principalitie'.

[106] For example, above n.94; *Idwal Iwrch* (Ll, ff. 25,26) and *Tewdwr Mawr* (Ll, 52v) occur only in BBB; Llwyd's omission of 'Hirmawr' as in BBB and Pen. 213 (note f. 77v.), 'Griff' remained in Mone' (Ll, f. 85v) is nearest to BBB *a gedwis*, and 'nothinge dismayed' (f. 105) is close to *nid argysurodd* (*BS*, xxvii, 131.9–10n.).

[107] Above pp. 18–20; notes ff. 14, 77v, 141.

[108] *CW* has the prose tribute but not the eulogy in verse; *Pen20Tr*, lxi; below, note f. 159.

material. That circumstance in itself does, however, make it remarkable
that Llwyd hardly ever notes such alternative accounts and, moreover,
on the very rare occasions when he does so, that the respective conflicting sources are not indicated.[109] He allows to pass without comment
instances where *Brut* accounts other than his own apparent source copy
give directly opposite versions;[110] and, even more remarkably, he
remains silent when similar serious discrepancies occur in fields of very
special interest to him such as the details of family connections[111] and
Welsh place-names. Most of Llwyd's errors in identifying places mentioned in his source copy relate understandably to south Wales. Some
examples are referred to above and some are given in the notes.[112]
Others of particular interest include 'Blaen Porth Gwydhan', most
probably deriving from a *BS* source, though which version is unclear,[113]
and Rhys ap Gruffudd's winning of the castle of 'Dynevwr' as in *BS* but,
more correctly, 'Nevern' in *Pen20* and *RBH*, as is also testified by
Giraldus Cambrensis when recording the same event.[114] Particularly
surprising, in that it refers to a place-name in north Wales and is an
omission by Llwyd, is that he makes no reference to 'Hirmawr' (or
'Hirfawr') in connection with the great battle of 'Gurgustv' (Llanrwst)
on the river Conwy in 952, although the name occurs in all the main
Brut versions including *BS*. Additionally interesting, however, is the
omission of this gloss in the BBB version of *BS* and in the Peniarth 213
version of *Pen20*.[115]

[109] See above n.51; also Ll, f. 104 *s.a.* 1116 'Abercomyn or Aberkorram', *BS s.a.* 1113
Abercouuyn, BBB Comwyn, *Pen20* Abercorram, *RBH* Abercofwy.
[110] Above, p. 20; note f. 185v; Ll, f. 85, Magnus stroke Hughe earl of Shrewsbury:
RBH, BS *s.a.* 1094, Earl Hugh was wounded by Magnus; *Pen20 s.a.* 1096, Earl Hugh
wounded Magnus; Ll, f. 152, Cadwaladr slain 'pryvely': *BS s.a.* 1186 *yn lledrat* 'by stealth';
RBH yn gyhoedawc 'openly'; Ll, f. 145 *s.a.* 1172, Seisyll ap Dyfnwal and Ieuan ap Seisyll ap
Rhirid got the castell of Abergevenny upon the sodeine, and toke the Kinges garrison
prisoners': *BS s.a.* 1173 Seisyll ap Dyfnwal and Ieuan ap Seisyll ap Rhiryd seized the castle
of Abergavenny and imprisoned the garrison; *RBH, Pen20* Seisyll ap Dyfnwal and Ieuan
ap Seisyll ap Rhiryd seized by the king's men (correctly).
[111] For example, notes ff. 109, 115v, 198, 203; also Ll, f. 137 (blinding of the two sons
of Owain Gwynedd and Rhys ap Gruffudd as in *Pen20* not as, more correctly, in *RBH*,
BS; see *Pen20Tr*, 63.40–64n.
[112] See notes ff. 86v, 92v, 135, 192v, 205.
[113] Ll, f. 105: *BS Blaen Porth Gwydni*, BBB *Gwyddno*, *RBH Hodnant*, from *Hoddni*. See
HW, II, 434 n.116. On Llwyd's misplacing of the river *Hodny* (Brecs.), *Twmbarlum* (Mon.)
and *Worme's Heade* (Glam.) on his map of Wales see North, 'Humphrey Llwyd's maps',
51.
[114] Ll, f. 153v *s.a.* 1191; *Giraldus Cambrensis Opera*, vi, 111–12 (*Itin. Kambriae*, II, ii). The
Mostyn MS 143 version of *Pen20* also has 'Dinevwr' : for its probable derivation from an
original *castellum de Niver*, through forms such as *CW* 'Dynneuore', see *Pen20Tr*, 74.9n.
[115] Ll, f. 47; see *BS*, 34, n.3, *Pen20*, 9 n.11; note f. 77v.

Llwyd's special interest in Welsh place-names and topography is not
only in line with the concern already noted for such matters, and with
the greater significance being given in western Europe to vernacular
tongues, but is in its own way a manifestation also of the priority still
being attached in his age to the authority of antiquity. One cannot but
sense also that, in putting 'thees thinges into the Englishe tonge',
prominent among the 'goode men and honeste natures' that Llwyd
hoped to please, to enlighten and to convince were his scholarly friends
and colleagues in the Arundel household at Nonsuch. These several
motives would apply at least as closely to his concern to introduce into
his account details of family connections and particularly the links with
Wales of his noble employer and patron Henry Fitzalan, earl of Arundel.
Among the more noteworthy additions that he makes to the material he
found in the *Brut* in this respect are those which recall common ground
shared with those of the Montgomery line who had been in their day
earls of Arundel and Shrewsbury, the links with the English Crown and
the Welsh royal line through the Mortimers and with Powys through
both these great houses and the Audley family, and the Arundel
connections in north-east Wales with the lordships of Bromfield and
Yale and Chirk, Whittington and Oswestry, and especially with Llwyd's
native town of Denbigh.[116]

It is not surprising either that most of Llwyd's observations on the
genealogy of other families relate also to north and north-east Wales, the
area most familiar to him.[117] He adds to his list of the sons of Rhodri the
Great the traditional version of the division of Wales among them;
naming the sons of Idwal Foel enables him to explain the right to
kingship of both Hywel Dda and Llywelyn ap Seisyll; the death of
Madog ap Maredudd ap Bleddyn is an opportunity to trace the history
of the division of Powys, and that of Owain Cyfeiliog to explain again
the names Powys Wenwynwyn and Powys Fadog.[118] The detail of
family matters and to a lesser extent the explanation of place-names

[116] Ll, ff. 81v, 201v, 202, 207v, 216; 11v–13, 174v, 183, 194, 199; 10v.

[117] An exception worth noting is the reference (Ll, f. 187) to the offspring of William
Marshal the elder, earl of Pembroke and lord of Striguil, and the naming of his five
daughters with details of their marriages. Another is the pedigree of Rhys ap Tewdwr
(f. 76); this does not occur in *Pen20*, *RBH*, *BS* but is given in Pen.213 (for other such
examples see note f. 77v). Like Peniarth 213 Llwyd omits Rhys ap Tewdwr's father,
Cadell, as do Powel (*HC* (1584), 13–14; (1811). The error could possibly be an instance of
Llwyd's lack of familiarity with south Wales, but, in any case, it is the more surprising in
that Giraldus Cambrensis, whose work Llwyd claims to know, has it correctly (*Giraldus
Cambrensis, Opera*, vi, 167 (*Descr. Kambriae*, I, iii)); *HW*, II, 393 n.116.

[118] Ll, ff. 44v, 132v, 162; above, n.51; note f. 36v.

provide the occasion also to introduce some of the traditional tales which at times lend flavour to Llwyd's account. His anecdote explaining the name 'Crogen' is one of many occasions when he seeks to redress any ill repute attached to his countrymen, whereas the tale of the monk of 'Cummer' (Cwm-hir) records yet another failure on his part to recognize a place-name in the southern part of Wales.[119] A tale rooted in traditional north Wales lore and first given cohesive utterance in the 'Cronica Walliae' is that which tells of the discovery of the New World by Madog, claimed to be the son of Owain Gwynedd, the twelfth-century prince of Gwynedd. It is not intended here to dwell on the story nor on the remarkable validation it affords of Llwyd's own judgement that it is a tale which in the retelling 'the commen people do use in distance of place and leingth of tyme rather to augment than to dyminish'.[120] It is worth noting Llwyd's quoting of a source, 'Francys Loues'; the restraint of his reference to Spain, for he was after all writing in a strongly Catholic household and doing so while Mary reigned or very soon afterwards; and the stress, itself possibly a veiled defence of indigenous languages and customs, laid on the 'non-colonial' nature of the discovery and the subsequent settlement.[121] Part of the genealogical past in a particular area of Wales is mirrored, albeit with much distortion, in the tale of the winning of Glamorgan by the Normans under Robert Fitzhamon.[122] It could well be that Llwyd's version was an integral part of his main Welsh source, but, however that may be, it is unique by virtue of several differences which distinguish it from other sixteenth-century accounts written in English, all of which have a south Wales provenance and which therefore have been seen as being

[119] Ll, ff. 168–168v, 192v–193; see note f. 192v.
[120] Ll, ff. 141–2. Llwyd's version was published, with additions, in Powel, *Historie of Cambria*, by which time the legend had already been printed and given a political edge in a pamphlet: Anon [Sir George Peckham], *A True Reporte of the late discoveries . . . wherein is also briefly sette downe her Highnesse lawful Tytle thereunto . . .* (London, 1583). For a discussion of the treatment of the legend in the sixteenth and seventeenth centuries see Williams, 'Ysgolheictod hanesyddol', 122 n.48, 222 n.71; and, in later centuries, David Williams, 'John Evans' strange journey', *THSC*, 1948, 105–46. Latterly, some more voluminous works, aimed it would seem at capturing a wider American audience, are R. Deacon, *Madoc and the Discovery of America* (London, 1967); G. A. Williams, *Madoc, The Making of a Myth* (London, 1979).
[121] The author is listed in Jayne and Johnson, *Lumley Library*, no. 1128 as Francisco Lopez de Gomara, *De La Historia Generall de Las Indias* (Antwerp, 1554). Madog arrived there without intent but 'by reason and order of cosmographie', and a second time in company with 'suche men and women as were desirouse to lyve in quietnes' and who 'folowed the maners of the lande they came unto and used the language they found there'.
[122] Ll, ff. 20v, 80–81.

probably close to an original version of the tale.[123] According to Welsh
native tradition, as reflected in the works of fifteenth-century poets such
as Lewys Glyn Cothi, Einion ap Gollwyn, whose conflict with Rhys ap
Tewdwr facilitated the Normans' coming to Morgannwg, had his roots
in Gwynedd and had family connections with Iestyn ap Gwrgant.
Ironically Llwyd, obviously knowing nothing of this north Wales
tradition, seems to blame the main legend for his own scant knowledge
of this part of south Wales when he first mentions it in the Description:
'of this [Morgannwg nowe Glamorgan shire] youe shall reade very litle
for one Iestyn . . . called one Robert Fitzhamon with a.great number of
strangers to his succoure . . . which . . . liked so well the countrey that
they . . . inhabited the countrey them selves and ther heires to this
daye'.[124] Llwyd introduces another such interjection with the words,
'here I thinke hit good to let the reader understande what the Britishe
Cronicle saithe of Northwales . . . that three tymes hit came by
enheritannce to women'; and he marks the end with 'By this youe maye
understand that Northwales hathe bene agreat wheile the chieffest seat
of the last kings of Britaine'.[125] The triad which lies at the heart of this
tradition speaks, not of north Wales, but of the three women rulers of
Gwynedd.[126] Although claiming the 'Britishe Cronicle' to be his source,
Llwyd takes his account out of any historical context by placing it in the
introductory section, the Description of Wales. He makes no mention
of the tradition at the most appropriate point in his historical account,
the succession of Merfyn Frych and Esyllt, the last of the three women
rulers; but he does, however, seek to demonstrate Merfyn Frych's right
to rule Gwynedd jointly with Esyllt by virtue of his noble descent.[127]

---

[123] These are the accounts in Leland, *Itinerary in Wales*, 38; Sir Edward Stradling, 'The
winning of the lordship of Glamorgan', as printed in *HC* (1584), 122–50; (1811),
192–214; and Rice Merrick, *Morganiae Archaiographia: A Booke of the Antiquities of
Glamorganshire*, ed. B. L. James (South Wales Record Society, 1, 1983), 19–30. Some
noteworthy differences concern Llwyd's references to Iestyn ap Gwrgant and Einion ap
Gollwyn. He alone refers to the latter as Einion ap Cadifor ap Gollwyn, relates that he fled
to Iestyn, that Iestyn was given the barren and rough mountain land and that the Normans
arrived and, after completing their task, set out to depart by sea. It should be added that
Llwyd's own account varies as between the 'Cronica Walliae' and *Commentarioli . . .
Fragmentum*, 100–1.
[124] See Ll, f. 20v. Interestingly enough the apparent cultural isolation within Wales of
Glamorgan in the twelfth and thirteenth centuries, the meagre references to it in the *Brut*
and the absence of the large genealogical collections which characterize other regions have
been remarked upon in G. J. Williams, *Traddodiad Llenyddol Morgannwg* (Cardiff, 1948), 8,
183; also ibid., 34–5, 118 n.119.
[125] Ll, ff. 14, 16v.
[126] *TYP*, 258; see note f. 14.
[127] Ll, ff. 30–30v and note f. 16v.

Thus Llwyd displays once more his support of 'right heires' and by implication of the primacy of north Wales.

In fact Merfyn's reign, regarded within the overall significance of the division of the 'Cronica Walliae' narrative by reigns, provides the first clear instance of Llwyd's wish to elaborate upon the detail in his *Brut* source in order to present his views on those issues, and also later on related matters such as the title and status of 'king' and 'prince'.[128] Although here again the possibility cannot be entirely ruled out that reign headings had already been introduced into the particular *Brut* version which was Llwyd's main source, enough is known of his own interest in these matters to make it more than likely that they were added by Llwyd himself. To the evidence of the frequent and lengthy genealogical glosses in the 'Cronica Walliae' can be added Llwyd's own compositions on genealogy and heraldry[129] and the nature of some of the works in the Lumley catalogue bearing his signature.[130] There is also the intriguing implication in a letter by Hugh Thomas of Brecon to Edward Lhuyd describing his visit to the great-great-grandson of Humphrey Llwyd when he borrowed a book by Llwyd containing, among other materials, 'some Notes upon the Welsh Chronicle in English from the Death of Cadwalader to the conquest of Wales by King Edward the first with the Liniall descent of all the British and Welsh Kings from Adam'.[131] On the whole the *Brut* is inexplicit about the succession of rulers, apart from providing an annal concerning their end,

[128] In recent years several important discussions have been published on the political and legal aspects of these concepts in medieval Wales. Although our sole concern here is with Llwyd's perceptions of these issues as manifested in his treatment of his *Brut* source, it may be useful to note briefly some of these which make reference also to other relevant discussions. They include R. R. Davies, 'Law and national identity in thirteenth-century Wales', in R. R. Davies *et al.* (eds), *Welsh Society and Nationhood: Historical Essays Presented to Glanmor Williams* (Cardiff, 1984), 51; J. Beverley Smith, *Llywelyn ap Gruffudd, Prince of Wales* (Cardiff, 1998), chap. VI; and idem, *The Sense of History in Medieval Wales* (Aberystwyth, [1989]). For the nomenclature, D. Jenkins, 'Kings, lords and princes: the nomenclature of authority in thirteenth-century Wales', *BBCS*, 26 (1974–6), 451–62. David Powel gives a summary of Llwyd's treatment as he sees it at the end of the section describing the reign of Cadwaladr in *HC* (1584), 6; (1811), 5.
[129] Gruffydd, 'Humphrey Llwyd', 66–82; M. P. Siddons, *The Development of Welsh Heraldry*, 3 vols (Aberystwyth, 1991), I, index under Llwyd, Humphrey.
[130] These include Jayne and Johnson, *Lumley Library*, no. 951, *Aurea Bulla Caroli Quarti Imperatoris* (Mainz, 1549); no. 1073, David Holland, 'Of the discent of Kinge Edwarde the Sixt by the father, from Brute' (MS); no. 1233, G. Boccaccio, *De Certaldo de Claris Mulieribus cum figuris* (Berne, 1539); no. 1243, J. Funck, *Chronologia ab Initio Mundi ad annum 1553* (Basle, 1554); no. 1334, M. Ritius, *De Regibus Francorum . . . De Regibus Hungariae* (Basle, 1570): also above n.48.
[131] Bodleian Library, Ashmole MS 1917B f. 5; see Gruffydd, 'Humphrey Llwyd', 85–6.

and it appears to take for granted a consensus on the question of 'right inheritance' as it does on that of the primacy of the 'kingdom' of North Wales. It describes Ifor the son of Alan of Brittany (and therefore not a 'right heire') as ruling not as king but as prince or leader (*pennaeth, tywysog*). Rhodri Molwynog succeeded as Cadwaladr's grandson, and Llwyd adds his own account of Rhodri's forced migration from the West country 'to seeke his owne inheritaunce in Northwales',[132] which thus initiated compliance with both criteria. Rhodri is described at his death in 754 by the *Brut* and Llwyd as 'Kinge of the Britons'; but, whereas his son and successor Cynan Dindaethwy is named simply 'king Cynan' by the *Brut* at his death, Llwyd makes clear his own view of Cynan's rightful status by that time as 'chief King of the Britons or Welshmen'.[133] Cynan's successor, however, was Merfyn Frych of the royal line of Powys, the first of several notable rulers during the following two centuries who were 'out of line' in the strict sense of descent in the royal line of Gwynedd or North Wales. In Merfyn's case, whereas the *Brut* mentions only his death and gives him no title, Llwyd, as already noted, cites his noble descent at some length and at the end of his reign in 844 names him 'Kinge of Britons'.[134] Thereafter, in the case of 'rightful heirs', Llwyd continues to amplify the *Brut's* vague entries by giving them full titular recognition; and he deals in turn with those not of the royal line of Gwynedd by describing the alternative 'right to rule' claimed or imposed in each case.

An eminently notable instance is, of course, Hywel Dda son of Cadell, king of South Wales, who became 'the noblest and worthiest Kinge of Wales' by virtue of his 'godly behaveor, discret and just rule' despite the claims of the true heirs.[135] His grandson Maredudd ab Owain, according to Llwyd, conquered North Wales as an instrument of God's justice and died 'Kinge of Wales'.[136] His successor Aeddan ap Blegywryd, who 'by force had taken upon him the rule of Northwales', was slain together with his four sons by Llywelyn ap Seisyll who 'havinge no respecte to Jago or James the sonne of Idwall and righte heire, tooke upon him the name and authoritie of Kinge of Wales', claiming the right and title by descent on his mother's side from the kings of Wales and claiming south Wales through his wife, the only

---

[132] Ll, f. 27v; for *pennaeth, tywysog*, see *Pen20*, 1 (*Pen20Tr*, 1); *RBH*, 1–2.
[133] Ll, f. 30, *BT, s.a.* 817.
[134] Ll, f. 32v.
[135] Ll, ff. 45, 46.
[136] Ll, ff. 50v, 53.

daughter of Maredudd ab Owain.[137] Llywelyn's son Gruffudd was able
to oust his father's successor, the 'right heire' Iago son of Idwal, because
'the more parte and the better souldiors were with Griffith for the love
they bare to his father'.[138] Following the death of Gruffudd ap Llywelyn
in 1061 (*recte* 1063), Llwyd's account is concerned largely with the
restitution of rule by right of inheritance, which was gained at last, by
Llwyd's reckoning exactly two decades later, with victory at the battle of
Mynydd Carn, when 'Griffith the sonne of Kynan . . . joyned with Rys
ap Tewdur as twoe right heires, Griffith of Northwales and Rys of
Southwales descendinge from Rodericke the Greate'.[139] It is worth
observing here that Llwyd, who rarely has much of his own to add to
the *Brut* in matters concerned with south Wales, includes as part of his
account of the reign of Rhys ap Tewdwr the tale of the winning of
Glamorgan by Fitzhamon and his Norman followers;[140] but in the case
of the reign of Gruffudd ap Cynan he follows closely the very sparse
account in the *Brut*, which for most of this period has more to say of
south Wales and Powys than of Gwynedd.[141] As a consequence he finds
it necessary to correct an impression of secondary status which the *Brut*
account seems to bestow now and then on Gruffudd and to place much
more emphasis than does the *Brut* on Gruffudd's right to reign in

---

[137] Ll, f. 59v.

[138] Ll, f. 62v.

[139] Ll, f. 76v; Llwyd erroneously gives 'mountains of Carno' for 'Carno'.

[140] Ll, ff. 79v–81.

[141] Where the *Brut* versions differ, Llwyd's particular source seems to vary; for example:
Ll, f. 77v Sulien '. . . the secunde tyme' occurs in *Pen20* (*Pen20Tr*, 17.32n); Ll, f. 78v
'Llechryd' only in *BS* (note f. 77v); Ll, f. 83 'Kelhy Tarvawc' in *Pen20* (*Pen20Tr*, 20.10.n.;
note f. 83); Ll, f. 84v the sobriquets 'Hugh Goch' and 'Hugh Fras' and the naming of
Owain ab Edwin as traitor occur only in *Pen20* but the building of Aberlleiniog occurs
only in the *Historia Gruffud vab Kenan* (below n.143) and not in *Pen20*; Ll, f. 87v Magnus
landing in Môn for timber follows *Pen20* not *BS*, (see *Pen20Tr*, 24.32–3n.); Ll, f. 109
'Owen was begotten . . . Edwyn' is in *BS* only (*BS*, 135.33–4n.; note f. 109); Ll, f. 112
'Ithell ap Ryryd . . . cold not come by hit' has no parallel in *BS* (note f. 112). This
apparent variety of *Brut* sources lends weight, of course, to a supposition that Llwyd was
translating an 'edited' composite version. As to the fewer references to Gwynedd, Powys
was predominant in Wales at that time; Llwyd himself, Ll, ff. 87–87v, like the *Brut*, names
Iorwerth ap Bleddyn as the 'greatest man off power in Wales', and the main (Latin) source
of the *Brut* between about 1100 and 1175 was a Llanbadarn Fawr document (see *HW*, II,
411 ff.; and *Pen20Tr*, xli). With the sole exception of Hywel Dda, Llwyd's chapter
headings refer steadfastly to the rulers of North Wales despite the overriding influence in
their time of others such as Rhys ap Tewdwr, Iorwerth ap Bleddyn and Rhys ap Gruffudd
(the Lord Rhys).

Gwynedd.[142] It seems clear by all this that Llwyd did not have recourse to the biography accorded, uniquely among Welsh princes, to Gruffudd ap Cynan. In fact, despite a few references which seem to derive from *Historia Gruffud vab Kenan*, there is other evidence to support a view that Llwyd did not know of that work. He takes no account of the *Historia*'s many references to place-names, nor of the several opportunities it offers to cast Gruffudd in a heroic mould as in the tale of his eagerness, compared with the reluctance of Rhys ap Tewdwr, to engage the common enemy at Mynydd Carn. More important, Llwyd makes no reference to Gruffudd's many years of imprisonment in Chester gaol: he would surely have related the tale of the prince's escape with the aid of Cynwrig Hir had he known of it.[143] Moreover, Llwyd gives no indication of knowing anything of the 'Statute of Gruffudd ap Cynan'. As its omission in the text below confirms (f. 116v), it was Powel himself who added, misleadingly as though it was part of Llwyd's account, the sentence 'He [Griffith ap Cynan] reformed the disordered behavior of the Welsh minstrels by a verie good Statute which is extant to this

---

[142] Llwyd (Ll, f. 76) includes the Brut's 'Rys the sonne of Tewdur . . . right heire to the kingdome of Southwales', and hastens immediately afterwards to equate Gruffudd and Rhys 'as twoe right heires' respectively of North and South Wales. Earlier, at the beginning of the reign of Trahaearn ap Caradog (Ll, f. 75), he had altered the *Brut's* description of Gruffudd simply as 'grandson of Iago' (*Pen20 s.a.* 1073, *BS* erroneously 'James's nephew') to 'Griffith sonne to Kynan, sonne to Iago . . . right enheritor of Northwales' ; and later Ll, f. 77; *Brut, s.a.* 1079, after the battle of Mynydd Carn, he adds 'and so the kingdomes of Wales came under the rule of the righte heirs againe', which provides a corrective for the secondary role given by the *Brut* to Gruffudd. When Rhys is killed Llwyd (Ll, f. 80) records that the kingdom of South Wales fell, as do *Pen20* and *BS*, but does not then comment that the 'kingdom of the Britons' and 'the kingdom of Wales' fell (*Pen20Tr, BS s.a.* 1091). Later, in Ll, f. 82, again as an addition to the *Brut*, when Llwyd links Gruffudd with Cadwgan ap Bleddyn, Gruffudd becomes 'King of Northwales and chief and onely ruler of all Wales' (*Brut, s.a.* 1092); and when Magnus lands in Môn for timber, Llwyd adds (Ll, f. 87v) that he was 'reaceved of Griffith ap Kynan'.

[143] See D. Simon Evans (ed.), *Historia Gruffud vab Kenan* (Cardiff, 1977) where (cxix *et seq.*) the context and composition of the work are examined in detail, and the essays in K. L. Maund (ed.), *Gruffudd ap Cynan: A Collaborative Biography* (Woodbridge, 1996), and cf. Ll, ff. 76–116v. Llwyd (f. 75) names the two brothers who helped Gruffudd's first expedition to Môn, and gives the list of his children (f. 116v) as it appears in the *Historia*. Elsewhere in the 'Cronica Walliae' the name *Bonp y don* is also reminiscent of the *Historia*, 2; see note f. 222. Among the place-names are those of the landings of Porth Clais and Porth Honddu, Gruffudd's early victory at Gwaederw (Y Tir Gwaedlyd), Erw yr Allt as another name for Bron yr Erw, and Mynydd y Garnedd for Mynydd Carn (*Historia*, 9.5n., 11.15n., 13.19n., 16.14n., 18.22n.). For Gruffudd's imprisonment and release, see *Historia*, 16–18. Llwyd's citation of material closely akin to that of the *Historia* is not readily explained; it may be attributable to its inclusion in his source copy.

daie', presumably as a prelude to his own additional note on the statute.[144]

Llwyd does, however, seem to have fulfilled his overriding purpose of laying greater emphasis on the *Brut*'s passing reference to the return to rule by 'right heires' in both South and North Wales, and in that process to have strengthened the role given by the *Brut* to North Wales under Gruffudd ap Cynan. On the death of that ruler Llwyd describes him as 'Kinge and prince of Northwales'; and his son and successor Owain Gwynedd as 'Prince of Northwales', adding 'for the name of kinge is no further used in the British Booke'.[145] While this is not entirely true of the *Brut*,[146] Llwyd thenceforth adheres strictly to the title 'prince', and diligently brings consistency to the *Brut*'s sometimes eccentric application of titles: Owain Gwynedd is never other than 'prince of North-wales' and his contemporaries Gruffudd ap Rhys and Madog ap Maredudd ap Bleddyn, less regularly, prince of 'Southwales' and prince of Powys respectively; the briefer epithet 'the prince', however, is given only to Owain as prince of 'Northwales'. Also by his own interpretation of events, having called attention to the 'enviable' state of unity gained in North Wales,[147] Llwyd avails himself of the opportunities afforded by the *Brut*'s account of the later reigns to underline in his own way the several occasions when Wales as a whole was united under the leadership of the prince of North Wales. When, according to the *Brut*, Llywelyn ap Iorwerth in 1202 'summoned all his kinsmen and his leaders' to make war on Gwenwynwyn of Powys, the motives attributed to him clearly reflect Llwyd's own view of the historical force of Welsh traditional usage and law in relation to the issue of the overlordship of North Wales:

---

[144] *HC* (1584), 191; (1811), 140. For the 'Statute of Gruffudd ap Cynan', a late tract on the bardic order, of which the earliest text appears to be that in the hand of Gruffudd Hiraethog, see T. Parry, 'Statud Gruffudd ap Cynan', *BBCS*, 5 (1929–31), 25–33; D. Klausner, 'Statud Gruffudd ap Cynan/The Statute of Gruffudd ap Cynan', *Welsh Music History*, 3 (1999), 282–98. A comparison of Powel's text with Llwyd's at this point shows that Powel has added also to Gruffudd's offspring 'by an other woman' one 'Elen the wife of Hova ap Ithel Velyn of Yal'.

[145] Ll, ff. 116v, 117. *HC* 'king or prince of Northwales' weakens the sense of overlordship of Wales which Llwyd seems to imply, especially when he adds (f. 116v) the encomium 'the onely defence and sheelde of all Wales'. Llwyd (f. 82) had previously described Gruffudd as 'Kinge of Northwales and chief and onely ruler of all Wales'. For the styles, Jenkins, 'Kings, lords and princes', 451–62.

[146] See above, p. 19.

[147] For example, Madog ap Maredudd 'envyed at the libertie of Northwales, which knewe no lorde but one' (Ll, f. 129).

And Lhewelyn ap Ierwerth Prince of Northwales, callinge to memorye his estate and title, and howe all the princes of Wales, by the ordinnance of Rodrike the Great, and after by the lawes of Howell Dha, ought of right to acknowledge the Prince or Kinge of Aberfrawe and Northwales as their liedge lorde, and holde their landes of him and of non other, and howe of late yeres, by neglygennce of his predecessors they did not use their accustomed duetie, but some helde of the Kinge of Inglande, and other ruled as supreme powers within their owne countreys, therfore he called a parliamente of all the lordes in Wales, which for the moste parte appeared before him, and swore to bee his liedge men.[148]

It was such a meeting assembled later at Aberdyfi in 1216, described by J. E. Lloyd as 'virtually a Welsh parliament', that confirmed Llywelyn's supremacy over the whole of Wales. Llwyd does not mention directly the presence of other princes and leaders of Wales nor of the 'learned men of Gwynedd', so that Llywelyn appears to be the sole arbiter in the division of lands between the sons and grandsons of Rhys ap Gruffudd.[149] Later, during the reign of Llywelyn ap Gruffudd, Llwyd seems to imply more than once that as a consequence of the prince's leadership the nobles of Wales were now moved by motives of a patriotism which was loftier than sectional loyalties or mere self-interest: swearing allegiance to Llywelyn and maintaining loyalty and agreement together, as in the *Brut*, becomes swearing an oath 'to defende their countrey to the deathe'[150] and a little before that he had described the refusal of the heir to the throne of England, the Lord Edward, to engage in battle with Llywelyn ap Gruffudd, who had with him 10,000 armed men, 'every one sworne to suffer death . . . in the defence of their countrey'.[151]

---

[148] Ll, ff. 167–167v; *Pen20Tr*, 81–2 (*s.a.* 1202).

[149] Ll, f. 181v–182, *Pen20Tr*, 92 *s.a.* 1216. See also *HW*, II, 649. Cf. also Llwyd's omission of the *Brut*'s clear emphasis that both the siege of Carmarthen and the razing of Trefdraeth were done by the 'common consent' of the princes; his claim that John sent to Reginald de Breos and to the prince for friendship rather than to 'the princes of Wales' as in the *Brut*; and his own emphasis on the modified homage done to Henry at Ceri by the prince rather than by 'the leading men of Wales' in *BT* (Ll, ff. 181, 183, 191; *Pen20Tr*, 91 (1215); 93 (1216), 101 (1228).

[150] Ll, f. 208, *Pen20*, 111 (1259). Cf. also 'it was, no doubt, with the assent of this gathering that he (*sc.* Llywelyn) now began to style himself "prince of Wales"' (*HW*, II, 723–4, and nn.42, 43, 47).

[151] Ll, f. 205v. This does not occur in the *Brut*; it is reproduced from Paris, *CM*, V, 597: *Erant namque equites ad decem milia eorum armati . . . Qui mutuo confoederati tactis Evangeliis juraverant se strenue et fideliter usque ad mortem pro libertate patriae suae et avitis legibus decertare.*

This seems a far cry from the days when Owain Gwynedd ruled North Wales and Rhys ap Gruffudd held powerful sway in South Wales. At that time Llwyd had interpreted the *Brut* account of an accord such as those mentioned in the previous paragraph, but aimed at restoring the ancient division of Wales so as to throw off the rule of the Normans, as one intended also to enable the Welsh 'to serve princes of their owne nation'.[152] Even after that stirring declamation attributed to Llywelyn ap Iorwerth in 1202, but while the prince was still in the process of making his authority secure, Llwyd describes him as appealing to his peers from south Wales and the whole of Powys to join with him so that they, who were subject to a stranger, but were 'wont to have a prince of their owne nation', might 'defende their auncient estate still'.[153] In all this, while no great weight should perhaps be given individually to what might be seen as no more than fine distinctions in Llwyd's phrasing, taken together they give a clearer impression than does the *Brut*'s account of a progression towards an acceptance of the overlordship of the prince of Gwynedd or North Wales. It cannot be entirely without significance in this connection that Llwyd keeps closely to the *Brut*'s brief account of the treaty of Montgomery and therefore presents only those two clauses which redefine, probably to his mind in a manner consonant with the tribute due to the king of Aberffraw according to the laws of Hywel Dda, the relationship of the prince of North Wales to the other lords in Wales and to the Crown of England. It is this achievement which brings Llywelyn ap Gruffudd to 'the hiest and most honorable staye that any Prince of Wales was in of many yeres before'.[154]

(b) Material relating to England and elsewhere
So far this examination of Llwyd's main Welsh source, despite underlining significant complications in the nature of its relationship to the *Brut*, has confirmed that most of the historical matter relating to Wales in Llwyd's text derives ultimately from some version or versions of *Brut y Tywysogyon* and, in the earlier section especially, from a version similar to *Brenhinedd y Saesson*. In considering Llwyd's material concerned with the history of the 'other inhabitants of this Ile', not only the English but

[152] LL, ff. 135–135v.
[153] Ll, ff. 175v–176. It is interesting to note that, near the end of the reign of Llywelyn ap Iorwerth, Llwyd (like *BS* alone, and that section of the 'Cronica Walliae' where *Pen20* was the usual source) names Joan his wife 'princess of Wales', and for the first time refers to Wales as a 'princedome' and 'principalitie' respectively in the reigns of Dafydd ap Llywelyn and Llywelyn ap Gruffudd: Ll, ff. 198, 203v, 204; see also above n.105.
[154] Ll, ff. 43v, 216v.

also the Scots and Irish, it must of course be borne in mind that much of this material derives from sources other than the *Brut*, sources that will be considered briefly later; also that it is necessary to distinguish between, on the one hand, those references which are common to *Brut y Tywysogyon* and *Brenhinedd y Saesson* and, on the other, those which are unique to the latter and which in Thomas Jones's edition appear, most helpfully, in smaller type.

To deal first with the references common to all three versions of the *Brut*: most of these occur also in Llwyd's account though seldom in the exact form that they are found in the *Brut*.[155] This is true from the earliest annals, those recording natural phenomena such as earthquakes in the Isle of Man and the discolouring of the moon and some terrestrial objects, which in Llwyd are placed before the reign of Rhodri Molwynog not after, as in the *Brut*, even though the dating is later.[156] From then onward, however, the entries in Llwyd's account differ in the main by attaching additional and sometimes different information usually from English chronicle sources; but the links with the *Brut* are implicit in the positioning of each entry of this kind, as in the *Brut* itself, precisely within the chronological sequence of the Welsh references. Instances are frequent and widespread. An early *Brut* annal, that recording the death of Bede in 735, is typical of many: it is dated (incorrectly) 733 in Llwyd,[157] with added details, commonplace in English chronicles, about his upbringing, his writings and his Northumbrian connections; it is, however, placed exactly as in the *Brut* between the battle of Mynydd Carno and the death of Owain, king of the Picts. Another is the *Brut* reference to the sacking of York, placed between the death of Cynan of Nanhyfer and the destruction of the tower of Alclud (Dumbarton), to which Llwyd adds that the two kings Osberht (Osbright) and Ælle (Ella) were slain.[158] These appear to be straightforward instances of endeavours to improve or enlarge a bare *Brut* annal. Similar examples occur regularly in Llwyd's account, at least as far as the entry recording Henry III's fruitless expedition to France in 1242 'to recover some of that which his

---

[155] Those omitted are concerned in the main with ecclesiastical matters and with the Crusades; also the occasional 'repetitious' annal such as the English kings' visits to France (for example, Henry III in 1259, *BT s.a.* 1259). It is also the case, of course, that just as some of Llwyd's text referring to affairs outside Wales derives from Welsh chronicle sources, so do some of the references to Welsh affairs derive from English chronicle sources.

[156] For the basic chronology see note f. 26v.

[157] Ll, f. 27.

[158] Ll, ff. 35–35v *s.a.* 868; *s.a.* 866. Osberht and Ælle are named in *HH* and *RW s.a.* 867.

father had lost', placed between the record of the imprisonment in London of Gruffudd son of Llywelyn ap Iorwerth and of the fortifying of the castles of Garth Grugyn, Builth and Maelienydd.[159] In the same way, most of the usually brief references to events in Ireland and Scotland common to all three *Brut* versions can be shown to occur in Llwyd, differing occasionally in some details but generally carefully synchronized with the Welsh entries as in the *Brut*.[160] Here too the differences are usually due to additions from English chronicle sources. One instance is the account of King John's voyage to Ireland in 1210, based mainly on the *Pen20* version but with some detail added, probably from Nicholas Trevet, who mentions the winning of Connaught and the capture of Cathol its prince.[161] Another is the recording under the year 1234 of the death in Ireland of Richard, earl of Pembroke, which has details not found in the *Brut*, such as the reference to Geoffrey de Marisco and to the disposal of Richard's lands – details given also by Roger Wendover, Matthew Paris and more briefly by Trevet.[162] There are occasions, however, when it becomes more difficult to ascribe the references in Llwyd's account mainly to a *Brut* source, at least with the same degree of certainty. This is especially the case if a common source is sought for a sequence of related events, as instanced by Henry I's involvement with Normandy during the earlier part of his reign, to which Llwyd's account refers on five occasions; or the four *Brut* references to the reign of Richard I which Llwyd includes among others in his account; or again events in the *Brut* relating to the reign of John,

---

[159] Ll, ff. 198v–199, *Pen20Tr*, 106 *s.a.* 1242. Though Llwyd's account of Henry III's expedition to France has little in common with the *Brut* apart from its position and its stated purpose, Ll's 'he lost a great number of his men' seems to reflect *Pen20* 'after losing (*colli*) earls and barons' (*Pen20Tr*, 106.10–11n.). Instances like those in the text above are: Robert de Bellême's cruel nature and his imprisonment, Ll, f. 98v *s.a.* 1111, *Brut s.a.* 1109; Henry I's marriage to Adela of Louvain, Ll, f. 110v *s.a.* 1121, *Brut s.a.* 1118; the landing in England of the Empress Maud, Ll, ff. 118–118v, *Brut s.a.* 1137; the deaths of Robert, earl of Gloucester, and Gilbert, earl of Clare, Ll, f. 124v, *BT s.a.* 1147; and of the 'Earle of Glocester', Ll, ff. 210v, *BT s.a.* 1262; the Pope's interdict on worship in England and the banishing of William de Breos, Ll, f. 170v, *BT s.a.* 1208; Henry III's marriage to Eleanor of Provence, Ll, f. 196, *BT s.a.* 1235.

[160] Early annals include the death of Owain king of the Picts (Ll, f. 27 *s.a.* 736,), the Danish invasion of Ireland (Ll, f. 29 *s.a.* 786), the death of 'Submon Cubin' (Ll, f. 37v *s.a.* 889) and the plague of locusts (Ll, f. 39v *s.a.* 897). Others follow (see notes ff. 52, 57v, 88, 138, 139, 142, 144, 171v, 195).

[161] Ll, f. 171v; *NT*, 182 *s.a.* 1210.

[162] Ll, f. 195; *RW*, IV, 306–7; *CM*, III, 279, 288–9, 292; *NT*, 220.

and especially to the king's conflict with the barons.[163] Whereas most of
Llwyd's descriptions of these events have much in common with the
Brut, some differ so much in their detail as to give the appearance of
quite separate accounts,[164] and others demonstrate yet again the
confusing mixture of sources discernible in so much of Llwyd's work.
Such is his very brief reference to the sinking 'by the misgoverment of
the maister' of the ship carrying home to England Henry I's sons (named
as William and Richard), his daughter and niece together with some 150
others. *Pen20* refers to two sons and 200 others, hinting at
mismanagement in that the ship bore down on the rocks 'unknown to
the sailors'. *BS* gives no such explanation but does add a reference to
Henry's daughter as one of those drowned. English chroniclers add a
daughter and niece and name the sons as does Llwyd, but give no
number for the others and attribute the disaster to the vengeance of God
because the ship's passengers were guilty of the sin of sodomy.[165] In
general, however, despite such complexities, it is clear that in the
content as well as in the pattern of these common 'non-Welsh' entries
Llwyd's account relates mainly to a *Brut* version source.

Those references to English affairs unique to *BS*, however, have far less
in common with Llwyd's account in the 'Cronica Walliae', strangely in
view of the seeming significance otherwise of *BS* as an important source.
The differences in the accounts become immediately apparent if, for
instance, a few of the longer sections in *BS* referring to some of the
events deemed to be among the most momentous in Anglo-Saxon
history are looked at alongside the equivalent accounts by Llwyd. The
undated opening description in *BS* of the conquest of Britain by the
Saxons and of the later consolidation of England under Ecgberht's rule
into one country bears little relationship to Llwyd's version of the same
events;[166] Llwyd's account of Godwine's part in the coronation of
Edward the Confessor and of his subsequent exile is very brief and differs
from *BS* in much of the content;[167] and the two versions of the sequence

[163] These few are typical examples. They are to be found respectively in *Brut s.a.*
1103–1117: Ll, ff. 90–110v; *Brut s.a.* 1189 (*RBH*, 1187–99): Ll, ff. 152v–64; *Brut s.a.*
1207–1216: Ll, ff. 170–183v.
[164] See, for example, the account of King Henry's expedition to Normandy Ll, f. 109v,
Pen20, BS s.a. 1114; and of Richard's capture and release Ll, f. 154v, *Pen20, BS s.a.* 1193.
[165] Ll, f. 110v *s.a.* 1120, *Brut s.a.* 1117; also *HH*, 466–7; *RW*, II, 201. Names of
passengers drowned on *Le Blanche Nef*, 'The White Ship', are given in W. Farrer, 'An
outline itinerary of Henry I', *EHR*, xxiv (1919), 513.
[166] *BS*, 3–5, 14 (*s.a.* 828) (Ll, ff. 1–4, 31–2).
[167] Ll, ff. 63v–64, *BS*, 61–5 *s.a.* 1043–4.

of events beginning with the death of Edward and ending in the crowning of William the Conqueror have very little in common.[168] Similar clear differences between the 'Cronica Walliae' and *BS* accounts can be seen when the *BS* 'small type' entries in general (those that are derived from the BBB text) are examined. There are, of course, broad resemblances in traditional accounts such as the arrival in Britain of Ifor the son of Alan and his subsequent departure for Rome; and also in the way he is identified with Ina (Yue) of Wessex, as well as in some of the detail such as the building of a refectory at Glastonbury and of lands given to the church in Winchester. The versions differ significantly, however, in that Llwyd omits the details in *BS* concerning Ifor's gifts to the church, as he does also its emphasis on the religious significances of his journey to Rome, and he introduces additional material from English chronicle sources.[169] In *BS* the reference to Ifor's death is separated from the preceding account by three entries which do not occur in Llwyd's version;[170] and whereas Llwyd does note those events that follow until the beginning of Ecgberht's rule, with just one exception they differ from *BS* by omitting church matters and by adding material from English chronicles.[171] The successive accounts in *BS* of the reigns of Anglo-Saxon kings from Ecgberht to William I are considerably longer than the equivalent references in the 'Cronica Walliae'. These, whilst agreeing by and large in their dating and their synchronization with Welsh affairs, correspond in little else apart from the occasional anecdotal entry common to many English chroniclers and even these are by no means identical.[172] Though the sections concerned with the reign of Athelstan show a greater degree of correspondence, notably in the erroneous reference common to both in the account of the battle of Brunanburh, in the detail of the tribute exacted from the Welsh and in the brief notices of Athelstan's death and the succession of Edmund, nevertheless the

[168] Ll, ff. 71–3, *BS*, 72–5.

[169] *BS*, 5.26–8n.; note f. 26v.

[170] *BS* s.a. 701, 709, 714.

[171] Ll, f. 26v–27v, *BS s.a.* 721 Æthelbald, 725 Cuthred, 749 Sigbert, 750 Cynewulf. For Offa's rule, above, pp.20–1. The reference to Ceolred of Mercia, Ll, f. 26v, *BS s.a.* 722 is a rare example of an entry matched in 'Cronica Walliae' in both content and dating.

[172] They include, among others, Alfred's division of the day *BS*, 23 (by candles changed every eight hours), Ll, f. 40v (by tapers changed every twenty-four hours), and his translation of the laws of the Britons *BS*, 25, Ll, f. 39v (Ll adding a reference to Dyfnwal Moelmud and to Marsia 'Queene of Britaine'); the murder of Edmund Ironside *BS*, 53 (by a servant), Ll, f. 59v (by the son of Edric); and the account of Cnut's visit to Rome *BS*, 57 (Cnut's devout injunctions to his subjects), Ll, f. 61v (bitingly scornful of Cnut's motives).

differences in Llwyd's account in terms both of what is added and what is omitted would make BS at most a partial source only.[173]

The relatively fewer and much shorter entries in BS after the Norman Conquest, from 1070 to their ending in 1168, are concerned in the main with ecclesiastical matters and have no counterparts in the 'Cronica Walliae'. A notable exception is an annal in each text referring to the death of Robert Courthose, neither of which significantly enough makes any reference to Church matters, but in this instance again there is disagreement in the detail.[174] It is significant also as the only entry in the 'Cronica Walliae' of four entries in BS relating to Wales and to south-west England bordering on Wales noticed by Thomas Jones. The three entries not included by Llwyd all refer to these matters and it is of interest therefore to note that, of certain passages in BS which are shown to correspond to entries in Corpus Christi College, Cambridge, MS 339, all but one contain references to the Church; and that in this instance again the odd 'non-Church' entry is the one to which an entry in BS corresponds and also corresponds to that in Llwyd's account, though without being identical.[175] It is also worth remarking here that virtually none of the frequent references in BS to Winchester and to St Swithin and his church in that city are to be found in Llwyd's account.[176] It will be recalled that the purpose behind these three sets of comparisons by Thomas Jones was to demonstrate the links between the passages unique to BS containing English historical matter and passages in the Annals of Winchester.[177] The omission of the BS references from Llwyd's account in these instances is in keeping with the tendency throughout the 'Cronica Walliae' to omit many of the ecclesiastical details which abound in the Brut, a tendency which would have the

---

[173] BS does not at this point give the battle a name but does refer later s.a. 937 to 'the battle of Brune'. Both accounts refer to the slaying of twelve earls, not seven as in the Anglo-Saxon Chronicle and other medieval chronicles. BS does not refer to the king of Ireland nor mention that Athelstan made all England and Scotland subject to him and defined England's boundaries with Cornwall and Wales. Ll makes no mention of Athelstan's sister Eadhild nor gives details of the gifts Athelstan received from abroad and those he bestowed on the Church. Ll, ff. 43–4; BS s.a. 924; also BS 29.31–2n.

[174] BS, 145 s.a. 1133 died at Gloucester, Ll, ff. 113v–14 at Cardiff. See BS, 145.10–11n. The few non-ecclesiastical events not found in Ll occur in BS, 87, s.a. 1094, 145 s.a. 1133, 171 s.a. 1168; all three are very brief.

[175] BS, xliii–xlvi. The entry referred to concerns the resistance of the three earls Hereward, Morcar and Siward. BS, 77 s.a. 1069, in common with such English chroniclers as HH and Paris, adds a fourth, the bishop of Durham. Ll, ff. 74–74v, names the three earls as Edwyn, Marcher and Hereward but makes no reference to the bishop of Durham.

[176] BS, xli–xlii.

[177] Ibid., xli–xlii, xlv–li.

effect of diminishing, if not actually eradicating, evidence of such links
with the Annals of Winchester in Llwyd's translation and which might
account in some measure for the introduction of material from medieval
chronicles other than the Annals here and elsewhere.

3 The main text and its relationship to English chronicles
It has already been mentioned more than once that some at least of
Llwyd's references in this respect are commonplace in medieval English
chronicles, and his customary reticence in disclosing his sources adds to
the difficulty of precise identification. Even the few clues he provides are
themselves somewhat misleading. His one and only appeal to the
authority of Henry of Huntingdon[178] does not in any way suggest the
considerable body of evidence to be found in Llwyd's text pointing to
the *Historia Anglorum* of Henry of Huntingdon as a very substantial
source for the 'Cronica Walliae' up to the reign of Stephen. Even if
many of the earlier resemblances are regarded with proper caution
because of broad similarities with other chronicles, the content of
important and lengthy sections such as those dealing with the Danish
invasions and especially with the reigns of Alfred and of Æthelflæd of
Mercia provide clear evidence of their dependence on Henry of
Huntingdon's work. This dependence is most apparent perhaps in
Llwyd's rendering of the verse epitaphs to each of these rulers, even
though remarkably he gives no indication that he knows the source: he
introduces the one as the work of 'a certayne clerke' and the other
baldly with the words 'her Epitaph was this'.[179] It can be remarked here
that Llwyd gives no indication either that he knew of Asser's *Life of
Alfred* or indeed that he was aware of Asser's connection with Alfred.
His only reference follows that of the *Brut* in recording the death of

---

[178] See above pp. 16–18 for Llwyd's few references to his sources. Llwyd (Ll, f. 8) quotes
HH's use of the name *Eubonia* for the Isle of Man (*HH*, 12–13) to emphasize Polydore
Vergil's confusion over the names Môn and Man.

[179] Ll, ff. 40, 43; *HH*, 298–9, 308–9. The few differences in Llwyd's versions are due to
minor copying errors, the most serious of which are the addition in Alfred's epitaph of a
first half-line, and in that of Æthelflæd the attachment of the first half of the first line to the
end of the second line, so making the epitaph one line shorter; see note f. 40.

'Asser Archebishop of Wales' in the year 906.[180] Years later in 'De Mona druidum insula . . . Epistola' Llwyd mentions Asser as one of several who, after the Saxons had conquered 'that part of the island', wrote of Wales, but again gives no indication that he knew of the connection with Alfred.[181] As to the dependence of the 'Cronica Walliae' on Henry of Huntingdon, it can be shown that many of its other entries relating to Alfred's reign correspond closely to the text of the chronicle.[182] The same is true also of Æthelflæd's reign, for instance in the recital of her victories where the similarities are clearly marked by the errors which characterize the two accounts. Among these is the description texts of Æthelflæd's husband Æthelred as her father, an error compounded later by describing her daughter 'Ælfwynn' as her sister.[183] The faulty chronology of the 'Cronica Walliae' in listing Æthelflæd's conquests reflects that of Henry of Huntingdon and is probably due to a misunderstanding of Henry's inexplicit dating sequence which he begins with the death of Æthelred 'in the eighteenth year of King Edward'. One result is to imply in both accounts a date of 922 for the battle of 'Brecananmer'.[184] That is also the date for the battle of Dinasnewydd with which Llwyd identifies it. The *Brut* chronicler's date for that battle, however, is 919, which is five years later than his date for the death of Æthelflæd. This is a rare example in the 'Cronica Walliae' of failure to

---

[180] Ll, f. 41: *BS*, 28 archbishop of the Britons, *Pen20Tr*, 6 archbishop of the Island of Britain. Giraldus Cambrensis knew of Asser as archbishop of Menevia and had access to the *Life* (Giraldus Cambrensis, *Opera*, iii, 422 (*Vita Sancti Ethelberti*); vi, 102 (*Itin. Kambriae* II, i)); Leland knew of Asser's *Life* (C. Brett, 'John Leland, Wales and early British History', *WHR*, 15 (1990–1), 174–5). Llwyd was acquainted with the works of both Giraldus and Leland. The copy of Asser's *Life* in the Lumley Library (Jayne and Johnson, *Lumley Library*, no. 945) has been identified as the one used by Parker for his edition of 1574 and probably therefore became part of the Library after Llwyd's death (see *Asser's Life of Alfred*, ed. W. H. Stevenson (Oxford, 1904; repr. 1959), xxxvii). It seems to be relevant here to recall Stevenson's description of *HH* as 'the only prominent twelfth-century chronicler who takes no matter directly or indirectly from the *Life*' (ibid., p. lxiv).

[181] Llwyd, 'De Mona druidum insula . . . Epistola', 124–5 (above p. 3 and n.11).

[182] For example, the phrase in Ll, f. 35v, 'slewe of the Danes one kinge and nyne earles' occurs only in *HH*, 284–5 (five earls). The events described in Ll, ff. 35v–6 are a precise summary of *HH*, 284–7, *s.a.* 872–6 as are those in Ll, ff. 36v–37 of *HH*, 286–91, *s.a.* 876–9, Ll, ff. 38–38v of *HH*, 292–3, *s.a.* 891, *HH*, 294–5, *s.a.* 893–4; also Ll, f. 39 of *HH*, 294–5, *s.a.* 895, with the intriguing exception of Ll's 'Quadring vel Euadring upon Sevarne' instead of *HH* 'Bridgenorth'. *ASCh* MSS have 'Bridge', except Corpus Christi College, Cambridge, MS 173 'Cwatbryeg'.

[183] Ll, ff. 42v–43, *HH*, 308–9 (Ælfwynn).

[184] Ll, f. 42v, *HH*, 306–7. Ll's dating from the death of Clydog ap Cadell in 917 (which is also the *BS* date) gives 918 as the date for the death of 'Adelrede her father', and 926 as that of Æthelflæd's own death, 'after she had ruled Mers 8 yeres'. Powel has 'silently' rewritten the whole account and rearranged the dating, and also changed 'Brecananmer' to 'Brecknoke', *HC* (1584), 47; (1811), 39.

synchronize with the *Brut*; it is extraordinary also in that, even so, it precedes closely an instance of matching the *Brut* so narrowly as to reproduce even its errors in the account of the battle of Brunanburh.[185] Such inconsistencies are untypical of Llwyd's meticulous attention to detail and again could be the result of his following an intermediate source copy. However that may be, there is clear evidence of the influence of Henry of Huntingdon's chronicle throughout the period of conflict with the Danes and in all probability extending also to the reign of Stephen.[186] Confirmation of such continuing influence seems to be provided in the annal in the 'Cronica Walliae' recording the marriage of Henry I's daughter to the son of the earl of Anjou.[187] These instances, taken together with the evidence provided by the later account of the battle of Northallerton,[188] serve to strengthen a conclusion that the intervening accounts of Stephen's dispute with his barons and with David, king of Scots, were also based on Henry of Huntingdon and not on other accounts showing less clear-cut resemblances.[189]

Furthermore, to a catalogue of similarities between the 'Cronica Walliae' and Henry of Huntingdon in their narration of events may be added many distinctive parallels in the naming of people and places and in the phrasing of the narrative. Despite a common origin in the Anglo-Saxon Chronicle of much of the content of medieval chronicles, it seems more than such coincidence that Llwyd's narrative should so frequently echo that of Henry of Huntingdon. He relates that, in the first year of his reign, Edmund brother of Athelstan won from the Danes 'which were then called Normaines', and converted to Christianity, the five cities of Leicester, Derby, Stamford, Lincoln and Nottingham, and converted also 'Aulaf, sonne of Sydric, Kinge of Northumberlande and Reynalde, Kinge of Yorke' in the exact order and phrasing of Huntingdon's account;[190] and he later describes the Northumbrians as 'a generation fickell and unconstant' and relates how Sweyn, having defeated Ulfcetel, returned later with three companions, 'fier sworde and spoyle', making England quake 'as a reede in the wynde' and 'devouringe suche vittaills as they

[185] See above, n.173.
[186] Instances abound in relevant passages such as those from the death of Edward (The Martyr): Ll. ff. 49–51, *HH*, 324–5; Ll, ff. 53v–57, *HH*, 330–53; Ll, ff. 59–60, *HH*, 360–3; or again in the accounts of the battle of Stamford Bridge Ll, f. 72, *HH*, 386–7; the battle of Hastings Ll, ff. 72v–73, *HH*, 388–95; the death of William the Conqueror and the character of his rule Ll, ff. 77v–78, *HH*, 404–7.
[187] Ll, f. 94; *HH*, 456–7.
[188] See note f. 118.
[189] For example, compare Ll, f. 114v *s.a.* 1135; Ll, f. 116 *s.a.* 1136; Ll, ff. 117–117v *s.a.* 1138–9 with *HH*, 707–21.
[190] Ll, ff. 44–44v, *HH*, 314–15.

founde in the houses, painge therfore with sworde and fier at ther dapartinge'.[191] In Edmund Ironside's second battle at 'Ceorstane' (Sherston),
Llwyd names one of his opponents as 'Almanl Derlinge', an echo of
Huntingdon's 'Almar Derling', Ælfmær Darling, among other close likenesses of phrase prior to the account of Stephen's siege of Lincoln in 1141
near the end of Huntingdon's chronicle, where the earl of Chester's Welsh
allies are described by Llwyd as being 'better couraged than armed' and by
Huntingdon as 'ill-armed but full of spirit'.[192] This selection, abbreviated
though it is, from the many close similarities between the 'Cronica
Walliae' and the *Historia Anglorum* serves to illustrate the role of the latter as
a very significant source and gives cause to question Llwyd's failure to
acknowledge it as such. More seriously, perhaps, it raises doubts here and
there, and most pointedly in the case of the verse epitaphs to Alfred and
Æthelflæd, as to whether Llwyd even recognized the source. He obviously
knew of Huntingdon's chronicle,[193] and a possible explanation here again,
as with some of the passages examined earlier, is that he was translating and
adapting as he saw fit a compiled version of the *Brut* which he regarded in
its entirety as 'the Britishe cronicle' or 'the Welsh historie'.[194]

It is fitting at this point to mention again two of Llwyd's own references
to sources. One, of course, is to the work of Matthew Paris, which he
names on several occasions. The other, with which it is proposed to stay for
the moment, is his statement that after the year 1270, when his own copy
of 'the Britishe booke' ended, he depended especially on the chronicle of
Nicholas Trevet among others 'written in the Latyne tonge'.[195] Not
surprisingly, in view of Llwyd's reticence otherwise concerning sources,
there are many indications of Trevet's influence much earlier than the
stated date of 1270. Indeed, soon after Huntingdon's chronicle comes to an
end, Trevet's *Annales* becomes Llwyd's paramount source other than the
Brut for the remainder of the 'Cronica Walliae' apart from a relatively brief
period discussed later when it was superseded in that role by Paris's
work.[196] While it is true, for instance, that Llwyd's accounts of the

---

[191] Ll, f. 47; *HH*, 316–17, 'with their usual fickleness'; Ll, f. 55, *HH*, 342–3
'accompanied by their usual attendants fire, slaughter and pillage; and all England trembled
. . . like the rustling of a bed of reeds shaken by the west wind' (cf. *RW*, I, 437 *s.a.* 1007
'like unto a bed of reeds agitated by the west wind').

[192] Ll, f. 58 *s.a.* 1015; *HH*, 356–7 'Almar Derling', derived from *ASCh* 'Aelfmer
Darling' (i.e. 'the beloved'). *RW*, I, 454 *s.a.* 1016 has Almer and Aldgar, but not 'Darling'.
Ll, f. 59 'fledde Engle flede Engle ded is Edmunde' is another instance of harking back to
ASCh through *HH*, 358–61.

[193] Above, p. 39; note f. 118.

[194] Above, pp. 16–22.

[195] For Llwyd's references to Paris see above, p. 16 and below pp. 43–55 and to Trevet,
see also below, pp. 56–9.

banishing of William Peverel of Nottingham in 1155, of the fortifying in the same year of the castle of 'Cleubur' (Cleobury) by Hugh Mortimer against the king and also of events surrounding the death of Roger son of Miles of Gloucester, earl of Hereford, are recorded too by others such as Roger of Wendover and Matthew Paris, some minor differences in his account, and especially the close correspondence in phrasing between Llwyd and Trevet, all tend to point to the latter as being his source.[197] The same can be said of some other entries during the reigns of Henry II and Richard, among them those concerned with Henry's consultations with his barons about the conquest of Ireland, Henry the young king's 'solempne feast', the dissension between King Henry and his eldest son, and Henry the elder's forsaking of his wife. Also Llwyd's version of the anecdote about King Richard's reaction to the siege of 'Verneuil' is that related by Trevet rather than by Wendover.[198] There are other similar instances of Trevet as a probable source during this period, and despite Trevet's own dependence on Roger of Wendover or Matthew Paris for much of his material for the barons' rebellions, Llwyd's description of events continues on occasion to bear closer resemblance to Trevet's account during the reign of John and for much of Henry III's reign. Thus the account of King John's defeat of

---

[196] The influence of Wendover and Paris is considered later; identifying Trevet as a source is often hazardous because so many of his annals are closely akin to those of other chronicles which include the *Flores Historiarum*, the chronicle of William Rishanger and the chronicle of Walter of Guisborough, and because also of Trevet's influence on later chronicles such as that of Thomas Walsingham. See, for instance, Thomas Hog's Preface to Trevet, *Annales*, pp. ix–x; A. Gransden, *Historical Writing in England c.550 to c.1307* (London, 1974), 504–7; Ruth J. Dean, 'Nicholas Trevet historian', in J. J. G. Alexander and M. T. Gibson (eds), *Medieval Learning and Literature: Essays presented to R. W. Hunt* (Oxford, 1976), 334; see ibid., 349–51 for a list of MSS of the *Annales*. About fifteen copies of Trevet's *Annales* are known. Dr Claire Bray, Curator, Department of Manuscripts at the British Library, very kindly examined Arundel MS 46 and Harley MS 29. The signatures noticed do not suggest an obvious association with the Arundel library in the period when Llwyd was in the earl's service, but further study of the provenance of the several manuscripts of the *Annales* may yet lead to an identification of the source used by Llwyd.

[197] Ll, f. 128 *s.a.* 1155, *NT*, 36–7. *RW*, II, 280–1 omits 'of Nottingham' and makes Hugh Mortimer fortify Gloucester, Wigmore and 'Breges' (Bridgnorth). Cf. also Ll, f. 128v 'but the Kinge kept the Earledom of Hereforde and the towne of Glocester in his owne hands' with *NT*, 37 *rege comitatum Herfordiae et urbem Gloverniae in manu propria retinente. RW* does not have this entry.

[198] Ll, f. 142v *s.a.* 1170, *NT*, 68–9 *s.a.* 1171; Ll, f. 144 *s.a.* 1171, *NT*, 69 (both entries virtually *verbatim*); cf. Ll, f. 145v 'the elder King was not discouraged' and *NT*, 73 *Henricus rex senior . . . non est fractus . . .* ; also Ll, f. 151 'Kinge Henrie the elder forsoke his wief for certeine consideratiouns and kept her in prison many yeres', *NT*, 90 *Henricus, Anglorum rex senior, abalienatus ab uxore sua, in custodia eam detinuit multis annis*; Ll, f. 155v *s.a.* 1184 (*recte* 1194, see note f. 155v), *NT*, 154.

the French fleet in Flanders in 1213 is virtually the same as Trevet's brief description, and differs from that of Wendover and Paris in extent and factual detail.[199] Much the same is true of Llwyd's account of the arrival in Thanet in 1216 of Louis the French prince, his triumphant progress to London, and his capture of the castles of Reigate, Guildford and Farnham on the way to Winchester.[200] Here again, however, the apparent complexity of sources underlying the 'Cronica Walliae' does not make for easy identification,[201] and these difficulties tend to increase in Llwyd's account during the reigns of Henry III and Edward I. Even so, the reference to the death in 1219 of William Marshal senior, leaving five sons who died without issue, and five daughters who inherited the estates and whose marriages are listed, follows faithfully Trevet's account. Also in relating a sequence of events concerning Richard Marshal, earl of Pembroke, beginning with his succession to the title, Llwyd seems to echo Trevet's words.[202] The same can be said of later events in that sequence, notably Richard Marshal's quarrel with King Henry and his alliance with Llywelyn ap Iorwerth against the king, and finally his death in Ireland followed by the succession of his brother Gilbert in 1234.[203]

Over the next twenty-five years of Henry's reign, however, as evidence of Paris's influence grows (up to his death in 1259), so do examples of Trevet's influence become markedly fewer and can be identified with any degree of confidence only in a relatively small number of events. These include the marriage in 1236 of King Henry to Eleanor, the second daughter of the earl of Provence, and that of the

[199] Cf. Ll, f. 177, '. . . Kinge John heringe howe the Frenche Kinge was in Flandres, and had a great navy at Dam . . . sent William de Longa Spata Earle of Boleyn and Hughe de Nova Villa . . . thither with a great navy which overthrewe the Frenchmen and returned home with great spoyle'; *NT*, 186: *Joannes rex Angliae copiosa classe navium parata, et praepositis eidem Willelmo de Longa-spata Saresberiensi, Reginaldo de Dammartino Boloniensi comitibus, ac nobili viro Hugone Novavilla cum viris navalis belli peritis, transmisit eam in Flandriam, ut Regis Francorum navigium destruerent . . .*, 272. *RW*, II, 78–9, *CM*, II, 548 are longer and like the shorter *HistAng*, II, 137–8 speak of the port of 'Swine' in Flanders where *NT* has *portum Damonis* (or *Damme*). See below, pp. 49–55, for a discussion of Matthew Paris's influence on Llwyd's work on the reigns of John and Henry III.

[200] Ll, ff. 182v–183, *NT*, 196–7. *RW*, III, 367–9 is again longer and differs in detail like the shorter account in *HistAng*, II, 179.

[201] Ll, ff. 183–183v; such is the case with Llwyd's lists of knights.

[202] Ll, f. 187, *NT* 205: . . . *quinque habuit filios . . . et quinque filias . . . Ad quarum heredes, deficiente fratribus successione, totius Marescalliae hereditas amplissima est devoluta*; Ll, f. 192, *NT*, 218 *s.a.*, 1231: *Obiit hoc anno Willelmus Marescalli junior cui successit in hereditate Ricardus ejusdem germanus* (cf. *RW*, IV, 224–5; *CM*, III, 201; *HistAng*, II, 331).

[203] The correspondence of phrase can be seen by comparing the accounts of those incidents in Ll, ff. 194v–195 with *NT*, 220 *s.a.* 1233. Both events are described in *RW*, IV, 265–6, 270–3, 275–94, 300–8; *CM*, III, 275, 288–92; *HistAng*, II, 361; and *Pen20Tr s.a.* 1233, but do not resemble Llwyd's to the same extent. See above n.162.

Emperor Frederick II to Henry's sister Isabella; the death of John the Scot, earl of Chester, without issue; the gift of the stewardship of England and the earldom of Leicester to Simon de Montfort on his return from France; William de Longspée's death in the Holy Land and his daughter's marriage to Henry Lacy, earl of Lincoln, and the Lord Edward's marriage in 1254 to Eleanor, daughter of King Alfonso of Castile. Several of these events occur in the *Brut* and all are to be found in Paris's work but details or phrasing in each case point to Trevet as Llwyd's source. Even Llwyd's account of Llywelyn ap Gruffudd's response to Geoffrey Langley's tyranny, when in 1256 he 'entred the Earles lands, and destroyed all to the gates of Chester', though probably based on Paris, seems also to retain an echo of Trevet's *intravit comitatum Cestriae . . . et omni usque ad portas Cestriae devastavit.* Llwyd's description of the Barons' War itself, though here and there resembling other chronicles such as those of William Rishanger and Walter of Guisborough, noticed later, clearly depends largely on Paris in the early stages until 1259. Nevertheless, it bears several close resemblances to Trevet's account of the later events, especially those from the capture by Simon de Montfort of Worcester, Gloucester and Bridgenorth in 1263 to much of the battle of Evesham in 1265, including the list of those slain in that battle, ending with Llwyd's reference to 'a great number of the meane people especially of the Welshmen', which compares with Trevet's *alii quoque minoris gradus in multitudine magna . . . et maxime Gallensium, numero excessivo.* Interestingly enough, this reference is one that in virtually the same terms occurs in the chronicles of William Rishanger and Walter of Guisborough; and Llwyd's description of 'Symon Fitsymons', captured at the earlier battle of Northampton in 1264, as 'the first man that barre enseigne against the Kinge', though probably based on Trevet's *qui primo vexillum erexerat contra regem* is described thus also by Rishanger and Guisborough.[204] These resemblances are discussed later, along with others which seem to

[204] Ll, f. 196; Ll and *NT*'s sequence for the marriage respectively of king and emperor differ from Paris and *Pen20*; and Ll's second daughter is matched by *NT*'s *filiam secundam*, cf. *NT*, 220, *Pen20Tr, 104*; *CM*, III, 318–21, 334–6; Ll, f. 196v: *NT*, 221 uniquely has the same details, *Joannes Scotus ultimus comes Cestriae moritur, et deficiente herede devolutus est in possessionem regiam comitatus*; Ll, f. 197: *NT*, 226 *Simon de Monte-forti . . . aufugit in Angliam, ubi gratiose receptus a rege, Leicestriae obtinuit comitatum cum senescallia Angliae* differs significantly from *CM*, III, 498 and especially from ibid., 566; Ll, f. 203: *NT*, 237–8 appears to be the source rather than *CM*, V, 196 etc. where no mention is made of the daughter's marriage to Henry Lacy; Ll, f. 203v: *NT*, 243–4 names Alfonso, king of Castile, but *CM*, V, 449–50 does not; Ll, f. 205v: *NT*, 245. Cf. *CM*, V, 594; see *HW*, II, 117 and n.8. For the Barons' War see Ll, f. 211–214v, *NT*, 251–66; but see below, pp. 56–9, for similarities with other chronicles especially Rishanger and Guisborough.

be more explicit pointers to the 'other cronicles written in the Latyne tonge' which Llwyd added to his acknowledgement of Trevet as a source after his copy of the 'Britishe booke' ended in 1270.

However, the many references already made to Matthew Paris are a reminder that he is the chronicler mentioned most frequently by Llwyd, and a close reading of the 'Cronica Walliae' confirms its many similarities to the work of that widely influential writer.[205] The detailed nature of the several closely related texts attributed to Paris again makes precise identification of source hazardous and often impossible, not only because of the relative brevity of the 'Cronica Walliae' entries but also by the way Paris's work, like Trevet's, bears the influence of other chronicles and in turn left its own mark on later medieval works. Entries very similar to some in Paris's texts, and which resemble also entries in the work of the English chroniclers, can be found in the 'Cronica Walliae' from an early stage within the period of Paris's writing. These occur predictably in the relation of major happenings such as the Norman Conquest itself; and also, more significantly, in view of the apparent motives for their inclusion, in Llwyd's account of some events of lesser moment. One such refers to the conspiracy against William I in 1074 (Ll, f. 74v) led by Ralph, earl of East Anglia, which Llwyd would have inserted probably in order to record the participation of Welsh confederates in the affair, an involvement due by implication to Ralph's Welsh descent on his mother's side, a particular feature recorded by Wendover and Paris, though not by Henry of Huntingdon.[206] Another is Llwyd's account of Stephen's succession 'by meanes of Hughe Pygod . . . the Archebishop of Canterburye and all the nobilitie of Englande (contrarye to their former othe made to Mawde)', linked, probably because of Llwyd's concern for the succession of 'righte heirs', to Stephen's truce with David of Scotland who would not swear allegiance to him 'for he had sworen allready to Mawde his neece'. Both events are described in similar terms by Henry of Huntingdon, Trevet and Paris, but the reference to Hugh Pigot – of particular interest to Llwyd because of other connections with the Welsh Marches – occurs only in Paris's account.[207] A later instance among several such entries is the combat appointed between Richard I and the French king, in 1195 according to Llwyd's reckoning, with five knights to support each monarch. While Trevet's very brief account and others by Wendover and Paris have features in common, Llwyd's indictment of

[205] The references occur in Ll, ff. 3v, 163v, 195v, 206v, 207v, 209v.
[206] Ll, f. 74v; *HH*, 398–9, *RW*, II, 14–16; *CM*, II, 12–13; *HistAng*, I, 19.
[207] Ll, f. 114v; *HH*, 702–9; *NT*, 7–8; *RW*, II, 216–18; *HistAng*, I, 251–2, 254.

the French king, who 'like a snayle, drewe in his hornes and forsoke the
battaill', is noticeably in the spirit of Paris's *Historia Anglorum,* which states
quod rex Francorum praecise agere recusavit; both descriptions tie in with
Llwyd's usually unflattering portrayals of the French.[208] Material from the
Brut itself is still, of course, the major component of the 'Cronica Walliae'
throughout the period of Paris's writings, and its influence, especially in
the recordings of affairs in Wales, can usually be traced with certainty.
Similarities to Paris's work and to that of other English chroniclers as well
as to the *Brut* come together from time to time. Llwyd's account of
William the Conqueror's only expedition to Wales contains elements of
the *Brut*'s description of the journey as a pilgrimage to St David's, but
implies also the view of the event as an armed invasion to subdue the
native princes given in several English chronicles and especially so in
those of Wendover and Paris.[209] There is another instance of an
elaboration on the *Brut* account, which, though similar to both Paris and
Trevet, seems to depend also on other sources. This concerns Henry II's
first invasion of Wales, into the north-east in this case, when a select
detachment from the king's army was so fiercely mauled in an ambush
laid by Dafydd and Cynan, sons of Owain Gwynedd, that the king's
safety was put at risk.[210]

These few selected examples, while illustrating again the difficulty of
isolating any one source, seem nevertheless to present a case for regarding
Paris as well as Henry of Huntingdon and Nicholas Trevet as a significant
influence on Llwyd's account from the late eleventh century onward.
Llwyd's first admission of Paris's direct influence comes with his brief
addition to the *Brut* version of the unsuccessful assault in 1198 by
Gwenwynwyn of Powys on Painscastle in Elfael: 'Mathias Parisiensis
sayeth this battaill was fought before the castell of Maude, and that, of the
Welshmen, there were slayne 3700.' Even before his interjection,
however, Llwyd has already added, as though they were part of his Welsh
base copy, Paris's references to 'William de Bruse' as lord of the castle and
to the lord chief justice of England as the commander of the English
forces. He makes no comment on the equation of Painscastle with the

[208] Ll, f. 157v; *NT*, 156–7; *RW*, III, 84–5, Luard, *Flores Hist,* II, 110; *HistAng*, II, 50–1.
[209] Ll, f. 77v: 'William Bastarde entred Wales with a great army as farre as Saincte Davies
where he offred, and toke homage of the kinges or princes of the lande'; *Pen20Tr,* 17
'. . . came on the Menevia pilgrimage'; *HH*, 400–1, 'led an army into Wales and subjected
it to himself'; *RW*, II, 20 '. . . led a large army into Wales and subdued it, receiving the
homage and fealty of the princes'; also *CM*, II, 17, *HistAng*, I, 25. See also *HW*, II, 393–4;
L. D. Nicholl, *The Normans in Glamorgan, Gower and Kidweli* (Cardiff, 1936), 177–8; R. R.
Davies, *Conquest, Coexistence and Change: Wales 1063–1415* (Oxford, 1989), 33.
[210] Ll, ff. 129–129v, 134v; see note f. 129v.

castle of 'Maude' or Matilda, but it is possible that he would, wrongly, have associated the name with that of the Empress Matilda, daughter of Henry I, the main events of whose troubled career are carefully if briefly charted in Llwyd's own account as they had been at greater length by Paris.[211] The interest of the latter would have been fuelled possibly by the justice of Matilda's claim to the throne and certainly by the attachment to her of her half-brother Robert of Gloucester, a patron of letters who also actively favoured the monastic movement. Matilda's status as 'right heire' to the English throne and also her links with Welsh affairs, notably in the Marches of Wales, would have focused Llwyd's interest on her, for they provided yet another strand in the historical relationships of the earls of Arundel, especially where they concerned also the Fitzalan lordships of Oswestry and Clun.[212] It is not without significance that it is in the same context, describing the Empress Matilda's return to England in 1139, that Llwyd first mentions the de Albineto (d'Aubigny) family in the person of William de Albineto, earl of Arundel through his marriage to Alice widow of Henry I, who welcomed Matilda to Arundel castle. Llwyd's interest, amply demonstrated by frequent reference to members of the family until 1243 when the last male member, Hugh de Albineto, died while still a minor, lay in the fact that, in the division of Hugh's possessions among his four sisters, the earldom of Arundel passed to Isabella, wife of John Fitzalan, thus establishing the right of the Fitzalan line to be earls of Arundel as well as lords of Oswestry and Clun. It is quite clear that Paris was Llwyd's source for all these references to the de Albineto family and equally clear that Paris's interest was linked to the family's patronage of Wymondham (co. Norfolk), a priory of the church of St Alban's, where most of the members were buried. The form 'de

[211] Ll, ff. 163–163v..The *RW* and *MP* accounts of the siege appear in *RW*, III, 129–30; *CM*, II, 447; *HistAng*, II, 70–1. *NT* does not mention it. On the name Castle Maud (i.e. Maud of St Valery wife of William de Breos) see *HW*, II, 585–6.

[212] On the whole the references are too brief and too commonplace in chronicles to hazard even a guess at Llwyd's particular source. What can be said is that the two comparable references in the *Brut* are plainly not his sole source (the return to England of Matilda Ll, f. 118, *Pen20Tr*, 22 and of her son Henry Ll, f. 127v, *Pen20Tr*, 58, see above n.159); that Llwyd's account of the sending of Matilda to be married to the count of Anjou reads much like that of *HH* (Ll, f. 13, *HH*, 476–7); but that his description of Matilda's landing at Arundel is very much like that by Paris (Ll, ff. 118–118v, *CM*, II, 170–1, *HistAng*, I, 262; and cf. *HH*, 722–3, *NT*, 11–12). Llwyd's following account of Stephen's unsuccessful siege of Arundel and Matilda's 'permitted' escape to Bristol is, however, paralleled by *HH*. The comparable description in Luard, *Flores Hist*, II, 60 is one example of many where that version is unlike both those of Llwyd and Paris.

Albineto' is the one used throughout by Llwyd as it is consistently, and virtually uniquely so, in Paris's *Historia Anglorum*.[213]

But to return to the siege of Painscastle in 1198. This first acknowledgement by Llwyd of Paris as a source does not signal any immediate increase in instances of his recognizable influence on the 'Cronica Walliae'. Not surprisingly, in view of the nature and brevity of Richard's reign, Llwyd's account during this period is concerned even more than usual with the *Brut*'s version of affairs in Wales; and much the same can be said of the reign of John, despite its greater length and John's more frequent involvement with Welsh matters. Indeed the *Brut*'s overarching influence on Llwyd's narrative extends here as elsewhere to the description of events outside Wales, among which during this brief period may be mentioned John's dispute with Rome over the election of an archbishop, his expedition to Ireland in 1210, the confederacy between the barons and Llywelyn ap Iorwerth and Llwyd's brief account of the death of John.[214] Although Trevet's chronicle continues to be the main source for Llwyd's references, additional to the *Brut*, to events outside Wales, there are some likenesses to Paris's work. During Richard's reign these tend to appear as popular anecdotes which occur also in other medieval chronicles, though not in Trevet's. Among them are Richard's quip about making a young earl of the ageing bishop of Durham and the brief reference to the ditch opened around the Tower of London by the ambitious bishop of Ely. The sad little tale of Symon de Thurnay's loss of his faculties, associated particularly with Paris's *Historia Anglorum*, is the only one of its kind in John's reign.[215] There are other accounts, however, concerned with matters of state in France which seem to owe more to Paris than to other chroniclers. They include Llwyd's accounts of the loss of Normandy, Anjou, Maine and Poitou due to the defection of Hugh de

[213] The name does not appear in the otherwise broadly comparable entries in *NT*, 11–12, *HH*, 722–3. Luard, *Flores Hist*, II, 154, 157, 219 differs here again from Llwyd in that it refers to the name on only four occasions, and then over the brief period 1215–36 as compared with Llwyd's much longer period of reference between 1139 and 1243. Remarkably, however, the form 'de Albineto' is given on three of the four occasions as it is in the *HistAng* and Llwyd. The following lists of folio references to the family name show that the pattern of occurrence in Llwyd also corresponds most closely to that of *HistAng* (references to links with Wymondham are marked ★) Ll. f. 118v, 147v★ (Arundel), 179, 183, 183v, 184, 184v, 186v (Arundel), 187v, 199 (Arundel): *HistAng*, I, 262; II, 87–8★, 163, 171, 195, 206 (Arundel) 209, 230 (Arundel), 411, 477; *CM*, II, 170–1, 298★, III, 1, 13 (Arundel); 67 (Arundel), IV, 243★.

[214] Ll, ff. 170v, 177–177v, 179, 184; *Pen20Tr*, 83–4, 89–90, 93; also above, pp. 35–6.

[215] The bishop: Ll, f. 153, *HistAng*, II, 11; Thurnay: Ll, ff. 169–169v, *HistAng*, II, 90. Madden, *HistAng*, III, xli, refers to the inclusion of the tale of Symon de Thurnay in Wendover's account.

Gournai, Robert Fitzwalter and Saer de Quinci and of the noble resistance of Roger Lacy.[216] Needless to say, a single source for some of the
events can be attributed only with even greater caution. Such is the case
with Llwyd's bare outline of the death of Richard; and his brief reference
to John's marriage to Isabel, daughter and heir of the earl of Angoulême, is
similar to that of both Trevet and Paris except for the description of the
rejected suitor Hugh de Brun: Paris's 'Counte of La Marche' (*comes
Marchise*) may possibly provide part of the clue to Llwyd's strange
identification of him as 'Vicount of Carce'. In Llwyd's equally brief
account of John's reconciliation with the Pope, with the French nobles at
La Rochelle and with the French king, his specific reference to 'Geffrey
de Landanano' seems to confirm Trevet as his source; and his 'peace with
the French kinge for 5 yeres' provides also another instance of his use of
the English chronicle account to correct as well as to enlarge the *Brut*
reference.[217] In point of fact the relatively few departures from the *Brut*
during these two reigns tend to throw into sharper relief other features of
Llwyd's use of English chronicle material, most especially, of course, his
obviously quite deliberate quoting from Trevet and Paris, but most
notably from the latter, of events and names associated with the Welsh
Marches as part of his constant endeavour to unveil the manifold Welsh
connections of the Fitzalan-Arundel line. In the instances already referred
to, such as John's loss of several French provinces and the flight of Robert
Fitzwalter and others, all those named fit into this pattern. Paris's mostly
lengthy lists of participants in the barons' rebellion are quoted to fulfil the
same purpose and begin in the early stages with the appointment of
Robert Fitzwalter as the leader of the barons. The accounts that follow
of their triumphant entry into Bedford and London, of the siege and fall of
Rochester, the imprisonment of the defenders in Corfe, the Pope's curse
on John's enemies, John's journey northward and the appointment of
governors of the north and of the city of York, and the death of Geoffrey
Mandeville, earl of Essex, while 'runninge at the tylte', are all drawn
directly from Paris's work and abound with the names of Norman knights
associated in some way or another with the Welsh Marches.[218] Nevertheless, again in these last few years of John's reign the *Brut* account is still
by far the main component of Llwyd's narrative and Trevet's chronicle is

[216] Ll, f. 169, *RW*, III, 172, *CM*, II, 482–3, *HistAng*, II, 98. Also Eustace de Vescy's
flight to France: Ll, f. 176v, *HistAng*, II, 128: according to *RW*, III, 249 and *CM*, II, 534
Vescy fled to Scotland and Fitzwalter to France. See also below, n.226.
[217] Ll, ff. 164, 166, 177–177v; *HistAng*, II, 146–52; *NT*, 186, 189–90; *Pen20Tr*, 89.
[218] Ll, ff. 179–179v, 183–183v; *HistAng*, II, 156–66, 169–72, 175. The equivalent
references in *RW* and *CM* do not match Llwyd's so exactly.

still the most significant ancillary source. Surprisingly, instances are few of any marked confusion arising out of such a complex and closely woven pattern of sources: Llwyd's identification of Hugh de Brun as 'Vicount of Carce' has already been remarked upon. In his account of the hanging in Nottingham by King John of '3 children which were pledges' he names them as Hywel ap Cadwallon, Madog ap Maelgwn and Meurig Barrech. These are described in the *Brut* as 'three leaders of gentle birth from Wales who were hanged in England', whereas Wendover and Paris agree that those hanged in Nottingham were twenty-eight youths. Llwyd's tale, already referred to in a different context, of the ambush 'at the woode called Coed Penarlage' in the reign of Henry II, is an earlier instance of confusions seemingly caused by a complexity of manuscript sources.[219]

It is remarkable, therefore, that from the crowning at Gloucester in 1216 of Henry III, when the five nobles named by Llwyd as being present are exactly as recorded by Paris, there should be a striking increase in the amount of additional material introduced into the 'Cronica Walliae' from English sources, mostly from Paris's work. Although the framework of Llwyd's account is still the *Brut* in its Peniarth 20 form, the balance of his dependence on Trevet and Paris changes rapidly and progressively throughout the reign. During the first decade, that is until the *Brut* annal recording the death in 1226 (*recte* 1227) of Maredudd, archdeacon of Ceredigion, the amount of additional material introduced which can with reasonable certainty be attributed separately to each of these two chroniclers reaches for the first time a rough parity. Over the second decade or so to the recording of the death of John the Scot, earl of Chester, in 1237, such entries deriving from Paris are twice as many as those from Trevet, over three times as many in the third decade, until the granting in 1248 of royal permission to bury Gruffudd ap Llywelyn in Aberconwy; and in the last decade ending with Paris's death in 1259 all except two early entries are taken from his work.[220] Throughout the whole period most of the

[219] For the hanging of pledges see Ll, f. 176v, *Pen20Tr*, 87 *s.a.* 1212, *RW*, III, 238–9, *CM*, II, 524, *HistAng*, II, 128. On the form of the name Meurig Barrech see *Pen20Tr*, 87.3n.; note f. 77v.

[220] Ll, f. 191, *Pen20Tr*, 101 *s.a.* 1227; Ll, f. 196v, *Pen20Tr*, 104 *s.a.* 1237; Ll, ff. 202v–203, *Pen20Tr*, 108; the two entries are the death of the earl of Salisbury in the Holy Land in 1250 and the marriage of the Lord Edward to Eleanor, daughter of Alfonso king of Castile, Ll, ff. 203–203v, *NT*, 237, 243–4; *CM*, V, 196 does not mention the marriage of the daughter of Salisbury to Henry Lacy whose link with the Welsh Marches was significant for Llwyd, and *CM*, V, 449–50 gives different details of the royal connections of Edward's bride; Llwyd places this marriage before 1254.

relatively few additions introduced from Trevet are concerned, like the last two mentioned, with matters relating to the king and his family and to events overseas. It may perhaps be no more than coincidence that these are among the list of matters which Paris directed his assistants to take out when revising the *Chronica Majora* into this briefer form as the *Chronica Minora*, or *Historia Anglorum*.[221] However that may be, it so happened that elsewhere also events recorded in the *Chronica Majora* but which are missing in the *Historia Anglorum* are missing from the 'Cronica Walliae'. One such is part of the account of the end of Gilbert Marshal in 1241, who died, according to Llwyd, 'by misfortune fightinge at the turney at Herforde'. The *Historia Anglorum* does no more than enlarge a little on the misfortune, whereas the *Chronica Majora* provides also a broad hint of foul play.[222] Llwyd's enlargement of the *Brut* entries for 1245 derives mainly from Paris's account which refers specifically to the slaughter of 300 Welshmen and the death of Herbert Fitzmathew near Montgomery, and to a campaign immediately afterwards in which an army of Englishmen and 'Gascoynes' remained embattled at Degannwy and the Irish overran Anglesey. The *Chronica Majora*'s description of these events is much longer than that of the *Historia Anglorum*, which omits, for instance (as does Llwyd), the account of the siege of Montalt (Mold) by Dafydd, prince of Gwynedd. It is also surprising, to judge by his regular practice elsewhere, that Llwyd omitted the reference to a member of the Arundel family; and these omissions again could be due to their occurrence only in the *Chronica Majora*.[223] All the examples quoted so far and many others beside demonstrate also that the 'Cronica Walliae' matches consistently the brevity of the *Historia Anglorum*, which, of course, differs widely in that respect from the *Chronica Majora*.

[221] For the abridgement see Luard's preface to *CM*, IV, xi–xv; R. Vaughan, *Matthew Paris* (Cambridge, 1958), 110–24. Some of the references introduced by Llwyd occur in both *CM* and *HistAng*, but there is good reason for assuming Trevet to be the source; for example, as already indicated (above, n.204), Trevet alone refers to the 'second daughter' (*filiam secundam*) of the earl of Provence.

[222] Ll, f. 198v; *HistAng*, II, 451, *CM*, IV, 135: *erant autem nonnulli qui veraciter affirmarent, ipsas habenas ab aliquo invido seditiose praecisas*. The account in *NT*, 230–1, though similar to Llwyd's, is longer and gives no location for the tourney.

[223] Ll, ff. 200–200v; *HistAng*, II, 499–500, 504–5, 507–8; *CM*, IV, 408–9, 423, 481–4, 486–8. The much briefer *Brut* account (given only in *Pen20Tr*, 106–7) places the reference to the succession to the patrimony of William Marshal (*recte* Walter Marshal as in Ll and *MP*) before the account of the conflict in Wales. *NT*, 130–1 (but not Paris) refers to the division between five sisters (above, n.202) The two omitted references are: 1246, death of Robert Arundel, Latin and Hebrew scholar, *CM*, IV, 553; 1252, Isabella (widow of Hugh), Countess of Arundel's unsuccessful appeal to the king (*CM*, V, 336).

These various parallels which can be drawn between Llwyd's work and the *Historia Anglorum*, set alongside the fact that all the entries in the 'Cronica Walliae' which are safely attributable to Paris are to be found also in the latter, suggest powerfully that the *Historia Anglorum* could well have been, until it ended in the year 1253, the specific source of material from Paris's work added by Llwyd to the 'Cronica Walliae'. The most convincing argument of all perhaps is the circumstance that quite a number of such entries by Llwyd can be shown to occur only in the *Historia Anglorum*. Some instances have already been suggested, notably a phrase in the account of the abortive duel between Richard I and the French king, and the many references to the de Albineto family.[224] A more specific example is Llwyd's brief addition to the otherwise fairly commonplace statement (*c.*1143) that King Stephen had taken Geoffrey Mandeville prisoner at St Albans, an addition to the effect that 'the Earle of Arundell a worthye knight was like to be drowned by defaulte of his horse', an Arundel reference clearly of interest to Llwyd and one to be found only in the *Historia Anglorum*.[225] Likewise the previously mentioned flight to France in 1212 of *both* Robert Fitzwalter and Eustace de Vescy is described thus only in the *Historia Anglorum*, just as it is there, uniquely, that an exact match can be found for Llwyd's account of the siege of Grosmont (not 'Builth' as elsewhere) in 1220, and for the comment additional to the account of the death in 1234 of Robert Fitzwalter that he died despite the 'stone aboute his necke of such vertue that he coulde not dye as longe as hit was there'.[226]

Llwyd's text seems to demonstrate that Paris's work influenced him mainly, and probably wholly, through the *Historia Anglorum* until that chronicle ended. Moreover, it can be shown that Llwyd's text also provides quite firm evidence that the *Chronica Majora* took its place for the ensuing five years until Paris's death in 1259. Within the short period between Llywelyn ap Gruffudd's advance into the Perfeddwlad

[224] Above, nn.208, 213.

[225] Ll, 120v; *HistAng*, I, 270–1: *unde comes de Harundel, miles licet egregius, in medio aquae, . . . simul cum equo suo prostratus est, totis membris attritus et fere submersus.* Cf. *CM*, II, 175; *NT*, 16 *s.a.* 1143; William of Newburgh and William of Malmesbury *s.a.* 1142.

[226] This phrase of Llwyd (Ll, f. 195v.) echoes the account of Fitzwalter's last words to his wife in *HistAng*, II, 385: *Tolle lapidem pretiosum, quem gero circa collum, et da primogenito et heredi meo, quia dum illum gessero, mori non potero, nec ille vel aliquis, qui ipsum gestaverit*; cf. *CM*, III, 334. References to the occurrence in Ll and *HistAng* of the other examples and to the contrasting versions elsewhere are as follows: Ll, f. 176v: *HistAng*, II, 128, *CM*, II, 534 (de Vescy to Scotland, Fitzwalter to France); Ll. f. 187v: *HistAng*, II, 247, *CM*, III, 64 (Grosmont).

or the Four Cantreds in November 1256 and his unsuccessful offer of
peace two years later (Ll, ff. 205–209v) Llwyd introduces a remarkably
long sequence of matters additional to the *Brut*'s account, details mostly
concerned with Wales and having close counterparts in the *Chronica
Majora*. They arise in the main from Welsh responses to injustices such as
those perpetrated by Geoffrey Langley, the Lord Edward's 'lieftenant',
and to the several invasions by the king and his son acting together with
their allies; the responses themselves have mostly to do with the Spartan
measures taken in the Welsh countryside to withstand these oppressions.
Special emphasis is laid on the discomfiture of the English and on the
awakening sense of unity and patriotism in Wales, a sense deepened
rather than otherwise by the non-adherence of the Welsh princes of
Powys.[227] Llwyd's dependence on the *Chronica Majora* extends beyond
the events themselves to the terms in which they are recounted. His
succinct condemnation of Edward as a 'cruell and unjuste manne,
havinge no regard to right, promise or othe' crystallizes Paris's lengthy
and damning portrait; when he attributes to Paris words expressing
God's protection of the poor, they call to mind here, as elsewhere in
these passages, Llywelyn's noble exhortation to his countrymen; and in
describing Llywelyn's offer of peace he quotes the exact terms as given
by Paris, while in the king's scornful rebuff – 'what is this to oure losses?'
– he reflects Paris's *Quid est hoc . . .*[228] These and other close parallels
with the *Chronica Majora*, despite shadowy possibilities of recourse to
other minor sources implied in the occasional anomaly, would appear to
confirm the overwhelming influence of Paris's *Chronica Majora* on Llwyd
at this stage in his account, that is between the end of the *Historia
Anglorum* in 1253 and the death of Paris in 1259.[229] Quite certainly
Llwyd would have seized with enthusiasm the opportunity to reflect

[227] Cf. Ll, f. 205v and *CM*, V, 613 (Langley); Ll, f. 207 and *CM*, V, 639–40 (invasion of
Wales); Ll, f. 208 and *CM*, V, 645–6 (Welsh resistance). See above n.150; also *HW*, II,
723; Smith, *Llywelyn ap Gruffudd*, 100–1.
[228] Ll, f. 206, *CM*, V, 597–8 (Edward); Ll, f. 207v, *CM*, V, 646 (Llywelyn's
exhortation); Ll, f. 209v, *CM*, V, 727–8 (offer of peace): *Quid est hoc: unus homo laudabilis
pluris est quam quod offerunt pro pace postulato.*
[229] Other such likenesses include Edward's refusal to fight Llywelyn's 10,000 armed men
sworn to suffer death at need in defence of their country (Ll, f. 205v, *CM*, V, 597: *erant
namque equites ad decem milia eorum armati . . . Qui mutuo confoederati . . . juraverant se strenue
et fideliter usque ad mortem pro libertate patriae suae*); and also the respective accounts of the
scarcity of beef and salt (Ll, ff. 208–208v, *CM*, V, 656–7, 677). Of uncertain origin are the
phrase 'one either side the water' when Llwyd describes Llywelyn's destruction of
Edward's territory to the gates of Chester (Ll, 205v); and his figure of 15,000 footmen in
each of Llywelyn's 'twoe battailles' which he admits to being less than Paris's 30,000 in
each: *et in utraque parte recensiti sunt triginta armatorum* (Ll, 206v, *CM*, V, 614).

views which differed from those of Trevet, in that they were sharply critical of the English king and his heir,[230] and which also paid rare tribute to the people of Wales for their fortitude, their patriotism and their noble descent; and especially so when those views were expressed by a most influential chronicler writing in England during the course of the events being related. It is intriguing to suppose that Llwyd might well have depended throughout on just one manuscript of Paris's work, the text now known as MS Reg.14 Cvii preserved among the Royal MSS in the British Library. This contains a complete copy of the *Historia Anglorum* together with a copy of just that section of the *Chronica Majora* concerned with its final five years, that is, from 1254 to 1259. Known as the Arundel MS because it was purchased in 1563 by Llwyd's employer Henry Fitzalan, earl of Arundel, it bears the signature of John, Lord Lumley (Llwyd's brother-in-law), who inherited Arundel's library, and it was transcribed for Archbishop Parker in 1568. After its removal from St Albans, where it had been written, the manuscript passed through several hands until by the mid-sixteenth century it was in the old Royal Library where, among others, Bale and Polydore Vergil are known to have used it. Though purchased by Arundel after Llwyd had completed the 'Cronica Walliae' in 1559, Llwyd could certainly have had an opportunity to read the manuscript fairly soon after his appointment to the Arundel household in 1553, with the aid of a growing circle of fellow antiquarians added, of course, to the powerful influence of his patron. Indeed, as part of his duties Llwyd might well have encouraged Arundel to purchase it after the death of Bale, who had 'borrowed' it from the Royal Library, so that it became part of Arundel's private library.[231]

---

[230] Trevet's respect for Henry III and his admiration of Edward I are noticed by Hog, preface to *NT*, x; Grandsen, *Historical Writing*, 504–5; Dean, 'Nicholas Trevet', 328–52.

[231] For Llwyd's work in helping to improve the Arundel and Lumley library at Nonsuch see Jayne and Johnson, *Lumley Library*, 6–8; Gruffydd, 'Humphrey Llwyd', 84; Williams, 'Ysgolheictod hanesyddol', 112. On MS Reg.14 Cvii see F. Madden in *HistAng*, I, xxxviii–xliv; H. T. Riley in Rishanger, *Chronica*, xx–xxi. Llwyd's two specific statements that Paris wrote from the Norman Conquest to the later years of the reign of Henry III (Ll, ff. 3v, 209v) would seem to exclude such popular compilations as the *Flores Historiarum* as possible sources. The Lumley Library catalogue strengthens this view: the three copies of the *Flores Historiarum* it lists (attributed to Matthew of Westminster) were published after completion of the 'Cronica Walliae'. Two printed works of Matthew Paris in the catalogue, Jayne and Johnson, *Lumley Library*, no. 1322, M. Paris, *Historia Maior* (London, 1571); no. 1326, M. Paris, *Historia Vetusta* (Zurich, 1589) appeared after Llwyd's death.

As already indicated in the brief reference to the Barons' War, soon after the end of Paris's chronicle in 1259, although Nicholas Trevet's work again becomes the paramount English influence on the 'Cronica Walliae', Llwyd's account seems even this early to imply some acquaintance with 'other cronicles written in the Latyne tonge', especially those of William Rishanger and Walter of Guisborough. Some of the events described in such parallel accounts are, of course, commonplace in medieval chronicles, quite apart from the outright plagiarism of such as Thomas Walsingham. One such is the reference to the papal absolution of Henry III from his oath to maintain the Provisions of Oxford.[232] Llwyd's named three barons from among those pledged to 'put those statutes in execution which they were sworne to at Oxforde' are not taken from Trevet but bear a close resemblance to, or could be a compilation from, the same references by Rishanger and Guisborough.[233]

The capture by Edward of the castles of 'Hay, Breknoke and Huntingdon' is related exactly as by Rishanger and Guisborough, but Trevet adds the castle of Hereford. The comment that follows that 'Robert Ferrers Earle of Derby [was] true to nether parte' is, however, closer to Rishanger's *fidus nec regi nec baronibus* than to Trevet's *qui comiti Symonii adhaesit*.[234] Llwyd's version of the tale of the king's discomfiture at the hands of the Londoners as he 'passed by water from the towre . . . [but was] compelled to return to the towre againe' is, however, closely comparable to Trevet's, which refers to the king and queen travelling to Windsor (*ad castrum de Windelsore*), whereas Rishanger indicates that the queen alone undertook the voyage.[235]

It is noteworthy also that in the account of the 'peace concluded betwixt the Earle and the Kinge' Llwyd omits, as do Rishanger and Guisborough, Trevet's first two conditions requiring the freeing of Henry son of the king of Germany and the releasing to the barons of all of the king's castles.[236] Also the account of the stout defence of the walls of Northampton by the 'schollers of Oxforde, which the barrons had removed thither' is closely similar to Guisborough's *clerici vero universitatis Oxoniae que quidem universitas iussu baronum ibidem translata fuerat*; and

---

[232] Ll, f. 209v, *NT*, 249; Rishanger, *Chronica*, 4–5; Guisborough, *Chronicle*, 187; the dates differ. For the text of Pope Alexander's Bull of 13 April 1261, I. J. Sanders, *Documents of the Baronial Movement of Reform and Rebellion 1258–1267* (Oxford, 1973), 238–41.

[233] Ll, ff. 209v–210, *NT*, 251; Rishanger, *Chronica*, 7–8; Guisborough, *Chronicle*, 187.

[234] Ll, f. 210, *NT*, 254; Rishanger, *Chronica*, 13.

[235] Ll, f. 211, *NT*, 251; Rishanger, *Chronica*, 18.

[236] Ll, f. 211–211v, *NT*, 252; Rishanger, *Chronica*, 18.

Llwyd's reference to the wounding of Roger Leybourne at the siege of Rochester occurs only in Guisborough.[237] The account of the battle of Evesham, as already indicated, follows in the main that by Trevet. Of the differences between these two accounts the most significant are probably Llwyd's reference to the dismemberment of Leicester's body, omitted by Trevet but included in similar terms by both Rishanger and Guisborough; and also his omission of Trevet's reference to the honourable burial of the slain, each no doubt a reflection of the chroniclers' differing views of the adversaries.[238] At the same time Llwyd's admiration of Leicester's courage and love of justice and godliness, expressed in the assertion that he did not despair despite the odds but was 'readye to dye in Goddes cause, and for justice sake', echoes Guisborough's *verumtamen, ut credo, moriar pro deo et iusticia*.[239] The later reference to 'a statute made at Glocester called Quo Warrante' is to be found in both Trevet and Guisborough, but it is the latter alone that adds the anecdote of the Earl Warenne's spirited response.[240]

Apart from a few instances of Llwyd's use of other 'cronicles written in the Latyne tonge', his account from 1270 onward is based on Trevet, even where the accounts of William Rishanger and Walter of Guisborough bear a close resemblance to his narrative. The tale of the Lord Edward's brush with the highwayman Adam Gurdon is a late instance of Trevet's influence before Llwyd's explicit indication, in his discussion of the year 1270, of his dependence on Trevet, and examples multiply after that date.[241] They begin with the slaying, in 1270 according to Llwyd, but two years earlier in Trevet's account, of Alan la Zouche in Westminster Hall by John, Earl Warenne,[242] and continues with that of the marriage of Edmund, earl of Lancaster, to the daughter of the earl of Holderness,[243] the departure of the Lord Edward and his brother Edmund to the Holy Land and the attempted assassination of Edward at Acre; the death in 1272 of Henry III and Edward's coronation on his return to England two years later,[244] and the capture at

---

[237] Ll, f. 212–212v, 190, 192, Guisborough, *Chronicle*, 190, 192.

[238] Ll, f. 214v, *NT*, 266; Rishanger, *Chronica*, 37; see also Gransden, *Historical Writing*, 505.

[239] Ll, f. 214v, Guisborough, *Chronicle*, 201.

[240] Ll, f. 221, *NT*, 299; Guisborough, *Chronicle*, 216; for the Earl Warenne's alleged declaration, note f. 221.

[241] Ll, f. 215, *NT*, 269.

[242] Ll, f. 217, *NT*, 273.

[243] Ll, f. 217, *NT*, 274.

[244] Ll, ff. 217–217v, *NT*, 274–5.

sea of Simon de Montfort's daughter Eleanor and her brother Amaury, who was imprisoned at Corfe castle and then at Sherborne.[245]

Llwyd clearly depended wholly on Trevet's account of the treaty of Aberconwy in 1277.[246] His reliance is reflected in matters of detail such as the comment that Dafydd ap Gruffudd had been made a knight 'contrarye to the maner of Wales' (*contra morem gentis suae*). More important, however, is the extent to which Llwyd incorporated detailed matter that Trevet had drawn from the record evidence of the treaty.[247] Trevet's account of the thirteenth century, like that of Matthew Paris, was informed by access to the documentary sources but, apart from his exceptionally full account of the agreement between Edward I and Llywelyn ap Gruffudd in 1277, Llwyd does not make any significant use of the chroniclers' citations of records.[248] Neither did Llwyd seek out documentary material on his own behalf. Recourse to original documents would be a conspicuous part of David Powel's contribution to the development of Welsh historical study. Llwyd's description of the war of 1282–3 and the later rebellions of the reign of Edward I adheres to the narrative approach of his entire work and reflects particularly the contributions of Trevet and Guisborough. Yet intriguingly he is able to add detail that is not drawn from the main narrative sources. His account of the forcing of the Menai Straits by means of 'a bridge of boates' is drawn from Guisborough, but additionally Llwyd locates the crossing at 'Bonp y don' (in later writing described as Moel-y-don) where, he says, Julius Agricola had once led Roman forces upon their invasion of Anglesey.[249] Again, his account of the death of Llywelyn is drawn from Trevet and Guisborough, though he attributes the fatal blow to Adam Frankton rather than to the Stephen Frankton named by Guisborough and, in concluding that the prince was 'betrayed by the men of Buelht', Llwyd gave the narrative a personal touch that it would bear for many years to come.[250] The details of Llwyd's description of the rising of Rhys ap Maredudd in 1287, with the exception of an error in attributing the leadership of the royal army to Edward, earl of Cornwall, rather than to Edmund, earl of Cornwall, are identical with those of Trevet, noting the

[245] Ll, f. 218, *NT*, 294; see note f. 218.

[246] Ll, ff. 218–20, *NT*, 296–8.

[247] For the record of the terms of the treaty, Smith, *Llywelyn ap Gruffudd*, 438–45, with chroniclers' summaries, including that of Trevet, noted ibid., p. 438 n.181.

[248] Paris's use of record evidence concerning, for example, Dafydd ap Llywelyn's submission in 1241, is noted ibid., 34 n.118.

[249] See note, f. 222.

[250] See notes, ff. 223–223v.

taking of Dryslwyn castle and the death of William de Monte Caniso.[251] Similarly, several details of Trevet's account of the rebellion of Madog ap Llywelyn in 1294–5 are reflected in the 'Cronica Walliae'. Madog 'sonne to Prince Lhywelyn' reflects, though inaccurately, Trevet's identification of Madog as a kinsman of the late prince (*quemdam de genere Lewelini principis ultimi*), closely similar to that of Guisborough (*de sanguine principis Leulini*).[252] Details such as those that describe the attack on Caernarfon and the killing of a number of Englishmen attending a fair, Maelgwn ap Rhys's rising in Pembroke and Carmarthen, or Morgan ap Maredudd's expulsion from Glamorgan of Gilbert de Clare, earl of Gloucester, who had disinherited Morgan's ancestors, are entirely derived from Trevet. Edward's counter-measures, including the earl of Warwick's tactical use of bowmen and horsemen in combination during the course of the engagement which saw the defeat of the insurgents, and the building of Beaumaris castle, are taken from the same source. Even so, Humphrey Llwyd rearranges his material to some extent so as to enable him to close his history of Wales with a late advance by Madog ap Llywelyn to the March of Wales in the neighbourhood of Oswestry, recounting his first defeat of English forces near Knockin and then a second 'overthrowe' of his adversaries before the prince, advancing towards Shrewsbury, was confronted with superior power and was finally taken at Cefn Digoll near Caus and sent to perpetual imprisonment in the Tower of London.[253] Llwyd's concluding paragraph, differing from the known sequence of events and certainly citing, in its reference to Cefn Digoll, a matter of detail that he did not draw from any of the known chronicle sources, enabled him to complete his narrative with a description of a last spirited resistance on the part of a Welsh prince before the author felt constrained to admit that thereafter 'there was nothinge done in Wales worthy memory, but that is to bee redde in the Englishe Cronicle'.

---

[251] Ll, 225v; *NT*, 314–15. It might be noticed that Llwyd follows Trevet in recording the death of this knight and makes no mention of the death in the same engagement at Dryslwyn of 'John Peulard', named in the continuation of *Brut y Tywysogyon* in the Peniarth 20 MS (incorrectly given as 'John Pennardd' in *Pen20Tr*, 121), identified as John de Bevillard in Arnold Taylor, *Studies in Castles and Castle-Building* (London, 1985), 209–27. Llwyd's text carries no indication that he had access to this continuation of the *Brut*. See note f. 225v.

[252] Ll, ff. 226–227v; *NT*, 333, 338; Guisborough, *Chronicle*, 250–2.

[253] See note f. 227v.

CRONICA WALLIAE

Humphrey Llwyd

[1] After that Cadwaladr[1], the laste kinge of the Britons, descendinge frome the noble race of Troians, by extreme plagues of deathe and famyne dryven to forsacke this his realme and native countrey and with a greate numbre of his nobles and others, hade remayned awheile with his cosin Alan, Kinge of litle Bryttayn, whiche is called in the Brytish tonge Lhydaw, was certifeid howe a greate number of strangers as Saxons, Angles and Juthes had arryved in Britane and finding hit desolate, and without inhabitantes savinge a fewe Saxons whiche had called them in, and certeine poore Britons that lyved by rootes in rockes and woodes, had over runne a greate parte thereof and devidinge hit to dyverse territories and kingedomes inhabited that whiche was then and is nowe at this daye in the Britishe or Welshe tonge called Lloyger, and in the Englishe tonge Englande, with all the cities townes castelles and villages which the Britons had builded ruled and inhabited by the space of 1817 yeres under divers kinges and princes of greate renoume, thought to returne and by streingth of Britishe knightes to recover his owne lande againe. And after he had made redye his navye for the transportinge over[2] of his owne men with suche succoures as he had founde at Alans hande, beeholde the angell of the highest appeared unto hym and declared to him that hit was the will of God that he shoulde not take his [1v] viage towardes Britaine but to Rome to Sergius then Pope, where he shulde macke an ende of his lief and be afterwarde numbred amonge the blessed, for God had appointed that the Britons shulde have no more the rule and governaunce of the whole Ile untill the prophecie of Merdhyn, or as the Englishe men call him Merlyn Ambrose, shulde be fulfilled. Whiche vision, after Cadwalader had declared to his frind Alan, he sent for all his bookes of prophecies, as the woorkes of bothe Merdynes, or Merlines Ambrose and Silvester or Weilde Merline, and the woordes which the eagle spake at the buildinge of Caer Septon, nowe called Chaftesbury, and after longe studie founde the tyme to be come whiche they had so longe tyme synce[3] prophecied of, and therfore counselled Cadwalader to fullfill the will of God whiche did so, and takinge his journey to Rome lyved ther 5[4]★ yeres in the service of God and died the yere after mans redemption 688. So that the Britons ruled this Ile with the oute Iles of Wighte, Mone, called in Englishe Anglesea, Manawe, in Englishe Man, Orkenay and Ewyst, 1137 yeres before Christe unto the yere of his incarnacioun 688. And this ended the rule of the Britons over the whole Ile.

[1]C preceded by 'Cronica Walliae a Rege Cadwalader ad an[num] 1294 Humfredo Floid authore', in the hand of Sir Robert Cotton

[2]C – over

[3]Ll – synce

[4]C 8

[2] Because★ I have taken in hande to wrrite the lives and actes of the kinges and princes of Walles whiche ruled that countrey from Cadwalader to Lhewelyn sonne of Gruffith ap Lhewelyn, whiche was the laste of the Britishe bloodde that had the governaunce of Wales, I thinke hit nessessarie to sette furthe the perfecte discription of the countrey as hit was in olde tyme and as hit is at thees dayes that therby the readere may the more playnely and easely understande the woorke following. Therefore after the three sonnnes of Brutus had devided the whole Ile of Britaine into three partes, that parte conteined within the Frenche seas, with the ryvers Sevarne, called in Britishe Haveren, Dee and Humber, fill to the eldest sonne Locrinus whiche[1] after his name is[2] called Lloyger, which name hit hathe in the Britishe tonge to this daye and nowe is called Ingland, and the meares augmented northwarde to the Ryver Tweede. The second sonne Albanactus had all the lande frome Humber northwarde to the Sea Orkenay (called in the Britishe tonge More Werydh, and in the Latine[3] Mare Caledonicum). The thirde sonne Camber had to his parte all that whiche remayned undevided[4], lying[5] within the [2v] Spanishe and Irishe seas, and seperated frome Ingland with the ryvers Sevarne and Dee, and this parte was after his name called Cambry, and an inhabitante therof Cambro, and ther language Cambraec, and so are at this daye. So that they have kept the same countrey and language 2690 and odde yeres without connuixion with any other nation specially in Northwales, as hit shall hereafter appere.

And because the name therof is changed or rather mistaken by the inhabitantes of Ingland and not of them called Cambry, naminge hit Wales, I thinke hit necessarie to declare the occasion therof which is, that where the Saxons, a people of Germanie, were the firste that after the Britons enhabited and ruled the greatest parte of this Ile, and drove the Britons to that corner which according to the maner of ther countrey they called Wales and the people Walshemen and the tonge Walshe, that is to saye strange or not of them understanded. For at this daye the inhabitant[6] of the Lowe Countreys calleth his[7] next neighboures language of Henander,[8]★ or other that speake Frenche, Walshe, as a language to them unknowen. Likewise the dwellers of Tyroll and other the hier[9] countreys of Germanie nameth the Italian his

[1]C + was
[2]C – is
[3]C + tonge
[4]C + and
[5]C lying *deleted*; being *inserted above line*

[6]C inhabitants
[7]C their
[8]C Henegaw;
[9]C hier *deleted*; hieha *inserted above line*

next neighboure a Welshman and his language Walshe. And [3] this is
an evident proffe that they whiche harped upon a Queene Gwalaes and
of a Prince Wala (of which nether Britishe, Latine nor Anglishe historie
makethe mention) were foule deceaved. Likewise was a greate
historiographer of late dayes, whiche saythe hit was called Wallia, quasi
Italia, because the reste of the Romaines which remayned in the Ile
were dryven thether. Nether is this any newe invention although
Polydore Virgile with an Italian bragge dothe glorie him self to be the
firste that espied hit out, for diverse auncient writers do alledge the same
cause of the name of Walles, of whom Silvester Giraldus is one, who
wrote in the tyme of Henry the Secund after the conqueste, 380 yeres
passed, which is an evident token that the said Polydore dyd ether never
see nor reade the auncient histories of this realme or dissemblethe the
same to the advauncement and praise of himself, and his countrey,
which to the learned and indifferent reader shall appeare to be thonly
occasion he toke that woorke in hande, for all his booke redoundith
onely to the praise and honor of the Romaines, as well spirituall as
temporall, and to blase furthe ther actes and deedes within this realme,
and upon the other parte dothe ether openly sclaunder orels prively [3v]
extenuate or shamefully denye the martiall[1]★ and noble actes aswell of
Saxons, Danes and Normanes as of the Britons, all inhabiters of this Ile.
Which thinge he that liste to prove let him reade and confer Casars
Commentaries, Cornelius Tacitus, Herodianus and other auncient
writers as well in Latine as in Greeke with his woorke, and as for the
aunciente writers of the British Historie as the British Cronicle, the
Historie of Gyldas, Virinnius Ponticus, yea the golden woorke of
Mathias Parisiensis monke of Sainte Alban, which wrote frome William
Bastarde to the laste yeres of Henry the Thyrde. I dare well saye he
never sawe them for they be in divers places to be had where the truth
maye be easelye proved. But to make an ende I saye that he being firste
a stranger borne, and aswell ingnorante in the histories of this realme as
of the diverse tonges and languages used therin, colde never set furthe
the true and perfecte cronicle of the same. But having[2] a good grace and
plesaunt stile to utter thinges[3]★ in the Latine tonge and finding him selfe
in a countrey where every man ether lacked knowledge or sprite to set
furth the historie of ther owne countrey, toke this [4] enterprise in hand
to ther greate shame and litle to his owne praise, because he a bleinde[4]
leader shall drawe a greate number of undiscrete and rash followers, as

---

[1]C materiall *deleted* martial *in margin*
[2]C – having, *inserted above line*

[3]C – to utter things, *inserted in margin*
[4]C blynde

well geographers and cosmographers as croniclers and historiographers, to the darke pitte of ignorannce where I leve them at this tyme, remittinge the reader to the apologie of the Britishe historie againste the calumniouse and sclanderouse tauntes of the said Virgile writen by Sir John Price Knight where the[1] reader shall see all his erroures confuted at large.* And to returne to my former matter which was of the name of Wales, which name to be gevyn by a strange nation and to be of late yeres, it[2] may be otherwise proved for the Welshmen them selves do not understande what thees woordes Wales and Welshe signifie, nor knowe non other name of ther countrey nor of them selves but Cambry nor of ther language but Cambraec, which is as muche to saye as Cambers language or speeche. As lickewise they knowe not what[3] Ingland nor Englishe meaneth, but comenly calle the countrey Lloyger, an Englisheman Says and in[4] the plurall number Saysson and the Englishe tonge Sayssonaece, which is [4v] an evident token that this is the same language or tonge which the Britons spake, for the woorke of Merdhyn or Merlyn and of Taliessyn, which wrote above a 1050 vel 1500[5] yeres agoe, are allmoste the same woordes which they use at this daye, or at the leaste easy to be understanded of every one that speke[6] perfectlye the Welshe tonge specially in Northwales.

Beside this, where at this daye ther doe remaine three remenantes of the Britons devided ether frome other with the seas which are Wales, Cornwaill called in Britishe Kerniw, and Little Britaine, yet all the particuler woordes of thees three people are all one, althoughe in pronunciation and writinge of the sentences they differ somewhat, which is no marvaile seinge that the pronunciation in one realme is often very diverse so that the one canne scaunte understande the other. But[7] hit is rather a wonder that the Welshmen being seperated frome the Cornishe welnye thees 900 yeres and the Britons frome ether of them 290 yeres before that, and havinge small traficke or concurse togeather since that tyme, have still kepte their owne British tonge. Therefore let them for shame holde ther peace that denye the Welshe to be the olde British tonge. And here I can not passe over what one of thees fyne croniclers wrote of late of the name of Britaine, affirminge hit sholde be so [5] called of Britaine in France as the elder name. But surely he had never seene Ptholome,[8] no nor Casar nor any other auncient writer for

---

[1]C the saide
[2]Ll – it
[3]C – what, *inserted above line*
[4]C – in
[5]C – vel 1500

[6]C speake *deleted*; speaketh *inserted above line*
[7]Ll – But
[8]C Ptholonce

there he mighte have learned that when this land was called Britaine the other was called Armorica, and howe in Maxentius tyme Conan Meriadoc was the first that gave hit that name and inhabited hit with Britons out of this Ile. Other dednitions* of thees woordes Britaine and Albion out of Greeke and Latyne I am ashamed to reherse, for unto such erroures doe they commonly fall that, ether puffed up with vayneglorie of ther owne wittes or pynched with dispite and envye at other mens woorkes or blynded with ignorance, goe about to sette furth any historie or cronicle. But passinge over this matter till an other tyme I will returne to the description of Wales which, as I said, was of olde tyme compassed welnye about with the Irish seas and the ryvers Dee and Sevarne although afterwarde the Saxons wanne by force frome the Britanes all the plaine and champaigne countrey over the ryvers and speciallye, Offa, King of Mercia, who made a diche of greate breadethe and depth to be a meare betwixt his Kingdome and Wales. Which diche beganne at the Ryver Dee by Bassinge warke¹ and ranne alonge the hilles sides to the southe sea alitle frome Bristowe aboue an hundred [5v] miles in length and is in many places to be seene at this daye bering the name of Clawdh Offa, that is to saye Offas Diche, and the countrey one this side comenly called in Welshe Mers* at this day, allthough the greateste parte of hit be nowe inhabited of² Welshmen especally in Northwales, which countrey at this daye kepeth his olde meres to the ryver Dee and in some places over hit. Other, as Silvester Giraldus, make the Ryver Wy, called in Welshe Gwy, to be the mere betwixt England and Wales one the southe parte called Southwalles, and he measureth the breadth of Wales frome Salowe or Wyloweforde called Rhyd yr Helig upon Wy to Sainte Davids in Menevia 100 miles, and the leingth frome Caerlhion upon Wyske in Gwentlande to Holy Heade, called Caergyby in Anglesea, called Mon, above 150 myles. And thees be the commen meres at this daye allthoughe the Welshe tonge is commenly used and spoken one this side thees olde meares a greate way, as in Herforde shire, Glocester shire and in a greate parte of Shropshire.* And thus for the generall description of Wales which afterwarde aboute the yere 870 Rodericus the great, Kinge of Wales, devided hit into three territories which they called kingedomes which remayned till of late dayes. Thees three were [6] Gwyneth, in Englishe Northwales, Dehevbarth, in Englishe Southwales, and Powys Lande and in eather of them he ordeined a princely seat or courte for the princes to remayne at moste commonly,

---

¹C passing *deleted*; Bass Basing *inserted above*   ²C by *deleted*; of *in later hand.*
line

as in Gwyneth, which some olde writers call Venetia and Venedotia for
Gwynedhia, Aberfrawe in the Ile of Mone in Englishe Anglesea; in
Dehevbarth, which likewise is called Demetia in Lattine, Caermerdhyn,
frome whens it was afterwarde removed to Dynevwr 8 myles thence; in
Powis Pengwern called Ymwythig and in Englishe Shrewisburie, frome
whence it was removed to Mathravall in Powis Lande. And because the[1]
hystorie dothe aswell entreate of the warres betwixt every of[2] thees
three princes as betwixt them and the Saxons, Northmannes[3] and the
Fleminges I thinke it good to sett furth the perticuler description of
every parte by hit selfe.

And firste of Northwales as the chieffeste parte which he gave to his
eldeste sonne ordeininge that either of the other twoe shulde paye hyme
yerely 66[li]* of tribute, as it appeareth in the Lawes of Howell the Good,
which are to be had both in Welshe and also in Latine. Therefore
Gwynedh, [6v] called Northwales, had upon the northside the sea frome
the Ryver Dee at Basingwerke to Aberdovy and upon the weste and
southweste the Ryver Devy which devideth hit frome Southwales and
in some places frome Powis Lande. And then south and easte hit is
devided frome Powys sometymes with mountaines and sometymes with
ryvers till hit came to the Ryver Dee againe. And this lande was of olde
tyme devided to 4 partes, of which the chieffeste was Mone, called
Anglesea, where the Princes chief house was at Aberfrawe, and is[4] an
ilande seperated from the maine lande with an arme of the sea called
Menai,[5] and had in hitself three cantredes or hundredes which were
subdevided to sixe comotes as Cantref Aberfrawe to Comote Lhion and
Comote Malhdreth, Cantref Kemais to the[6] comotes Talebolion and
Twrkehelyn, Cantref Rhossyr to the comotes Twydaethwy[7] and
Menay. And at this daye there is a prety towne in that ile called
Beavmarys and a commen passage to Ireland at Caergybi, called
Holyhead. But here[8] I can not wynke at that notable erroure of
Polydore which, after his accustomed fashion, denieth this ile to bee
called [7] Mona but Anglesia or Anglorum Insula because hit is called in
Englishe Anglesey, and geveth this name[9] of Mona to Manne and so
hathe loste the name of either ile. Which ignorance and forgetfullnes
might be forgeven him, yf he hade not drawen a great numbre to this
erroure with him which in ther chartes doe dayly wronge name thees

---

[1] C this
[2] C – every of
[3] C Normaines
[4] Ll – is
[5] C Manai *deleted*; Menai *in margin*

[6] C + two *inserted above line*
[7] C Tindaethwy
[8] Ll – here
[9] Ll – name

iles, which may be easlye proved. First because the inhabitantes of the Ile
doo knowe non other name but Mona, and hit is called throughe all
Wales Tyr Mon, that is to saye the Lande of the Mone* unto this daye,
so that neither by memory of manne, nether by any monument in
writinge in the Britishe tonge can hit appeare that ever hit had any other
name but Mone, yet ther be manifest monuments for thees 1000 yeres.
Hit is also growen to a proverbe throughe Wales for the fertilnesse of
the grounde, Mon Mam Cymry, that is to saye Mone Mother of Wales.

Yf this bee not sufficient, reade* the anncient historie of Cornelius
Tacitus,* which by lyke age hade beaten out of Polydores headde, who
saieth that the souldioures [7v] of Paulinus Suetonius and afterwarde of
Julius Agricola after they had passed throughe Northwales they came
over againste Mona, where they dyd swymme over the arme of the sea,
and so by force wanne the ile.* Nowe whether is hit* more reasonable
thus to swymme over 200 passes[1] or 20 myles, I knowe ther is no man
that beleueth Polydore in this pointe: let them therefore by this[2] judge
the reste. As for that which he saieth of the greate woodes it is nothinge,
for bothe the Romaines and after when the Christen faieth toke place in
thees realme the Christians dyd out roote them for the idolatry and
cruell religion used ther. That the Kinge of Man sende[3] for tymber to
Mone, reade the lief of Hughe Earle of Chester, as hit is evident by the
greate beeches and other trees founde in the earthe at thees dayes. His
other reasone is because hit is called Anglesey in Englishe, so is Lloyger
Englande, and Cymbry Wales, are those therfore the olde names? No
surely. And what yf the inhabitantes called hit so, as they do[4] not, had
hit not aname before the Angles wanne hit? Yes I warrant youe, but he
hade forgotten that well.* To the [8] name of Manne hit was ever, or at
the lest thees 1000 yeres named in Britishe Manawe, of which cometh
the Englishe name Manne. The inhabitantes thereof calle hit so and no
nation about hit dyd ever calle hit Mone. No, nor[5] any wrriter but
Polydore whiche was to yonge a godffather to name so olde a cheilde.
For Gyldas who wrote aboue 900 yeres passed which writinge[6] Polydore
never sawe but untruely fathers upon him his owne[7] devise, Gyraldus in
his Description of Irelande to Henrey the 2, Henry Huntingdon, dothe
plainely calle Man in Latine Eubonia,[8] adding thereto ether Manawe or
Man for the better understandinge of the name. Will youe beleve them

[1] C pases
[2] C + point *inserted above line*
[3] C sende *deleted*; sent *added*
[4] C dye *deleted*; do *in margin*
[5] Ll more
[6] Ll – writinge
[7] C newe *deleted*; owne *in margin in another hand*
[8] C Eabonia; Eubonia *in margin in another hand*

or Polydore? Other argumentes there are which I will passe over, till I have more leasure and occasion to write of this matter.

The secunde parte of Northwales was called Arvon which is asmuche to saye as over againste Mone and had in hit 4 cantredes and 10 comotes. Cantref Aber had in hit 3 comotes: Y Llechwedh Vcha, y Llechwedh Issa and Nankonwy; Cantref Arvon had 2 comotes: Ywch Gwyrvai and Is Gwirvai; Cantref Dunodic had 2 comotes: Ardvdwy [8v] and Eivyonedd; Cantref Lhyn conteineth 3 comotes: Kymytmaen, Tin Llayn and Kanalogion. This is[1] nowe called Caernarvon shire as Mone is called Anglesey Shire and have the same devisions at this daye. Also in this shire are Snowdon hilles, called Eryri, nether in height, frutefullnes of grasse,* woode, cattell, fishe and foule geving place to the famouse Alpes, and without contraversi the strongeste countrey within Britaine. Here is the towne of Caernarvon called in the[2] olde tyme Caersegonce.* Here is also Conwaye called Caer Kyffyn, and the see of Bangor with divers other auncient castelles and places of memorye and was the last peece of Wales that came under the dominion of the kinges of Englande. Hit hathe one the north the see and Menai* upon the easte and southeaste the Ryver Conwey which devideth hit frome Denbigh Shire althoughe hit nowe passe the ryver in on place by the sea shore, and is southwest[3]* and weste separate from Myryonydd by highe mountaines and ryvers and other meres.

The thirde parte of Gwynedh was Meryonydh conteininge 3 cantredes and every cantre 3 comots, as Cantref Meirion hathe thees [9] comots: Tal y bont, Pennall and Ystvmaneir; Cantref Arwistli had these: Uwchcoet, Iscoet and Gwarthrenion; Cantref Penllyn had these: Vwch Meloch, Is Meloch and Micnaynt, and this kepethe the said name till this daye but not within the same meres and is full of hilles and rockes and hathe upon the northe the sea, notable at this daye for the greate resorte and number of people that repaire thither to take hearinges.[4] Hit hathe upon the easte Arvon and Denbighe Lande, upon the south Powis, and upon the west the Ryver[5] Dyvi and Caerdigan shire apeece of [South]wales. In this countrey standeth the towne of Harlech and a great lake called Llyn Tegyd, through which the Ryver Dee runneth and myngleth not with the water of the pounde, which is 3 miles longe, and also the salmones, which are comenly taken in the ryver harde by the lake, are never seene to enter the lake. Likewise a kinde of fishe called Gwyniayd, which are like to whitinges, and are full in the

[1]Ll – is   [4]C herings
[2]Ll – the   [5]C – river
[3]Ll southeast

pounde, are never taken in the river. And not ferre frome this pound is a place called Caergay, which was the house of Caye, Arthures foster brother. This shire, as Arvon, is full of catell, foule and fishe, [9v] withe great number of redde dere and roos but ther is great scarsitie of corne.

The fourthe parte of Gwynedh was called Y Bervedhwlad, which maye be Englished the inlande or mydle countrey, and hit conteined 5 cantredes and 13 comots, as Cantref Ryvoniok had in hit thees comotes: Vwchaled and Isaled; Cantref Ystrad had Hiraethog and Kynveirch; Cantref Ros thees: Vwch Dvlas, Isdvlas and Y Krevddyn, and thees comotes, savinge Y Kreuddyn, are at this daye in the Lordshipp of Denbighe, for hit is in Caernarvon shire and in that standeth the castell Dyganwy which was the Earles of Chester and is¹ comenly called in the Latine and English Cronicle Ganioc²★ And therefore when Edwarde the First wanne Wales he added that peece to Caernarvon shire because it was his owne ground. The fourthe cantref was Dyffryn Clwyd (in English the valleye of Clwyd and nowe called the Lordeship of Rythyn) and hathe thees commotes: Gologion, Llanarth and Rythyn.★ The 5 cantref is Tegengle and is nowe apeece of Flyntshire having thees comotes: Kwnsallt, Prestatyn, and Rudlan. And in this part is one of the fayrest valleyes within this Ile conteining 18 myles in length and [10] 4, 5, 6 or 7 myles³ in breadth as hit chanceth, havinge easte west and south highe hilles and northwarde the sea, plentifull of catell, fishe and foule, corne, haye, grasse and woode and devided alonge with the Ryver Clwyd to whome rune Clvyedoc,⁴ Ystrad, Whilar, Elwy and a great number of other ryvers frome every hill. In this valley 2 myles frome the sea is the towne and castell of Rudlan, where sometymes a parliament hath bene kept, and 2 miles aboue hit is the See of Saincte Assaph, betwixt the ryvers Clwyd and Elwy, called in olde tyme the Bishops see of Llanelwy. 3 miles thence and 2 miles frome the ryver is situate upon a rocke the prety towne of Denbighe, where is one of the greatest markettes within the marches of Wales, and 3 fayre parks adjoininge to the towne, and one of the fairest and strongest castelles within this realme for situation, with highe and huge towers, stronge and thike walles, largenes in compasse and faire prospecte, which being the house of David brother to Llewelyn, the last prince of Walsh bloodde, was enlarged and streingthened by Henry Lacy Earle of [10v] Lyncolne, who was lord of the countrey by Kinge Edwardes gifte. And after his decesse⁵ came to Thomas Duke of Lancaster and after him to Hughe Lorde

¹Ll – is
²C Gannoc
³C – myles
⁴C Clywedoc
⁵Ll successe; C successe *deleted*, decesse *later correction*

Spenser and at laste was gevyn to Roger Mortymer Earle of Marche.
After whose deathe hit was gevyn to the Lorde Montacute Earle of
Salysburie, but shortely after was restored againe to the Mortymers
frome whome hit camme with the Earledome of Marche to the House
of Yorke and so to the crowne. Hit is called one of the greatest and best
lordships in Englande and nowe of late is joyned with other and made a
shire. Fyve miles above this is the towne of Rythyn with afaire castell
which belonged sometymes to the Lordes Graye Earles of Kent. And so
this peece of North Wales hathe upon the northe the Ryver Dee and
the sea, vpon the west Arvon and the Ryver Conwy, south and east
Merionyth and the countrey then called Powis. And thees bee the
meares and bandes[1] of Gwynedh or Venedocia, for the name of
Northwales conteineth beside this all Powys at thees dayes, and thus ther
was under the territorie [11] of Aberfrawe 15 cantredes, and in them 38
comotes.

   The secunde kingedome was Mathravall, which in right order was the
thyrde as that which came to the thyrde brother, yet for the beter
understanding of the woorke I have placed hit here.* To this kingdome
belongeth[2] the countrey of Powys and the land betwixt Wy and
Sevarne. And this parte had upon the south and west Southwales with
the ryvers Wy and Towy and other meares, upon the north Gwynedh
and upon the east the Marches of England frome Chester to Wy a litle
above Hereforde, and therefore hit was moste troubled with warres as
well of the Saxons as afterwarde of the Normanes Lordes Marchers, who
dayly wanne some parte thereof, and by that meanes hit was the first that
served the kinges of England and therefore lesse estemed of all the rest.
This parte called Powys was againe subdevided into two partes Powys
Vadoc and Powis Wenwynwyn and so ther remained three partes[3]* in
this territorie. Powys Vadoc conteined in hit selfe fyve cantredes and 15
comots. The cantreds[4] and comotes bee these: Cantref y Barwn, [11v]
whiche hath three comotes: Dymael, Y Deirnion and Glyndyfyrdwy,
which be nowe in Merioneth shire savinge Dymael; Cantref y Rhyw,
whose comotes were these: Ial nowe in Denbigheshire, Ystradalyn and
Hope nowe in Flyntshire; Cantref Vwchnant hathe thees comots:
Merfordh in Flyntshire, Maylor Gymraec, in Englishe Bromefelde,
nowe in Denbighe shire and Maylor Saesnec in Flyntshire; Cantref
Trefred conteneth thees comotes: Croesvayn, Tref y Wayn, in Englishe
Chirke and in Denbighe shire, Croesoswallt, in Englishe Oswester and

in Shropshire; Cantref[1] Rayader* with his comotes Mochnant Is Rhaiader, Kynllaeth and Nanheudwy all in Chirkelande and in Denbighe shire. Also the Lordeship of Whittington was in this part of Powys which parte at this day hath lost the name of Powys and is situate in divers shires as hit appeareth by the discourese before passed. In this parte is the castell of Holte in Bromefelde, which was buylte by William Earle Waren which with Bromefelde and Ial came by juste discent to the Fitzalens, Earles of Arundell, frome whome it passed, [12] againe for lake of issue male. Ther is also the castell of Chirke buylded by Roger Mortymer Earle of Marche which likewise cam by the daughter of Roberte Mortymer to the said Earle of Arundell. Likewise the Lordship of Whittington which came by mariage to Fulke Fitzwaren and so continued for many yeres in that house till hit came to the Kinges hand in oure tyme and nowe is in the hande of the Right Honorable Henry Fitzalen Earle of Arundell. There is beside these, the Lordeship of Oswester of the which the Fitzalens have bene Lordes thees 300 and odde yeres and of diverse other lordshipes in those Marches as Shrarden, the Eleven Townes, Clun and many other which be all nowe in Shropshire.

The secunde parte called Powys Wenwynwyn had like wise 5 cantredes and 12 comotes. Cantref Yvyrnwy had thees comotes: Mochnant Uwch Rhaydyr, Mechayniscoed and Llannerch Hudwl; Cantref Ystlyc had these: Deudhwr, Gordhwr Issa and Stradmarchelh; Cantref Llyswynaf [12v] had these: Caereinion and Mechayn Uwchcoed; Cantref Kedewen hathe Comote Kynan and Comote Haverne; Cantref Kynan hathe* Comote Kevelioc and Mawddwy which is nowe in Merionydh shire. And the 3[2] firste cantredes doe onelye at this daye bere the name of Powys which are upon the northe side of Sevarne and are all fyve saving the comote of Mowddwye in Mountgomery shire. This is a countrey full of woodes, hilles and ryvers and hathe in hit thees townes: the Poole, Newetowne and Machyn-llayth. Arwystli was in olde tyme in this parte but afterwarde hit came to the Princese of Gwynedh. Thees lordeshippes came by just discente frome the princes thereof to a woman named Hawys, the[3] daughter of Owayn ap Gryffidh, and she by the comanndement of Kinge Edwarde the Secunde maryed one John Charleton, a yoman of the Kinge, who therby was made Lorde of Powys and so hit contynued in that name 4 discents. At whiche tyme hit came to two daughters [13] of the whiche,

[1]Ll – Cantref [3]Ll – the
[2]C three

the eldest maryed with Sir John Graye Earle of Tangerfelde in which name that parte called[1] Powys is at this daye. For the moste parte Arwystly and Kevelioc came to the Baron of Dudley and was solde to the Kinge.

The thyrde[2]★ parte belonging to Mathraval was the lande betwixt Wy and Sevarne conteyninge foure cantredes and 13[3] comotes. Cantref Melienyth hathe thees comotes: Kery, Swydhygre, Riwlalht and Glyin Iethion; Cantref Elvel hath these: Uwch Mynydh, Ismynydh and Llech Dhyfnoc; Cantref y Clawdh these: Dyffryn Tyveydiat, Swyddhynogen and Pennwelht; Cantref y Bualht hath these: Swydhyvam, Dreulys and Isyrwon. Of this parte there is at this daye some in Mountgomery shire, some in Radnor shire, and some in Breknoke shire. In this parte and the lordshipes Marchinge to hit, which althoughe at the tyme of this devision, which was in the tyme of the last Prince, were not in his subjection, yet to this daye speake Welshe and are called Wales, are theese townes and castells: Mountgomery called in Welsh Trevaldwyn, a prety towne and a faire castell, [13v] the castell of Clunne called Colunwy, which is the earles of Arundell, the towne of Knighton, the castell of Kymaron, Prestene, in Welshe Llanandras, the towne and castell of Radnor, in Welshe Maysyved, at this day the shire towne, the towne of Kynton, and the castell of Huntyndon, called in Welsh Castell Mayn, which were the Bohunes Earles of Hereforde and after the Dukes of Buckyngham, Castell Payn, Haye, and Llanvair in Buelht. Thees lordeshipes, with Breknocke and Abergevenni, were belonginge to the Bruses Lordes of Breknocke, and after came diverse tymes and by sundrye meanes to the Bohunes, Nevyls and Mortymers.

And so, as I have reahersed, in this territorie or kingdome were founde 14 cantredes and 40 comotes, and two of thees partes which are bothe Powis and Gwynedh are at this daye callyd Northwales and devided into 6 shires: Mone called Anglesey, Caernarvon, Meryonedh, Denbighe, Flynt and Mountgomery shire and are all one the north side Sevarne savinge apeece of Mountgomery shire. And [14] here I thinke hit good to let the reader understande what the Britishe Cronicle saithe of Northwales, which affirmeth that three tymes hit came by enheritannce to women.★ First to Stradwen daughter to Addeawn ap Kynan ap Endaf and wiff to Coel Godebaugh mother to Kenav and Dyvyr and Gwawl. The secunde tyme to the said Gwawl wief to Edyrn ap Padarn and mother to Cunedha Wledic, which Cunedha,

---

[1]C of
[2]C third; Ll thyrde *amended to* secunde;
[3]C xiii

correct form thyrde *restored in text; see note*

enhabitinge in the north partes of Englande aboute the yere 540 after the
incarnation and heringe howe the myngled nations of Irishe Scottes and
Pictes had overrunne the sea shore of Caerdigan which was parte of his
enheritannce, sent his sonnes thyther to enyoie ther enheritannce, of the
which Tybiawn his eldest sonne dyed in Manne which landes¹ the said
Irishe Scottes had wonne. For Guildas saeith that of the children of
Glam Hoctor, which people a great parte of Ireland, Ystoreth²★ with his
people enhabited Dalrienda, [14v] whiche is a parte of Scottelande.
Buylke with his people came to Manne but I thinke hit good to put in
Guildas woordes whiche saieth★: Buylke cum filiis suis inhabitavit
Euboniam insulam vulgo Manaw que est in meditullio maris inter
Hiberniam et Britaniam. That is to saye: Buylke with his children
inhabyted the Ile Eubonia, commenly called Manawe, for so hit was and
is named in Britishe, which lyeth in the meeddell of the sea beettwene
Irland and Britaine. This was not called Mona as Polydore fayneth. The
children of Bethan enhabited Demetia which is Southwales with Gwyr
and Cydweili till they were chaced thence by the children of Cunedha.
This farre Guildas. Therefore the sonnes of Cunedha being arrived in
Northwales, aswell I thinke beinge dryven by the Saxons as for ther
enheritaunce, devidede the lande betwixt them. And first Meyriawne,
the sonne of Teibiawne the sonne of Cunedha, had Cantref Meyriawn
to his parte, Arwystel ap Cunedha had Cantref Arwystli, Keredic ap
Cunedha had Keredigyon nowe Cardigan shire, Dunod had Cantref
[15] Dunodic, Edyrn³★ had Edyrnion, Mael had Dynmael, Coel had
Goleiowvn,⁴ Dogvael had Dogveilin, Rvawn had Ryvoniog nowe
Denbighe Lande, Einion Yrch had Caereiniawn in Powis, Ussa had
Maesusswalht nowe Oswester. For suerlye that they saye commenly of
Oswalde King of Northumberlande to be slayne ther and of the well
that spronge where his arme was caried is nothinge so. For Beda and all
other writers testifie that Peanda slewe Oswalde at Maserfelt in the
Kingedome of Northumberland and howe his bodie was buried in the
abbey of Bardeney in the province of Lyndeseyt. But to my former
matter. These names gevyn by the sonnes of Cunedha remayne to this
daye. After this the Irishe Pictes or Scottes, which the Britons called Y
Gwydhyl Fychtiaid which is to saye the Irishe Pictes, dyd overrunne the
Ile of Mone and were dryven thence by Caswallon Lhawhir, which is to
saye Caswallon with the Longe Hand, the sonne of Einion Yrch ap
[15v] Cunedha, who slewe Serigi ther Kinge with his owne handes at

¹C lande   ³C Edwyn
²C Ystroeth   ⁴C Goleiowon

Llan y Gwydhel which is the Irishe churche at Holy Heade. This
Caswallon was father to Maelgwn Gwyneth which the Latine calle
Maglocunus, Prince and Kinge of Britaine.

In this tyme★ was the famouse clerke and greate prophecier Taliessyn
Ben Bardh vel Beirdh,[1] that is to saye chieffest of the wysardes, for this
woorde bardh in Caesares tyme signified, as Lucan bereth witness, such
as had knoweledge of thinges to come and so[2] hit signifieth at this daye.
This Maelgwn had a sonne called Rhun in whose tyme the Saxons
invited Gurmond into Britaine frome Ireland who had come thyther
[from] Afrike.★ And he with the Saxons was the utter destruction of the
Britons and slewe all that professed Christe and was the first that drove
them over Sevarne. This Rhun was father to Beli, who was father to
Iago, for so the Britons calle James, who was father to Kadvan and not
Brochwell [16] called Brecynall, as the Englishe Cronicle saieth. For this
Brochwel Ysgithroc, that is to saye, longe tothed, was chosen leader
with suche as mette with Adelred alias Ethelfryd, Rex North[umbriae
et] Ethelbertus Cantie[3]★ and other Angles and Saxons, which Austyn
had moved to make warre againste the Christon Britons. And thees put
Brochwell twise to flighte not farre frome Chester and cruelye slewe
1000 pristes [and] monkes of Bangor and a great number of laye
bretherene[4] of the same house which lyved by the laboure of ther
handes and were come barefooted and woolwarde to crave mercie and
peace at the Saxons handes. Youe shall understand that this was not
Austyne Bishope of Hippona the great clerke, but Austyn the monke
called the Apostle of England. Then this Brochwel retired over Dee
harde by Bangor and defended the Saxons the passage till Cadvan, Kinge
of Northwales, Mredith, Kinge of [16v] Southwales, and Bledrus, Prince
of Cornwall, came to succour him and gave the Saxons a sore battell and
slewe of them the number of 1066 and put the rest to flight. And after
this fight Cadvan was chosen kinge of Britaine and was chieff ruler
within the Ile. And after him his sonne Cadwalhawn, who was father to
Cadwalader, the last of the Britishe[5] bloodde that bare the name of
Kinge of Britaine. The thyrd tyme Northwales came to a woman was to
Esilht, the daughter of Kynan, the sonne of Rodri Malwynog[6] the sonne
of Cadwalader.★ She was wief to Mervryn Vrych and mother to
Roderike the Great, as shalbe hereafter declared.

By this youe maye understand that Northwales hathe bene agreat

[1]C – vel Beirdh   Rex Cantie
[2]Ll – so   [4]C bretherne
[3]C Ethelfryd, Rex North', Ethelbert   [5]C Brutes
    Cante; *reading corrected*; HC Ethelbertus   [6]C Idwal

wheile the chieffest seat of the last kings of Britaine because hit was and is the strongest countrey within this Ile, full of highe mountaines, craggyd rockes, great woodes [17] and deepe valleys, strayt and dangerouse places, deepe and swifte ryvers as Devi, whiche springeth in the hilles of Meryonydh and runneth northwest throughe Mowddwy and by Machynllayth and so to the sea at Aberdevy, devidinge North and Southwales asunder. Dee, called in Welshe Dyvyrdwy, springing also in the other side of the same hilles, runneth easte throughe Penllyn and the Lake Tegid downe to Corwen and Llangolhen throughe Chirke land, and so boweth northwarde towarde Bangor, to the Holte and to Chester and thence northwest to Flynt castell and so to the sea beinge the mere betwixt England and Wales frome the Holte to the sea. Ther is also Conwy, rising in Meryonydh shire and deviding Caernarvon frome Denbighe shire, runneth under Snowdon northeaste by Conwy to the sea. Also Clwyd, which risinge in Denbigh Land, and runneth downe to Rythyn and playne north not ferre from Denbighe to Saincte Assaph, and so by Rudland and to the sea. There be manye other fayre ryvers of which some runne [17v] to the sea, as Mawr at[1] the Traethmawr and Avon y Saynt at Carnarvon and others that runne to Sevarne, as Murnwy in Powis and Mvrnwy Tanet, some to Dee, as Kyrioc betwixt the lordships of Chirke and Oswester, Alyn throughe Ial and Hopes Dale and Moldes Dale and so to Dee a little above Chester. And this shall suffice for the perfecte description of that which was in the olde tyme called Gwynedh and Powis and at thees dayes the six shires of Northwales.

Nowe remaineth the laste kingdome of Wales called Dinevwr, which althoughe hit was the greatest, yet was hit not the best, as Giraldus witnessith, chiefflye because hit was much molested with Flemings and Normannes, and also that in diverse partes thereof the lordes wolde not obeye ther prince, as in Gwent and in Morgannwg, which was ther owne confusion as shall hereafter appere. This was devided to six partes of the whiche Keredigion was the firste and conteined 4 cantredes and 10 comotes, [18] as Cantref Penwedic had in hit thees comots: Genevrglyn, Pervedh and y[2] Kreudhyn; Cantref Kanawl had these: Mevenydd, Anhunawg and Pennardh; Cantref Castell had thees comotes: Mabwynion and Caerwedros; Cantref Syrwen had these: Gwenionydh and Iscoed and this parte is at this daye called in Englishe Cardiganshire and in Welshe Swydh Abertivi. This is a[3] champion

countrey without much woode and hathe bene diverse tymes overrunne
with Flemynges and Normannes, which builded manye castells in hit
and at the last were beaten out of them all. Hit hathe one[1] the east
Northwales with the Ryver Devi and parte of Powis, upon the south
Caermerdhyn shire, upon the west Penbrooke shire, with the Ryver
Tivi, and upon the north the Irishe Sea. In this parte is Caerdigan upon
Tivi not ferre frome the sea, Aberystwyth upon Ystwyth by the sea,
Lhanbatern, whiche was a great sanctuary and a place [18v] of religiouse
and learned men in tymes passed. And in[2] this shire were a great number
of castelles, as the castell of Ystrad Meurig, of Wallter, of Llanrystyd, of
Dynerth, of the sonne of Wynnyon, of Aber Reidiol, and a great
number more, with the townes of Tregaron, and Lhandhewi Brevi as
youe shall understande in the historie folowing.

   The secunde parte was called Dyvet, and at this daye Penbroke shire,
and had in hit 8 cantredes and 23 comots The cantredes with ther
comotes were these: Cantref Emlyn hathe thees comotes: Uwch Kuch,
Is Kuch and Elevethyr; Cantref Arberth hathe these: Pennrhyn ar Elais,
Esterolef and Talacharne; Cantref Daugledhau had these: Amgoed,
Pennant and Evelfre; Cantref y Koed had these: Llanhayaden and
Castelh Gwis; Cantref Penvro hathe these: Koed yr Haf, Maenorbyrr
and Penvro; Cantref Rosse hath these: Hwlfordh, Castell Gwalmai and
Y Garn; Cantref Pebidioc hathe these: Mynyw, Penkaer and Pebidioc;
Cantref Kemais hath these: Uwchnever, Isnever and Trefdraeth. In this
parte are diverse townes and [19] havens at this daye as Penbroke, Tenbi
in Welshe Dinbigh, Haverforde-west in Welsh Hwlfford, with the fayre
haven of Mylford called in Welsh Aberdavgleddav, Saincte Davies in
Menevia called Mynyw, the chieffest see in all Wales. Then Fiscarde
called Abergwayn and Newporte called Trefdraeth. Thees be all alongest
the sea coste or not verey farre of. Beside thees ther be diverse castelles
as Kylgeran, Arberth,[3] Gwis, Llanhayaden, Walwyn and diverse other.
This parte was wounne first by Debelenos★ Earles of Shrosbrie and after
geven to the Marshalles and so to Valence. And frome thense were the
princes of Wales moste troubled with Normannes and Flemings who
inhabite aboute Tenbi, Penbroke, and in Rosse to this daye for they
cane speke[4] neither Welsh nor good Englishe as yet. Dyvet, for so will I
calle hit hereafter, hathe one the west and north the Irishe Sea and upon
the south the Spaynishe sea and upon the easte [19v] Caermerdhyn shire
and the north east Caerdigan shire.

The thyrde parte was Caermerdhyn shire having[1] 4 cantredes and 13 Comotes as: Cantref Finioc with the comotes of Hirfryn, Dervedh and Iskenem; Cantref Eginoc with thees: Gwyr nowe in Glamorgan,[2] Kydweli and Carnwilhion; Cantref Bychan with thees: Mallaen, Kaeo, and Maenor Deilo; Cantref Mawr with these: Ketheinioc, comote of the sonne of Elviw, [commote] of the sonne of Uchdrud and Widigada. In this shire are the townes and castelles of Caermerdhyn, Dynevwr, which was the Princes seat of the countrey, Newtowne, Llandeilo, Llanymdhyfri,[3] Emlyn, Swansey, nowe in Glamorgan called Abertawy upon the sea, the castell of the sonnes of Uchdryd, of Llanystyffan and others. Hit hathe upon the west Dyvet or Penbrokeshire, one the north Caerdygan, upon the southwest the sea, and upon the southeast Glamorgan and upon the east Breknockeshire. This was[4] counted the strongest parte of [20] all Southwales as that which is full of highe mountains, great woodes and fayre ryvers, specialy Towi. And in this and the other two[5] parts of Southwales were the notablest actes that this historie entreteth of atchived and done.

The fourth is called Morgannwg nowe Glamorgan shire conteyning 4 cantreds with 15 comots as: Cantref Croneth* with thees comotes: Rwngnedh ac Avan, Tyr yr Hwndrwd, Tyr yr Iarlh and Maenor Glyn-ogwr; Cantref Pennychen with these: Meyskyn, Glynrhodne, Maenor Dalyvan and Maenor Rythyn; Cantref Brenhinawl with these: Kybwrn, Saynhenydd Uwchkaeach and Iskaeach; Cantref Gwentlhwg, which is nowe in Monmouthshire with thees comotes: Yrhardh,[6] Kenawl and Eithafedylygyon. In this parte are thees townes and castells: Lhandaff, the Bishops see, Cardyff called Caerdhydd, Cowbridge called Pontvaen, which is to saye Stonbridge and not Cowbridge, Lantwid [20v] called Lhanilhtyd, Neth, Dynwyd, Caerffyli and others and hathe diverse ryvers which runne to the southe sea as Lay, Taff, Tawy, Neth, Afan, Ogwr and Lhychwr. Hit hathe on the southe the sea of Seavarne which devideth hit frome Devenshire and Cornwall, upon the west and north-west Caermerdhyn shire, upon the northeast Breknocke shire and upon the east Monmouth shire. Of this youe shall reade very litle for one Iestyn, beinge chieff of the country, and having warre with his neigh-boures, called one Robert Fitzhamon with a great number of strangers to his succoure which after they had atchived the enterprice, liked so well the countrey that they founde occasion to fall out with Iestyn and inhabited the countrey them selves and ther heires to this daye.

---

[1] Ll have
[2] C Glamorganshire
[3] C Llandhyfry

[4] C is
[5] Ll to; C towe
[6] C yr haidh

The fyfth parte was called Gwent and nowe Monmouth shire, which
had 3 cantredes and 10 comotes as: Cantref Gwent which had thees
comotes: Y Mynydd, Iscoed, [21] Lhevynyd and Tref y Gruc; Cantref
Iscoed these: Bryn y Buga, Uwchcoed, y Teirtref and Erging ac Evas,
nowe in Herefordeshire; Cantref Cochywthees,[1]* Y Seythved of
Cantref Morgannwc which is nowe in Glocester shire and called the
Forest of Deane. In this parte is the ancient citie of Caerlhion upon the
Ryver Uske, wherin was the Archebishops see of Wales. Here are also
diverse townes and castells as Chepstowe, *olim* Strygil,* Rosse, Tynterne
upon the ryver Wy. Ther is also Newporte called Y Castell Newydd,
Uyske called Bryn Buga, Crosomont, Raglan, Whit Castell, Abergevenny and many other. This is a[2] fayre and fertile countrey of which
likewise the gentilmen were never obedient to ther prince which was
the cause of ther owne destruction. Hit hathe one the west Glamorgan
and Brecknocke shire, upon the north Herforde shire, upon the east
Glocester shire with the Ryver Wy, and upon the south and southeast
Seavarne.

Last of all cometh Brecheinog, [21v] nowe Breknocke shire, which
hath three cantredes and 8 comotes: as Cantref Selev, which hath these
comotes: Selif and Trahayarne; Cantref Kenawl these: Talgarth,
Ystradyw and Eglwys Iail; Cantref Mawr these: Tir Raulph, Lhywell
and Kerrig Howell. In this parte is the towne of Breknocke upon the
meeting of Uske and Hodni and is called Aberhodni, and Hay called Y
Gelly with Talgarth, Buelht and Lhangors. Hit hathe one[3] west
Caermardhyn shire with the Ryver Towy, upon the north Radnor shire
with Wy, upon the east Herforde shire and Monmouth shire and upon
the south Glamorgan. This for the most parte is full of mountaines
woodes and ryvers especially Buelht. And the lordes of this countrey
called Bruses with the Mortymers most of all other[4] Lordes Marchers,
sometymes by fight but more oftene by treason, have molested and
greaved the princes of Wales as youe shall understande by the hystorie
folowinge. This Lande came after Bruse to the Bohumes Earles of
Hereforde, and so to the Staffordes Dukes of Buckingham. [22]

Thees 6 shires beinge subjecte to the territorie of Dynevwr with
Radnor shire, which was belonging to Mathraval, are nowe commenly
called South Wales, which countrey is bothe greate and large, with
manye fayre playnes and valleyes for corne, highe mountaines and
rockes full of pasture for catell, great and thicke woodes with forestes

[1]C Cochyvotheese; see note   [3]C – one
[2]Ll – is a   [4]C others

and parkes for redde deere and fallowe, cleare and deepe ryvers full of
fishe of which Sevarne is the chieffest, which with Wy and Reidiol
spring out of ahighe mountaine called Plymlhymmon in the edge of
Caerdigan shire and are called commenly the three sisters. And Sevarne
runneth full east throughe[1] Kedewen and by the Poole and under the
castell of Shrarden to Shrewesburye, frome whence hit turneth south
and runneth [to] Bridgemorffe, Bewdleye, Wocester, Glocester and to
the sea by Bristowe. The secunde sister is Gwy, in Englishe Wy, which
toke here journeye south east by Rhayder Gwy to Buelht wher Irvon
meeteth her and thence to Glasburye and so to Hereforde and
Monmouth and to the sea of Sevarne at Chepstowe, for so they [22v]
calle More Hafren the sea which separateth Wales frome Somerset,
Devenshire and Cornewall. The thyrde sister [named Reidol] ranne
northwarde to the sea beinge not farre of at Aberystwyth. Ther be other
fayre ryvers as Uske, which risinge in a highe mountaine called Mynydd
Du in the southwest parte of Brecknocke shire runneth to Breknocke
and so throughe Monmouth shire to Uske, Caerlhion and Newporte
and so to the said south sea. Towi also risinge not ferre frome Wy
runneth south to Lhanymddyfri and thence southwest by Lhandeilo and
Dinevwr and to Abergeweili and Caermerdhyn and at Lhanystyffant to
the sea. Tivi likewise which riseth in the edge of Caermerdhyn shire and
runneth northwest by Emlyn, Gilgeran, Abertivi called Caerdygan, and
so to the north sea. In Tivi above all the ryvers in Wales were in
Giraldus tyme a great numbre of castors, which maye be Englished
bevers, and are called in Welshe avanke, which name onelye remayneth
in Wales at this day, [23] but what hit meaneth very fewe cane tell. Hit
is a beast not muche unlike an otter[2] but that hit is bigger, all heary
savinge the tayle which is like a fishe tayle as broade as a mans hand.
This beast useth aswell the water as the lande and hath very sharpe
teethe and bytethe cruelly till he perseave the bones cracke. His stones
be of great efficacie in phisick. He that will lerne what stronge nestes,
which Giraldus calleth castelles, they builde upon the face of the water
with greate bowes which they cute with ther teethe and howe some lye
upon ther backes holdinge the woode with ther foure feete which the
other drawe by a crosse sticke, the which he holdeth in this mouth to
the watter side, and other particularities of ther nature, let him reade
Giraldus in his Topographie of Wales. Therbe besides thees a great
numbre of ryvers of which some runne to the south, and some to the
west and north sea as Taf, Laye, Lhychwr and Tawai in Glamorganshire,

---

[1]C + Arwistly *inserted above line*   [2]Ll another

Taf also in Caemerdhyn shire which runneth [23v] to Cleddau, two
ryvers either called Gledhau which geve Milforde the name of
Aberdaugledhau in Penbrocke shire, Arth, Aeron and Ystwyth in
Caerdiganshire. Therbe also divers lordshipes which be added to other
shires and were taken here to fore for partes of Wales and in moste parte
of them at this daye Welshe [is] spoken as Oswester, Knockinge,
Whittington, Ellesmere, Masbroke, Chureburie, Carrs, Clwn, which are
nowe in Shropshire, Evas Lacy, Evas Harolde, Clifforde, Wynforton,
Yerdley, Huntingdon, Whitney, Logharneys in Herforde shire. Also this
countrey of Southwales as all the rest of Britaine was first inhabited by
the Britons, whiche remaine ther to this daye saving that in diverse
places especially alongest the sea shore they have bene mingled with
Saxons, Normannes, which the Welshe historie calleth Frenchmen, and
Flemings, so that the princes of Wales never sith the conquest of the
Normannes colde [24] have quiet possession therof, but,[1] what for
strangers and what for disloyaltie of ther owne people, have had
continuall trouble and vexacioun and were for the moste parte
compelled to kepe them selves in Caermyrdhyn shire.

And this shalbe a sufficient description of Wales with the partes
thereof for the parfectest[2] understanding of [the] historie following,
which I shall desire the readers not enviousley to smatter at but gentlye
to admonish me of the errors which by ther advise and helpe shalbe
amended, and in so doing they shall do me a great pleasure, whiche I[3]
partely deserved because I was the first that tocke the province in hande
to put thees thinges into the Englishe tonge. For that I wolde not have
the inhabitantes of this Ile ignorant of the histories and cronicles of the
same, wherein I am sure to offende manye because I have oppenede ther
ignorance and blindenes thereby and to please all goode men and
honeste natures that be desirouse to knowe [24v] and understand all
suche thinges as passed beetwixt the inhabitantes of this lande frome the
first inhabiting therof to this daye.★

[25] Yvor the sonne of Alan, Ina de Stirpe regia filius Kenredi sorori regis Cadwaladri

After that Cadwalader had taken his journey towards Rome
accordinge to the comanndement receaved by the angell as is before

declared, leaving his sonne Idwall Iwrch, that is to saye Idwall the Roo, and his people with his cosine Alan, who, not yet despairinge of the conquest of Britaine, manned his shippes as well with a great number of his owne people, as with those which Cadwalader had brought with him and appointed Yvor his sonne and Ynyr his nevewe to be the leaders who sailinge over the narwe[1] seas landed in the west parte[2] which, when the Saxons understoode, they gathered agreat number and gave Yvor battaell wher they were put to flight and loste a great number of ther people, and Yvor wonne the countreys of Cornwall, Deven shire and Somerset shire and inhabitede them with Britons. Which, when Kentuinus Kinge of West Sexe sawe, he gathered a great power of Saxons and Angles[3] togeather [25v] and came against the Britons which were readye to abeyde the battelle. But when the armies were bothe in sight they were not very desirouse to fight but felle to accomposition and agreament that Yvor sholde tacke Ethelburga to wife, which was cosine to Kentwine, and quietly enjoye all that he had woonne, which was kept all the reigne of Yvor. This Yvor is he which the Englishe Cronicle calleth Yve Kinge of West Saxons that reigned after Cedwall and they saye he was a Saxon, for Kentwine reigned but 5 yeres after Yvors cominge to England. And after hyme his nevewe Cedwall who, after he had reigned over the Weste Saxons 2 yeres, went to Rome and lefte his kingedome to Yve his cosine. Which Yve or Yvor, whome the Britons call the sonne of Alan and the Saxons the sonne of Kenred, beinge Kinge of the Saxons and Britons which inhabited the west parts of England, and after manye victories [26] atchived against the kinges of Kent, Southsexe and Merse, left his Kingedome[4] to Adelred, or as some calle him Adelerdus, his cosine, and toke his journeye to Rome where he made a godlye end the yere of oure Lorde 720. This Yvor made the Fratrie at Glasenburie called in British Ynys Avalon and gave great landes to the Church of Wynchester. In the secunde yere of his reigne dyd Bryth, a subjecte to Egfride King of Northumberlande, cruellye overrunne and destroye agreat parte of Irelande. And in the furthe[5] yere of his reigne there was agreat earth quake in the Ile of Man. And the yere folowinge hit rayned bloode in Britaine and Irelande and the milke and butter turned to the color of bloode. And the secunde yere after that the mone lokede all like bloode. And so as before is declared after the departure of Yvor, Adelarde or Adelred toke the rule of the Saxons and

[1]C narrowe
[2]C + of Britain *later added above line*
[3]C angells *deleted*; Angles *later added above*
[4]C – Kingdome *later added in margin*
[5]Ll 4

Rodri Malwynog, the sonne of Idwall Ywrch the sonne of Cadwalader, did take the rule over the Britons in the west parte of Englande.

[26v] Rodrycke the sonne of Idwall the sonne of Cadwalader

This Rodrycke begane his reigne the yere 720 againste whome Adelard[1] Kinge of Westsex reised a great armye and destroyinge the countrey of Devenshire entred Corwayll where Rodericke, with the Britons, gave him battell in whiche the Britons had the victorie. Likewise the same yere beinge 721* obteined the Britons twoe other victories against the Saxons, one in Northwales at a place called Garth Maelawg and another in Southwales Pencoet. Also this yere dyed Beli the sonne of Elphin a noble man amongest the Britons. The yere folowing dyed Celredus Kinge of Merse and Ethelebaldus[2] was made kinge after him. And the yere 728 was the great battaile and warre betwixt Ethelbaldus[2] and the Britons at a place called Mynydh Carno not ferre frome Abergevenny. [27] The yere 733 died Beda priest, brought up in the Abbey of Wyrynindham,[3] a great clercke and that wroote manye woorkes amonge which ther is one entituled the Ecclesiastical Historie of the English Nation, dedicated unto Cleolwolf Kinge of Northumberland. This yere did Adelard Kinge of Westsex [and] Athelbald Kinge of Merse joyne ther powers against the Britons and after longe fight and great slaughter upon either parte obteined a blooddy victorie. The yere 735 Adelard King of Westsex died and Cudred reigned in his place. And the yere folowing dyed Owen King of the Pictes. And in the yere of 746 was ther a great battaille fought at Hereforde betwixt Cudred and Adelbaldus where after longe fight Cudred had the victorie. Also the next yere ensuynge he gave the Britons an overthrowe and after dyed.

And the yere 749 was Sigebert created Kinge in his place and, for his evyll behavior, expulsed by his nobles out of his Kingedome and [27v] was miserably slayne by a swynhearde. After whom Kynewlfe was made Kinge of Weste Saxons the yere 750. And at that tyme dyed Teudwr the sonne of Beli a Britone of great estimation. And ther was a great battaill betwixt the Britons and the Pictes at a place called Megedawc where Dalargan King of the Pictes was slayne. And aboute this tyme was[4] Rodri or Rodrycke Malwynoc dryven by the Saxons to forsake the west

[1] C Adelred   [3] C Wyrnamdham
[2] C Ethebaldus   [4] Ll – was

countrey and to come to seeke his owne inheritaunce in Northwales where reigned the chyldren of Bletrus[1] Prince of Devenshire and Cornwall, who was one of them that gave Adelrede and Ethelbert the overthrowe at Bangor upon the ryver Dee. And after Cadvan was chosen Kinge of Britaine had the governaunce of Northwales till this tyme. And Roderike Kinge of the Britons dyed the yere of 754 leaving two sonnes after him, Kynan Tyndaethwy and Howell.

[28] Kynan Tindaethwy sonne to Rodryck

Kynan Tindaethwy began his reigne over the Britons the yere of Our Lord 755, and twoe yere after was there a great battaill at Herforde betwixt the Britons and Kynewlf with the Saxons where Dyfynwal the sonne of Teudwr was slayne. And this yere dyed Athelbalde[2] King of Merse and Bearnvet reigned in his steed. And the yere folowing was there an order taken for the right kepinge of the feast of Easter in Wales, by Elbodius a man both godly and learned. For the Britons ever before that tyme differed frome the Churche of Rome in celebratinge the feast of Easter and the diversitie was this. The church of Rome by order of a generall counsell at Nicene had agreade that every the next Sondaye after the 14 daye of the mone shulde be Easter Day, so that Easter shulde be ever ether the 15, 16, 17, 18, 19, 20, or 21 of the aege of the [28v] mone and never the 14 daye hitself nor never passe the 21 daye. And the Britons dyd use to kepe their Easter upon the 14 daye and so to the 20 as it fell, so that sometymes when hit was Easter Daye with the Britons it was but Palme Sondaye with the Saxons. Of which [diversitie][3] grewe a great contention betwixt Colman and Hilda upon the one parte, defending the rites of the Britons, and Agilbert and Wilfride upon the other parte in the yere 664 where in they seeme scant to call the Britons and Scottes Christians because they kept not Easter within the dayes appointed and afterwarde they brake hit them selves, for nowe Easter is some yeres kept out of the dayes ordined by the generall Councell 4 or 5 dayes. Whether hit be well or no, let them that have charge lock to hit for suerlye this erroure yf hit be one, came because either[4] they understoode not the coures of the mone or because they wolde not correcte the place of the prime or golden number comenly set forth[5] very false in the Kalander.

[1] C Bletons
[2] C Athelbert
[3] C diversitie *inserted above line in similar* *hand*
[4] C – either
[5] Ll – forth

[29] But to the historie. In the yere 763 was Offa made Kinge of Mers and Brichtrich Kinge of West Saxons. And this yere dyed Fernael, the sonne of Idwall, and the yere folowinge dyed Cemoyd the Kinge of the Pictes. And the yere 775 died Sainct[1] Cutberth monke and abbat. And the next yere after dyd the men of Southwales destroye a[2] great parte of Mers with fier and sword. And the somer folowing a great number of Welshmen entred the Kingdome of Mers and dyd muche hurte there. Werefore Offa caused a great dyche, large and deepe, to be made frome sea to sea betwixt his kingdome and Wales wherby he might the better defend his countrey frome the incursions of the[3] Welshemen, and this dyche is to be sene in manye places as yet and is called Clawdh Offa, which is Offas Diche at this daye. In the yere 786 came the Danes first into England and 6 yeres after they came againe and destroid a great parte of Lyndsey and Northumberland and also they overrunne a great part of Ireland and destroyed Rechreyn. [29v] Also aboute the same tyme was ther a battell fought at Rudland[4] betwixt the Saxons and the Welshemen where Caradawc[5] king of Northwales was slayne. This Caradawc was the sonne of Gwyn, the sonne of Colhwyn, the sonne of Ednywayn, the sonne of Bledhyn, the sonne of Bletrus Prince of Cornwall and[6] Devenshire. Also this yere died Offa King of Mers and Egfert his sonne reigned in his steede. And the yere 787 dyed Meredudh King of West Wales or Dyvet.[7]★

The yere of Our Lord 800 was Egbrutus[8] made Kinge of Westsex. The yere folowing was Kenewlf created King of Mers. And Arthen the sonne of Sesylt, the sonne of Clydawc, King of Caerdygan dyed. And in the yere 808 died Run King of Dyvet and Cadelh King of Powys. And the sonne was eclipsed and the next yere dyed[9] Elbodius Archebishop of Northwales. In the yere of 810 was the mone eclipsed upon Christmas Daye and Saincte Davyes was brent by the West Saxons and ther was a generall deathe of cattell throughe all Wales. [30] And the next yere ensuinge died Owen the sonne of Meredyth, the sonne of Tewdos. And the castell of Deganwy was destroyd by thunder. And the next yere was agreat fight betwene Howell and Kynan wherin Howell had the victorie. And the yere 815 was there muche hurte done by thunder and diverse places brente to the earth. And the same yere died Gryffith the sonne of Run, and Griffri the sonne of Kyngen was slayne by the

[1]C – Sainct
[2]Ll – a
[3]C – the
[4]C Rudlan
[5]C Caiadanoke

[6]C + of
[7]C – And the yere . . . dyvet
[8]C Ebgetius
[9]C – dyed

treason of Elisse his brother. And Howell gave his brother Kynan an
other battaill and slewe agreat number of his people. And in the yere
817 was Howell, by the force of his brother, chaced out of the Ile of
Mone or Anglesey to Man. And a litle after died Kynan Chief King of
the Britons or Welshmen leaving behinde hyme a doughter called
Esylht, which was maryed to a nobleman called Mervryn Vrych the
sonne of Gwyriad, the sonne of Elydyr and so furth in the right lyne to
Belinus the brother of Brennus Kinge of Britons. And his [30v] mother
was Nest the doughter of Cadell King of Powis, the sonne of Brochwel,
which descended by just lyne frome that Brochwel Ysgythrog, that
fought with the Saxons at Bangor, who was Prince of Powys.

Mervryn Vrych and Esilht daughter to Kynan

The first yere of the reigne of Mervryn Vrych and Esylht his wieff dyd
Egbrute enter Wales with agreat armye and destroyed the whole
countrey of Snowdon hilles and wonne the countrey of Ryvonyauc to
himself. And the yere folowing was a great battaill fought in Anglesey at
Llanvaes. And the yere 819 dyd Kenewlf[1] destroye West Wales and the
somer folowing was Deganwy brent and Powis overrunne by the Saxons
of Mers. And this yere died Kenwlph King of Mers and Kenelme
reigned in [31] his place. And Howell King of Man died also. The yere
825 was Cedwolf mad Kinge of Mers and reigned 2 years. And then was
Beornwolfe created Kinge who was overthrone at Ellodowne by
Egbrute King of West Saxons who also wanne the countreys of Kent
and West Angles. And the yere 828 was Beornwolfe slayne by the East
Angles and Ludecen reigned in his steede who was the yere folowing
likewyse slayne by the East Angles. And this yere was a great battaill
fought at a place called Gavelford betwixt the Britons and the West
Saxons of Devenshire and manye thousandes cruely slayne upon either
seyd and the victorie uncerteine. And the yere 829 dyd Egbrute
overthrow Wylaf Kinge of Mers and made him trubutarie to him. He
also passed Humber and wonne the land, and so was the first monarche
of the Saxons, and brought the 7 kingedomes to one and changed [31v]
the name of Britaine to Englande and called the people Englishmen and
language Englishe. For the people that came into this Ile frome
Germayne were three:[2] Saxons, Angles and Juthes. And of the Saxons
came the people of Estsexe, Southsex, Myddelsex and West Saxons. Of

---

[1]C Kewiste   [2]C these

the Angles came the Est Angles, Myddelangles or Mersyans and all one the northside Humber. And of the Juthes came the inhabitantes of Kent and the Ile of Wyghte. And the seven Kingdomes★ were these: the first Kent. The secunde Southsex conteinynge Southsex and Southrey. The thyrd East Angles conteinynge Northfolke, Southfolke and Cambridge-shire. The fourth Westsex conteininge Barkeshire, Hameshire, Wilshire, Dorsetshire,[1] Devenshire, Somersetshire and Cornwall. The fyfth Mers, conteining Glocestershire, Herfordshire, Woscestershire, Shropshire, Staffordshire, Chestershire, Warnvycheshire,[2] Leycestershire, Derby-shire, Notyngamshire, Lyncolneshire, Northamptonshire, Oxfordeshire, Buckinghamshire, Bedfordshire and halfe [32] Hertfordshire. The sixth was East Saxon conteininge Essex, Meeddelsex and the other half of Hertfordeshire. The seventh kingdome was all the lande upon the north seide Humber which was also devided into 2 kindomes, Deyra and Brenecia. Deyra was the lande betwixt Humber and Tyne, Brenecia frome Tyne to the Scottes Sea.

And those weere all brought under subjection of Egbrute Kinge of West Saxons. And this realme called England the yeare after the comynge of Brute to this ile 1968, and after the comynge of Hengist 383, and after the departure of Cadwalader 142 yeres, whiche name althoughe hit hathe continued to this daye for the space of 730 yere was not very luckye or fortunate to the Saxons enhabiters of this realme. For even upon this change of ther name and unition of their kingedomes folowed the terrible and cruell plage[3] of the Danes. And after that the conquest of the Normannes of whome the kinges of this tyme have descended. But to returne to my matter againe. [32v] The yere 833 did the Danes lande in divers places of this realme and fought diverse battailles with Egbrute or Egberte and sometymes they and sometymes he had victorie. And the yere 836 they landed in Westwales and so passed throughe Wales to England and at[4] Hengestdowne were overthrowen by Egbrute who dyed the yere folowinge. And his sonne Ethelwolfe reigned in his place and he gave his doughter to Beurnrhed[5]★ his tributarie King of Mers. He had great warre with the Danes which destroyed with fiere[6] the sea coste of Ingland. And the yere 842 dyed Idwalhon a noble man of Wales. And twoe yeres after was the battaill of Ketill beetwixt Beurnrhed Kinge of Mers and the Britons. And this yere dyed Mervryn Vrych★ Kinge of Britons leaving behinde hyme a sonne called Rodri Mawr, that is to saye Rodericke the Great Kinge of Wales.

---

[1] C – Hameshire . . . Dorsetshire
[2] C Warwykeshire
[3] C plages *deleted* vexasion *above in another hand*
[4] Ll – at
[5] C Berthred
[6] C + and sword *above line in another hand*

Roderick Mawr: Rodricke the Great sonne to Mervryn and Esilht

[33] Rodrike the Great begane his reigne over Wales the yere after Christs incarnation 843. This prince devided all Wales to the three territories of Aberfrawe, Dinevwr, and Mathraval and had great warre withe Burhred Kinge of Mers, which by the ayde of Ethelwolfe entred Northwales with a great power and destroyed Anglesey and fought with the Welshmen dyvers tymes and slewe Meuric a great prince amonge them. And the yere 846 dyd the Danes overrunne a great parte of England and fought withe Athelstan, Ethelweolfes brother, Kinge of Kent, and remained that winter at the Ile of Tenet, which was the firste tyme they wyntred in England.[1]* This yere also was Ithell Kinge of Wentsland slaine[2] in fighte by the men of Brekenocke. And the yere 850 was Kyngen slayne by his owne men.* And foure yeres aftire dyed Kyngen King of Powis at Rome, and twoe yeres after dyed Cemoyth Kinge of Pictes and Jonathan Lorde of Abergele. And the yere 856 Ethelwolfe toke his journey to Rome and made his Kingedome tributarie to the Pope, [33v] and was the first that payd the Peter Pens to the Churche of Rome. The old Saxons do bringe the genelogie frome this Ethelwolfe to Adam after this maner: Ethelwulf the sonne of Egbrute, the sonne of Alciunnid, the sonne of Eaffa, the sonne of Eappa, the sonne of Inglis, the sonne of Kenrede, the sonne of Ceolwalde, the sonne of Cudd, the sone of Cudwyne, the sonne of Ceanlyn, the sonne of Ciricke, the sonne of Cerdicke, which was the first king of West Saxons, the sonne of Elesse, the sonne of Esly, the sonne of Gewy, of whome the people were called Gwysses, the sonne of Wyggy, the sonne of Freweyn, the sonne of Fridegare, the sonne of Frondy, the sonne of Beldegy, the sonne of Woden, of whose issue came the kinges of manye nations, the sonne of Fredewall, the sonne of Ffredelase, the sonne of Ffynny, the sonne of Godwlphe, the sonne of Gety, the sonne of[3] Recty the sonne of Boorne, the sonne of Sceldy, the sonne of Sceafe, which reigned in a countreye called Angle beetwixt Gothes and Saxons, and was the sonne of Heranode, the sonne of Stermon, the sonne of Hadrye, the sonne of Gwale, the sonne of Bedegy, the sonne of Sem, the sonne of Noe, and so furth to Adam.

[34] This genelogie have I sette here that the reader may hereby understand that not onelye the Britons or Welshmen but all other nations

---

[1]C and remained that winter at Wintred in   [3]Ll – of
    England; see note
[2]C – slaine

have beene ever desirouse to sette furthe ther antiquitie and progenie, whiche was not verye harde to suche nations as were not myngled with other and that had ever amonge them suche as dyd oneley frome tyme to tyme professe that arte and did customablye write the progenie, wives, children of all suche as were of any estimation in the countrey. In which twoe thinges Wales hathe ever passed all other nations as they which have not myngled with any other till of late yeres with Englishmen, and also ever had[1] suche as dyd professe the arte of genelogie, which although they have erryd or rather willinglye flattred some in bearinge wronge[2]★ genelogies, yet suerly are able by ther bookes to bring any gentyllmans genelogie of that countrey to suche as have lyved nyne hundred yeres passed and but fewe further excepte suche as descendeed of the kings of Britaine. The Italians before they myngled with the Vandales, Gothes and Lumbardes brought ther genelogies to Aeneas, [34v] the Hispaniards to Hesperus before the Gothes and Moors overranne the land, the Saxons to Woden before they myngled with the Danes and Normannes, yea the Frenchmen and Turkes rejoyce at this daye to bringe them selfes to the Troianes,[3] and the Germaines to the chyldren of Twiston, and hit is possible they maye so doe because they have not myngled with any other and have not bene overrunne with any other nation. Therefore let suche disdaynfull heades as scant knowe ther owne grandfather leave ther scoffinge and tauntinge of Welshmen for that thinge that all the worthye nations[4] in the worlde do glorie in. And lette them reade the auncient writer Birosus (to whome the wise Grecians for the knowledge they learned at his hande made an image of coper and set hit up in Athens in memorye of hyme). And ther they shall finde the beginninge of all the moste parte of the nations of the world. And if they beleeve hyme let them not denye oure[s]. And yf they credite hime not let them beleve no more but what they see with ther eies or that pleaseth ther fonde fantasies. But to the matter.

[35] This yere dyd the Danes chace Burhred oute of his kingedome who also went to Rome and ther deyd. In whose place reigned Celwolf by the[5] appointment and election of the Danes 7 monothes.★ And the yere 857 dyed Ethelwolfe and lefte his sonnes Adelbolde Kinge of Westsex and Adelbright Kinge of Kent and of East Saxons. And after Adelbalde had reigned 5 yeres he dyed and Adelbright his brother toke the rule of his kingedome. And that yere dyd the Danes spoyle Wynchester and after a great fight were dryven out of the land. But

[1]C have ever
[2]C learning false
[3]C Territories
[4]C all wordly nations
[5]C – in whose place ... by the

returninge to Tenet they remayned ther for the wynter and spoyled by incursions all the sea shore. And this yere was the battaill of Gweythen★ betwixt the Britons and the Englishmen, and a great number slayne one either side. The yere 865 dyed Kynan Nant Nyver, and the yere folowinge came Hungar and Hubba with a great armye of Danes into Englande. And the yere 867 dyed Adelbright and Ethelred his brother reyned in his steed. And the next yere ensuinge dyd the said Danes★ spoyle Yorke and slewe the twoe kinges of Northumberlande [35v] Osbright and Ella. And afterwarde the Danes spoyled the countrey unto Notyngham and returned to Yorke, and from thence to East Angle and slewe Edmonde the Kinge. And the 6 yere of Ethelrede came an other hoste of Danes throughe Westsex [to] Redinge with Basrecke and Aldinge and fought 5 battailles with Ethelred and Alvryd his brother, in two of the which the Danes were overcome at Hengleffelde and Estendowne. And in the three other the Englishmen were overthrowen at Reading, Basinge, and at Mereton. And the same yere dyed Ethelred and Alfrede his brother reigned in his steed.

And in the first yere of his reigne he fought 11 battailles against the Danes upon the south side of Themes, and slewe of the Danes one kinge and nyne earles. And this yere dyed Gwgan Kinge of Caerdygan. And the towne of Alclyd★ was destroyed by the Danes, and they wonne London and Redinge and all the inlande and kingdome of Mers, and one kinge or leader of them toke the countrey of Northumberland to him and his people, and dyd muche trouble the Pictes. And the yere folowinge the [36] three kinges of the Danes went frome Cambridge to Warrham in Dorsetshire. And Alfred wolde have geven them battaill but the Danes desired peace and forswore England, which they never dyd before, but the same night their horsemen toke ther journey towardes Excester and their fotemen which went to the sea were all drowned at Sandwich. And the yere 873 dyd the Danes enter Wales where Rodericke gave them twoe battailles and at a place called Banngole and an other at Emergyd in Anglesey. And Einion Bishop of Menevia or Saincte Davids dyed and Humbert was stalled in his place. And two yeres after was Dangarth kinge of Cornewall drowned by misfortune. And the yere 876 dyd the Englishmen enter Anglesey and fought with the Welshmen a sore battaill. And the yere folowing they slewe Rodericke Kinge of Wales and Gwyriad his brother or, as some saye, his sonne.★ This Roderik had by his wief Yngharad the doughter of Meuric, the sonne of Dyfenwall, the sonne of Arthen ap Seysylht, dyvers sonnes as Anaraud his eldest sonne, to whome he [36v] gave Aberfrawe with Northwales, Cadell the secunde sonne, which had Dynevwr with

Southwales and also [tooke] Mathraval and Powis lande by force frome
his brethren. Rodericke had also Roderike, Meuric, Ydwall or Tudwall,
Gwyriad and Gwydhelic of which youe shall here in the historie
following.

Anaraud eldest sonne to Rodrick

Anaraud reigning over the Britons, came Rollo with his Normaines
to France, and wonne and enhabited that countrey which is called to
this daye Normandy. And the Danes which had fledde to Excester were
dryven thence by Alfrede[1] and they after entred the Kingdome of Mers
and remained their. And the yere folowing the Danes wonne all the land
upon the northseide of Themes and helde hit to them selves. And after
they passed the ryver to Chipenham in Westsex* and the Englishmen
fledde before them, yet Alfrede fought with a number of them and slewe
the prince and wonne their standard which they called Raven. [37] And
after he overthrewe them at Edendowne and they gave him pledges and
ther King Godrun receaved the Christen faithe, and after reigned in the
East Angle. The yere 878 dyed Aedh the sonne of Melh a noble man of
Wales. And the twoe yeres folowinge was their a great battaille fought
betwixt the Danes and Englishmeen of Mers against the Welshmen
upon the ryver of Conwy and this was called the Revenge of the Deathe
of Rodricke. And the yere 882 was also fought the battaill of
Catgwethen* and this yeres the Danes that laye at Fulenham by London
passed the sea to France by the Ryver Seyne, and spoled the countrey
aboute Paris and overthrewe the Frenchmen in battaill but afterward
they were all slayne and drowned by the Britons of Armorica. And
Alfrede gote London and chaced away the Danes that besyeged
Rochester, but at the same tyme he loste a great navye of shippes
whiche the Danes toke and drowned at Sturemutham. [37v] And the
yere 889 Submon Cubin the greatest clerke in Scottelande dud. And[2]
the yere folowing came the Black Normanes,* for so the Britishe[3]
booke calleth the Danes, to Northwales. And here I thinke hit
necessarye to let the reader understande frome whence suche a wonderfull number of Danes and Normaines dyd come. The Kingdedome of
Denmark had under hit not onely Denmarke, which is a small countrey
separated with the sea into iles and half iles as that which joyneth to

[1]C – were ... Alfrede   [3]C Britons
[2]Ll – And

Saxonye and Holsake[1] and runneth like an arme to the sea called
Chersonesus Cimbrica, and the Ile of Selande and Fuinen with apeece of
the maineland joyninge to Swethenlande, but also Norway and the great
countrey Suetia, or Swethenlande, which reacheth to Moscovia and
welny to the North Pole This countrey, beinge scant knowen to the
worlde at that tyme, powred oute of hit self, as the Trojane horse,
diverse people, that at divers tymes overrunne and spoyled all Europe
with a greate parte [38] of Africa, like a sodeine tempest or an odiouse
storme. From thens came the Gothes that overrunne Germaine, France,
Hispaine, Afrike and Italie. Frome thens came the Vandales of no lesse
worthines. Frome theme came the Lumbardes, the Alames, the
Swythsers, the Borgonions, the Danes, and the Normaines, whiche
came out of Norwaye and diverse other, I meane frome the countrey
subjecte[2] to the Danes, and the sea shore of Eastlande by Prussia frome
whence [came] the Vandals.* He that is desirous to understand the
mervelouse historie of Swethynlande let him reade the woorke of Olaus
Gothus, and Johnes Maznus and frome thees countreys, as I declared
before, came the people which wee called the Danes and not onely
frome Denmarke. And the yere 888[3] came 250 sayles frome thees
countreys and landed in Lymene in Kente harde by the greate woode
called Andredesleg, and builded a castell at Auldre. And the same tyme
came Hastinge with 80 sailes to Themmes Mouth, and buylded a castell
at Myddelton [38v] and made an othe to Alfrede that [he] never would[4]
annoy him nor his subiectes. But shortlye after he buylte a castell at
Beamflete and made mansions* upon the countrey, wherefore Alfrede
overthrewe his castell and toke his wief and to sonnes whiche he had
christened and sent them to their father againe.

And this yere dyed Henneth the sonne of Bledrig a baron of Wales.
And the yere 893 came Anaraud King of Wales with a great number of
Englishmen to make warre against his brother Cadelh and spoyled the
countreys of Caerdygan and Ystradtywy.[5] And the Danes asseydged
Exancester againste whome, when Alfrede went, they which were at
Auldre passed over to Essex and builded a castell at Scobrith, and frome
thens toke their journey to Budyngton upon Seaverne and when Alfred
came to Exancester the Danes fledde to the sea and spoyled the sea coste
of Wales. And they which were in Budingtone[6]* heringe of the Kinges
comynge flede bake to their castell in Estsex. And the fourth companie
came to Leycester, wher Alfrede dyd besiedge them till they were

[1] C Holesate
[2] C – other . . . subiecte
[3] C 880
[4] Ll to; C dyd; HC would
[5] C Ystradwy
[6] Ll – upon Seavarne . . . Budingtone

dryven to eate their owne horses. [39] And the yere 895 the Danes which were in Leycester, with all the rest of them that were in Northumberland, passed by the northe seas to Mereseig an ile in Essex. And the winter folowinge they entred the ryver Lyne by the Themes and their buylded a castell 20 miles frome London. And as they came to spoyle the countrey, they were overthrowen and lost foure of their princes and fledde to the castell. Then Alfrede devyded the ryver into three partes so that the water was so diminyshed that their sheppes colde not returne to the sea. Which thinge when the Danes sawe, they left their wyves and children in Essex and passed spoylinge throughe the land to Quadring vel Euadring upon Sevarne[1] and so passed the ryver, and spoyled the countries of Breknocke, Gwentsland and Gwentlhwg. Also this yere went a great number of them[2] to France by the ryver Seyne and other of them spoyled the coastes of Devenshire wher they lost 6 shippes after a longe conflicte. [39v] And the somer folowing was the countrey of Ireland destroyed by strange wormes with two tethe which consumed all that was greane in the lande. Thees seeme to be the locustes, a rare plage in thees countreys and oftene seene in Afrike and Italy, and other hote regions. And the yere 900 came Igmonde with a great number to Anglesey and the Welshmen gave him battaill at Meleriam.

And the same yere dyed Alfrede which some call Alured makinge the v: a vowell which sholde be a consonant. This prince translated the ancient lawes of Dyfynwall Moelmud, Kinge of Britons, and Marsia, Queene of Britaine and wief to Kehelyn, oute of Britishe into English and called hit Marsian lawe, which lawe was afterwarde called West Saxon Lex, and kepte in a parte of Merse and in all the countreys by south Temmes. For the other parte of land had an other lawe called Danlex and remained to Edwarde Confessor, who of thees two lawes made one. [40] Also this Alfrede dyd devide the daye to three partes by a taper which brente continually in his chappell and endured iust xx iiij hours. And the firste parte he bestowed at his booke, the secunde in the affaires of the common welthe, and the thirde parte to take his rest and repose him self. And aftere his deathe a certayne clerke made his Epitaph as here foloweth*

> Nobilitas innata Christi probitatis honorem,
> Omnipotens Alfrede, dedit probitasque laborem,
> Attulit atque labor nomen, cui mixta dolori
> Gaudia semper erant, spes semper mixta timori.
> Si modo victor eras, ad chrastina bella parabas.

[1] C Suadring upon Sevarne; HC   [2] C – of them
   Quadbryge upon Seauerne

Cui vestes sudore madent, ensisque cruore
Tinctus erat iugi validus quam tua facta probarunt.
Non fuit immensi quisquam per climata mundi,
Cui tot in adversis vel respirare liceret.
Nec tamen aut ferro contritus ponere ferrum,
Aut gladio potuit vite finisse dolores.
Iam post transactos vite regnique labores,
Christus sit vera tibi, sit quies sceptrumque perenne.

[40v] After Alfrede reigned Edwarde hes sonne, againste whome Edelwolde made a cruell warre, beinge his brother, for fleinge to Northumberlande he was chosen kinge as well of the Danes as of the Angles which by that tyme had grown to one people. And after he subdued the East Saxons and with a great armye spoyled Mers, and passing over Themes at Cricklade¹ destroyed Brythende and returnede home with a great spoyle. And at this tyme was Rodericke the sonne of Huneth slayne in Arwistly. And Edwarde pursued his brother and overrunne all the lande betwixte Ouse and Duke, and returned backe with all his army savinge the Kentishmen which tarried to spoyle. And the Danes came upon them and fought a sore battaill and slewe a great number of them and put the rest to flight. And the yere 905 dyd the Danes fight with the Irishmen and slewe Cormot Kinge and Bishope of all Ireland. And the sonne of Culennan, a man both godly and relygiouse and Kyrnalt, the sonnne of Murgan Kinge of Lagines, was slaine also. [41] And the yere after dyed Asser Archebishop of Wales and at this tyme Edward sent a great army to Northumberlande, which spoyled the countrey and returned home. And the Danes folowed and destroyed a great parte of Merse but Edwarde overthrewe them in battaill and slewe their kinges Aldene and Edelwolfe and a great number of their nobles. This yere dyed Edred Duke of Merse, wherfore Edward seised London and Oxford with all the lande of Merse into his owne handes. The yere 907 dyed Cadelh secund sonne of Rodericke and Kinge of Southwales leaving behinde him three sonnes: Hywell Dha, that is to saye Hywell the Good, who succeaded his father, and Meurig and Clydawc. And twoe yeres folowinge dyd Edward builde the castell of Hertforde² betwixt the ryvers Benefyc, Minier and Towy and also the Boroughe of Whitam in Essex, and lay at Weauldyne and subdued those countries. And the yere folowinge the Danes of Leycester and Hampton slewe a great number of Englishmen [41v] at Hochenertune and spoyled all Oxfordshire and returned home. And the next yere came a greate

¹C Crickland   ²Ll Herforde

navie frome Tydwycke with Uther and Rahalde, and past by west to
Wales, and destroyed Saincte Davyes, and ther fought the battaill of
Duneir wher Mayauc, the sonne of Peredyr Cam, was slaine. And
afterwarde they entred Herfordeshire where they were fought with all
and Rahalde slaine, and compelled to forswere the Kinges lande, and the
King caused the southside of Sevarne to be kept with a great army. Yet
dyd the Danes twyse enter his lande, ones by the east at Wered, and an
other tyme at Portagan but they were at eyther tyme overthrowen by
the Englishmen. And frome thens they departed to the Ile of Stepen
frome whence they were dryven by hungar★ to Southwales, and being
beaten thence they departed to Ireland. And the yere folowinge[1] was a
great battaill fought betwixt the Kentishmen and the Danes at Holme
but who had the victorie hit is not knowen. [42] And the yere 913 was
the mone eclipsed and Anaraud chieff king of[2] Wales dyed and left
behinde him twoe sonnes Idwal Voel, which reigned after him, and
Elysse.

Idwal Voyl sonne of Anaraud

   After Idwal Voyl begane his dominion over Northwales, Howell Dha
beinge Kinge over Southwales and Powislande, appeared a terrible
comete in the firmament. And the yere folowinge was Leycester newe
built and Ireland spoyled by suche as inhabited Develyn and the next
somer dyd the same people destroye the Ile of Anglesey. And the yere
917 was Clydauc, the sonne of Cadelh, slayne by the handes of his
brother Meuric. And aboute the same tyme the Englishmen dyd
overthrowe the Danes after a great fight at Tottenhalle. And the same
yere dyd Edelflet lady of Mers builde the castell of Brumesburithin. And
the yere folowinge dyed [42v] Adelrede her father which had bene
longe sicke and made her his heire for he had no sonne. And the yere
919 dyd she builde a boroughe at Storiat and another at Brugge by the
forest of Morphe. And the yere folowinge she builded Tamworth and
Stafforde and the[3] yere after that Edelbirith and Werigewic,[4] and the
winter folowinge Cirebirith and Warebirith, and the next somer[5]
Runconen. And at that tyme sent she her whole army to Wales and
fought with the Walshmen and wonne Brecananmer[6] and toke the
queene and 33 men. This is hit which is called in Welsh Gwayth y

[1]C ensuynge   [4]C Wernigewic
[2]C – of   [5]Ll – somer
[3]Ll – the   [6]C Brecamner

Dynas Newyth, that is to saye The Battaill of the Newe Citie.* Also she wonne the towne of Derby with the countrey but ther she lost 4 of her chieffest captaines. And the yere insuinge she wonne Leycester and subdued to her the hoste that laye ther and they of Yorkeshire dyd her homage and service. And after she had ruled Mers 8 yeres she dyed at Thamworth [43] and lyeth buried at Glocester by Sainte Peters Porche and her Epitaph was this:*

O Edelfleda potens, [O terror virgo virorum,
Victrix nature,] nomine digna viri.
Te quo splendidior fieres, natura puellam,[1]
Te probitas fecit nomen habere viri.
Te mutare decet, sed solam, nomina sexus,
Tu regina potens rexque trophea parans.
Iam nec Caesarei tantum meruere triumphi;
Caesare splendidior, virgo virago vale.

After her death dyd Edwarde disherite her sister Alfynen and toke the lande to him self and, after he had builded Glademuthin, he dyed at Ferandyn and Aulforde his sonne at Oxforde, and were bothe buried at Wynchester the yere 924. After Edwarde reigned Adelstan his base sonne, which was the woorthyest prince of Saxon bloodde that ever had reigned before him. He did overcome Cudfryd the father of Rynald Kinge of Danes at Yorke. And the secunde yere of his reigne he gathered a great army against Haulaf Kinge of Ireland, who came with a great[2] power of the Scottes [43v] and Danes against him and gave him battaill at Bunesburych, wher Adelstane gate the victorie and slewe the said Kinge Haulaf and the Kinge of Scotts and 5 kinges of the Danes and Normaines and 12 earles and brought all the lande of Inglande and Scottelande in subjection to him which none of his predecessors had ever attempted. This yere went Howell the Goode, King of Southwales, to Rome and shortly after returned home. The yere 933 was Owen the sonne of Gruffyth slaine by the men of Caerdigan. And Athelstan dyd enter Wales with a great armye and brought the kinges of the countrey to subjection and receaved yerely of tribute 20[li] in golde, and 300[li] in sylver and 500 head of cattell. Yet the lawes of Howell Dha appointe to the Kinge of Aberfrawe to paye yerely to the Kinge of London 66[li] and no more for a tribute and that bothe the Kinge of Dynevor and the King of Powys shulde paye a licke some of 66[li] yerely to the King [44] of Aberfraw, and thees lawes were made aboute this tyme or litle after. To this Adelstan dyd the kinges of Norway and France and the Duke of

---

[1]C natura puella   [2]C the whole

Gascoyng sende great and riche giftes to winne his frendeship.* And the
yere 936 dyed Hymeith the sonne of Clydawc, and Meuric the sonne of
Cadelh. And Adelstane dyd remove the Britons that dwelled in Excester
and ther abouts (till that tyme) to Cornwall and appointed the ryver of
Tambia¹ to bee ther utter mere towardes England, and he had before
appointed the Ryver Wy to be the mere of England and Wales. And the
yere 939 dyed the noble Prince Adelstane and was buried at
Malmesburie and his brother Edmunde borne in wedloke reigned in his
place. And the first yere of his reigne he wonne 5 cities of the Danes:
Leycester, Derby, Stamforde, Lyncolne and Notyngham and turned all
that unfayethfull people to the Christen fayeth. And then the Danes,
which were then called Normaines, toke first the Christen fayeth. [44v]
Then dyd Aulaf, sonne of Sydric, Kinge of Northumberlande, and
Reynalde, Kinge of Yorke, receave the Christen fayeth,²* Edmund
beinge ther godfather and so he returned to Westsex with much honor.
And at this tyme dyed Abloic chief Kinge of Ireland. And the yere
folowing was Cadelh, the sonne of Arthvael, a noble Briton imprisoned.
And Idwal Voyl the sonne of Anaraud and Elisse his brother were slayne
in a battaill which they fought against the Englishmen and Danes. This
Idwal had 6 sonnes, Meuric, Ieaf which some call Ievan, Iago which is
James, Kynan, Idwal and Rodericke, but after his death Howell Dha
ruled all Wales for his lief tyme, who was cosine germaine to Idwal. Also
Elisse his brother had a sonne called Kynan, and a dougher called
Traust,³ whiche maried Seysilht and was mother to Kynan, the sonne of
Seysilht, and to Llewelyn ap Seysilht whiche was afterwarde Kinge of
Wales.

[45] **Howell Dha sonne to Cadelh secunde sonne to Rodrycke
the Great**

   After the deathe of Idwall dyd Howell the Good take upon him the
rule of all Wales althoughe the sonnes of Idwall dyd somewhat murmure
against him, yet for his godly behaveor, discret and just rule he was
beloved of all men. This Howell made and constituted lawes to be kepte
throughe his dominions which were used in Wales to suche tyme as they
reaceved the lawes of England in the tyme of Edwarde the First and in
some places therof longe after. Thees lawes are⁴ to bee seene at this daye

¹C Cambia   ³C Graust
²C – Then dyd Aulaf . . . fayeth   ⁴Ll be

both in Lattine and in Welshe. And in his tyme dyd the forsaid kings
Aulaf and Reynalde enter the lande of Edmunde, contrarye to their
promise, and returned home with a great spoyle. Wherupon Edmunde,[1]*
gatheringe his streingthe together, folowed them into Northumberland
and overcame them in playne battaill and chaced them out of the land
and remained a whole yere, [45v] settinge orders and lawes in those
partes and spoyled the countrey of Cumberlande because he coulde by
no meanes bringe the inhabitantes thereof to lyve by any honest order
and committed hit to the rule of Malcolme Kinge of Scotlande upon
condicon that he shulde sende him succoures in all his warres both by sea
and lande. Also the yere 942 dyed Humbert Bishop of Saincte Davyes,
and the yere folowinge dyed Morclais Bishop of Bangor, and Ussa the
sonne of Llaur. And the yere 944 dyd the Englishmen enter Wales with a
stronge armye, and spoyled Stradclut and returned home. And at that
tyme was Kyngan the sonne of Elisse put in daunger of death by poysone
and Evevris Bishop of Saint Davies deceased. And the yere folowinge was
Edmunde Kinge of England slaine by treasone, as some writers[2] saye,
upon Saincte Augustines daye at dynner. Other writers saye that he
espied an outelawe sittinge in haull and as the Kinge drewe him by the
heare [46] frome the table the outelawe slewe the kinge with a knife and
he lyeth buried at Glastenbury. And his brother Edred or Edfrede was
crowned in his place, who made an expedicioun to Scottelande and
Northumberlande and subdued them both and receaved fealtie and
homage of the Northumbers and Scottes by othe, whiche was not longe
kepte. And the yere 948 dyed Howell Dha the noblest and worthiest
Kinge of Wales, whose death was sore bewayled of all men for he was a
prince that loved peace and good order, and that feared God. And he
lefte behinde him foure sonnes, Owayn, Rem,* Roderycke, and Edwyn,
betwixt whome and the sonnes of Idwall was great warres for the chief
rule of Wales as shall appeare in the historie following.

[46v] Ieaf and Iago sonnes to Idwall Voyl

After the death of Howell Dha, dyd his sonnes devide Southwales and
Powis betwixt them. And Ieaf and Iago the secunde and third sonnes of
Idwall Voyl ruled Northwales, because their brother Meuric was not a
man worthie to have the rule of the lande and also, they cominge of the
ealder house, wolde have had the chief rule of all Wales which the

[1] C – contrarye to ... wherupon Edmunde   [2] C – writers

sonnes of Howell Dha deneyd them. And therupon Iago, or James, and Ieaf[1] entred Southwales with a great power, against whome came Owen the sonne of Howell and his bretherne and fought together at the hilles of Carno where Iago and Ieaf[2] had the victorie. And the yere folowing the same brethrene dyd twise enter into Southwales and spoyled Dyved and slewe Dunwalhon the prince therof. And a wheile aftere dyed Roderike one of the sonnes of Howell Dha. And the yere 952 dyd the sonnes of Howell gather all their streingth together against Iago and Ieaf[2] and entred [47] their lande to the ryver of Conwy, wher they fought a cruele battell at a place called Gurgustv, and ther was a great number slaine upon either seide as Anaraud the sonne of Gwriad, the sonne of Rodericke the Great, and Edwyn the sonne of Howell Dha. And in this battaill were overthrowen the sonnes of Howell, and Iago and Ieaf pursued them to Caerdigan and destroyed the countrey with fier and sworde. And about this tyme was Hayardhur the sonne of Mervryn drowned and the yere folowinge was Congelach Kinge of Irelande slaine. But to returne to Edrede, Kinge of Englande. As sone as he was returned to his owne lande dyd Aulaf with a great armye lande in Northumberlande, and was reaceved of the people with much gladnesse, but, as a generation fickell and unconstant, they banished him the lande againe and tocke to their kinge one Hyrch, the sone of Haralde, who lickewise after 3 yeres they expelled, and willingly submitted them selves to Edred, which after he had ruled the whole lande 8 yeres dyed and was buried at Winchester. [47v] And after him reigned Edwayne the sonne of Edmunde in whose tyme chaunced nothinge worthye to be put in writinge, but that he maried an other mans wife, her husband beinge alive, and after he had governed the realme 4 yeres dyed and his brother Edgar was crowned in his steed. And the yere 958 was a wonderfull hote sommer, and Gwgon the sonne of Gwyriad, the sonne of Rodericke, dyed. And the yere folowinge was ther a sore plage in Marche and Iago and Ieaf[3] dyd governe the whole land of Wales by their great force, and the sonnes of Abloic Kinge of Irelande dyd brenne and spoyle Holyheade and the countrey of Lhyn. In the yere 972[4] were the sonnes of Gwyn,[5]★ the sonne of Kalhwyne, slayne after they had destroyed to Towyn,[6] and Meuric the sonne of Cadvan dyed. And the yere ensuinge dyed Rytherch Bishop of Saincte Davies and shortlye after Cadwalhon the sonne of Owen deacessed and the countrey of Northwales was sore spoyled by the army of Edgar Kinge of England.

[1]C James and Jeffe
[2]C Ieaff
[3]C Jesse

[4]C 961
[5]C Edwyn
[6]C Towy

[48] And the yere 966 was Roderik the sonne of Idwal Voyl slaine by the Irishmen and Aberfrawe destroyed. And the next yere ther fille a great debate beetwixt the twoe sonnes of Idwall, Iago and Ieaf,[1] which had ruled joyntly togeather frome the death of Howell Dha to that tyme. And Iago toke his brother Ieaf[1] by force and very cruelly imprisoned him longe tyme after. And aboute this tyme dyd Enion, sonne to Owen Kinge of Southwales, conquere to him self the lande of Gwhir. And the yere 969 did Mactus the sonne of Harolde, with an army of Danes being Panyms, enter the Ile of Anglesey and spoyled Penmon. Thees Danes were suffred by Edgar to enhabite quietly throughe all England till they were as stronge as the Englishmen, and then they felle to suche riotousenes and drinkinge that muche mischief ensued therof. Wherupon Edgar made a lawe, that every man shulde drinke by measure and caused a certaine marke to be sette in every potte, howe deepe they shuld drinke, and so by thees meanes did somewhat staye that immoderate ingurgitacioun. And at this tyme dyd Godfryd the sonne of Harolde subdue to him [48v] self the whole Ile of Anglesey which he enjoyed not longe. And the yere 972 dyd Edgar send a great navie to Caerlhion upon Uyske which shortlye turned backe without doinge of any notable acte. And the yere 973 dyd Howell, the sonne of Ieaf, rayse a great powere against his uncle Iago, for the delyuerance of his father out of prisone and overcome his uncle in fight and chaced him oute of the lande, and toke his ealdest uncle Meuric, the sonne of Idwall, and put out bothe his eyes, and put him in prisone where he dyed shortly after, leavinge behinde him 2 sonnes, Idwal and Ionoval, of which Idwall came afterwarde the most worthie princes of Wales. Also this Howell set his father at libertie, yet toke upon him self the whole rule of the lande for his lyef tyme. He had three brethrene, all men of great estimacion, Meuric,[2] Ieaf and Cadwalhon whose lyves shall ensue hereafter.

[49] Howell the sonne of Ieaf

After Howell the sonne of Ieaf had expelled his uncle frome the land, he toke the rule of it him self. And at that tyme dyd Dwnwalhon Prince of Stradclud take his journey to Rome. And Idwalhon the sonne of Owen dyed, and Edgar Kinge of England dyed after he hade builded many monasteries, after whome succeded Edwarde his sonne 4 yeres,

[1]C Jesse　　　　　　　　[2]Ll Meig

and was traytorouslye slayne throughe the meanes of his stepmother, that her sonne Edred or Edelred might enioye the kingdom, which after his brothers death was crowned kinge of the lande. And the yere 976 dyd Enion sonne to Owen, Kinge of Southwales, destroye the lande of Gwyr the secunde tyme. And the yere ensuinge Howell the sonne of Ieaf, with a great number in[1] armye both of Welshmen and Englishmen, made warre againste such as succoured and defended his uncle Iago and spoyled the countrey of Lhyn and [49v] Kelynnawg Vawr. And shortlye after was Iago taken by Howell the sonne of Ieaf[2] his men who enioyed his parte of the lande peaceablye. And the yere 979 was Idwall Vychan the sonne of Idwall Voyl slayne by his nevewe Howell and at this tyme Custennyn Dhu, that is to saye Constantyne the Blacke, sonne to Iago (beinge prisoner), hyred Godfryde the sonne of Harolde with his Danes against his cosine[3] and bothe togeather they destroyed Anglesey and Lhyn. And Howell gather his army togeather and fought with them at a place called Hyrbarwhich[4] and overthrewe them, and their Constantyne was slayne. Aboute this tyme dyd the Danes, with 7 shippes, lande at Southampton and spoyled the towne and a litle after dyed Saincte Dunstan, who prophecied the utter destruction of the lande by the Danes. The yere 981 dyd Godfryde the sonne of Harolde gather a great armye and landede in Westwales [50] and spoyled Dyved with Saincte Davies and Llanweithefavr.[5] And the next yere ensuing dyd Duke Alfrede with a great power of Englishmen spoyle and destroye Breknocke and a great parte of the landes of Owen Kinge of Southwales, against whome dyd Enion sonne to the said Owen and Howell Kinge of Northwales reyse all their power and overthrewe them in plaine battell and slewe the greatest parte of Alfredes armye and put the rest to flight. And the yere folowing dyd the gentillmen of Gwentesland rebell against their prince and cruelly slewe Enyon the sonne of Owen, which had come thither to appease them. This Enion was a worthie man and dyd many notable actes in his fathers tyme and leafte behind him 2 sonnes, Edwyn and Teudur Mawr, of whome came afterwarde the kinges of Southwales. And in the yere 984 dyd Howell the sonne of Ieaf Kinge of Wales enter England where he was fought with all and slaine valiantly [fighting]. This Howell had no sonne but his brethren reigned in his place.

[1] C number in *deleted*   [4] C Hyrbaruch
[2] C the sonne of Ieaf *deleted*   [5] C Llanweith Fawr
[3] C cosigne

[50v] Cadwalhon the secunde sonne of Ieaf and Meredydh
sonne to Owen sonne to Howell Dha

After the death of Howell dyd his brother Cadwalhon take in hande
the governance of Northwales and first made warre with Jonavaul his
cosine,[1] the sonne of Meuric and right heire to the lande, and slewe
him, but Idwall the youngest brother escaped away prively. And the
yere folowinge dyd Meredith the sonne of Owen kingke[2] of
Southwales, with all his power, enter Northwales and in fight slewe
Cadwalhon the sonne of Ieaf, and Meuric[3] his brother and conquered
the lande to him self. Here youe may see howe God punished the
wronge, which Iago and Ieaf, the sonnes of Idwall Voyl, dyd to ther
eldest brother Meurig, who was first disherited and afterwarde his eyes
put out and one of his sonnes slaine. For first Ieaf was imprysoned by
Iago and the said Iago, with his sonne Constantine, slaine by Howell,
the sonne of Ieaf, [51] and afterwarde the saide Howell with his
bretheren Cadwalhon and Meuric[3] slaine and spoyled of all their landes.

But to the historie.* The yere 986 dyde Godfred, the sonne of
Harolde, the thyrde tyme enter the Ile of Anglesey, and robbed
Lhywarch, the sonne of Owen, of his eyes and toke 2000 prisoners in
the Ile and caused Meredyth the Prince to flee with the rest to
Caerdygan. And the same yere was ther a great deathe of cattell
throughe all Wales. Aboute this tyme dyd the Danes enter Englande
with divers armyes and at Weshport and Witest overthrewe twoe[4] dukes
of England, Godan and Brichtwolde, so that the Kinge was compelled to
geve the Danes 10000[li] for peace, and that they wolde lyve quietlye in
the lande. Yet awhile after the Kinge brake[5] the peace, and prepared a
great navie to meete the Danes by sea, where also he was overcome and
all the shippes taken with Affricke the capteine of them. After this the
Danes spoyled Yorke, with Lyndsey, and Northumberlande where they
were put to flight by Godwyn and Fridegist. And at the same tyme dyd
[51v] Aulaf and Swayn enter the Themes with 94 sayles, and beseiged
London which was valiantly defended, wherefore they lefte their
sheppes and entred the lande and cruelly, with fier and sworde,
destroyed all Kent, Sussex, Surrey and Hampshire. Whereupon Kinge
Adelred sende[6] to them for peace which he obtained for great somes of
money and vittaill. And they laye peaceblly at Hampton that winter. And
Aulaf, upon composition, came to Aldred, who reaceved him worthely

[1]C cosigne	[4]C the
[2]C Kynge	[5]Ll – brake
[3]Ll Meig	[6]C sent

and dyd so enterteine him that he promised to depart the lande and never to returne, which promise he fayethfully kept.

And the yere 987 dyed Ieaf the sonne of Idwall, which had lyved many yeres a pryvate lief. And the same yere dyed also Owen the sonne of Howell Dha, Kinge of Southwales. This Owen had 3 sonnes: Enion, which died in his fathers tyme, Llywarch, which loste both his eies, and Meredith, which as before is declared had wonne Northwales and after his fathers death toke also to his possession all Southwales [52] havinge no respecte to his brothers sonnes, Edwyn and Teudwr. And at this tyme dyd the Danes sayle frome Hampton alongest the coaste, spoylinge Devenshire and Cornwall and so at the laste landed in Southwales, and destroyed Saincte Davies, Llanbaderne, Llanylltut* [and] Llandydoch, which were all places of religion, and all the countrey. And Meredith dyd paye them of tribute a peny for every man within his lande, which was called the tribute of the Blacke Armye. And at this tyme was Glwmaen,[1]* the sonne of Abloec Kinge of Irelande, slaine and a great number of people dyed for very hunger. And the yere 989 was Owen, the sonne of Dyfynwal, slayne and the yere after dyd Meredyth Kinge of Southwales destroye the towne of Radnor, and his nevew Edwyn the sonne of Enion, throughe the helpe of Duke Adelfe and a great army of Englishmen and Danes, spoyled all the landes of Meredith in Southwales [52v] as Caerdygan, Dyved, Gwyr, Kydwely and Sainct Davies. And Edwyn toke pledges of[2] the chief men of those countreys. And in the meane tyme dyd Meredith with his people spoyle Glamorgan, so that no place was free from fier and sworde. But at the last Meredith and Edwyn fille at an accorde and Cadwalhon the only sonne of Meredith dyed. And the yere 992 was the Ile of Anglesey destroyed by the Danes and Idwall the sonne of Meuric, as right heire, was reaceved as Kinge of Northwales. And the yere ensuinge was ther greate famyne though all Southwales. And Meredith* gathered togeather all his power to get againe Northwales, but Idwall mete with him at Lhangwn and overthrewe him in playne battaill. And there was slayne Teudur Mawr his nevewe, who lefte behinde him twoe sonnes Rys and Rytherch and a daugher called Elen. And a litle after this dyd Swayn, the sonne of Harorlde,[3] destroye the Ile of Man, [53] and entring to Northwales slewe Idwall the Kinge thereof, which left after him a sonne named[4] Iago. And the yere 998 dyd the Danes againe spoyle Saincte Davies, and slewe Morgeney the bishop and in the same yere dyed Meredith the

[1]C Elwmaen   [3]C Harald
[2]C for   [4]C called

sonne of Owen, Kinge of Wales, levinge behinde him one[1] onely
daughter called Ingharad which was maried to Llewelyn ap Seysilht, and
after his death to Kynvyn Hirdref and had by either of theim children,
which was the cause [of] much ware and mischief in Wales as shall
appear hereafter.

Addan the sonne of Blegrwyd

The death of bothe thees princes (of which Meredith had no issue
male, and Idwall left behinde him a childe within yeres not able to tacke
the charge of a commonwealth) dyd cause muche mischief to ensue. For
in Northwales dyverse dyd aspire for the rule of the lande as Kynan the
sonne of Howell, and Addan the sonne of Blegrwyd, who tried the
matter in open fielde wher Kynan was slaine the yere 1003. [53v] And
the yere folowinge were Gulfath and Ubiad Iryshe lordes taken by the
Scottes, and their eies put out, which Scottes dyd also destroye the
countrey and the towne of Develyn. And likewise the Danes, which had
againe destroyed Westwales, spoyled and brennyd the lande in
Somersetshire, Dorsetshire and so throughe Hampshire and Sussex they
came towardes the ryver of Themes, without any lette or staye, and so
sayled alongest the ryver to the place [where the river][2] of Mydwey
entreth to the Themes, alongest which watter they came to Rochester,
wher they overthrewe the Kentishmen that badde them battaill. And at
this tyme was Edelred in Cumberlande, the chief deenne of the Danes,
which lande he brought to subjection. But in the meanwhile another
armye of Danes, whose leaders were Mers and Vlean,[3] fought againe
with the men of Somersetshire and gote the victorie and ruled the
countrey at their pleasure. Then Edelred, hearinge of the great
worthienesse of Richarde Duke of Normandye, [54] sent to him for his
daughter Emme in mariagie which he obteined, thinkinge thereby to
have succoures. But God,[4] who wolde punishe the great sinnes and
enormities of the Saxons, dyd move the Kinge therto, that like as they
beinge instrumentes of Goddes wrathe, under the colour of frendes and
hired souldiers, had trayterouslye and cruelly slayne the Britons and
dryven them oute of their lande, so shulde the Normaines, by coloure of
this affinitie, first enter the lande as frendes and bringe succoures against
the Danes and afterwardes as foes and be the[5] utter destruction of the

[1]C an
[2]Ll – to the place, *supplied from* C; Ll –
    where the river, *supplied from* HC
[3]C Vulean
[4]Ll – God
[5]Ll – the

Saxons and Angles, which was then forseene, and tolde the kinge by
Anachorate[1] a holye man* which, inspired with the spirite of God, sawe
the plages that he had certeinly appointed to fall upon the Saxons. But
the Kinge, puffed up with pride and hope of his affinitie, dyd pryvely
wryte to all the Englishe rulers throughe the realme, to kyll the Danes in
one nighte which then lyved peacebly, which murther was cruelly
executed upon Saincte Bryces[2] Day at night. [54v] And the yere folowing came an army of Danes to Devenshire and overranne[3] the lande with
fier and sworde, sparing nothinge that bare lief to revenge the murther
of their cosines, and rased the Citie of Exceter and slewe Hughe the
Normaine whome the Queene had appointed governoure there. Then
dyd Duke Alfrede geather a great armye of Hampshire, Wilshire and all
the countries aboute, and mete the Danes, but he and his were put to
flight, and the Danes pursued them to Wylton, and destroyed hit and
Salisburie, returninge to their shippes with riche spoyles and great
triumphe.

And the yere folowinge beinge 1004 Swane, a mighte prince of
Denmarke, to whome God had predestinated the crowne of Englande,
came with a great number of sayles to Norwiche, and spoyled hit, with
whome Wlfketell Duke of the land made peace. Yet the Danes, after
they had rested awheile, went to Tedforde which they also spoyled and
returninge to their shippes with their praye and overthrewe Duke
Wlfketel, who had gathered [55] and prepared an armye to fight with
them, and so sayled to their countrey. And two yeres after returned
againe with ther companions, fier, sworde and spoyle and landed at
Standwich[4] and brenned hit and made Englande quake, as a reede in the
wynde. And thens sayled to Wycht, where they wintred till Cristmas
and then entred Hampshire and passed in diverse bandes alongest the
land to Redinge and Wallingeforde and Colsey devouringe suche
vittaills as they founde in the houses, painge therfore with sworde and
fier at ther dapartinge. And at their returne they mete upon Esumdowne
the armye of West Saxons which did nothinge but trouble them with
kylinge, and ladde them with spoyle and so they passed the gates of
Winchester with muche triumphe to Wight. And all this while was
Kinge Edelrede at his maner in Shropshire full of cares and troubles. And
then the nobilitie of England bought peace of the Danes for 30000[li]
[55v] In which tyme of peace Edelrede toke an order that of everye
300 hiddes[5] of lande thrughe the realme ther shulde be a shipe made,

[1]C Anachorat   [4]C Sandwiche
[2]C Brickes   [5]C hides
[3]C overthrewe

and furnyshed, and of every 8 hides a corselet and a helmet. A hyde conteyneth as muche grounde as a ploughe may ere by the yere. Beeside thees the Kinge had a navie frome Normandy, which being all togeather at Standwych was one of the greatest that ever was seene in Britaine. But hit happened so that where the Kinge had banished one Wlnod[1] (a noble yonge man of Southsex) he fell arovinge upon the sea and troubled all passagers and vittaylers, and one Brichtrich brother to the traytoure Edryc Duke of Mers promised the Kinge to bringe before him Wlnod, either alyve or deade. But hit happened otherwise, for ther fell suche atempeste, that he was dryven of force to the shore and manye of his shippes lost, and the rest dyd Wlnod[2] and his companie set one fier and brenned them and so the rest of [56] the navy, beinge abashed of this infortunate beginninge, came alongest the Themmes to London.

And shortlye after came a navy with Danes to Sandwiche, and so passed by lande to Canterburye mindinge to destroye the citie, but the citezens bought peace for 3000.[li3] And the Danes passed furthe[4] thrughe Kent, Sussex, Hampshire and Barkeshire wher Kinge Edelrede, with all the power of Englande, mette them, but being persuaded by the traytoure Edric wolde not fight with them and they returninge backe by London, which citie deffended hit self manfully, went to their sheppes. And the yere folowinge they landed at Ypsewiche upon the Ascention Daye and put to flight Duke Wlfketell who fought with them, and passinge to Cambridgeshire overthrew the Kinges sisters sonne with his armye, whome they slewe and with him Duke Oswy, and Edwy, and Wlfric Earles, and after toke their wayes by Essex (56v) to Themmes, leaving no parte of crueltie unpractised by the waye. And alongest the ryver syde they went to Oxfforde which they had burned the yere before and so to the three castells upon Ouse, Buckingehm, Bedforde and Huntingdon, and destroyed Godemuncester,[5] then a fayre towne, and burned Northampton, and at Cristmasse returned to their shippes. And the yere folowinge, after they had spoyled all the lande from Trent southwarde, at length they wanne the citie of Cannterbury by treason of one Almar, which Alfei the Archebishop had delyvered from deathe, and leaft nothinge behinde them but bloode and ashes, caryinge the Archebishop (with many other) to their shippes, whom they slew afterwarde cruelly. And shortly after came Swane Kinge of Denmark alongest Humber to Genesburch, to whome Vitred Duke of

[1] Ll Wlnodi   [4] C first
[2] C Wlnine   [5] C Godminchester
[3] C 30000[li], HC 30000[li]

Northumberland with all his people and all Lyndesey[1] [57] and all that
dwelled north of Watlyngstreete became subjectes and gave him
hostages. Which when he sawe, he committed his navie to Knot[2] his
sonne, and went him self to Oxforde and Winchester, which cities with
all the countreys about acknowledged him for Kinge. Then he came to
London wher Kinge Edelred was, but the citizens defended the citie so
manfully and valiantly that Swaine returned backe to Wallingforde and
so to Bathe, and reaceved homage of all West Saxon and afterward
comynge to London reaceved the citie to mercye, and was called Kinge
thrughe the lande. And Edelred fledde to Normandy to his wief and his
two sonnes Edwarde and Alfred, whome he hade sent thyther before.
And Swane, as sone as he had brought the whole lande to his obeysance,
dyed sodenlye after whose deathe the Danes chose Knot for their kinge.
And the Englishmen sent for Edelred againe, and he with a great army
destroyed Lyndesey because the province was become subjecte to Knot.
Which when Knot understoode, being at Ipswich, he cutte of the
handes and noses of all the pledges that he had and returned to
Denmarke.

[57v] And aboute this tyme dyd Brian Kinge of Irelande, Murcath his
sonne and other kinges of that lande to him subjecte, gather a great
power against Sutric,[3] the sonne of Abloic, Kinge of Develyn, and
Mailmorda, Kinge of Lagenesse. Which Sutric hired a number of
strangers, all armed men and rovers upon the seas, to his succoures and
gave Brian battaill wher were slaine the said Brian and his sonne, and of
the other Mailmorda and Broder capteine of the strangers. And this yere
1015 cam Knot frome Denmarke and landed in Westsex, and spoyled all
the countrey and Edryc with Edmunde, Kinge Adelredes bastarde
sonne, gathered an army but yet they durst not geve him battaill. Then
went Edmunde to Vitred Duke of Northumberlande and togeather they
spoyled Staffordeshire, Leycestershire and Shopshire. And upon the
other parte Knot came downe throughe Buckinghamshire Bedfordshire
and Huntingdonshire and so by Stafforde passed towardes Yorke, to
whome Vitred cam and yelded him, yet he lost his lief. [58] And Knot
made one Hyrc Duke in hes steede and Edmunde went to his father,
which lay sicke at London and Knotte returned to his shippes and sayled
to Themmes mouth and upon the ryver towardes London, but before
he came thyther Edelred was departed, after he had reigned with muche
trouble and misery 37 yeres. After whose deathe the[4] Englishmen chose

Edmunde his bastarde sonne for their Kinge. This Edmunde was surnamed Ironside for his streingth and tolerance in warre. This Edmunde
went to[1] Westsex and subdued all the countrey to him and the Danes
layde their siedgie to London and made a great trenche rounde about hit
that no man colde escape out and gave Edmunde battaill who came to
reise the siedge at Proman by Gyllenhes, wher Edmunde had the upper
hande. The secunde battaill they fought at Ceorstane, wher Edryc and
Almanl Derlinge were against Edmunde and after longe fight the night
departed bothe armyes. The thyrde battaill was at London where
Edmunde persued the Danes to their sheppes and entred [58v] the citie
tryumphantlye. And 2 dayes after they fought the 4th battaill at
Brenforde, from whens Edmunde bare the honor awaye and went to
gather a newe army, whiles Knot dyd beseidge London by watter and
lande. But hit was manfully defended and Edmunde, with his army
passed Themmes at Brenforde and entred Kent and fought the fyveth
battaill wher the Danes fledde as shepe before him. But he stayed the
pursute by the wicked rede of the traytor Edryc, whome he had
reaceved to mercye and made stewarde of the lande. The 6th battaill was
fought at Essedowne in Essex, with all the whole power of the Danes
and Englishmen, wher Edmunde shewed his prowesse and forsakinge his
place, which is betwixt the dragon and the standarde, he entred the
armye of his enemyes and brake the thickeste rankes of them and
compelled the prowdest of them to turne their backes. Which when
Edric sawe, fearynge the overthrowe of the [59] Danes, cryed alowed
fledde Engle, flede Engle, ded is Edmunde, and therupon fledde with his
people, whome all the army folowed to the great murther of
Englishmen. And ther were slaine Ednod, Alfirc, Godwin, and Vlfcetel
all Dukes and all the chyvalrye of England. After whiche victorie Knot
entred London and was crowned Kinge of the lande and Edmunde
gathered his army together and they mete in Glocestershire but, either
army fearinge other, were loth to fighte but moved the kings to make an
ende of this cruell bloodshed by combate. Wherunto ether prince
agreed and the place beinge appointed, fought togeather manfully and
either of them were founde so valiannt and worthie men as fewe then
the like, but Knot fearing the incomparable strength of Edmunde moved
him to accorde, whereunto he agreed and peace was made with muche
joye, upon condicioun that Edmunde shoulde reigne in Westsex and
Knot in Mars. And so they departed, Knot to London and Edmunde to
Oxforde where he was traytourouslye murthered [59v] by the sonne of

[1] Ll – to

Edric, as he was at the pryvey, with a sharpe knief. And Edryc came to
Knot with great joye and greeted him as onely Kinge of Englande,
declaringe howe Edmunde was slayne. And I saide Knotte will[1] rewarde
thee* accordinge to thy desertes and sette thee above all the nobles of
Englande, and furthwithe caused his hed to be cutte of, and to be sette
upon a poull upon the hiest towre in London, and dyd execution of all
the other that were consentinge to the murther.

And the yere 1016[2] dyd Llewelyn the sonne of Seysylht rayse a great
power against Aydhan or Addan which by force had taken upon him the
rule of Northwales and slewe hyme and his four[3] sonnes in battail and,
havinge no respecte to Jago or James the sonne of Idwall and righte
heire, tooke upon him the name and authoritie of Kinge of Wales. This
Llewelyn was descended from the kinges of Wales by his mother side,
whose name was Traust daughter to Elisse, secunde sonne to Anaraud,
which was the eldest sonne of Rodericke the Great and also he had to
wief Ingharad the onely doughter of Mredith Kinge of Southwales and
by thees meanes claymed and enioyed the right and title[4] of either
countrey, as hereafter shalbe declared.

[60] Llewelyn the sonne of Seysylht and Ingharad the daughter of Meredith Kinge of Wales

After Llewelyn the sonne of Seysylht had taken into his handes the
governance of Wales, all things dyd prosper in the lande, for the earthe
brought furthe her fruite[5] double to the tymes before passed, the people
prospered in all their affayres and multiplied wunderouselye, the cattell
increased in great number so that their was nether begger nor poore
slave from the southe to the north sea, but every man had plentie, every
house dwellers and every towne inhabiters. Nowe in this tyme had Knot
maried Emme, sometymes wief to Edelred, and Edmund and Edwarde,
the sonnes of Edmunde Ironside, he sent to Hungrie to be slaine, but
the Kinge cherished them as his owne children. Kinge Knot also seased a
great subsidie upon the land of 72000li besides 11000li which the citisens
of London payed. And the yere 1019 dyd Meyrig the sonne of Arthvael
rayse a great armye against Llewelyn Kinge of Wales, which mete with
him in the fielde and manfully slewe him and disconfited his people.

[1] Ll wee
[2] C 1015
[3] Ll 4or
[4] C – and title
[5] C – her fruite

Also this yere dyd Knot sayle with a great navie [60v] to Denmark and made warre against the Vandales which had a great armye in the felde, but Knot overthrewe them by the prowesse of Earle Godwyn, and the Englishmen, wherefore he loved and trusted¹ them the better ever after.

In the yere 1020 dyd a Scotte of lowe birth come to Southwales, and named him self Reyn the sonne of Meredithe their last kinge. And the nobilitie which loved not Llewelyn exalted him to the regall throne and toke hym as ther Kinge. Which thinge, when Llewelyn herde, he gathered his power in Northwales and came towardes Reyn which was with all the strength of Southwales at Abergwili. And with great pryde abode Llewelyn their and, when bothe armyes were redye to joyne, Reyne, full of bragges and crakes as the nature of the Scottes is, encoraged his people to fight promisinge them the victorie. But he him self accordinge to the proverbe, sette one thy dogge² but folowe him not thy selfe,★ gave them not³ the lokinge one, where[as] upon the contrarye parte Llewelyn, [61] like a bolde and chivalrouse prince, came before his people, callinge for the vyle Scotte Reyn that durst belye a kinges bloode. And so bothe the armyes joyned togeather with muche malice and hatred, for the one partie were so not couragiouse to defende the quarell of so worthie a prince of their owne bloodde, as the other were obstinate in the cause of a strange slave. But after great slaughter upon either parte the Northewales men, remembring their olde victories and encoraged by the prowesse of their prince, put their enimyes to flight and pursued Reyn so narowely that all his Scottes wiles colde not save his lyef, and so returned home with a great spoyle and praye. And Llewelyn ap Seysylht ruled all the lande quietly and the yere folowinge he was slaine by Howell and Meredith the sonnes of Edwyn, levinge behinde him one sonne named Griffith ap Llewelyn.

[61v] Iago the sonne of Idwall the sonne of Meirig the sonne of Idwal Voyl

After the death of Kinge Llewelyn dyd Jago or James the sonne of Idwall take upon him the rule of Northwales as right heire therof, and Rytherth the sonne of Iestyn governed Southwales by stronge hande. And this tyme dyd Knot make his viage to Denmarke and Swethen against Vlf and Alaf who hade sturrede the Fynlanders againste him, with

¹C – and trusted   ³Ll – not
²Ll eagge

whome he hade a cruell fight and lost a great number of his armye, as well Englishmen as Danes. And after his returne to Englande he made his journey to Rome with muche pomp and glorye not because he thought by that journey to be clensed of his sinnes, but that his ambitiouse minde might have the prayse and fame of the worlde for his[1] riche giftes and princely behavior. And what holynesse he learned there hit appeared at his returne, for furthwith he entred Scottelande with a great armye against Malcolyn the King[2] thereof, who desired peace and became his subjecte with twoe other Kings of the Orkneyes Ewyst, Melbeath and Iermare.

And this yere 1031 dyd the Irishe Scottes enter [62] Southwales by the meanes of Howell and Mredith the sonnes of Edwyn, the sonne of Einon, the sonne of Owen, the sonne of Howell Dha, who hired them against Rytherche ap Iestyn. And he boldley mete with them, and was disconfited and slayne and so those two brethren dyd joyntly reigne in Southwales, but not in quietnesse, for the sonnes of Rytherch gathered a number[3] of suche as were their fathers frendes to revenge his deathe, with whome Howell and Meredith meete at Hirathwy and after longe fight putte them to flight. And the yere ensuing 1033 was Meredith, one of the Kinges of Southwales, slayne by the sonnes of Kynan the sonne of Seysylht, brother to the worthie prince Llewelyn, to revenge their fathers death, whome Mredith and his brother hade slaine. And the yere folowing was Caradawc the sonne of Rytherch ap Iestan[4] slayne by the Englishmen that entred Gwent lande. And shorteley after dyed Knot the moste famouse and mightiest prince [in] the west partes of the worlde as he that had under his dominion the great countrey of Swethen frome Germaine to the North [62v] Pole with Norwaye and Denmarke and all the noble Ile of Bryttaine. And after him Harolde Harfoote was created Kinge sonne to Knot, and to Alwyne daughter to Duke Alfelyne. For Hardy Knote, his other sone borne of Emme, was then in Denmarke, and Harolde the firste yere of his reigne banished Emme his stepmother out of the realme. And this yere 1037 dyd Griffith sonne to Llewelyn ap Sysylht, sometymes Kinge of Wales, rayse a great number of people against Iago then enjoying the Crowne, and likewise Iago[5] geathered all his streingthe to fight with him. But the more parte and the better souldiors were with Griffith for the love they bare to his father. And after the armyes mette Iago was soone overthrowen and slayne. This

---

[1] Ll – his
[2] C prince
[3] Ll – a number

[4] C Iestin
[5] Ll – Iago

Iago left behinde him a sonne called Kynan by his wief Avantret, doughter to Gweir ap Pylh.

[63] Griffith the sonne of Llewelyn ap Seysylht and Ingharad

Griffith ap Llewelyn, after he had slayne Iago, governed Northwales worthelye, in all thinges folowinge his fathers steppes, and he overcame bothe the Danes and the Englishmen divers tymes and defended his people and countrey manfully all his reigne. And the firste yere of his kingedome he fought with the Englishmen and Danes at Crosforde upon Sevarne, and put them to flight, and frome thence he ledde his army to Llanbadarne Vawr in Caerdiganshire, and destroyed hit utterlye. And frome thence passsed all Southwales throughout and receaved the people to his subjection for Howel ap Edwyn their Kinge fledde before his face, and forsooke the lande, and when he had brought all Wales under his dominion he returned to Northwales againe. And the yere ensuing 1038 dyed Hermin,[1] the Bishop of Menevia, a man both lernyd and godlye. [63v] And the yere next folowinge Howel Kinge of Southwales gathered a great power of his frendes and strangers and entred the lande, entendinge to recover hit againe but Griffith like a worthie prince came with all speede to succoure his people, and meettinge with Howell at Pencadair, after he had encouraged his souldiors, gave him battaill and overthrewe him and pursued him so narowely that he tooke Howelles wief which he hade brought to the filde to see the overthrowe of Griffith which chaunced contrarye and Griffith likede her so well that he tooke her to his wife.

And aboute this tyme dyed Harolde Kinge of Englande and his brother Hardy Knot reigned in his steede, a noble and liberall prince he caused his tables to be covered and furnished foure tymes every daye for strangers and all comers, and after he had reigned twoe yeres he dyed at Lambeth in the floure of his age. After whose death the Englishmen sent for Alfrede the eldest sonne of[2] Edelred, frome Normandye. But[64] that message pleased not Earle Godwyn, which was the mightiest man in the lande, because he knewe the yonge prince to be couragiouse and stoute and therfore one that wolde not suffer him to rule the lande as he entendede to doe. Therfore he perswaded the people that Alfrede, who hade come well accompanied withe Normaines, had promised them the whole rule of the lande, and therupon they tooke all the Normaines and

[1]*Pen20* Heruini (Erfyn); *HC* Hernum   [2]Ll – of

bound them and afterward tythed them,* puttinge every tenth man to deathe. And yet they thought ther were to manye, wherefore they teythed them the secunde tyme and ledde Alfred from Gyldeforde,[1] where this crueltie was committed, to Gillengham and there put out his eyes and removed him thence to Ely, where he was pittifullye murthered. And afterwardes they sent for Edwarde the youngest sonne which they receaved as Kinge the yere folowinge. But first he maryed Godwynes doughter and the first yere of his reigne he banished Earle Swein sonne to the saide Earle Godwyn who [64v] was receaved of the Earle of Flanders. In the yere 1041 dyd Howell come againe to Southwales and remayned there awhile and shortlye after dyd a number of strangers lande in Westwales and spoyled the countrey, against whome Howell gathered a number of people and fought with them and drove them to their shippes with muche loss.[2]

And at this tyme dyd Kynan the sonne of Iago, who had fledde to Irelande to save his lief, with the power of Afloedh[3] Kinge of Deuelyn (whose doughter Ranulht he had maryed) entred Northwales and by treason had taken Gruffith the Kinge, and caried him towardes their shippes. But when hit was knowen the countrey rose and folowed the Irishmen and overtooke them and rescowed their prince and pursued their foes with muche slaughter to their shippes, who returned streight, with Kynan, to Irelande. And the yere folowinge dyed Howell the sonne of Owen Lorde of Glamorgan full of yeres, [65] and Howell ap Edwyn called to his succoures Danes and Englishmen with all the power he colde make in Southwales to be revenged upon Griffith Kinge of Wales.[4]* Who[5] heringe this gathered his power togeather in Northwales and came couragiouslye to meete his enimeyes, which he hade twise discomfited, as farre as the springe of the ryver Tywy, where, after a longe and dangerouse batteill, Howell was slayne and his army discomfyted, and so narowely pursued that fewe[6] escaped alyve. And after his death dyd Rhytherch and Rhese the sonnes of Rytherch ap Iestyn aspyre againe to the rule of Southwales, which their father had ones obteined, and gathered a great armye as well of strangers as of Gwentlande where they were Lordes, and Glamorgan, and mette with Griffith king of Wales. Who, after his accustomed fashyon detracted no tyme, but couragiousely animatinge his men with the remembrance of their former fortune and diverse victories under his standarte [65v] joyned battaill, where they founde their enemyes disposed to abide and

[1]C Gileforde
[2]Ll lose
[3]C Alfredh

[4]C – to be revenged . . . Wales
[5]C who *deleted*; Griff *inserted above line*
[6]Ll – fewe

to wynne againe the honor they had before loste, wherefore the fight
was cruell and bloddy that hit continued tyll night, whiche departed
easely both armyes beinge wery of fight, and either fearinge other they
returned to their countreyes to geather more streingth. And this yere
dyed Joseph Bishop of Teilo at Rome. And the lande was quiet for two
yeres. And Griffith ruled all Wales without any trouble tyll the
gentillmen of Ystradtywy dyd by treason kill 140 of the Kinges best
souldiors. To revenge whose death the kinge destroyed all Dyved and
Ystradtywy. And this yere fill suche a snow that hit laye upon the earthe
frome the Calendes of Januarii¹ to the 14 of Marche. And about this
tyme dyd Lothen and Hyrlinge lande at Sandwiche with a great number
of Danes and after they had spoyled the towne they returned to their
shippes and sayled to Flandres and solde their buttyn and so sayled to
their countrey. [66] And at this tyme dyd Earle Sweyne returne to
England and came to his fathers house at Pevenese, and humbly
besought his father and his brethrene Harald and Tosti, and Earle
Beorne to bee meanes to the Kinge for him, and Beorne² promised to
entreate the Kinge for him, and went with Sweyn to his shippes, where
he was traytourously murthered and his body leaft upon the shore, and
by his frendes buryed by his uncle Kinge Knot at Winchester. And
Sweyn sayled againe to Flanders but the yere folowinge he obteined the
Kinges favor by his fathers meanes.

   And this yere 1050 dyd Kynan sonne of Iago gather an army of his
frendes in Ireland, and as they sayled towarde Wales ther arose suche a
tempest that hit scattered his navy abroade and drowned the most parte
of his shippes and so he lost his labor. And shortly after Roberte
Archebishop of Canterburye accused Earle Godwyn and [66v] his
sonnes Sweyn and Harolde of treasone and the Quene of adultrye and
therefore, because they refused to appeare before the Kinge, he banished
Godwyn and his two sonnes and put the Queene frome him. And
Godwyn, with Sweyn, fledde to Flandres and Harolde to Irelande. And
the King gave to Odonon the Earledome of Devonshire, Somersetshire
and Dorset and to Algar sonne to Earle Leverycke the Earldome of
Harolde. But Godwyn and Sweyn gote men and shippes in Flanders and
sayled to the Ile of Wight and spoyled hit and so they dyd Portlande.
And Harolde cominge frome Irelande and spoylinge alongest the shore,
mette with them, and they burned Pevenesieinesse, Romnei, Hith,
Folkestone, Dover and Sandwiche and entringe the Themes destroyed
Chepei³ and landinge in Kent burned the Kinges house at⁴ Middeltunne

¹C – of Januarii   ³C Sheppeye
²C – to be meanes . . .and Beorne   ⁴C houses of

and afterwarde sayled up towardes London and mette with the Kinge
and so sayled with him. And [67] when they were ready to fighte an
accorde was made by meanes of Bishop Stigan, and the kinge restored
them their landes and goodes, tooke home the Queene, and banished
the Archebishop with all the Frenchemen which had put that suspition
in the Kinges headde.

And shortly after Oswarde Earle of Northumberlande, when he herde
his sonne was slayne in Scottelande whither his father had sent him to
conquere hit, asked whether his death wounde was in his breste or in his
backe, and they saide in his brest, and he answered I am right gladde
thereof for I wolde not wishe mee nor my sonne to dye otherwise. And
Kinge Edwarde entred Scottelande, overcame the Kinge in battaill,
destroyed the lande and subdued hit to him self. And the yere folowinge
Godwyn dyed at the Kinges table choked with a pece of breade and
Harolde his sonne hade his Erldome and Algar Earle of Chester had the
Earldome of Harolde. And about this tyme the worthie Earle Siwarde,
being brought to the pointe of deathe with the bluddy [67v] fluxe,
bewayled his mischance, that he had escaped in many a dangerouse
battaill, and nowe shulde dye suche a filthy and cowardly death, called
his frendes and his men aboute him commanding them to sett hyme in
his chayre and to arme him at all pointes to put his sheelde[1] in hys leeft
hand and his axe in his right hande[2] and made an ende of his worthie
lief. And because his sonne was within yeres his Earldome was geven to
Tosti Godwynes sonne.

And the yere 1054 dyd Griffith the sonne of Ritherch ap Iestyn
gather a great number as well strangers as other against Griffith ap
Llewelyn Kinge of Wales, but commenly called Kinge of Northwales,
who, detractinge no tyme, mette with him, fought with him and slewe
him. And shortely after was Algar Earle[3] of Chester convicted before the
counsaill of treason to the kinges person, and fledde to Griffith Kinge of
Wales which Griffith had gathered his power to revenge the often
wronges he had receaved at the Englishmens handes which ever
succoured his enimyes against him. Therefore he entred Herfordeshire
and spoyled all [68] the waye with fyer and sworde to the citie, whither
all the people hade fledde. And they boldley yssued furthe, Earle
Randulf beinge their leader, and gave him battaill which Griffith wished
for above any other thinge, as he that had wonne fyve sette feeldes, and
couragiously receavinge his enimyes fought with them. Which fight was

[1] C childe   [3] C Knige
[2] C – and his axe . . . hande

longe and doubtefull tyll suche tyme Griffith encouraged his people
with the remembrance of the prowesse and worthie acts of the ancient
Britaines theyre forefathers and howe hit was the same enimye whose
backes they had so[1] oftene seene before tymes, which doubled their
streingth and force, and so sore pressed forwardes that their foes were
compelled to forsake the feeldes and trust to their feete, where their
handes prevailed not, and thought to have taken the towne for their
defence. But Griffith and his men pursued them so harde that they
entred with them and after a great slaughter returned home with many
worthie prisoners, great tryumphe and riche spoyles, leavinge nothinge
in the towne but bloodde and asshes and the walls rased to the grounde.

[68v] And this tyme came Edwarde the sonne of Edmunde Ironside
to Englande with his wief and children, Edgar, Edelyng (which worde
signifieth in the Britishe tonge a yonge lorde or prince) and Margaret
which was afterwarde Queene of Scottes and mother to Mawde, wief to
Henrye the First Kinge of Englande, and this Edwarde dyed shortly
after. And twoe yere after came Rodericke sonne to Harolde Kinge of
Denmarke with an army to Wales, and ther beinge frendely receaved of
Kinge Griffith and joyninge their powers togeather entred Englande,
and cruelly spoylled and burned a great parte of the lande. But shortely
Roderike was compelled for great causes to returne to his shippes and to
sayle to Denmarke and Griffith returned home with spoyles. This yere as
Harolde Godwyns sonne wolde have saylede to Flannders, he was
dryven by force of tempest to lande in Poytiers, where he was taken and
conveyd to William [69] Bastard Duke of Normandye, to whome
Harolde declared his journey to bee onely thither to offer him his
service in the affaires of Englande and toke a solempne othe, first to
marrye the Dukes doughter, and after the death of Edwarde to reserve
the Crowne to the Dukes use, and shortely after receaving riche giftes
with muche honor he returned to Englande. And this yere dyed Owen
the sonne of Griffith ap Rytherche. And Harolde and his brother Tosti
by the procuring of Caradawc (sonne of Griffithe ap Rytherche), and
others, gathered a great power and entred Southwales, and subdued a
great parte therof and wrought so with those that were aboute Griffith
the Kinge that as sone as he had gathered his people in Northwales and
tooke his journey to meete with Harolde, he was cruelly and
traytorousely slaine[2] by his owne brother,[3]* and his hed brought to
Harolde, who appointed and placed Meredith, the sonne of Howell, the

[1] Ll – had so
[2] Ll – slaine

[3] Ll + Mariarig Scotus

sonne of Edwyn in Flyntshire, Kinge and ruler of Southwales. And he
with his brother [69v] Tosti returned home.

This Griffith ap Llewelyn had governed Wales 24 yeres valiantly and
worthelye, he never fought but he bare awaye the victorie. He was
gentill to his subjectes and cruell to his foes, loved of the one and feared
of the other, liberall to strangers, costly in his apparell, and princely in all
his doinges and unworthie of [1] that cruell ende [2] that the ambitiouse
desire of rule did provoke his unkinde subjectes and unnaturall cosins to
prepare for so noble and victoriouse a prince and so gentill a master as he
was.

Blethyn ap Kynvyn and Meredith ap Owen

After the deceasse of Kinge Griffith did Meredith the sonne of Owen
the sonne of Edwyn, which Edwyn some writers saye was the sonne of
Howell Dha, take upon him the rule and governance of Southwales and
Blethyn and Rhwalhon the sonnes of Kynvyn and [70] halfe bretheren
to Kinge Griffith ap Llewelyn (as they which were borne of Ingharad
doughter to Meredith Kinge of Wales) dyd governe Northwales, Kynan
the sonne of Iago beinge all this tyme with this father in lawe in
Irelande. And hit fortuned that as Harolde served the Kinge with drinke
at Windesor, his brother Tosti moved with envye that his younger
brother shulde be preferred beefore him, pulled him by the heare of the
headde and overthrewe him. And afterwarde departinge full of rancor
and malice to Hereforde, where Harolde had prepared great cheere for
the Kinge, he slewe all Haroldes servauntes and cut of their heads,
armes, leggs, noses, feete and handes and fylled all the vesselles of wyne,
meath, beere, and ale therwith and sent the Kinge worde, that he shulde
lacke no powdred and sawced meates when he came, lette him provide
for other thinges himself, for which heniouse offence the Kinge
banished him the lande [70v] for ever. He and his brother were chief
justicers of the lande and they used, when they sawe any manor house or
ferme that pleased them, to cause the owner to be murthered by night
with all his children and householde, and then to sease the landes to
their owne handes. Nowe when the people of Northumberlande herde
the exile of Tosti, which was their Earle, they rejoyced muche for they
hated him to the death, and cominge to Yorke they slewe all his familie

---

[1] Ll – of   [2] C death

as well Englishmen as Danes, and joyninge to them the men of
Lyncolneshire, Notyngham, and Derbyshire, they made Marcher sonne
of Earle Alfgar their capteine and to theme came his brother Edwyn
with his people and a great number of Welshmen. And they went
spoylinge and brenninge to Hampton where Harolde mete with them,
sent frome the Kinge to knowe their willes, and they saide they wolde
have Marcher Earle over them, which the Kinge grannted and
confirmed, wherupon they returned the one parte [71] to the north and
the other to Wales, spoylinge and burninge all the countrey and leade
with them many thousande prisoners.

   And the yere folowinge beinge 1066 dyed Kinge Edwarde and was
buried at Westminster. This Edwarde was the last Kinge of Saxons, or of
Englishe bloodde, that reigned in this lande, which frome Cerdike
Kinge of Westsaxons had continued 571[1]* and from Egbrute the first
monarche 271 yeres. And after the death of Edward some wolde have
preferred Edgar Ethelinge as right heire to the crowne but Harolde,
beinge of greater power, more rich and better frended, obteined hit,
nothinge wayinge his othe and promise to William Duke of Normandy.
Which Duke callinge all his nobles togeather, declared them the
wronges that the hade reaceved at Haroldes handes as first, the death of
his cosin Alfred, the banishment of the Archebishop Roberte and Earle
Odon, with all the Normaines, and thirdly his othe and promise broken,
and also the titles he had to Englande [71v] as well by the former
promise of Edwarde made to him in Normandy that yf ever he enioyed
the crowne of England William shulde be his heire as also by cosynage,
and by othe and promise of Harolde. Which matters considered by the
nobilitie of Normandy, with all the daungers and difficulties of this
expedicion, the most[2] parte feared the ende. And William Fitzosbert, the
Dukes sewer, seinge howe they were bent, dissuaded them frome that
vyage, wherfore they agreed all, that he shuld declare their mindes to the
Duke and promised the Duke, that what he wolde doe, they were
readye to folowe. Then he spake to the Duke[3] and saied I with all my
men and power am redye to lyve and dye with thee in this jorney.
Which when the other herde, upon their promise they were readye to
folowe, and so made readye a great navy. And in the meane while Tosti
entred Humber with 40 saile but Earle Edwyn mette with him and put
him to flight who, as he sayled towardes Scotland, mette with Harolde
Kinge of Norwaye [72] withe 300 saile cominge towardes Englande and

[1]C 171
[2]C more   [3]C – and promised the Duke . . . spake to
                                 the Duke.

joyned with him, and entred Humber and landed their army and came
to Yorke, where bothe[1] Earles Edwyn and Marcher gave them battaill
upon the south parte of the towne. But Harolde and Tosti bare away the
victorie and spoyled the citie and came forwardes to Stanfordes bridge
where Harolde Kinge of Inglande, with all his power, mette with them
and their armyes fought togeather from morninge till noone, at what
tyme the Norwayes retyred backe over the watter. And one of them not
worthye to be forgoten kept the passage upon the bridge with his axe
against all the armye of Englande tyll 3 of the clocke and slewe fortie
men, and at the last one gote about and came[2] under the bridge, and
with a spere gave him his deathes wounde thrughe the bridge in the
fundement. And then the army passed over the bridge, and put the
Norwayes to flight and slewe their Kinge Harolde and Tosti and let not
one man escape of all the number but ether killed them or brenned
them. [72v] And Harolde entred Yorke with great joye and triumphe
and as[3] he sate at dynner cam in a post, which tolde him howe Duke
William was landed at Suwerhyde and had fortified him self with a
trenche at Hastinges. With which tydings Harolde beinge nothinge
dismaied, made expedicion thitherwarde, where William had devided
his army to fyve battailles and after a longe oration to his people, where
he declared the worthinesse of their forefathers the Danes and Norwayes
as well against the Englishmen, who were never able to abyde their
force, as against the Frenchemen and other nations. And howe they
were accustomed to overcome at all tymes and beinge well horsed, well
armed, and good archers had to doe with a nation onley taught to truste
to their feete, evyll horsed, unarmed, and that knewe not howe to
occupey their bowes. He brought his people to the felde, where
Harolde who had couched all his armye in one battaill as nighe
togeather as [73] they colde well stande. But after longe fight William
caused his men to retire as yf they fledde, and the Englishmen folowed
apase and brake their array. And so[4] a battayll of fresh Normaines entred
their battaill and after longe fight Harolde was hurte with an arrowe, and
afterwarde slaine. And so the Englishmen leaft the Normaines the felde
and victorie. And William went streight to London where he was
receaved peaceablye and crowned at Westminster Kinge of the lande.

   This last battaill and utter destruction of Englishmen was fought the
14 day of October in the yere 1066 which change was before declared
by a comete that appeared in the beginninge of this yere of the which
one made thees verses:

Anno millesimo sexagesimo quoque seno
Anglorum metae flammas censere cometae.

And the yere folowinge William passed the sea to Normandy, and Edgar
Ethelinge came out of Scoteland to Yorke, for the people of the
countrey had slaine Roberte, to whome William [73v] had geven the
Earldome, and 900 men with him, and they receaved Edgar. But
William returninge frome Normandy destroyed all the north and chaced
Edgar to Scottelande againe.

And this yere 1068 dyd Meredith and Ithell the sonnes of Griffith ap
Llewelyn rayse a great power against Blethyn and Rywalhon Kinges of
Northwales and mete with them at a place called Mechayn. And in that
fight were slaine upon the one parte Ithell and upon the other Rywalhon
and Meredith put to flight, whome[1] Blethyn pursued so straytly that he
sterved for colde and hunger upon the mountaines. And so Blethyn the
sonne of Kynvyn was onely Kinge of Powis and Northwales.

And about this tyme came Sweine, Kinge of Denmarke, and Osbert
his brother to Humber with 300 saille and to them came Edgar
Ethelinge and Earle Waltelf and togeather they came to Yorke and
wanne the castell and laye that winter betwixt Ouse and Trent till [74]
the Kinge came thither and chaced the Danes to their shippes and
destroyed the inhabitantes of the countrey, but Earle Waltelf he
receaved to mercy.

And Caradawc sonne to Griffith ap Ritherch ap Iestyn hyred and
procured a great number of Frenchmen (for so the Britishe booke
calleth the Normaines) to enter Southwales, to whome he joyned his
power of Gwentlande and gave battaill to Meredith the Kinge thereof
and slewe him upon the ryver of Rympyn. Also at this tyme was
murthered Dermud Makmael[2] the worthiest and noblest prince that had
ever ruled in Ireland.[3] And the twoe Earles Edwyn and Marcher with
Herewarde gathered an armye against the Kinge but Edwyn was slayne
of his owne people and the other toke the Ile of Ely which the Kinge so
sore beseeged that he shortely tooke Marcher and his complices, but
Herewarde escaped manfully to Scottelande, whom shortely the Kinge
folowed and made [74v] Malcolyn Kinge of the lande his subjecte and
vassall. And after the Kinge passed to Normandy and reaceved Edgar
Ethelinge to his mercye. And about this tyme dyd the Normaines leade

[1]Ll when; *corrected to HC* whome   [3]C Ingland
[2]C Makeinanel

a great power to Westwales by sea and destroyed Dyved and the countrey of Caerdygan, and caryed away muche spoyle, and so they dyd likewise the yere folowinge. And Bleydhad Bishop of Menevia or Saincte Davies dyed, and Sulyen was bishop in his place. And aboute this tyme Radulphe Earle of Eastangles conspired against the Kinge, with Roger, the sonne of William Fitzosbert, and Earle of Hereforde, and Earle Waltelf. And at the maryage of the saide[1] Radulphe with Rogers sister in Essex the matter was opened, but hit pleased not the rest. Therefore Radulphe toke shippinge in Norwiche and fledde to Denmarke and the Kinge sodeinly cominge over toke Waltelf and Roger, of whome Waltelf was beheded, and Roger committed to prison, and the people all slaine, amonge whome ther were a great number of Welshmen.

And the yere 1073 was Blethyn ap Kynvyn Kinge of [75] Wales traytorouslye and cowardely murthered by Rees ap Owen ap Edwyn and the gentillmen of Istradtywy,[2] after he had worthely governed Wales 13 yeres. This man was very liberall and mercyfull, and loved justice and equitie all his reigne. This Blethyn had by diverse women many children, first Meredith by Haer doughter of Gylhyn, Llywarche and Cadwgan by an other woman, Madocke and Ryryd by the thirde and Ierwarth by the fourthe.

Trehayarn ap Caradoc

After the death of Blethyn, Trehayarn ap Caradoc his cosine germaine toke upon him the rule of Northwales and Rees ap Owen and Rytherch ap Kradoc dyd joyntlye rule Southwales. And Griffith sonne to Kynan, sonne to Iago or James, right enheritor of Northwales, came from Irelande, with succoures which his brethrene Ecumathun[3] Kinge of Ulton and Ranalht and Mathawn had delivered him, and landed in the Ile of Mone or Anglesey and brought hit to his subjection. [75v] And Kynvric ap Rywalhon was slayne in Northwales.

And this yere dyd Gronwe and Llewelyn sonnes to Cadwgan ap Blethyn joyne ther powers with Caradawc ap Griffith ap Rytherche against Rys ap Owen ap Rytherch ap Kryadoc to revenge their grandfathers death. And they fought at aplace called Camdhwr, where the sonnes of Cadwgan obteined the victorie. And shortely after dyd

[1] Ll – saide   [3] C Encumalhon
[2] C Ystradtywy

Griffith ap Kynan passe over the water from Mone to the maine land, and Trehayarn ap Caradoc mete with him at Bron yr erw, where Griffith was put to flight and retyred backe to the Ile. And the yere 1074 Rytherch ap Kryadoc was slaine by treason of his cosine germaine, Meyrchyawn ap Rys ap Rytherch, and Rys ap Owen ruled Southwales alone. Yet the sonnes of Cadwgan gathered their power and fought with him the secunde tyme at Gwayn Yttul, and put him to flight. [76] But he gathered a new power and kept the lande still, tyll Trehayarn ap Caradoc, Kinge of Northwales, moved his power against him, and Rys with all the streingth of Southwales boldeley mete him at a place called Pulh Guttyc, and there after longe fight Rys after his accustomed maner trusted his feete, and after the great slaughter of his men fledde frome place to place, fearinge all men like a stagge that had bene lately chaced which mistrustethe every noyse. And at the last he, with his brother Howell, fell in the handes of Caradoc ap Griffith, who slewe them bothe to revenge the death of the wise and noble prince Blethyn ap Kynvyn. And this yere dyd Sulyen forsake his bishopricke and Abraham was made bishop in his place. And the yere 1077 dyd Rys the sonne of Tewdur, the sonne of Enyon, the sonne of Owen the sonne of Howell Dha, as right heire[1] to the kingdome of Southwales clayme the same, and the people reaceved him with much joye and made him their prince. [76v] And the next yere was Menevia all spoyled and destroyed by strangers, and Abraham the bishop dyed, and Sulyen was compelled to tacke the bishopricke againe. And the yere folowinge dyd Griffith the sonne of Kynan bringe a great armye of Irishmen and Scottes in to Wales, and joyned with Rys ap Tewdur as twoe right heires, Griffith of Northwales and Rys of Southwales descendinge from Rodericke the Greate. And against them came Trehayarne ap Caradoc and Caradoc, Griffith and Meylyr the sonnes of Rywalhon ap Gwyn, his cosine germaines, for Gwyn ap Blethyn was their grandfather, for thees ruled all Wales at that daye. And after they had mete at the mountaines of Carno, they fought a cruell battaill, for upon that laye the lyves and honor of either partie, and at the leingth the victorie fell to Griffith, and Rys, and Trehayarne with his cosines were all slaine and the most parte of their people. [77] And so the kingdomes of Wales came under the rule of the righte heirs againe. And at this tyme was a noble man of Wales called Urgeney ap Seisylht slayne by the sonnes of Rys Says, which is to saye Rys the Englishman, for so they used to name all suche as had served in England and coulde speake the Englyshe tonge.

[1]C inheritore

Griffith the sonne of Kynan

And after the death of Trehayarn dyd Griffith ap Kynan rule Northwales and Rys ap Tewdur Southwales quietly. And about this tyme Malkolyn Kinge of Scottes spoyled Northumberland and caryed a great number of prisoners with him. And the people of Northumberlande slewe Walker Bishop of Durham and 100 men with him as he sate ministringe justice. And Roberte Curthoys overthrewe his father William Bastarde in battaill. [77v] And the yere folowinge William Bastarde entred Wales with a great army as farre as Saincte Davies where he offred, and toke homage of the kinges or[1] princes of the lande. And about this tyme dyd Thrustan Abbot of Glasenbury cause three of his monkes to be slaine upon the highe aulter. And this yere dyd Sulyen forsake his bishopricke the secunde tyme and Wilfred was stalled in his place. And this tyme was Caerdiff buylt* and Terdelach Kinge of Irelande dyed. And the yere 1083[2] dyed William Bastarde Kinge of all Britaine and Duke of Normandy, after he hade leaft never a noble man of Englishe blood within Englande, but had robbed, spoyled and slayne or banished them all and gave their landes to his owne men. For God had brought in the Normaines to revenge his anger upon the Englishe[3] and Saxons, which Normaines were accompted the cruellest people in the worlde, [78] for ever when they had brought their enimyes to subjection that they were not able to rebell against them, they commenlye destroyed one another, and so ever excercised their crueltie upon themselves as hit appeared in Englande, Normandy, Apulia, Calaber, Sicilye, and Antiochia, which landes they brought to their subjection. And William appointed and ordeined suche officers that they spoyled the whole lande by color of justice yet he brought the lande in suche awe of him that a childe mighte have caryed golde thrughe the realme openly without dannger of theeves (for all suche offenders lost their handes, and yf any oppressed his neigbor he shulde lose his stonnes). This William leaft England to William Rufus his sonne and Normandy to his eldest sonne Roberte and he gave his treasure to Henry his thirde sonne.

And this yere dyd all the sonnes of Blethyn ap Kynvyn (sometymes Kinge of Wales) gather their streingth together against Rys ap Tewdur, who not beinge able to meet with them [78v] fledde to Irelande and there he gate him selfe great frinds and an army of Irishmen and Scottes to whom he promised great rewardes yf he dyd obteine his kingdome

---

[1] C and the
[2] C 1087
[3] C Angles

and landed in Southwales with thees stranngers. Which when his frendes herde they drewe to him, and the other came in all haste to meete with him[1] thingkinge to fight before his power shulde encrease and at Llechryd they gave him battaill where they lost the victorie, and 2 of the brethrene were slaine, Madoc and Ryryd, and the other fledde and forsake the countrey and when Rys was in quiet possession he sende home his strangers with great rewardes. And at this tyme was the shryne of Saint Davy stolen out of the churche, and all the jewelles and treasure taken awaye and leaft not ferre of. And the Normaines rebelled against their kinge in diverse places at one tyme. For Odo bishop of Bayl, chief governor of England, beganne the rebellion in Kent and burned the Kinges townes. [79] So dyd Roger Earle of Mortymer at Pevenese, Bishop Galfride destroyed Bath and Berklaye, Rogerus dyd his endevor in Norfolke and Suffolk, Hughe in Leycester and Northamptonshire, and the Bishop of Durham was not behinde in his quarters. Likewise the Earles[2] of Hereforde and Shrewisburie with the Welshmen burned all Worcestershire and Glocestershire to the gattes of Worcester Then the Kinge gathered his streingth together and promisinge the people their auncient liberties proceaded towardes his enemyes and firste wanne the castell of Tunbridge, and after beesieged Odon, and Roger Mortymer in the castell of Pevenese sixe weekes, at which tyme his brother Robert came with an armye from Normandy and wolde have landed but he was dryven backe by suche as kept the sea coastes and Odo yelded Pevenese to the Kinge, and promised to departe the lande which he dyd. And afterwarde the Kinge wanne the castell of Rochester, and leade his armye to Durham and toke it and banished all his enimyes the lande. [79v] And this yere 1088 was their a terrible earthquake thrughe all the lande And the yere folowinge dyed Sulyen the godliest and wysest man and the greatest clerke in all Wales at the age 80 yeres and this yere dyd strangers which were rovers upon the seas lande at St. Davyes and robbed hit and burned the towne.

About which tyme dyed Kedyvor the sonne of Kollwyn Prince of Dyved, and his sonnes Llewelyn and his bretheren[3] moved Griffith the sonne of Meredithe to make warre against their lorde and Prince Rys ap Tewdur, and joyninge all their streingth against him came to Llandydoch where Rys was and he gave them battaill and put them to flight and pursued them so sore that he toke Griffith ap Mredith and put him to death, and Enyon sonne to Kedyvor ap Kollwyn fledde to Iestyn lorde of

[1] C – to meet . . . him
[2] C Earle
[3] C bretherne

Morganwc, who rebelled likewise against Rhes ap Tewdur. And they
[80] agreed to be revenged upon Rhes for which purpose Enyon
promised to bringe to their succours an army of Normaines for he had
served in England before and was well knowen there (upon condicioun
that he shulde marye Iestyns daughter which Iestyn graunted). And so
Einon went to Englande and wrought suche meanes that he allured
Roberte Fitzhamon with 12 other knights to make a great armye of
Frenchemen, or Normaines, and to lande in Glamorganshire, where
Iestyn ap Gurgant lord of the lande reaceved them with muche honor
and joyninge his men to them brenned and spoyled the Kings lande and
people, which when hit came to Kinge Rhes his eares, hit greeved him
muche, and upon the sodeine gathered his power, and meette with them
not farre from Breknocke. And ther after a terrible fight was discomfited
and slaine, with whome fill and decayed the kingedome of Southwales.
For this [80v] Rhes had by his wief daughter to Rywalhon ap Kynvyn
but a sone called Griffith, which at his fathers death was but a very childe,
and one Grono that was in the Kinges prison. And thees Normaines,★
after they hade reaceved their promised salarie and great rewards of
Iestyn, returned to their sheppes, and Enyon burthened Iestyn with the
promise to have his daughter, and Iestyn laughed him to scorne and tolde
him he wolde bestowe her otherwise. Where upon Enyon, full of anger
and despite, folowed the Normaines and when he came to the shore they
were all one shipborde and he hovyd to them with his cloke, and they
sent to knowe his meaninge, who went to the cheefest of them
declaringe howe easye hit was for them to wyn that fayre and plesant
countrey from Iestyn, who for his treason to Rhes non other prince of
Wales wolde succor and they were easely persuaded therto, and falsely[1]
and ingratefully turned all [81] their power against hym for whose
defence they hade come thither and at whose hands they had bene well
interteined and reaceved riche giftes and great rewardes. And first they
spoyled him easely of his countrey (as he that mistrusted them not) and
tooke all the fertile and valley grounde to them selves, and leaft him the
barraine and rough mountaines for his parte. And the names of thees 12
that came with Roberte Fitzhamon were these: Londres or London as
the Welshe booke nameth him,★ Stradlinge, Seynt John, Turbevylle,
Grenevylle, Humfrevylle, Seintquintyn, Sore, Sully, Berkeroll, Sywarde
and Flemynge. Also they gave parte of the lande to Einon, and they and
their heirs have enjoied hit to this daye and thees were the first strangers
that ever inhabited Wales sith the tyme of Camber.

[1]C – falsely

And at this tyme William Rufus and Roberte his brother were made
frendes and both togeather came into England and leade an army into
Scottelande against Malcolyn the [81v] Kinge, who had entred
Northumberlande and spoyled hit in the Kings absence and he yelded
himselfe to William and by othe came his vassaill and subjecte. And
William[1] reedified Caerlyle and brought people from the south to
enhabite hit, and shorteley after as Malcolyn returned into Englande,
spoyling the lande, and beinge fought withall was slayne, and his sonne
Edwarde also, and Denecan his sonne, which was pledge with Kinge
William, was crowned in his steede. And this tyme dyd Cadwgan sonne
to Blethyn ap Kynvyn destroy all Dyved in the ende of Aprill and
shortely after the same somer dyd the Normaines in great companie[2]
lande in Dyved or West Wales and Caerdygan and buylded castells their
and begane to inhabite the countrey upon the sea shore. And Roger de
Montgomeryke (to whom the Kinge hade geven the Earledome of
Arundell and Shrosburie) dyd enter Powys lande, and wanne the castell
and towne of Baldwyn, which he fortified [82] and called hit
Montgomerye after his name. And this yere William Rufus dyd goe to
Normandye againste his brother Roberte and sent to England for 30000
fotemen, of which, when they came to the sea shore, the Kinge toke
10s. a peece and returned them home, and he came shortely after and
made a viagee[3] into Northumberlande against the Earle which rebelled
and after he had taken Newe Castell and Bamberough he toke the Earle
at Tynmouth, and returned homewarde. And this yere dyd Griffith ap
Kynan, Kinge of Northwales and chief and onely ruler of all Wales,
wyth Cadwgan ap Blethyn, who ruled Southwales, enter the lande of
Caerdygan and killed a great number of the Normaines (not beinge able
any longer to suffer their great pride, and crueltie). And after ther
returne the captaines send[4] for more men to Englande, and thought
pryvely to make a rod to Northwales, whiche [82v] journey beinge
discovered to Cadwgan he gathered his power and mete with them in
the wood or forest of Yspys, and sette upon them with great hew and
crye. And they defended them selfes manfully, but in the ende they were
commpelled to flee with great losse and Cadwgan folowed the pursute
and spoyled all the countrey of Caerdigan and Dyved, and destroyed all
the castells savinge 2 which were Penbroke and Rydkors which he
coulde not gete and returned to Powis with much joye.

And this yere 1093 dyd the Normaines that inhabited Glamorgan
spoyle the countreys of Gwyr, Kydwely, and Ystradtywy, and leaft them

[1] Ll – William
[2] C compaines
[3] C viaage
[4] C sent

without any inhabiters, and William Rufus, heringe the great slaughter
of his subjectes as well in Cheshire, Shropshire, Worcestershire and
Herefordeshire as within Wales, which Griffith ap Kynan and the sonnes
of Blethyn ap Kynvyn had done, gathered his power togeather and
entred Wales at [83] Montgomery, which castell, lately overthrowe by
the Welshmen, he reedyfied againe. But the Welshmen kept so the
straites of the mountaines with the woodes and the ryvers that the Kinge
dyd no good but lost his labor and his men. Therefore he returned backe
to his great dishonor. And the yere 1094 dyed William the sonne of
Balwyn who had builded the castell of Rydkors by the Kinges
commandement, and after his death the castell was forsaken by his men,
and the inhabitantes of Gwyr, Brechynog, Gwent, and Gwentlhwg cast
of their neckes the burthen of the Normaines that had wonne their
countreyes and held them in subjection and chaced them out of their
countreyes and they returned againe with great streingth of Englishmen
and Normaines. But the countrey men, which abhored their pride and
cruell rule, meete with them at a place called Kelhy Tarvawc,★ and
fought with them manfully and put them to flight and with great
slaughter chaced them backe [83v] againe oute of the lande. Yet for all
this they stayed not, but doublinge their streingth returned againe to
Brekenockeshire mackinge a vow to leave no lyvinge thinge within that
countrey. But it happed¹ otherwise, for the people fledde before them
and at strayts and narrowe passages dyd gall² and kill a great number of
them.

Therefore when they sawe they had all the losse they manned and
vittailled the castelles they had before tyme builded there, and returned
backe. And the sonnes of Idnerth ap Cadwgan, Griffith and Ivor, meette
with them upon the sodeyne at Aberlhech and fill upon them, and slewe
the most parte of them, and the rest escaped to Englande and the
capteines of the castelles defended them manfully and kept them tyll
they were dryven by force to forsake them and to save ther lyves and so
the auncient dwellers enjoyed their countrey quietly. And shortely after
dyd certaine lordes of Northwales as Uchtryd the sonne of Edwyn ap
Grono, and Howell ap Grono, and the children of Cadwgan ap Blethyn
of Powis lande gather a number of men, and passed thrughe [84]
Caerdyganshire to Dyved and spoyled destroyed and burned all the
countrey save³ the castell of Penbroke and returned home with great
butty. The Kinge had geven the lande of Dyved or Westwales to

¹C happened
²C – and narrowe . . . gall
³C savinge

Ernulfe, secunde sonne to Roger Montgomery Earle of Arundell and
Shrosburie, and he had appointed one Geralde stewarde thereof, and he
had geven him the kepinge of the castell of Penbroke. This Geralde,
after the rule of the Welshe lordes, dyd issue out of the castell and
spoyled the lande of St. Davies, and toke many prisoners, and returned
to the castell againe.

And[1] the yere ensuinge William Rufus returninge from Normandy to
Englande, and heringe the great slaughter of his men done by the
Welshmen, gathered all his power, and with greate pompe and pride
entred Wales. But the Britons, fearinge the great streingth of the Kinge,
put their hope onely in the almightie Lorde, turned to him in fastinge
and prayer, and repentaunnce of their sinnes, and he, that never
forsaketh the penitent and contrite herte, herde their prayer, so that the
Normaines and Englishmen durst [84v] never enter the lande but suche
as entred were all slaine and the Kinge returned with small honor after
he hade builte certaine castelles in the Marches. And this yere folowinge
beinge 1096 dyd Hughe de Montgomery, Earle of Arundell and
Shroseburie, which the Welshmen calle Hughe Goch, that is to saye
Hughe the Redheaded, and Hughe Vras or Hughe the Fatte, Earle of
Chester, and a great number of nobles more, gather an huge[2] armye and
entred into Northwales, beinge moved therto by certeine lordes of the
countrey. But Griffith ap Kynan the Prince and Cadwgan ap Blethyn
toke the hilles and mountaines for their defence because they were not
able to meette with the earles nor durst not well trust to their owne
men. And so the earles cam over against the Ile of Mone or Anglesey
wher they dyd builte a castell at Aberlhiennauc. Then dyd Griffith and
Cadwgan goo to Anglesey thinkinge to defende the Ile and send for
succoures to Irelande and reaceved very small. Then dyd treasone appere
[85] for Owen ap Edwyn (who was the Princes cheef counsaill, and his
father in lawe, for Griffith had maryed Yngharad his daughter, and also
Owens wief was Ewerydh verch Kynvyn aunte to Cadwgan) was the
chief caller of the strangers, and there openlye went with all his power to
them and leade them to the Ile of Anglesey which, when Griffith and[3]
Cadwgan sawe, they[4]* sayled to Irelande mistrustinge the treason of
their owne people. And the Earles spoyled the Ile and slewe suche as
they founde their. And at the same tyme was Magnus sonne to Harolde
with a number of shippes hoveringe upon the seas thinkinge to lande in
some parte of Englande, and by channce[5]* wolde have landed in Mone

[1]C – the castell . . . And   [4]C he
[2]Ll hugy   [5]C – to lande . . . by chance
[3]C ap

but the Earles kept them frome the lande. And ther Magnus with an arrowe stroke Hughe Earle of Shroseburie in the face that he dyed thereof and sodeinly eather parte forsoke the Ile and the Englishemen returned to Englande and leaft Owen ap Edwyn prince in the lande, who hade allured them thither.

[85v] And the yere 1098 returned Griffith ap Kynan and Cadwgan ap Blethyn frome Irelande, and made peace with the Normaines and gave them parte of their inheritannce, for Griffith remained in Mone, and Cadwgan had Cardygan and apece of Powis lande, and the men of Breknoke slewe Llewelyn the sonne of Cadwgan, and Howell ap Ithell of Tegengill went to Irelande. And Rychmarch Bishop of St. Davies (sonne to Sulyen Bishop) dyed the godliest wisest and greatest clerke that had bene in Wales many yeres before (savinge his father) who had brought him up, and a great number moe of learned disciples.

And William Rufus* after he hade walled the towne of London, and builded Westmynster hall, went to Normandye and after he hade brought all the countreye to his subjection returned home and was slaine with an arrowe by Walter Tyrell as he shotte at a stagge in the Newe Forest. And Henry his brother was crowned in his steede for Robert the elder brother was all [86] this while in the Holy Lande, but shortely returned and landed at Portesmouth. And Henry came against him with great power but they were agreed upon condicioun that Henry shulde paye yerely to Robert 3000 marces and the longest lyver shulde bee the others heire. This Henrye maryed Mawd, Malcolyns daughter of Scotteland of Margaret daughter to Edwarde sonne to Edmunde Ironside. And this yere dyed Hughe Earle of Chester and Richard[1] his sonne* was made Earle in his place, and this yere dyed Grono ap Cadwgan, and Gwyn ap Griffith. And in the yere 1101 dyd Robert de Belesmo, sonne to Roger de Montgomerye Earle of Shroseburie, and Ernulph his brother Earle of Penbroke rebelle against the Kinge, which when the Kinge herde, he sent for them to come to him, and they made blinde excuses, and gathered their strength and fortified their castelles and they gave riche giftes and made great promises to the sonnes of Blethyn ap Kynvyn, Jerwerth or Edward, Cadwgan and Meredith and entised them to joyne their powers to theirs. [86v] And Roberte fortified foure castelles, Arundell, Tekingill,* Shrosburie [and] Brugge, which was the cause of the warre, for Roberte had builded hit without the Kinges leave and Ernulph fortified his castell of Penbroke, and then

---

[1]C Roger, *above in another hand* Richard;
   HC Richard; Ll Roger, corrected in text
   to Richard

they entred the Kinges lande, and burned, and spoyled and caryed away riche buttyes. And Ernulph to have more streingth sent Geralde his steewarde to Murkard Kinge of Irelande to desire his daughter in mariage which he obteined with promises of great succours which dyd encourage him the more against the Kinge. And then the Kinge gathered a great army, and first besieged the castell of Arundell, and wanne hit, and likewise he dyd with Tekingill, and afterwarde leade his power before Brugge, which for the situation and depth of the diches, being also well manned and vyttailled, the Kinge doubted the speedye wynninge therof. Wherfore he was counsailled to send pryvely to Ierwerth ap Blethyn promisenge him great giftes, yf he wolde forsake the Earle and serve him and also [87] remembringe what wronges the Earles father Roger and his brother Hughe had done to the Welshmen. And the Kinge gave him all the lands the Earle had in Wales without tribute or othe, which was a peece of Powis, Caerdygan, and halfe Dyved, and the other half hade the sonne of Balwyn with Ystradtywy and Gwyr. And Ierwerth receaved thees offers joyousely, and commynge him self to the Kinge he sent his power to the Earles lande, which doinge their masters commaundement destroyed and spoyled all the countrey, for the Earle had caused his people to convey all their cattell and goodes to Wales not remembringe the mischeefe the Welshemen had reaceved at his fathers and brothers handes. And when thees newes came to the Earle, and to Cadwgan and Meredith, Ierwerthes bretherene, they were all dismayed and despayred to be able to withstande the Kinge, for Ierwerth was the greatest man [87v] off power in Wales. And in this tyme was Ernulph gone to Irelande for his wief and succours and also a litle before had Magnus againe landed in Mon (and reaceved of Griffith ap Kynan) [and] hewyd downe as muche tymber woode as was needfull for him and returninge to Man, which he had wonne, builded three castelles their, and sent to Irelande to have the daughter of Murcarde in maryagee[1] to his sonne, which hee obteined and made his sonne Kinge of Man. And Earle Roberte heringe this sent to him for helpe, but he reaceved non.[2] Therefore seinge no remedy he sent to the Kinge, desiringe him he might forsake the realme, which the Kinge graunted, and he sayled to Normandye and likewise the Kinge sent woorde to his brother Ernulph, that ether he shulde folowe his brother, and departe the lande, or yelde him selfe to the Kinges mercye and pleasure, but he chose to departe the lande, and so he dyd.

[1]C mariage   [2]C none

And after this the Kinge returned home. Ierwerth [88] toke his brother Meredith, and sent him to the Kinges prison, for his brother Cadwgan agreed with him and Ierwerth gave him Cardigan,⋆ and a peece of Powis and Ierwerth him self came to the Kinges courte to remember the Kinge of his promise. But the Kinge when he sawe all quiet forgate the service of Ierwerth and his owne promise and contrarye to his promise toke Dyved from Ierwerth, and gave hit a knight called Saer, and Ystradtywy, Kydwely, and Gwyr he gave to Howell ap Grono, and Ierwerth was sent home emptie handed. And this yere dyed Grono the sonne of Rhes ap Tewdur in prison. And at this tyme Magnus sonne of Harolde entred the countrey of Lenoux in Scottelande, and after he hade goten a great praye returned to his shippes but the inhabitants pursued him so harde that they put his people to flight and slewe him and rescowed their goodes and cattell. And in the ende of this yere dyd the Kinge sende dyverse of his counsaill to Shrowisburie and willed Ierwerth ap Blethyn to [88v] come meete with them there to consulte about the Kinges busines and affaires. And when he came thither all the consultacioun was against him, and against all right and equitie they condemned him of treason because the Kinge fearyd his streingth and that he wolde avenge[1] the wrongs he had receaved at the Kinges hande and so they commytted him to prison.

And this yere beinge 1103 dyed Owen ap Edwyn after great miserie and longe sickenes, and Richarde (the sonne of Baldwyn) dyd fortifie the castell of Rydcorse, and chaced Howell ap Grono oute of the countrey to whome the Kinge had geven the custodie thereof, but he shortely after returned and burned all the countre, houses, corne, and heye, and slewe a great number of the Normaines as they returned homewarde and kept all the countrey in his subiection, excepte the castells and their garrysons. And at this tyme dyd the Kinge take the rule of Dyved from Saer to whom he had committed hit and gave hit to Geralde [89] who had bene sometymes steewarde there under Ernulph. And the Normaines which were in the castell of Rydcors and other castelles their aboutes seinge they colde not have the overhande of Howell ap Grono in open fight, they fill to their accustomed practise of treason and so atchived the purpose in this maner. There was one Gwgan ap[2] Meyryg, who had norished a sonne to Howell ap Grono, and therefore very well trusted and loved of him, as the maner of Wales is. This traytor (beinge corrupted by the Normaines) procured his

---

[1]C revenge   [2]Ll and

masters deathe, for he badde him one night to his house, whether[1] he came gentlye, and Gwgan sent the garrisons of the castells woorde therof and in they dawninge of the day they entred the towne and came aboute the house, and gave a great shoute, wherwith Howell awoke and coragiousely lepte out of his bedde, and sought his weapons, but the traytor Gwgan had conveyde them awaye when he was asleepe. Then he called for his men but they were all fledde to save their lyves and as he wolde have gotten awaye he was taken [89v] by Gwgan and his company and strangled, and his body delyvered to the Normaines who cut of his heade and brought hit to the castell of Rydcors and this traytorouse murther of the Kinges Lieftenannt was leaft unpunished. For what faulte the Normaines committed, whatsoever hit was, was alwayes wynked at and yf the Welshmen dyd never so litle offende the lawes of [the] Kinge hit was thought an henyouse fault which was the cause that afterwarde they rebelled against the Kinge, who sought nothinge but their utter destruction.

And about this tyme dyd Anselme Archebishop of Canterburie call a Synode at London where amonge other thinges hit was ordeined that priests shulde not marrye, which was not before forbidden in Britaine and to some hit seemed very clenly and honest, and to other hit was thought perilouse and daungerouse, lest by[2] seekinge to be to cleane and honest (as they termed hit) they shulde fall into horrible unclenlynesse and dishonesty abhominable to a Christen manne[3] and [90] this was 1100 and odde yeres after the Incarnnacioun of Christ.

And Henrie, the 5th yere of his reigne, sayled with a great power to Normandy and ther his brother Roberte with Roberte de Blesmo,[4] Ernulf [and] William Earle of Mauritania gave him battaill, where the Kinge hade the victorie and toke the Duke his brother and William de Mauretania prisoners, and caryed them to Englande, and committed them to perpetuall prison, where he caused his brothers eies to bee put out. And shortely after dyed Edgar Kinge of Scottes and Alexander his brother was crowned in his place by consent of Kinge Henrie. And Meyryg and Griffith sonnes to Trahayarne ap Caradoc were both slaine by Owen sonne to Cadwgan ap Blethyn. And Meredith ap Blethyn brake the prison where he had been longe tyme, and came home, and gote his owne enheritaunce againe and enioyed hit quietly. And the yere 1108 dyd the rage of the sea overflowe, and drowne a great parte of the lowe countrey of Flanders [90v] that the inhabitantes were dryven to

[1] C whyther
[2] C they
[3] Ll name
[4] C Belesmo

seeke them selves other dwellinge places, and came to Kinge Henrie and desired him to geve them some voyde place to remaine in. And he very liberall of that which was not his owne gave them the lande of Rose[1] in Dyved, or Westwales, where Penbroke, Tenby and Haverforde are nowe builte and they remayne there to this day and hit may well be perceaved by their speeche and condiciouns ferre differinge from the rest of the counntrey. And then dyd Geralde steewarde builde againe the castell of Penbroke in a place called Kengarth Vechan, and brought thither all his householde stuffe, and other goodes[2] with his wief and his children.

And this tyme dyd Cadwgan ap Blethyn make a greate feast at Christmas and bidde all the lords of the countrey to his house in Dyved amonge whome came Owen his sonne and he beinge [91] at his fathers house hearde the beautie of Nest, wief to Geralde stewarde of Penbroke, praysed above all the women in the lande, and therefore being desirouse to see her came thither with afewe under the color of frendship, for Gwladus, wief to Rhes ap Tewdur, and mother to Nest, was daughter to Rhywalhon ap Kynvyn and cosine germaine to Cadwgan, father to Owen, and so they were cosines. And findinge trueth to surmmont the rumour he came home all enflammed with love of the woman and returninge that night with a sorte of wilde companions, entred the castell pryvely, and compassed the chamber about, and sette the house one fyer wherwith Geralde and his wief awooke, and wolde have issued out to knowe what that noyse ment, but his wief fearinge some treason stayed him and counsailled him to goe to the pryvey and pullinge up the borde she helped him out that waye. And then [91v] she came to the dore of the chamber,[3] and sayed ther was nowe but she and her children, and they entred in and sought all about and when they colde not finde him they toke her, and her twoe sonnes and a sonne and a daughter borne by a concubyne to Geralde, and caryed them awaye to Powys and burned the castell, and spoyled all the countrey. And when Cadwgan herde this he was very sorye, and feared the Kinges displeasure, and went to Powis, and willed his sonne to sende home to Geralde his wief and children with his goods, but Owen in nowise wolde departe with the woman, yet at her requeste he sent to Geralde his children againe. And when Richarde Bishop of London (whom the Kinge hade appointed president of the Marches) beinge at Shroseburie, herde this, he was very sore offended, and sendd[4] for Ithell and Madoc (the sonnes

[1] C Rost
[2] C goods
[3] C the chamber dore
[4] C sent

of Ryryd ap Blethyn) to him, and promised them riche giftes, and great
rewardes, besides the rule of the whole [92] countrey, yf they colde take
or kill Owen to revenge the dishonor he hade done to the Kinge, and to
them added Lhywarch the sonne of Trehayarne ap Gwyn (whose two
bretherne Owen had slaine) and Uchtryd the sonne of Edwyn, and thees
foure promised the bishop to bringe him Owen and his father either
alyve or dead and furthwith gathered their power to destroye the whole
countrey. But Uchtryd send pryvey woorde before, that all suche of the
people as wolde have their lyves saved to come to him and when the
countrey herde this some fledde to Arwystly, some to Melyenydh, some
to Ystradtywy, and some to Dyved, where Geralde was destroinge the
countrey. And at that tyme dyd Wa[l]ter Bishop of Glocester★ by the
kinges commission gather an armye to defende Caermerdhyn and mette
with such as fledde to Arwystly, and Melyenydh, and destroyed a great
number of them. Those that went to Ystradtywy [92v] were gently
reaceved by Meredith ap Rytherch, and Uchtryd saved all suche as came
to him and so thees foure came with their powers to the castell of
Rydcors,★ and thought best to have entred the countrey by night, and
to take Cadwgan and Owen his sonne unawarres,[1] but Uchtryd
dissuaded them from that, and thought hit danngerouse to enter the
countrey by night for ferde of embushmentes, and counsailled them to
enter in the light with their men in good order. And in the meane while
Cadwgan and Owen gate a shippe at Aberystwyth[2] which was lately
come from Ireland with changes, and escaped awaye and the daye after,
when they entred into the lande, they founde none of them that they
sought. Therefore puttinge all the faulte upon Uchtryd they burned and
spoyled all the countrey savinge the sainctuaryes of Padarn and
Llanddewi Brevi yet they tooke dyverse men out of those places and
[93] caryed them prisoners to their countreys and then returned to their
owne castelles againe.

And Owen with suche as had bene with him at the burninge of the
castell fled to Irelande to Kinge Murcarde who reaceved him joyousely,
for he had bene there before, in the tyme of the warre of the twoe Earles
in Anglesey, or Mone, and had brought the Kinge riche giftes from
Wales. And Cadwgan kepte himself pryvely in Powis and send to the
Kinge to declare his innocencie and the Kinge was content he shulde
remaine in the countrey, and enjoye the towne and landes that he had
by his wief, for she was daughter to a lorde of Normandy called Pygod
de Say. And Madoc and Ithell his twoe nevewes devided suche landes as

[1]C unawares   [2]BT, Pen20; RBH, Aberdyfi, HC Aberystwyth

he and his sonne Owen had in Powys betwixt them, and ruled hit very evyll for they colde never agree amonge them [93v] selves. Yet dyd Cadwgan make suche frends to the Kinge painge 100^{li} fyne [that] he shulde enjoye againe his landes in Caerdygan, and that the inhabitantes shulde returne againe to their houses and till the grounde, for the Kinge had geven commaundement,[1] that no man Welshman nor Norman shulde dwell within Caerdygan. And when they that were in Irelande understoode this, they returned home prively, and hyde themselves in their cosins houses. And shortely after Owen came to Wales but not to Caerdygan (for his father had reaceved that lande upon suche condicioun, that he shulde not suffer Owen to come therin, not succor him with ether counsaill, money nor men), but he came to Powys, and wolde fayne have sent messingers to the Kinge, but he culde finde no man that durst speake for him. And at this tyme fill their a variance betwixt Madoc [94] ap Ryryd and the Kinges president for certaine fellons of Inglande that had fledde to him for succor. And the bishop sent for them, but Madocke refused to delyver them, wherefore the president was sore offended with him and he understandinge that sent to Owen and desired his frendship whose greatest enemye he was before. And they were made frendes and swore either to other, that none of them shulde betraye the other, and that none of theim shulde by himself agree with the Kinge or with his officers. And therupon they burned and spoyled the landes of suche as they loved not and destroyed all thinges that they mette with all.

And this tyme dyd the Emmproure Henrie send his embassador to entreat of a mariage with Mawde daughter to Kinge Henrye and had her to his wief. And shortelye after the kinge banished and disherited Philip de Brus, William Mallet, and William Baynarde, and put to deathe the Earle of Mayne and there appeared a terrible comete. [94v] And this yere the Kinge remembred Ierwerth ap Blethyn, whome he had kept longe in prison, and sent to knowe of him what fyne he wolde paye to have his libertie and he promised the Kinge 300^{li} or the worthe therof in cattell or horses and the Kinge sette him at libertie, and gave him his lande againe and gave 100^{li} of that money to Henrie sonne to Cadwgan by the daughter of Pygod. And all this while were Owen and Madocke burninge and spoylinge the Englishmen and Normaines, and ever withdrew themselves to the landes of Ierwerth, which greved him greatly. And therfore he send[2] them woorde, and desired them to forsake his lande and Cadwgans land, for yf hit were knowen that they

---

[1] C comaundement   [2] C sent

came in any of theirs, the lande was forfecte to the Kinge. And they
heringe this used his countrey more often then they were wonte and
Ierwerth seinge that chaced them out of his countrey and they went [95]
to the countrey of Uchtryd in Meryonydhshire, and the sonnes of
Uchtryd send¹ worde to their people to kepe them out of their countrey
and so they did. For meetinge them by the waye they sette upon them
and Owen and Madocke defended them selves manfullye but at the last
they and their men fledde, Owen to Caerdygan to his fathers counntrey,
and Madocke to Powis and Owen with his companions made diverse
rodes to Dyved, and spoyled the countrey and caryed away the men and
cattell to the shippes that they came in from Irelande, and after ransomed
them, and gathered a great number to him, and sette upon a towne of
Fleminges, and burned hit and spoyled, and slewe all the people² and
returned to Caerdigan nothinge esteminge his fathers danger nor the
Kinges displeasure.

   And this time³ hit chaunced that Owens men amonge other
mischieffes layde wayte for a [95v] bishop that was towardes the Kinge
whose name was William de Brabant and slewe him, and all his men.
And hit chanced that Ierwerth and Cadwgan were this tyme at the court
to speake with the Kinge, concerninge certaine busines of their owne
and beholde, as the Kinge talked with them, there came in a Fleminge,
brother to the deade bishop, and he made an exclamacioun howe Owen
ap Cadwgans men had slaine his brother and a great number moe, and
howe they were succoured in Cadwgans lande, and the Kinge beinge
therewith sore offended⁴ asked Cadwgan what he coulde saye to the
matter, and he puttinge all the faulte in his sonne excused him self as
well as he coulde. Then saide the Kinge, Cadwgan, seinge thowe canst
not kepe thine owne lande, but that thy sonne and his compannions
shalbe reaceved and succoured therin, I will geve hit one that will kepe
him out and I will keep thee at [96] my charges all thy lief charginge
thee, upon thy allegyannce, thou enter not within Wales untill suche
tyme as I have taken further order. And so the kinge gave him 26
adaye⁵★ and lette him·at libertie to goe whither he woulde savinge to
Wales. And when Owen and Madocke herde this they went to Irelande
and the Kinge furthwith sent for Gilberte the sonne of Richarde
Strangebowe Earle of Strigill, which was a noble man, and a chivalrouse
knight, to whome the Kinge sayde this: Thowe hast bene diverse tymes

¹C sent
²C – and spoyled . . . people
³Ll – time; *supplied from HC*

⁴C displeased
⁵C 20 dayes

a suter to mee to have some landes in Wales, and nowe I geve thee all
the landes and enheritannce of Cadwgan ap Blethyn, wynne hit and take
hit.[1] Gilbert reaceved hit joyfullye and thanked the Kinge and gathered
all the power he might, and landed in Caerdiganshire and brought hit to
his subjection without any contradiction, then he builded twoe [96v]
fayre[2] castelles there one towardes Northwales upon the ryver Ystwyth
at the sea shore a myle from Llanbadarne, and an other towards Dyved,
upon the ryver Tyvi at a place called Dyngereynt, where Roger
Montgomery had began a castell before tyme. And shortely after
Madoke the sonne of Ryryd returned from Ireland as he[3] coulde not
awaye with the maner and condiciouns of the Irishmen, and Madocke
came to the countre of his uncle Ierwerth, and he heringe this and
fearinge to lose his lande, as his brother Cadwgan had done, made
proclamacioun that no man shulde be a meane for him but take him as
his enimye, which when Madocke had herde he gathered to him a
number of unthriftes and outlawes and kept him selfe in the rockes and
woodes, and cast to be revenged upon Ierwerth by any way that he
colde invent and entred frendship [97] pryvely with Llywarch ap
Trahayarn who hated Ierwerth to the death. And havinge knowledge
that Ierwerth laye one night at Caerenyon gathered all their streingth
and came aboute the house at midnight and Ierwerth and his men
awooke and defended the house manfully untill their foes sette feire[4] on
the house which, when Ierwerthes men sawe, every one shifted for
himself. For some escaped thrughe the feire, and the rest were ether
brent, or slaine or bothe and Ierwerth, seinge no remedie, adventured
rather to bee slaine than[5] burned and came out but his enimyes reaceved
him upon sharpe speares and overthrewe him in the fier, and so dyed a
cruell death. As soone as the Kinge understoode this he called Cadwgan
beffore him and gave him his brothers lande, which was Powys, and
promised his pardon to Owen and willed his father to send for him to
Irelande. [97v]

Nowe when Madock sawe his other uncle Cadwgan rule the
counntre, he hidde himself in roughe and deserte places. And addinge
one mischief upon an other determined also to murther him by one
waye or other. Therefore after Cadwgan had put the countrey in good
quiet, and sawe righte and justice ministred therin, havinge ever an eie
and respecte to the Kinge, he came to the Tralhung (nowe called Poole)
and the ealders of the countrey with him and, mindinge to dwell there,

[1] Ll – hit   [4] C fyer
[2] C fyne   [5] Ll or
[3] Ll + that

began to buylde a castell. And Madocke pretendinge nothinge but
mischief heringe this, came sodenlye upon him, and Cadwgan thinkinge
no hurte was slaine before he coulde eyther fyght or flee. And Madocke
sent streight to the Bishop of London, the Kinges Lyeftennte at
Shrosburie, and prayed him to remember what he had promised him
before tyme [98] when he chaced Owen out of the lande, for the Bishop
hated Owen and Cadwgan, and gave Madocke all suche landes as had
bene his brothers Ithell. Nowe Meredith sonne of Blethyn heringe the
deathe of bothe his bretherne spedde him selfe to the Kinge, desiringe of
him the landes of Ierwerth which Cadwgan had lately had. And the
Kinge gave him the rule therof untill suche tyme as Owen sonne to
Cadwgan was come frome Irelande who came shortelye after, and went
to the Kinge, and the Kinge receaved him to his peace and gave him his
landes. And Owen promised to the Kinge a great fyne and gave pledges
to paye hit. Likewise dyd Madocke fyne to the Kinge for his peace and
landes but the Kinge bidde him take heed of the kinffolke of suche as he
had murthered upon his perill. [98v]

And this yere 1111 was Roberte de Belesmo taken by the Kinge in
Normandy and committed to perpetuall prison in Warram, to gentill a
punishment for so cruell and bloodthursty a man, as he was, for all his
delite was therin, in so much that he putte out bothe the eies of his
owne childe with his thumbes for a pastime, as the boye played under
his gowne. And the yere 1112 Meredith ap Blethyn send a number of
his men to make a rode into the counntre of Llywarch ap Trehayarn ap
Gwyn, who was Meredith and Owens enimye, as he that succoured
Madocke to kyll his[1] uncles Ierwerth and Cadwgan, Meredithes
bretherne. And as thees men passed thrughe the counntrey of Madocke
in the night, they meette with one of Madockes men, and toke him, and
examined him where his master was, and he said he coulde not tell, but
beinge put in feare of death [99] he confessed that he was not ferre from
thence. Therefore they lay quietly there all the night, and in the
dawninge they came sodenly upon Madocke and his men and slewe a
great number of them and toke him prisoner and brought him to their
lorde, and he was right gladde thereof, and put him in saffe pryson tyll
he had sent woorde to his nevewe Owen, who came thither streight,
and Meredith delyverid Madocke to him. And Owen, remembringe the
frendeship and othe that had bene betwixt them twoe before tyme,
wolde not kill him althoughe he had slaine Owens father his owne
uncle, but put out both his eies and lette him goe and devyded his landes

[1]C + own

with his uncle Meredith, which was Caerenyon, Eberiw,[1] and the thyrde parte of Deydhwr.

And the yere folowinge Kinge Henrye [99v] prepared an armye againste Wales, beinge therto instigated by suche as wolde have the Welshmens landes, that was Gilberte Strangebowe Earle of Strigill, to whom the Kinge had geven Caerdygan, for he made sore complaintes upon Owen ap Cadwgan, howe he reaceved and maintained suche as robbed and spoyled in his countrey. And also Hughe Earle of Chester sayed no lesse by Griffith ap Kynan Prince of Northwales, and howe his men and the men of Grono ap Owen ap Edwyn Lorde of Tegengle spoyled and brenned the countrey of Chester and howe Griffith dyd nether owe service nor paye any tribute to the Kinge, wherefore the Kinge sware he wolde not leave one lyvinge creature in Northwales and Powis lande, but destroye the lande [100] utterly and put in newe inhabitantes and departed his army into three partes. And the leadinge of the first he gave to Gilberte Earle of Strigill, wherin was the whole power of all the fourth parte of Englande and Cornwaill against Southwales. The leadinge of the secunde had Alexander Kinge of[2] Scottelande and Hughe Earle of Chester and there was the power of Scottelande and the north, and they went against Northwales. And the Kinge leade the thirde himself wherein was the streingth of meedell Englande. And Meredith ap Blethyn heringe this came and yelded himselfe to the Kinge.

And Owen with his power fledde to Griffith ap Kynan to Northwales. Therefore the Kinge turned all his streingth that way and came him self as farre as Murcastell and the Kinge of Scottes [100v] as farre as Pennant Bachwy, but the people fledde to the mountaines and woodes, and caryed all their vyttailles and cattaill with them so that the Kinge coulde not folowe them, and suche as entred the landes were ether slaine or galled in the straytes. Then dyd the Scottishe Kinge sende to the Prince to come and yelde to the Kinge, and promised him the Kinges peace, but he was acquainted with suche promises and wolde not. And the Kinge, because he wolde not returne without doinge of somethinge, sent to Owen to come to him and to forsake the Prince, which was not able to defende himself but was ready to make peace with the Scottishe Kinge and the Earle of Chester. Yet for all this Owen wolde not truste the Kinge, untill suche tyme as his uncle Meredith came frome the Kinge to him and counsailed him not to forsake the Kinge of Englandes [101] offer, but to trust his promise and to macke

[1] C Y Beriw   [2] Ll – of

haiste, before the Prince agreed with the Kinge, who offered him all his landes without tribute. And Owen heringe this came to the Kinge and the Kinge receaved him thankefully, and toulde him that because he had trusted the Kinges woorde and promise, he wolde not onely performe that, but also exalte him above all his kinne and geve him his lande without tribute. And likewise the Prince, heringe of this, sende to the Kinge to have his peace, which because the Kinge coulde not come by him he obteined for a great some of money.

And the Kinge returned to Englande, and sayed to Owen, yf thowe wilt folowe mee to Normandy and serve me[1] I will performe all my promises with thee and make thee knight, and Owen dyd so and obteined all his desire at the Kinges hande at his returne from Normandy the yere folowinge. [101v] And at this tyme dyed Griffri Bishop of Menevia, and the Kinge made one Benarde, a Normaine, bishop in his place contrarye to the mindes of all the clergie of Wales, which were ever accustomed to chose there bishop. And at the same tyme was ther a talke thrughe Southwales of Griffith the sonne of Rhes ap Tewdur, which for feare of the Kinge had bene of a childe broughte up in Irelande, and had come over twoe yeres passed, which tyme he hade spent with his frendes and affines pryvely, as with Geralde Steewarde of Penbroke his brother in lawe, and others. And at the last he was accused to the Kinge, that he entended to have[2] the kingdome of Southwales as his father had enjoyed hit which was nowe in the Kinges handes, and that all the countrey hoped of libertie thrughe him. Therfore the Kinge sent to take him, but Griffith ap Rhes heringe this sent to [102] Griffith ap Kynan Prince of Northwales desiringe him of his ayde, and that he might remaine safely within his countrey, which he graunted, and reaceved him joyously for his fathers sake.

And when the kinge herde this he sent gentill letters to the prince desiringe him to come and speake with him which Griffith ap Kynan dyd. And the Kinge received him honourably, gave him riche giftes and precious jewelles after the usage of the Normaines when they entende to committe some treasone. And afterwardes talked with him of Griffith ap Rhes, and promised him mountaines of golde to sende him or his headde to the Kinge the which Griffith beinge deceaved with the fayre woordes of the Kinge promised to doe and returned home joyfully. And Griffith ap Rhes, Howell his brother (who had bene ever sith his fathers death kept in strayt prison by Ernulph Earle of Penbroke) had counsaill [102v] geven them to gette them out of the waye awhile, till they

---

[1] Ll – to Normandy, and serve me   [2] C – to have

understoode what the Prince wolde doe, for they suspected the Kinges
message, and so they dyd. And the Prince enquired for Griffith ap Rhes,
and learned wher he was, and sent horsemen for him to bringe him to
his courte, and as they came towardes the house, where he was, Griffith
had warninge, and with muche adoe escaped to the churche of
Aberdaron, and toke Sainctuarie there. And they returned and declared
hit to the Prince and he commaunded him to be pulled out by force, but
the clergie of the whole countrey withstoode that, and defended the
liberties of the churche and at night some (that pityed to see that yonge
innocent to be sought, as a lambe to the slaughter) conveyed him awaye
out of Northwales to Ystradtywi in Southwales, where he was
compelled for savinge his owne [103] lief to rebelle againste the Kinge
and to gather all the power he coulde to him, and to macke warre
against the Flemings and Normaines.

    And the yere insuinge 1116 dyd Griffith ap Rhes gather his power
and layed siedge to a castell that was over against Arberth, and wonne
hit, and made hit plaine with the grounde. Then he came before the
castell of Richarde de Pwns at Lhanymdhyfri (to whome the Kinge hade
geven Cantref Bychan) and wolde have burned the castell, but Meredith
ap Rytherch ap Caradoc, Richardes Lieftente, and the garryson
defended hit manfully. Yet Griffith burned the utterwarde and slewe
many of the garryson and likewise lost many of his owne men, and
returned without profytte. And furtherwith he came to Abertawy and
laye[1] siedge to the castell which Henrie Beaumont, Earle of Warwike,
[103v] had builte, and likewise burned the utterwarde, and the courte
house, and destroyed the countrey to Ystradtywy, where there drewe to
him a great number of wilde younge men from every place, that he
begane to waxe stronge, and made rodes into Rose and Dyved, and
spoyled and robbed all the countrey. Wherefore the Normaines and
Flemings consulted howe to remedye this and called to them all suche as
were the Kinges frends and lordes in the countrey, as Owen ap
Rytherch and Rytherch ap Tewdur, and his sonnes Meredith and
Owen, whose mother was Honydh daughter to Blethyn ap Kynvyn, and
Owen ap Caradoc, whose mother was Gwenlhian also daughter to
Blethyn ap Kynvyn, and Meredith ap Rytherch and asked them[2]
whether they were true and faythfull to the Kinge of Englande. And
they saide they were. If[3] youe bee, sayed they, youe moste kepe and
defende [104] the Kinges castell of Caermardhyn and that after this

¹C layede   ³Ll And
²C – them

maner. Firste Owen ap Caradock shall kepe hit a fortenight, and
Rytherch ap Tewdur and his sonnes an other fortenight, and Meredith
ap Rytherch the thyrde fortenight, and so by course, and they were
content so to doe. And Owen toke upon him the kepinge of the castell,
and the castell of Roberte Courtemayn in Abercomyn or Aberkorram
was committed to Blethyn vab Kedivor.

And shortely after Griffith ap Rhes sende spyes to understande the
state of Caermardhyn and the castell and brought him good tydinges.
Therefore he came with his power sodeinly upon the towne, and gave a
great shoute and Owen ap Caradock which kept hit ranne to the place
wher the shoute was geven, thinkinge his men wolde have folowed
him, but the most parte of them fledde, and Owen [104v] was slaine
fightinge manfully, and the towne wonne and destroyed all save the
castell which escaped very evyll. And Griffith returned to his
accustomed place with great spoyle and buttyn and upon this drewe
unto him a great number of lustie yonge men, and served him,
thinkinge that all was his. And he went to Gwyr and wonne a castell and
brent hit and William de Londres forsoke his castell, and fledde with his
men. But Griffith destroyed the castell and caryed awaye all the cattaill
and spoyle of the countrey. And when the men of Caerdigan herde this,
they sent for Griffith, chosinge him rather to bee their headde and ruler,
beinge their cosine and countreyman, than any other. And thither he
came beinge well reaceved of Kedyvor ap Grono and Howell ap Idnerth
and Trahayarn ap Ithell, for they had [105] forsaken Dyved, and left hit
full of Normaines, Flemynges and Englishmen. And likewise there were
many strangers in Caerdigan, and ruled the countrey, but yet the people
hated them, not yet forgettinge the wronges they had reaceved at their
handes, althoughe Henrie Kinge of Englande hade brought them all to
his subjection, some by force, some by banishment, and some by giftes
and rewardes. And Griffith beinge nothinge dismayed with this, but
boldly came to Caerdygan Iscoet, and layde siedge to a stronge holde,
which Earle Gilberte[1] and the Fleminges had builde at Blaen Porth
Gwydhan. And after longe fight, and diverse assaultes with the slaughter
of dyverse within, and but one of his men, they brenned the towne, and
brought the countrey to his subjection. [105v] And all the strangers
fledde away and left there houses, which the Welshmen brenned and
destroyed all to Penwedic. And there they assaulted the castell in
Ystradpychilh,[2] which was Rauffe Earle Gilbertes steewarde, and gotte

[1] C + Strangbow of Strigill *above line in*   [2] C Ystradpychdh
another hand

hit and slewe the men that were within. And frome thens they camped at Glascrug a myle from Llanbadarn and there they dyd wronnge to the churche, for they toke out some of the cattaill to vittaill themselves that were within the compasse of the Saintuarie. And they entended to laye siedge to the castell of Aberystwyth the daye folowinge, and Raffe steewarde, heringe that, sende pryvelye to the castell of Ystradmeyryg (whiche Gilberte hade builte) for succors which he reaceved by night. And Griffith came towardes the castell the daye folowinge out of all order for they feared nothinge, and dyd nott understande what [106] number of men was within. And the castell standeth upon a hill, and the ryver betwixt them and the castell with a bridge to passe over, where they stayed and consulted concerninge makinge of engines to assault hit till hit was[1] eveninge. At which tyme the Normaines (seinge there misorder) sent archers to the ryver syde to skyrmish with them, to entise the Welshmen to the bridge, that the armed horsemen might sodeinly yssue furth[2] upon the naked footemen. And the Welshmen approched neere to the bridge and skyrmished with them, and sodeinly yssued furth one horseman and wolde have passed the bridge but his horse was wounded with a pyke and begane to fayle, and as he returned to the fotemen he fill of his horse, and the Welshmen pursued him over the bridge. And when the Englishmen sawe that, they fledde towardes the castell, and the Welshmen [106v] folowed to the hill toppe, and sodeinlye the ambushe of horsemen that laye under the hill thrust betwixt them that had passed over and the bridge, and they that fledde turned bake with more streingth and so they were compassed about one either parte, and the bridge so kept that no rescowes coulde come to them, and slaine all for the most parte, for they were all naked men. And the rest, seinge the great number of men armed which they looked not for, turned backe and departed the countrey.

And when the Kinge herde all those murthers and spoyles he sent for Owen ap Cadwgan to him, to whom when he came the Kinge sayed, Owen I have founde thee true and faythfull unto mee, therefore I desire thee to take or kill that theeffe [107] and murtherer* Griffith ap Rhes, that doth so trouble my lovinge subjects. For I assure thee my cheeffe truste is in thee and in Lhywarch ap Trehayarn who shall goe with thee. And youe twoe shall wayte upon my sonne Roberte, whom I will shortlye sende against that traytor with an armye and looke howe thowe servest mee at this tyme, so will I recompence thee without fayle. And Owen was wonnderfull gladde that the Kinge put confidence in him,

1C were   2C out

and called his men,[1] and encouraged them to doe their endevor at this tyme to pleasure the Kinge, as they had done heretofore to offend him. And joyninge with Lhywarch they went towardes Ystradtywi to meete with the Kinges sonne and when they came to the confynes of the countrey, they made avowe that nether man, woman, nor childe shulde escape their handes alyve. [107v] And when the people understoode this cruell bande, they fledde out of the countrey[2] some to woodes, some to rockes and caves and some to the castells of the Kinges to save their lyves, for as the proverbe is, the dogge wyll like the weapon that shall kill him. And they devyded their people to enter the woodes and straytes, which be very many in that countrey. And Owen himself toke with him aboute 100 men, and entred the woode, and perceaved that men and cattaill had passed before them towardes Caermardhyn, and pursued them[3] to the castell, and slewe some, and the rest fledde, and he toke all their cattaill and returned backe towardes his companye. And beholde at that instant Geralde Steewarde of Penbrocke with all his power of Flemings was cominge to meete the Kinges sonne [108] and mette with them that fledde, and they cryed out upon him for helpe and declared howe Owen ap Cadwgan had spoyled them of all their goodes. And when Geralde and the Flemings understoode that Owen was there with so litle a companye they thought hit a meete tyme[4] to bee revenged of their olde wronges and pursued him to the woodes. And Owens men came to him and willed him to make haist for their is a great number[5] pursuinge us, and he understandinge that they were the Kinges frendes, doubtinge nothinge, but stayed, and when they came nighe they begane to shote at his men, who wolde have[6] had Owen to have fledde, but he turned to his enimyes manfully and encouraged his men sainge that althoughe their enimyes were 7 to one yet they were but Flemings [108v] and suche as feared their names and good for nothinge but to emptie cuppes, and with that sette upon them couragiousely. And hit chanced that at the first meetinge Owen was striken with an arrowe to the herte and slayne, which when his men sawe they fledde, and brought woorde to Lhywarch ap Trehayarn and their felowes, who suspectinge the Kinges army, and seinge they colde not trust them in the Kinges owne[7] service, returned to their countrey.

And after the death of Owen his bretherne devyded his landes betwixt them (except that which he had taken by force from his uncle Meredith,

---

·[1]C – and . . . men   [5]Ll – number
[2]Ll – countrey   [6]Ll – have
[3]C – towards Caermardhyn . . . them   [7]C – owne
[4]C thinge

and was the landes of Madocke ap Ryryd ap Blethyn). The names of his
bretherne were thees: Madocke by Gwenlhyan the [109] daughter of
Griffith ap Kynan, Enyon by Sannan[1] daughter to Dyfnaval, Morgant by
Eyrlhyw daughter to Kedyvor ap Kolhwyn lorde of Dyved, Henrie and
Griffith by the daughter of the lorde Pygot his wedded wife, Meredith
by Evron daughter to[2] Hoedlyw ap Cadwgan, and Owen was begotten
upon Iweridh daughter to Edwyn.* And upon this Enyon sonne to
Cadwgan and Griffith sonne to Meredith ap Blethyn dyd leade their
power against a castell that Uchtryd ap Edwyn had built at Kymer in
Meryonydh. For Cadwgan had geven to his cosin germaine Uchtryd
Meryonydh and Keveylioc, upon condicioun that he and his shulde bee
frendes to his frendes and foes to his foes in all causes, but contrary he,
and his sonnes, was against Cadwgans childrene in every enterprise
[109v] that they went aboute. Therefore [after they had] sett upon the
castell and after the slaughter of dyverse of the garrison the rest yelded to
them, and so they wanne all the countrey and devyded hit betwixt
them. This Griffith ap Meredith had Mowdhwy, Kevelyoc and half
Penlhyn, and the other half of Penlhyn[3] and Meryonydh came to
Enyon.*

And the yere 1116 dyd Kinge Hennry sayle to Normandy with a
great army against the Frenche Kinge, who with the Earle of Flanders
and others went aboute to make William, sonne to Roberte Courte-
hose, Duke of Normandy, but at Kinge Henryes arryvall they returned
home without honor. And this yere dyed William Strangebowe of a
consummption. And the yere ensuinge fill ther a great variannce betwixt
Howell ap Ithell Lorde of Roos [and] Rovonyog, nowe Denbighe
lande, and Ryryd and Lhywarch the sonnes of Owen ap Edwyn. And
[110] Howell sent to Meredith ap Blethyn and to Enyon and Madocke
(Cadwgans sonnes) for succours and they came downe from Meryonydh
with 400 men well appointed, and mette with the sonnes of Owen in
the valley of Clwyd their owne lande. And the sonnes of Owen sent for
their cosins germaines the sonnes of Uchtryd to send their powers to
succour them, and they mette together with cruell hertes and fought
manfully, but at the ende after great slaughter was Lhywarch (the sonne
of Owen ap Edwyn) slaine, and with him Ierwerth ap Nodh, which was
a noble man, and a worthy souldyer. And Ryryd fledde and so Howell
ap Ithell had the victorye, but he was so sore wounded that he dyed
within[4] fortie dayes after. And Meredith ap Blethyn and the sonnes of

[1] C Sannra   [3] Ll – and the other halfe of Penlhyn
[2] C – daughter to   [4] Ll with

Cadwgan made speed home for feare of Frenchemen that laye in garrysons about Chester.

[110v] And the yere 1120 dyed Murcarde the worthiest and greatest prince in all Irelande. And the same tyme was there a great battaill fought betwixt Kinge Henrie and the Frenche Kinge who was overthrowen, and a great nummber of his nobles taken. And shortely after as Kinge Henry returned towardes Englande, by the misgoverment of the maister, there was a shippe drowned wherin perished the Kinges twoe sonnes William and Richard, with his daughter and nyece with many other to the number of 150. And the yere folowinge dyd the Kinge marry Adelyc daughter to the Duke of Lovaine, and furthwith prepared a great army against Wales, and came to Powys lande, which when the lordes of the lande, Meredith ap Blethyn and the 3 sonnes of Cadwgan, Enyon, Madocke and Morgan sawe, they sent to Griffith [111] ap Kynan Prince of Northwales to desire succours at his handes. And he answered they shulde not receave any at him, nor enter within his landes, for he had made peace with the Kinge, and they heringe this purposed to defende them selves within their owne lande after the best maner they coulde. And they sette men to kepe and defende the straytes, where by there enimyes must needes passe. And as it chaunced the Kinge him self with a small number came to one of those defended places, for his whole army had gone a further waye aboute, because of their carryages. And beholde the men which kept the strayte skyrmished with the kinges men, and with their arrowes havinge the advantage of the grounde slewe somme and galled many. Amonge which one drew his bowe and shotte to his foes a stronge shotte[1] and by fortune stroke the Kinge a great blowe upon the breast, but by meane of his [111v] mace hurte him not. Neverthelesse he was wonderfully dismayed withall, and thought howe rashly by misfortune he might losse[2] in that wilde countrey the honor and fame which he had wonne before, and stayed his men streight, and sent to parle with them, and to will them under assurannce to come speake with the Kinge, which they dyd. And he asked them whose men they were and howe they durst be so bolde as to put the kinge in suche daunger. And they saide they were Meredith ap Blethyns men, and dyd nothinge but their masters commanndment in kepinge the passage. And the Kinge willed them to goo to their master and counsaill him to come to the kings peace, and he shulde receave no hurte. And so he and his cosins dyd and fyned to the kinge for their offences 10000 head of cattaill, and the kinge returned to England.

[1]C shute   [2]Ll – losse

And the yere ensuinge* dyd Griffith ap Rhes ap Tewdur kill Griffith ap Sulhayarn [112]. And Enyon the sonne of Cadwgan dyed and he gave his parte of Powis and Meryonydh, which he had wonne, to his brother Meredith. But Meredith ap Blethyn his uncle put him bake by force, and toke hit to him selfe. And at this tyme dyd the Kinge sette at libertie Ithell ap Ryryd ap Blethyn, which he kept in prison many yeres, and he came home thinkinge to have enioyed his owne landes, but he cold not come by hit.[1]* And when Griffith ap Kynan Prince of Northwales herde howe Meredith ap Blethyn had taken by force the landes of his nevewe Meredith ap Cadwgan, he sent his sonnes Cadwalhon and Owen with a power to Meryonydh, and they brought all the countrey to their subjection, and caried[2] the cheefmen and the catteill to Lhyn. And afterwarde the sonnes of Cadwgan destroyed the lande of Lhywarch ap Trehayarn, because he joyned with the sonnes of the prince. And about this tyme came one Johnnes Cremensis a cardinall of Rome [112v] frome the Pope, and after he had gotten many riche rewardes of bishoppes and abbottes he helde a Synode at London at the Nativitie of Our Ladye, where he inveyde bitterly againste the marryage of priestes, declaringe howe unseemely a thinge hit was to come from his woman to the aulter, and the same night was founde with a whore in bedde with him.

And the yere 1125 dyd Meredith ap Blethyn kill his brothers sonne Ithell ap Ryryd. And shortely after Cadwalhon ap Griffith ap Kynan slewe his three uncles Grono, Ryryd and Meylyr, sonnes to Owen ap Edwyn. And also Morgan ap Cadwgan slewe his brother Meredith with his owne handes. And Henry the emperor dyed, that had maryed Mawde, Kinge Henryes daughter and heire. [113] And the yere 1127 the Kinge sent his daughter to Normandy to bee maryed to Geffrey Plantagenet sonne to the Earle of Aniow[3] and folowed himselfe shortely after. And Griffith ap Rhes was put beside the landes, which the Kinge had suffered him quietly to possesse, by the false accusacioun of the Normaines, which comhabited with him. And then dyed Danyell Archdeacon of Powis, a man bothe learned and godly and that travayled all his tyme to sette peace and accorde betwixt his countrey men. And the yere 1128 dyed Griffith ap Meredith ap Blethyn and the same yere dyd Llewelyn the sonne of Owen ap Cadwgan take Meredith ap Llywarch and delyvered him to Payn Fitz John to be kept saffe in the castell of Brugge Morphe. This Meredith had slaine Meuryc his cosin

[1]C – But . . . hit
[2]Ll – caried

[3]Ll Arvove; C arvow *deleted*; aniow *in another hand*; HC Aniow

germaine, and had put out the eies [113v] off his twoe cosins germaines the sonnes of Griffri. And the yere ensuinge dyd Ieuen or Ieaf the sonne of Owen blinde 2 of his bretherne and banished them the countrey. And Llewelyn ap Owen slewe Ierwerth ap Llywarch. And Meredith ap Blethyn toke the same Llewelyn his nevewe and put out his eies and gelded him, because he shulde gette no children, that he might have his landes and he¹ slewe Ieaf ap Owen his brother. Also Meuryc slewe Lhywarch, and Madocke his sonne, his owne cosins. But he was blinded and gelded shortely after. And Morgan the sonne of² Cadwgan toke great repentannce for the murther of his brother Meredith, and toke his journey to Jerusalem, and dyed at his returne in Ciprus.

And in the yere 1132 dyed Roberte Curthose the Kinges [114] brother in the castell of Caerdyffe. And the yere folowinge Cadwalhon sonne to Griffith ap Kynan was slaine at Nanheudwy by Enyon, sonne to Owen ap Edwyn his uncle (whose three bretherne he had slaine) and Cadwgan ap Grono ap Edwyn. And that yere dyed Mredith ap Blethyn ap Kynvyn, the greatest lorde and chieffest man in Powis as he that had goten his bretherne and nevewes landes to his owne landes by hocke and by crocke. And the year insuinge there happened nothinge worthie to be noted. And the yere 1135 dyed Henrye Kinge of Englande, one of the worthiest and most victoriouse princes that ever reigned in the Ile of Britaine. And after him reigned Stephen Earle of Boloyne, his sisters [114v] sonne, a stoute knight and a hardy. For (by meanes of Hughe Pygod³ steewarde to Henry) the Archebishop of Canterburye and all the nobilitie of Englande (contrarye to their former othe made to Mawde) created⁴ and crowned Stephen Kinge. And shortely after Davydh Kinge of Scottes wanne by treason Caerleil and Newe Castell, against whome Stephen lede an armye, and Davydh yelded to him and restored Newcastell and kept Caerleill by composition. But wolde not sweare to him, for he had sworen allready to Mawde his neece, yet Henrye his sonne sware to Stephen, and had the earldome of Huntington geven him. And this yere was Richarde and Gilberte his sonne slaine by Morgan ap Owen. And shortely after Cadwalader [115] and Owen Gwynedh the sonnes of Griffith ap Kynan (in whome remained the hope of all Wales, for they were gentill and liberall to all menne, terrible and cruell to their enimyes, meeke and humble to their frendes, the succour and defence of wydowes, fatherlesse, and all that were in necessitie, and as they passed all other in good and laudable vertues, so

¹C – he   ³C Bygod
²Ll – of   ⁴C – created

they were paragons of streingth, bewtie and well proportionate bodyes)
gathered a great power against the Normaines and Flemynes, [who]
enterynge Caerdygan, wanne, destroyed and brenned the whole
countrey, with the castell of Walter Debec,[1] the castell of Aberystwyth,
which was verey stronge, and well manned. And thither came Howell
ap Meredith, with his twoe sonnes Mredith[2] [115v] and Rys, and
Madocke ap[3] Idnerth★ and they went forwarde and raysed the castell of
Richarde de la Mare, and the castell of Dinerth and Caerwedros, and
returned home with muche honor. And towards the end of the same
yere they returned againe with 6000 footemen and 2000 horsemen well
armed and to them came Griffith ap Res and Howell ap Meredith of
Brekenocke and his sonnes, and Madocke ap Idnerth, and they subdued
the countrey to Abertivi, and placed againe the olde inhabitantes [and]
chaced awaye the strangers. And against them came Stephen, Constable
of Abertivi, Roberte Fitzmartyn, the sonnes of Geralde, and Gwylym
Fitzorc★ with all the power of Normaines, Flemings and Englishmen
that were in Wales or the Marches. And after a cruell and bloody fight
the strangers, after their accustomed maner and use, put all their [116]
hope in their fortes, and forsake the felde, and the Welshmen folowed
harde that, besides 3000 that were slaine, a great number were drowned
and taken and caryed captyves awaye. And after this victorie Owen and
Cadwalader overrunne the whole countrey, and returned home with
riche spoyles as well in armor and horse, as in other thinges, with great
tryumphe. And at this tyme the perinrie[4]★ of the nobles begane to
appeare. For first Hughe Bygod kept the castell of Norwich but
furthwith farre against his will restored hit to the Kinge himself. After
the Kinge dyd besiedge Excester whiche Baldwyn de Redvers kept
against him, and wanne hit, and so he dyd the Ile of Wight, which was
the saide Baldwyns and banished him out of the lande.

   And the yere 1137 dyed Griffith ap Rys ap Tewdur the light, honor
and staye of Southwales, and he had by his wief Gwenlhyan, daughter to
Griffith ap Kynan, [116v] Rys comenly called the Lorde Rhes and
others. Also towardes the ende of the same yere dyed Griffith ap Kynan
Kinge and prince of Northwales, the onely defence and sheelde of all
Wales, after he had escaped many great daungers by sea and lande in
Ireland and Wales, and after many worthie victoryes, and after he had
brought Northwales (which he founde full of stranngers) to peace and
quietnes, and after he had bene confessed and communicated, full of

<hr>

[1] C de Bec   [3] Ll and
[2] C – with . . . Mredith   [4] C prince

yeres had ruled his realme worthely 50 yeres. This prince had many childerne by dyverse women. First by Yyngharad daughter to Owen ap Edwyn he had sonnes Owen, Cadwalader and Cadwalhon (slaine before his father dyed) and daughters Mareda, Susanna, Ranulht, Agnes and Gwenllyan. He also had by an other woman Iago and Islain, and Idwall abbot of Penmon, and Dwlinge which was also preest and well learned.*

[117] Owen Gwyneth sonne to Griffith ap Kynan

After the death of Griffith ap Kynan his sonnes devyded the lande betwixt them after the manner of Wales. And Owen, surnamed Gwynedh, the eldest sonne was made Prince of Northwales (for the name of kinge is no further used in the British Booke). And in the beginninge of his reigne he and his bretherne made the thyrde expedition into Southwales, and overthrewe the castelles¹ of Ystrad-meyryc and castell Stephen, and Humfreys castell, and brenned the towne of Caermardhyn, and returned home with much honor. And at this tyme dyed John Archpriest of Lhanbadarn, who for his godly lief is numbred² amongst the sainctes. This yere went Kinge Stephen to Normandy and made peace with the Frenche Kinge, and with the Earle of Anjou and returnned home. And the yere folowinge beinge 1138 Kinge Stephen made a viage against David [117v] Kinge of Scottes who had brenned and spoyled a great parte³ of Englande, but assoone as he herde the kinges comminge he returned home. And Stephen folowed him and destroyed all the south partes of Scottelande. And the somer ensuinge dyverse noble men of Englande fortifeid their castelles and rebelled against the Kinge, as William Earle of Glocester fortified Ledes and Bristowe, Raffe Luuel Cari, William Fitzalan Shrosburie, Paganellus Ludlehaw, William de Moun Dunestor, Roberte de Nichole Warham, Eustach Fitz Johnns Mertone, and Walkelyn Dover, which castelles the kinge gotte, some by assaultes, some by fayre promies and some by treason. And at this tyme, the Scottes heringe this busines entred Englande againe, against whome William Earle of Albermarle, William Pyppell of Notingham, Walter Esper, and Gilbert Laci gathered the power of the north, and beinge animated⁴ [118] with an eloquent oration (made and prominced⁵ to the whole army by Raffe Bishop of Orkeneys)*, sette upon the Scottes manfully at Almerton, and after great

¹C castell
²C counted
³Ll – parte

⁴C aminated
⁵C pronounced

murther of them put the Kinge to flight and returned with great tryumphe. And in the beginninge of the next yere the Kinge toke the castelles of Ludlehaw and Ledes, and kept the bishoppes of Salusbury and Lyncolne fastinge, tyll they had delyvered him the castelles of Devyse and Chyrburne, which the bishop of Salusbury had builde, and Newerke Upon Trent, and Elliaforde,[1] which twoe likewise the Bishop of Lyncolne had made. And upon this dyd Maude the Empresse, daughter and heire to Kinge Henrie (to whome Kinge Stephen with all the nobles of Englande had sworne fidelitie), land at Arundell with her brother Roberte Earle of Glocester, and there were reaceved [118v] honorably of William de Albineto, which had lately maryed Adelyz the Queene, late Kinge Henryes wife, and to whome Kinge Henrye had geven the Earldome of Arundell. And King Stephen layed siedge to the castell, but seinge hit was impugnable,[2] he raysed his siedge, and suffred the Queene and her brother to escape to Bristowe where they were reaceved.

And in the yere 1140 was Kenvryc the sonne of Owen slaine by the men of Madoc ap Meredith ap Blethyn ap Kynvyn. And the next yere after dyd Kinge Stephen with a great army besiedge Lyncolne. And thither came Raffe Earle of Chester and Roberte Earle of Glocester his father in lawe, with the barons (which were disherited) to reyse the siedge. But before they came the towne was wonne, and passinge a dangerouse marryse,[3] camped harde by the Kinge, ready to geve him battaill, who likewise brought furth his men in 3 battailles. [119] In the first were thees, Alace Duke of Britaine, the Earle of Mellent, Hughe Bygod Earle of Norfolke, Symon Earle of Hampton, and Earle Warrenne. In the secunde the Earle of Albemarle and William of Ypres, a noble man and a worthie souldyer. And in the thyrde the Kinge with Baldwyn Fitzgilberte, and a great number of nobles more. And of the other parte the disherited barons had the first place, the Earle of Chester with his succoures of Wales (better couraged than armed) had the secunde place, and the Earle of Glocester ledde the last battaille. And after a cruell fight they toke the Kinge prisoner. And afterwarde the Queene and William of Ypres, Bryan Fitzconte, William Martel, Geffrey de Mandevill gathered a newe army, and fought with the Empresse and her brother at Wynchester, and put her to flight takinge Earle Roberte prisoner, for [119v] channge of whome the Kinge was sette at libertie.* The yere folowinge the Kinge had an overthrowe at Wilton. And the same yere he besiedged thempresse at Oxenfurde, and

[1]*HC* Sleeford   [3]C marrise
[2]C impugnable *later corrected to* impregnable

she escaped to Wallingefurde. And the same yere dyed Madock ap Idnerth a man of great estimacioun in Wales. And the sonnes of Blethyn ap Gwyn slewe Meredith ap Howell.

And the yere 1142 were Howell ap Meredith ap Rytherch of the Cantref Bychan, and Rys ap Howell slayne by treason of the Flemyngs. And likewise Howell ap Meredith ap Blethyn was murthered by his owne men. And Howell and Kadwgan the sonnes of Madocke ap Idnerth dyd either kill other. And shortely after there fill a varyannce betwixt Anaraude, sonne to Griffith ap Rys, Prince of Southwales, and his father in lawe [120] Cadwalader sonne to Griffith ap Kynan and brother to Prince Owen Gwynedh. And from woordes grewe to fight, where Anaraud was slayne, the hope and streingth of Southwales. For which thinge Prince Owen toke suche displeasure at his brother that he and his sonne Howell gathered an army againste him, and destroyed all his countrey and brenned[1] his castell at Aberystwyth, for he had fledde to Irelande and had hyred Octor (sonne to Octor) and the sonne of Turkylh, and the sonne of Cherulffe, with a great number of Irishmen and Scottes for 2000 markes to his succours, and landed at Abermenay in Caernaunvonshire,[2]* against whome the prince came with a great power. But beefore the armyes mette there was a peace concluded betwixt the bretherne, which thinge, when the Irishmen understoode, they withhelde Cadwalader as prisoner for their wages and he [120v] delyvered them 2000 head of cattaylle besides many prisoners and great spoyles they had taken in the countrey. And as [soone as] the prince knewe his brother sette at libertie he fill upon the Irishmen, and slewe a great number of them, and recovered all the cattell with the prisoners and other spoyle, and as many as escaped alyve returned home with great shame and losse.

And aboute the same tyme dyd Hughe, the sonne of Randell, refortifie the castell of Kymaron and wonne Melyenydh to himselfe, and likewise the castell of Clun was fortified by a lorde Normaine and all Elvel brought to their subjection. And Kinge Stephen toke Geffrey Mandevyll prisoner at Saintalban, where the Earle of Arundell a worthye knight[3] was like to be drowned by defaulte of his horse. And Earle Mandevyll gave to the Kinge for his libertie the towre of London, with the castell[s] of Walden, and Plassey, who afterwarde lyved by spoyle of [121] abbeyes and was slaine in a skyrmishe against the Kinge, whom he had sore annoyde, and his sonne Arnulphe was banished the realme.

[2]C Caernarvonshire
[1]C burned
[3]C – a . . . Knight

And this yere dyd Hughe the Mortimer take Rhes ap Howell in a skyrmishe and dyverse other with him and imprisoned them. And at the same tyme Howell and Conan the sonnes of [1] Prince Owen gathered an army against the Flemyngs and Normaines and gave them an overthrowe at Abertivi, and brent[2] the towne, and returned home with great honor. And this yere dyed Sulyen ap Rychmarch a man of great knowelege, one of the College of Llanbadarn.

And Gilberte Earle of Clare came with a great power to Dyved and built the castell of Caermardhyn and the castell of the sonnes of Uchtryd. And Hugh Mortymer slewe Meyric ap Madoc ap Ryryd and Meredith ap Madock ap Idnerth. And Cadelh sonne to Griffith ap Rhes prince of Southwales gate the castell [121v] of Dynevor which[3] Earle Gilberte had builte. And after he and his bretherne Meredith and Rhes gathered their powers, and layde siedge to the castell of Caermardhyn which was yelded them, reservinge onely their lyves to the garryson. And from thense they brought their army before the castell of Llanstephant, where the Normaines and Fleminges mette with them and had a great overthrowe, and they wonne the castell. And here upon all the Fleminges and Normaines enhabitinge that countrey all aboute gathered their powers together and their capteines were the sonnes of Geralde and Gwylam de Hay and they layed siedge to the same castell upon the sodeine. And Meredith ap Griffith to whose custodye the castell was committed encouraged his men to fight, and to defend the place. And that which lacked in him of streingth (for he was of great yeres) he supplyed in courage and discretion, and suffered his enimyes [122] to skale the walles and when the ladders were full he gave the watch woordes and his souldyers dyd manfully with engines overturne all the ladders, and sodeinly issued furthe, and slewe[4] and maimed a great number of armed men, and tryed souldyors, and put the rest to flight. And shortely after dyed Rhun,★ the sonne of Prince Owen of North-wales, the fayrest and godliest gentilman that ever nature forged, bolde in battaill, and meke in peace, cruell and stoute to his foes, gentill and lovinge to his frendes, discreat and plesant in his talke, and wise in his deedes, and breefly a very paragon as well of good qualities, as forme and perfection of proportion and bewtie, whose death, when hit came to his fathers eares, dyd so trouble him, that no kynde of pleasure coulde comforte his heavy herte, but ledde the nightes in teares and the days in hevines [122v] till God, who toke compassion upon the poore leavinges

[1]C to
[2]C kept
[3]Ll – which
[4]C – and sodeinly . . . slewe

and remenantes of the Britons, even as he had discomforted the Prince
with the death of his sonne, so he dyd gladen[1] his sorowfull herte with
the overthrowe of his enimyes. For their was a castell at the Molde verye
stronge, and well manned, which dyd trouble the whole countrey
aboute, and had been oftentymes besyedged, but never wonne. Prince
Owen brought his power before hit, and layed his seedge unto hit,[2] and
the garryson defended hit[3] manfully and abode dyverse assaultes but at
the last, maugre their heades, the sight of the Prince did so encorage his
men that they entred by force, and slewe a great number, and toke the
rest of the deffendanntes, and raysed the forte to the earth, which
victorie acheeved dyd so please the Prince that he leaft his solitarie
plaintes, and fill to his accustommed pastymes.

[123] And the same yere[4] Kinge Stephen overthrewe his enimyes at
Ferendon. And the yere ensuinge were Randell Earle of Chester and
Kinge Stephen made frendes. But the Kinge toke him prisoner, and kept
him so (conntrarie to his promise) untill suche tyme the Earle had
delyvered to the kinge the castell of Lyncolne, with all other fortes of
the Kings that he had in his custodie. And this tyme dyd Cadelh,
Meredith and Rhes, the sonnes of Griffith ap Rhes ap Tewdur leade
their powers against the castell of Wyst or Gwys, which after they sawe
they coulde not wynne, they send[5] for Howell sonne of Owen Prince of
Northwales to their succour, who for his prowesse[6] in the felde and his
discretion in consultatioun was counnted the flowre of cheevalrye, and
whose presence was thought onely sufficient to overthrowe any holde.
And he beinge very desirouse to wynne honour gathered his men and
came [123v] to thees lordes before the castell Gwys who[7] reaceved him
joyfullye. And when he had vewed the place, he caused engines to be
made to batter the walles with force of men, and other to caste great
stones to their enimyes and to disquiet the garryson, which preparations,
when they within behelde, their stomakes fayled and furthwith they
yelded the forte and Howell returned home with great honor. And
shortely after there fill a great discention betwixt Howell and Conan,[8]
Prince Owens sonnes, and Cadwalader their uncle. Whereupon they
called their streingthe unto them and in twoe[9] places entred the
countrey of Meryonydh, and the people fledde to the sainctuaries to
save their lyves. And thees twoe yonge lordes made proclammacioun

[1]C glade
[2]C and siedge layed unto hit
[3]C – hit
[4]C – yere
[5]C sende
[6]C powers
[7]Ll – who
[8]C Dwnon
[9]Ll to

that no mane shulde hurte them that wolde yelde to them, whereupon
the people which had fledde returned to their houses, and had no hurte.
And so they brought all that countrey in to subjection to them, and lead
their [124] armye before the castell of Kynvaell, which Cadwalader had
builte and fortified, and wherin was the abbot of the Ty Gwyn, or the
White House, to whom the lorde had committed the defence of his
holde. And Howell and Conan[1] sommened the forte with great
threatninges, and they within defied them. Then they promised the
Abbot Morvan[2] great rewardes, to lette them have the house. But he
like a faythfull servant, that nether terrible manasses nor plesant proffers
shulde ever move him to untrueth, but as his lorde trusted him, so
wolde he continue, and not deceave his expectation, chosinge rather to
dy with honor than to lyve with shame. With which answere the yonge
lordes were greatly offended, that a priest shulde staye their prosperouse
expedicioun and therupon assaulted the castell so sore, that after they
had beaten downe the walles, they entred by force, and slewe and
wounded all the garryson (savinge the Abbot) [124v] who escaped away
pryvely by meanes of frendes that he had in Howelles army.

And the yere 1147 dyed Roberte Earle of Glocester and Gilberte
Earle of Clare, and Uchdrud, Bishop of Landaf. And after him Nicolas
ap Gwrgant was made bishop. And the yere 1148 dyed Bernarde,
Bishop of Sainct Davids or Menevia, and after came David Fitzgerald to
bee bishop there, which was before Archedeacon of Caerdygan. And the
yere ensuinge Owen Prince of Northwales dyd builde a castell in Ial,
and his brother Cadwalader built an other at Llanrhystud, and gave
Cadwgan his sonne his parte of Caerdigan. And towardes the ende of
this yere dyd Madocke the sonne of Meredith ap Blethyn builde the
castell of Oswaldestre* and gave his nevewes Owen and Meyryg sonnes
to Griffith ap Meredith his parte of Kevelyog. And the yere after dyd
Prince Owen [125] emprison Conan his sonne for certeine faultes
committed against his father. And Howell Prince Owens sonne toke his
uncle Cadwalader prisoner, and brought his countrey and castell to his
subjection.

And this tyme dyd Cadelh sonne to Griffith ap Rhes fortifie the castell
of Caemardhyn, and from thence lead his army to Kydwyly, and
destroyed and spoyled all the countrey, and after his returne he joyned
his power with Meredith and Rhes his bretherne, and entred
Caerdygan, and wonne the parte called Is Aeron. And not longe after fill
a discension betwixt Rondell Earle of Chester and Owen Prince of

[1]C Donan   [2]C Mervan

Northwales, and Rondell gathered a great power of his frendes, and hired souldyors of Englishmen. And also Madock ap Meredith, Prince of Powis, disdayninge to holde his landes of Owen, joyned all his powers to the Earles, and both togeather entred Prince Owens lande. And he like a worthie Prince (not sufferinge the spoyle [125v] of his subiectes) met them at Cunsylht and boldly bade them battaill, which they refused not, but beinge more in number, and better armed and weaponed, were gladde of the occasion. Yet before the ende they threwe awaye weapon and armor, and trusted ther legges, and the Northwales men dyd so pursue them that fewe escaped but were ether slayne or taken. And the yere 1150 Cadelh, Meredith and Rhes (sonnes to Griffith ap Rhes Prince of Southwales) wonne all Caerdygan from Howell sonne to Prince Owen (savinge the castell of Lhanvyanghell in Penwerne). And at the castell of Llanrhystud they lost many of their men, therfor they slewe all the garrison when they wonne hit, and from thence they went to the castell Ystradmeyryg, which they fortified and manned, and returned home. And Cadelh had a great pleasure in huntinge, and used muche that pastime [126] which, when the inhabitantes of the towne called Tenby (and in Welshe Dynbigh y Pysgod) in Penbrokeshire [knewe],[1] they layed an embushument for him. And so when this lorde had uncoupled his houndes and pursued the stagge with a fewe companyons, he fill amonge his enimyes and they sette upon him and his companyons[2]* fyersly, seinge they were but a fewe and unarmed and shortely put them to flight, and wounded Cadelh very sore, yet he escaped their handes by manfull fighte, and came to his house where he laye longe tyme at the pointe of death. And his bretherne Meredith and Rhes entred Gwyr and brenned and destroyed all the countrey, and wonne the castell of Aber Lhychwr, and raysed hit to the grounde. And returninge hom with great buttyn[3] they reedified the castell of Dynvwr. And the same yere dyd Howell sonne to Owen Prince of Northwales fortifie Humfreys castell in the valley of Caletwr.

[126v] And in the yere 1151 dyd Owen Gwynedh take Cunedha (his brother Cadwalhons sonne) and put oute his eies, and gelded him lest he shulde have children to enherite parte of the landes. And Lhewelyn (sonne to Madocke ap Meredith) slewe Stephen, sonne to Baldwyn, and aboute the same tyme dyd Cadwalader brother to Prince Owen escape out of his nevew Howelles prison, and subdued parte of the Ile of Mone or Anglesey to him. But his brother Owen sent an armye against him,

[1]Ll – knewe; *supplied from HC*   [3]C buttye
[2]C – he fill . . . companyons

and chaced him thence, and he fledde to Englande for succours to his
wives frendes, for she was daughter to Gilberte Earle of Clare. In the
same yere was Gaufryd Arthur made Bishop of Llanelwy[1] (nowe called
St Assaph in Englishe). And Symon Archeadecon of Clynnauc a great
clercke dyed. And the yere ensuinge Meredith and Rhes, the sonnes of
Griffith ap Rhes, lead their powers to Penwedyc before [127] the castell,
which was Howelles sonne to Prince Owen, and with great payne gotte
hit. And shortely after pryvely by night they came to the castell of
Tenby, which was in the kepinge of William Fitzegeralde, and skaled hit
upon the sodeine and got hit, and dyd avenge their brothers hurte. And
returninge thence they devyded their army, and Rhes went to Ystrad
Kyngen, and destroyed and spoyled hit. And Meredith layed siedge to
the castell of Aberavyn, and wonne hit, and came home with riche
spoyles, and furth with Rhes destroyed Kevelyoc. And this yere dyed
Rondell Earle of Chester and Hughe his sonne was created in his place.

In the yere 1153 dyed Meredith ap Griffith ap Rhes lorde of
Caerdygan and Ystradtiwy, in the 25th yere of his age, a worthie knight,
and fortunate in battaill, just and liberall to all men. And the same yere
dyed Geffrey[2] Bishop of Landaf. [127v] And the same yere ensuinge dyd
Henrye Shortemantell (the empresse sonne) enter Englande, and wanne
dyverse castelles as Malvelburye, Wallingeforde and Shreusburie, and the
same yere was drowned Eustace sonne to Kinge Stephen and therupon
the Kinge and Henrye concluded a peace.

And the yere 1154 dyed Stephen Kinge of Englande and Henry
Plantagenet thempresse sonne was crowned in his steed. This Henry was
wyse and learned, and besides a worthye knight, he never wore glove
exepte he bare a hauke on his fist, and never sate but at his meate, and
delited in haukinge, huntinge, and ridinge, and in all honest exercises. In
the beginninge of his reigne, and in the yere 1155 dyd Rhes ap Griffith
ap Rhes (which the Welshe booke surnamed the Lorde Rhes, and all
the Latyn and Englishe writers of that tyme name Kinge of Southwales)
gather all his streingth together to defend his [128] country from Owen
Gwynedh, whom he herde was levinge[3] of men to conquere Southwales, and Rhes came as farre as Aberdyvi over against Northwales, and
perceavinge the rumour to be false builte a castell there, and so returned
backe. And the same tyme dyd Madoc ap Meredith Prince of Powis
build a castell at Carenyon besides Kymer, and Meyrige his nevewe
escaped out of prison where he had longe bene kept. Also Terdelach
Kinge of Connach in Ireland dyed.

[1]C Lhanelweye   [3]C levyinge
[2]C Jeffraye

And at this tyme dyd Kinge Henrie banishe the Flemings, which Stephen had brought in, and sent some of them to their cosins in[1] West Wales. Likewise the Kinge banished William Peverell of Notyngham. And Hughe Mortymer fortified the castell of Cleubur against the Kinge, which the Kinge toke and rased. And Hughe yelded to the Kinge, and delyvered to his handes the castells of [128v] Wygmor and Brugge. Likewise Roger sonne to Myles of Glocester, Earle of Herforde, delyvered to the Kinge the towne[2] of Glocester, and dyed shortely after, and his brother Walter enjoyed his landes. But the Kinge kept the Earledome of Hereforde and the towne of Glocester in his owne handes. The yere folowinge Conan, Earle of Richemonde, sayled to Britaine, where he was reaceved of the most parte for their duke. And Kinge Henry and his brother Geffrey were agreed in Normandy, and the Kinge returned into Englande, and received of the Scottes Kinge Caerlyll, Newecastell, and Bamburgh with the countrey aboute and gave him the Earledome of Huntingdon. Also William Earle of Mortimer★ (and base sonne to Kinge Stephen) delyvered Henry the castell of Benonesey[3] and Norwiche and the Kinge confirmed to him his other landes.

And furthwith the Kinge gathered all his [129] power together, from all parties of Englande, thinkinge to subdue Northwales, beinge therunto provoked and moved by Cadwalader (whom the Prince his brother had banished out of the lande and bereved of his levinge)[4] and by Madocke ap Meredith Prince of Powis who envyed at the libertie of Northwales, which knewe no lorde but one. And so the Kinge leadde his armye to Westchester, and camped upon the marsh called Saultney. Likewise Owen, as a valiant prince, gathered all his streingth and came to the utter meres of his lande, entendinge to geve the kinge battaill, and he camped himself at Basingwerke. And when the Kinge understode that, he chose out of his army dyverse of the cheefest bandes, and sende certaine earles and lords with them towardes the Princes campe. And as they passed the woode called Coed Penarlage David and Conan, the princes sonnes, met with them, [129v] and set upon them fiersly and what for the advantage of the [ground]★ and for the sodeines of the deede the Englishmen were put to flight and a great number slaine and the rest were pursued to the Kinges campe. And the Kinge beinge sore displeased with that foylle, removed his campe alongest the sandes thinkinge to have passed betwixte Owen and his country. But Owen,

[1] C to
[2] C towre
[3] C Bensaye
[4] C lyvinge

foreseinge that, retired backe to a place which is called to this daye
Kilowen* (that is to saye the retyer of Owen), and the Kinge came to
Rudlan.

And Owen encamped and entrenched himself at Bryn y Pina,* and
skirmished with the Kinges men dayly. And in the meane while that the
Kinge was fortifyinge the castell of Rudlan, his navye, which was
gywded[1] by Madocke ap Meredith Prince of Powis, ankered in Mone,
or Anglesey, and put on lande the souldyers, whiche spoyled 2 churches
and a litle of the countrey aboute. And as they were [130] returninge to
their shippes all the streingth of the Ile sette upon them and killed them
all, so that non of such as robbed in the Ile brought tydinges howe they
spedde, and the shippemen, seinge that, liked not their lodginge, but
wayde up ancres, and awaye to Chester. And in this meane tyme was
there a peace concluded betwixte the Kinge and the Prince upon
conditions [that] Cadwalader shulde have his landes againe, and his
brother shulde be his frend. And so the Kinge leaft the castelles of
Rudlan and Basingwerke well fortified and manned, and built a house
thereby to the Templers, and returned to Englande.

And Ierwerth Goch ap Meredith gote the castell of Ial, and brenned
hit. And the yere folwinge was Morgan ap Owen slaine traytorouslye by
the men of Ivor ap Meyryg, and with him the best poet in the Britishe
tonge of his tyme called Gurgant ap Rhes, and his brother Ierwerth gote
the [130v] towne of Caerllyon, and the landes of Owen. And after the
Kinge had made peace with all the princes and lordes of Wales, except
Rhes ap Griffith ap Rhes Prince of Southwales, Rhes, fearinge the
Kinges power, caused the people to remove their cattell and goodes to
the wildernes of Towy and he still made warre againste the Kinge.
Therefore the Kinge sent to him, to come to his courte, and to conclude
a peace before the power of Englande and Wales shulde be sent for him.
Whereupon Rhes, after determination came to the Kinge, and an order
was taken that Rhes shulde enjoye the Cantref Mawr and an other
cantref,[2] as hit shuld please the Kinge, so that they shulde bee whole
together, and not in diverse places and shyres. But the Kinge did
contrary to his promise, for he appointed Rhes landes in dyverse places
and lordeshippes, entermedled with other mens landes. Which deceit,
althoughe Rhes perceaved hit well ynoughe, [131] yet he reaceved hit
peacemell as hit was, and lyved quietly untill Roger earle of Clare,
heringe this, came to the Kinge and desired his highnesse to geve him
suche landes in Wales as he colde wynne, which the Kinge graunted,

---

[1] C guided   [2] C – and . . . cantref

and he came with a great army to Caerdygan. And firste he fortefied the castell of Ystradmeyrig, and afterwardes the castell of Humfre, and of Dyvy, of Dynerth and Lhanrystyd. And when thees castelles were well manned and fortified, Walter Clyfforde, who had the castell of Lhanymdhifri, made a rode to the lande of Rhes, and returned with a butty after he had slaine dyverse of Rhes men.

And Rhes sent to the Kinge to complaine, and to have a redresse, and he had fayre woordes, and nothinge els, for the Kinge wynked at the faultes of the Englishe and Normaines and punished the Welshmen cruelly. Rhes seinge this layed siedge to Lhanymddifri, and in shorte space wonne [131v] the castell. And Enyon sonne to Annaraud brother to Rhes, beinge a lusti gentillman and seinge his uncle discharged of his othe to the Kinge, and also desyrouse to bringe his countrey men out of servitude, layed siedge to the castell of Humfre and by force wonne hit and slewe all the garrison, and founde therin horses and armour to furnishe a great number of men. Likewise Rhes, seinge he coulde enjoye no parte of his inheritannce, but that he wonne with the sworde, gathered his power, and entred Caerdygan and leaft not a castell standinge in the countrey of those which his enymyes had fortefied, and brought all to his subjection. Wherfore the Kinge beinge sore offended returned to Southwales and when he sawe he colde doe no good, he suffred Rhes to enjoye all that he had goten, and toke pledges of him to kepe the peace in his absence. And returninge to Englande he toke his jorney to Normandy and made peace with the [132] Frenche Kinge. And the next yere Rhes Prince of Southwales lead his power to Dyved and destroyed all the castelles that the Normaines had fortified there, and afterwarde layed siedge to Caermerdhyn. Which thinge when Reynalde[1] Earle of Bristowe the Kinges base sonne herde, he called to him the Earle of Clare, and his brother in lawe Cadwalader (brother to Prince Owen) and Howell and Conan (Owens sonnes) and twoe other earles, and came to reyse the siedge with a great army. But Rhes abode not their comminge and gote himself to the mountaines called Kevyn yr Eskayr Main,[2]* and there kept himself. And they camped at Dynwylheyr, and builded a castell there and after they colde not here of Rhes they returned home without doinge any notable acte. And the same [132v] yere King Henrie remayned in Normandy, and made warre against the Earle of Ewe for the citie of Thoulouse.

And the yere 1160 dyed Madoc ap Meredith ap Blethyn Prince of Powis at Wynchester. This man was ever the Kinge of Englandes frend,

[1]C Reynold   [2]C Kevein yrteskayr mayn

and was counted a very wise and discreate man,[1] on that feared God and
releeved the poore. His bodie was conveyde honorablye to Powis, and
buryed in the churche of[2] Tessilio in Myvod. This Madoc had by his
wief Susanna (daughter to Griffith ap Conan Prince of Northwales)
three sonnes, Griffith Maelor (that is to saye Griffith Bromfelde), Owen
and Elisse, and a daughter called Marred and he had base sonnes Owen
Brogyntyn, and Enyon Evell, which base sonnes were no lesse[3]
esteemed then the other, and had their parte[4] of their fathers
inheritaunnce, with [133] the rest throughe Wales, especially yf they
were stoute and noble couraged. And here youe shall understande howe
Powis lande came to be devided in many partes, and therby weakened
and so brought under the Normaines before the rest of Wales. Meredith
sonne to Blethyn ap Kynvyn Prince of Powis had by his wief Hunudh
verch Endodi 2 sonnes, this Madoc (of whome wee entreat) and
Griffith. Powys was devided betwixt them and Madocke had that parte
which after him was[5] called Powis Vadock, which parte was againe
devided betwixt his three sonnes after this maner: Griffith Maelor had
Bromfelde, Yal, Hopesdale, Nanheudwy, Mochnant ys Rhaiader,
Chirck, Kynlhayth, and Glyndoverdwy. Owen his secunde sonne called
Owen Vichan had Mechayn ys Coed, and Owen Brogynton (his base
sonne, for Elisse dyed) had Dynmael and Edeyrnon for his parte. The
other parte of Powis (called [133v] afterwarde Powys Wenwynwyn) was
in Griffith ap Merediths possession, and after his death his sonne called
Owen Kevelyog enioyed hit, as hit shall bee at large declared hereafter.

But to my matter. The same yere was Cadwalhon ap Madoc ap
Idnerth taken by his brother Enyon Clud, who delyvered him to Owen
Prince of Northwales and he sent him to the Kinges officers, to be
emprisoned at Winchester, from whence he escaped shortely after and
came to his countrey. And Kinge Henry remained in Normandy all this
yere, and his sonne Henrye maryed Margaret daughter to Lewis Kinge
of France. And the yere ensuinge dyed Meuryc bishop of Bangor, and
Kinge Henrie and the Frenche Kinge fill at discension, and shortely after
Kinge Henry went to Gascoyn to chastise certeine rebbelles there. And
the yere 1162 was there a peace conncluded beetwixt the kinges of
Englande and France. And Howell the sonne of Ieaf ap Cadwgan ap
Elyssan Gladrudh, gote the castell of Walwern in Kevelyog, and rased
hit, which newes, [134] when hit came to the eares of Owen Prince of
Northwales, hit displeased him wonderfully, and was so greved withall,

[1]C – and was counted . . . man   [4]C and he had part
[2]C – the churche of   [5]Ll – was
[3]C not baser

that nothinge colde make him mery, untill suche tyme as he had
gathered his power and came to Arwystli, to Llandhinan,[1] and thence
sette a great spoyle. And the people of the countrey came all to their
lorde Howell ap Ieaf, and he folowed the spoyle to Seavarn, where the
princes campe was. And the prince seinge suche an occasion [of
revenge][2] offered him, was right glade, and sette upon his enimyes and
slewe the most parte of them, and the rest with their lorde escaped to
the woodes and rockes. And the prince beinge joyfull of this reavenge
built up his castell againe, and fortified hit strongely. And the yere
folowinge Owen, sonne to Griffith ap Meredith (called Owen
Kevelyog) and Owen sonne to Madoc ap Meredith gote the castell of
Carreggova by Oswestre, and rased hit.

And the same tyme [134v] was there a combate fought betwixt
Roberte Mountforte and Henrie de Essexe to trye which of them had
begonne[3] the flight in a battaill fought[4] against the Welshmen in the
Marches, where the Kinge was present (and Eustace FitzJohnns and
Roberte Courcy twoe woorthie knightes slaine) for either of them
sclandered the[5] other. The said Henry of Essex bare the standarde of
Englande by inheritannce, and cast hit downe, and fledde, and so their
were slaine the twoe forsaide knightes Eustace and Roberte. (The Kinge
fledde himself, as sayeth any Frenche Cronicle.) And Henry was
overcome and afterwarde disherited and shaven a monke at Redinge.
And the Kinge gathered a great power against Southwales and came
himself as farre as Pencadayr besydes Breknoke. And Rhes came to him
and dyd him homage, and gave him[6] pledges and the Kinge returned to
Englande againe. And aboute this tyme was Enyon (sonne to Anaraud
ap Griffith and nevewe to Prince Rhes) murthered in his bedde by a
man of his owne, named Walter ap[7] Lhywarch. [135] And Cadwgan ap
Meredith was slaine after the like maner by one Walter ap Rikart. And
Lorde Rhes (as he is called in Welshe, or Kinge Rhes as the Latyn
authers name him) toke the Cantref Mawr, which is a great countrey,
and the lande of Dynevwr and enjoyed hit. And this yere dyed Kedyvor
ap Danyell Archedeacon of Caerdygan and Henry ap Arthen, which was
the worthiest clerke that had bene many yeres in Wales. The yere
ensuinge the Lorde Rhes (seinge he was not able to manteine his estate
with suche landes as the Kinge had appointed him) entred the landes of
Roger De Clare, Earle of Glocester (for by the earles meanes was his

[1]C Lhandinan   [5]Ll – the
[2]Ll – of revenge; *supplied from HC*   [6]Ll – him
[3]C begun   [7]C – Walter ap
[4]C – in . . . fought

nevewe murthered) and wonne the castells of Aberrheydiol and of the
sonnes of Wynyawn★ and rased them. And in shorte tyme he brought all
Caerdygan to his subjection, and from thence he made many rodes[1]
against the Fleminges, and gote great spoiles in their countrey. And all
Wales agreed to forsake the rule [135v] off the Normaines (whose
pride,[2] treason, and crueltie they colde not abide) and to serve princes of
their owne nation. And this yere Hamelym, base brother to Kinge
Henrye, maryed the countesse of Warrenne, which was wief to William
Earle of Mortimer, Kinge Stephens sonne, and this countesse[3] was
daughter and heire to William the thyrde[4] Earle of Warrenne. And this
yere dyed Walter Gifforde, Earle of Buckingham, without heires, and
therfore the Earldome fill to the kinges handes.

And the yere 1165 dyd David, the sonne of Owen Prince of
Northwales, destroye all Flintshire, which was the Kinges, and caryed all
the people and cattell with him to the valley of Clwyd,[5] nowe called
Ruthyn lande. Which when the Kinge understoode, he leveyed an army
in haist, and came to succour his castelles and people as farre as Rudlan,
and after he had layne there three daies, and colde doe no good, he
returned to [136] Englande, and gathered an other army of chosen men,
throughe all his dominions, as Englande, Normandy, Angyew,[6]
Gascoyn, and Gwyen, and sende for succours to[7] Flandres and Britaine.
And returned towardes Northwales, mindinge utterly to destroye all that
bare lyef in the lande, and came to Croesoswalt, nowe called
Oswaldestrie, and encamped there. And one the contrarie parte prince
Owen and his brother Cadwalader with all the power of Northwales,
and the Lorde Rhes with the power of Southwales, and Owen Keveliog
and the sonnes of Madoc ap Meredith with the power of Powis, and the
twoe sonnes of Madoc ap Idnerth with the people betwixt Wy and
Sevarn gathered them togeather to defende their countrey in
Edeyrnyon, at Corvaen. And the Kinge, understandinge they were so
nighe, was wonderfull desyrouse of battaill, and came to the ryver of
Kyriog,[8] and caused [136v] the woode to be hewen downe. And of the
Welshmen, understandinge the passage, came a great number of the best
men, unknowinge to their captaines, and mette with [the] Kinges
vawarde[9]★ where were placed the pyked men of all the army, and there
began a hote skirmishe, and diverse worthie men slayne one either syde.

[1] C roods
[2] C – pride
[3] C – King . . . countesse
[4] Ll 3de
[5] C Clud

[6] C Angie
[7] C from
[8] C Kyrig
[9] C warde

But the Kinge wonne the passage and came to the mountaine of Berwyn and laye there in campe certeine dayes. And so both armyes stode in awe of other. For the Kinge kept the open playnes, and was afrayed to bee in trapte in straytes and the Welshmen watched for the advantage of the place, and kept the Kinge so strayte that neither forage nor vyttaill might come to the campe, nor any souldyer durst sturre abrode. And to augemente thees myseries, there fill suche rayne that the Kinges men colde skant stande upon their feete, upon those slyppery hilles. And so the Kinge was compelled [137] to returne home without his purpose, and with great losse of men and munition besids his charges. And therfore in a great choler[1] he caused the pledges eyes (which he had reaceved longe before that) to be put out, and they were Rhes and[2] Cadwalhon the sonnes of Owen, and Kynvryc and Meredith the sonnes of Rhes, and others.

And after longe consultacioun the Kinge came the thirde tyme towarde Northwales entendinge to have his army conveyed by sea, and landed in some convenient place of the countrey. And so he came to Chester; and theire laye a certeine tyme till all his navye was gathered togeather,[3] as well hyred shippes of Irelande as his owne. And upon the sodeine he brake up his campe, and gave bothe shippes and men leave to departe. And the same yere dyd Rhes Prince of Southwales laye siedge to the castell of Abertivi, and wonne hit, and made hit flatte with the grounde and likewise wonne Kylgerran and rased hit and toke [137v] Roberte (the sonne of Stephen his cosine germaine) prisoner (for Nest his aunt, after the deceasse of Geralde maryed Stephen constable) and returned home with a riche spoyle. And aboute the same tyme dyed Lhewelyn sonne to Prince Owen, a worthie gentillman, and of great towardnes. And the yere ensuinge came the Flemynges and Normaines of Westwales with a great power against the castell of Kilgerran, which Rhes had fortified, and layed siedge to hit, and assaulted hit diverse tymes, but hit was so manfully defended that they returned home, as they came. And shortely after they came before hit againe, and lost many of their best men, and retyred backe with great losse and dishonor.[4] And the same yere Owen (Prince of Northwales) layed siedge to the castell of Basingwerke, [138] whiche the Kinge had fortified, and in shorte tyme wonne hit, and rased hit. And aboute the same tyme Dernyd sonne to Murchath was chased out of his dominion in Irelande, and he went to Normandye to Kinge Henry for succors. Also Ierwerth Goch was

[1] C collor
[2] C ap
[3] C together
[4] C – with . . . dishonor

spoiled of his landes in Powys by Owen Kevelyoc, sonne to Griffith ap
Meredith (and lorde of that which is nowe called Powis) and by Owen
Vychan secunde sonne to Madocke ap Meredith. And they devyded his
landes betwixt them, so that Owen Kevelyog had Mochnant above
Rhayader and Owen Vychan Mochnant benethe Rhayader. This yere
was there an earthquake in Northfolke, and Suffolke. And the Kinge
maryed Geffrey his sonne to Constance thonly doughter and heire of
Conan [138v] Earle of Richemonde and Duke of Britaine.

   In the yere 1167 Owen Prince of Northwales and Cadwalader his
brother, and Rhes Prince of Southwales brought their powers to Powys
against Owen Kevelyog, and wonne all his landes and chased him out of
the countrey, and gave Caerenyon to Owen Vichan sonne to Madoc ap
Meredith to houlde of Prince Owen and the Lorde Rhes had Walwerne
because hit stoode within his countrey. And shortly after returned
Owen Kevelyog, with a great[1] number of Normaines and Englishmen,
to recover his countrey againe, and layed siedge to the castell of
Caerenyon, and wonnne hit and brent hit to the grounde. And the same
yere dyd the forsaide princes, Owen, Rhes and Cadwalader, [139] laye
their siedge to the castell of Rudlan, which the Kinge had[2] latly built
and fortified. And the garryson defended hit manfully and worthely, yet
the princes woulde not departe till they had wonne hit, and rased hit at
the three[3] monethes ende that they came before hit. And afterwarde
they gote the castell of Prestatyn* and destroyed hit and then brought all
Tegengle to Owen's subiection[4] and returned home with muche honor.
And the yere folowinge Conan (sonne to Prince Owen) slewe Urgeney
Abbot of[5] Lhwythlawr, and Lhaudhen his nevewe. And at this tyme
Henrye Duke of Saxonye maryed Mawde Kinge Henryes doughter.
And the nobles of Pectew[6] rebelled against King Henrie[7] by ayde of the
Frenche Kinge and slewe Patrike Earle of Salysburye. And the King
created William his sonne earle in his steede. Also the [139v] Britons
rebelled against Kinge Henrye, and he destroyed a great parte of the
countrey. The next yere Henry, the Kinges eldest sonne, dyd homage to
the Frenche Kinge for the earledome of Angiowe, and Steewardeship of
France which belonged therto. And Geffrey dyd his brother homage for
the dukedome of Brytaine, and the Kinge made a great diche and
trenche beetwixte France and Normandy to defende sodeine incursions
and theves. And this yere Roberte sonne to Stephen was released out of

[1]C – great
[2]Ll – had
[3]C – twoe
[4]Ll – and destroyed hit and then brought

all Tegengle to Owen's subiection
[5]Ll – of
[6]C Peitew
[7]Ll – Henrie

his cosins prison, the Lorde Rhes, and was sent to Irelande with a great power to succor Dernyt sonne to Murchath, and they landed at Lochgarmon, and wonne hit and so went forwarde.

[140] In the yere 1169 was Meuric ap Adam of Buelht slaine and murthered in his bedde by Meredith Bengoch his cosine germaine. And this yere there were founde the bones of a gyant cast up by the sea, of such leingth that his body seemed to conteine 50 fote in height. And the Kinge caused his sonne Henrye to be crowned by the Archebishop of Yorke Kinge of England. And this yere Owen Gwynedh sonne to Griffith ap Conon, Prince of Northwales passed out of this worlde, and transitorie lief, after he had governed his countrey well and worthely 32 yeres. This Prince was fortunate and victoriouse in all martiall affayres, he never toke any enterprice in hande but he atcheved hit. He left behinde him many childrene goten upon dyverse women which were esteemed not by [140v] their mothers and birth, but by their prowesse and valiantnes. First he had by Gwladus, doughter to Lhywarch ap Trehayarn ap Caradoc, Ierwerth Drwyndwn (that is to saye, Edwarde with the broken nose), Conan, Maelgwn, and Gwenlhian, by Christian, doughter to Grono ap Ywayn ap Edwyn, he had David, Rodryk, Cadwalhon Abbot of Barsey, and Ingharad wief to Griffith Maelor. He had besides thees Conan, Lhewelyn, Meredith, Idwall, Rhun, Howell, Cadelh, Madock Enyon, two Kynvrykes, Phillippe, and Ryryd, Lorde of Clochran in Irelande by dyverse women, of which Rhun, Lhewelyn and Kynvric dyed before their father and of the rest youe shall here hereafter.

David the sonne of Owen Gwynedh

[141] After the death of Owen his sonnes fill at debate who shulde enherite after him. For the eldest sonne borne in matrimonye Edward or Erwerth Drwyndwn was counted unmeete for his maime upon his face. And Howell who toke upon him all the rulle was a base sonne begoten upon an Irishwoman. Therfore David gathered all the power he coulde, and came against Howell, and fought with him and slewe him, and afterwarde enjoyed quietly the whole lande of Northwales, untill his brother Ierwerth or Edwardes sonne came to age as shall hereafter appeare. And at this tyme an other of Owen Gwynedhs sonnes, named Madocke,★ lefte the lande in contention betwixt his bretherne, and prepared certeine shippes, with men [and] munition, and sought adventures by the seas. And sayled west levinge the cost of Irelande [so

far] north that he came to a lande unknowen, where he sawe many strange thinges. And this lande most needes bee [141v] some parte of that lande the which the Hispaniardes do affirme them selves to be the first finders, sith Hannos tyme. For by reason and order of cosmographie this lande to which Madoc came to, most needs bee somme parte of Nova Hispania, or Florida. And so hit was by Britons longe afore discovered before eyther Colonus or Americus lead any Hispaniardes thyther. Of this Madockes passage and returne therbe many fables fayned as the commen people do use in distance of place and leingth of tyme rather to augment than to dyminish, but sure hit is, that there he was. And after he had returned home and declared the plesant and frutefull countreys that he had seene without inhabitantes, and upon the contrarye parte what barreyne and wilde grounde his bretherne and nevewes did murther one an other for, he prepared a number of shippes, and gote with him suche men and women as were desirouse to [142] lyve in quietnes. And takinge his[1] leave of his frendes, toke his journey thytherwarde againe wherefore hit is to be presupposed that he and his people enhabited parte of those countreys. And hit appeareth by Francys Loues[2] that in Acuzanus,[3] and other places, the people honoured the crosse, and that Christians had bene there before the comminge of the Hispaniardes, and because his people were not manye they folowed the maners of the lande they came unto, and used the language they founde there.★

But to my hystorie. About[4] the same tyme, Elynor the Kinges doughter was maryed to Alfonce, Kinge of Castell. And Richarde Strangbowe (Earle of Strigill)★ went to Ireland without the Kings leave, and maryed the doughter of Diernyt, Kinge of Develyn, wherefore the Kinge ceassed all his landes in Englande to his owne handes and Diernyt dyed shortely after, and was buried at Ferna. And at the ende of this yere was Thomas Becket (Archebishop of Canterburye) slayne. [142v] And the yere ensuinge, Rhes Prince of Southwales came with a great power to Powis, and subdued Owen Keveliog the lorde therof, and toke 7[5] pledges★ of him and returned home with muche honor. And the Kinge called his nobles to consulte aboute the enterprise of Irelande, which had bene before determined to bee taken in hand, and to his[6] consultaciouns came messingers frome Richarde Strangbowe, and Earle of Strigill, and marshall of Englande, to delyver to the Kinges handes the citie of

---

[1]C – his
[2]C Lopes
[3]C Acuzanus *deleted*, Acujarniland yucutan
  inserted above in later hand

[4]C – About
[5]C -7
[6]C this

Develyn and the towne of Waterforde, with such other townes as he
had by the right of his wife. Wherupon the Kinge restored to him
againe his landes in England and Normandy, and made him Steewarde
of Irelande, and so conclusion was taken for the Kinges viage to Ireland.
And therupon the Lorde Rhes came to the Kinge, and the Kinge[1]
receaved him to his peace, and confirmed him all that he had and
therefore Rhes payed the Kinge 300 horses and 4000 oxen, and gave
him 14 pledges.* [143] And shortly after, the Kinge came to Southwales
and entringe Caerlhion upon Usk toke the towne from the lorde therof,
Ierwerth ap Owen ap Caradok, and kept hit to himself. Wherefore[2]
Ierwerth departed from the Kinge, and callinge his sonnes Owen and
Howell to him (which he had begoten upon Yngharad, doughter to
Uchtryd bishop of Landaffe) and his sisters sonne Morgan ap Seysilht ap
Dyvynwal, gathered a number of men and upon the Kinges departure
entred the countrey, and spoyled and brenned, as they went, and toke
the towne of Caerlhyon, and destroyed hit all,[3] save the castell which
they coulde not gette, and the Kinge kept his journey to Penbroke. And
there he gave Rhes all Caerdygan, Ystradtywy, Arwystly and Elvael.*
And Rhes was at Abertivi, which he had wonne from the Earle of
Glocester, and fortified of late, and from thence he came to Penbroke
the 7[4] calendes* of October, and spake with the Kinge, and returned
againe the day after, and chose out of [143v] the horses he caused to be
brought thither for the Kinge 86, and caused them to be brought to
Penbroke.* And the same daye the Kinge went to St. Davyes, and
offered there, and dyned with the Bishop David, sonne to Geralde
(cosine germaine to Rhes). And thither came the Earle of Strigill from
Irelande to speake with the Kinge. And after dyner the Kinge returned
to Penbroke and Rhes presented him the horses, and the Kinge chose 36
of the best, and sende the rest bake againe, with great thankes to Rhes.
And at the White House, the Kinge rendred to Rhes Howell his sonne,
which had bene longe for pledge with the Kinge. And also the Kinge
gave him day for the other pledges, and for his tribute, till he returned
from Ireland. And so the Kinge made ready his navye, and toke
sheppinge, but the winde was contrary, and he was compelled to returne
to the shore againe and the next day, beinge the xiiii calendes of
November, the Kinge toke shipping againe, and had faire passage [144]
to Irelande, where [he] laye quietly that winter. And the Christmas
folowinge, Henrie the younge Kinge kept a solempne feast where were

[1]C he   [3]C – all
[2]C Wherof   [4]C – 7

William SaintJohn (procurator of Normandy) and William Fitzhamon (seneschall of Britaine) and 110 knightes besides.

And the yere 1172 fill a great death in the Kinges army in Irelande, for the change of the ayre and vittailles, and therefore the Kinge returned and landed in Wales in the passion weeke, and remayned at Penbroke Easter Daye and the daye folowinge and upon Tuisday¹ toke his journey towardes Ingland. And the Lorde Rhes mette with him at Talacharne, and spake with him. And as he passed from Caerdyff throughe the newe castell upon Uske he sent for Ierwerth ap Owen ap Caradock to come speake with him, under saffe conducte to him. And his sonnes and frendes and Ierwerth toke his journey towardes the Kinge, and sent worde to Owen his sonne (beinge a lustie yonge gentillman) [144v] to meete with him by the waye. But as he came, at his fathers commaundment,² the Earle of Bristowes men, heringe that, came furth of the newe castell upon Uske and layed wayte for him by the waye and sodeinly sette upon him (being unarmed, and havinge but fewe in his companye, and trustinge the Kinges promise) and murthered him traytorousely and cowardly. And when his father herde this by some of his men that had escaped, he was verye sorye, and returned home with all his frendes, and his sonne Howell, and wolde never afterwarde trust nether the Kinges promise, nor any Englishman. And furthwith gathered his power, and his frendes also, and without mercy destroyed all the countrey with fyer and sworde to the gates of Hereforde and Glocester, to revenge³ the death of his sonne. And the Kinge made the lorde Rhes⁴ chief justice of all Southwales by commission and toke his journey to Normandy. [145] And the same yere dyed Cadwalader ap Griffith ap Conan, brother to Owen⁵ prince of Northwales. He had by his wief Ales doughter to Richarde of Clare (Earle of Glocester) Cunedha, Randwlf and Richarde, and by other women he had Cadvan, Cadwalader, Enyon, Meredith Goch and Cadwalhon. And toward the ende of this yere Seisylht ap Dyvynwal and Ieuan ap Seisylht ap Ryryt got the castell of Abergevenny upon the sodeine, and toke the Kinges garrison prisoners. And the yere ensuinge was the fayrest wynter that ever was seene.

And this tyme fill a discension betwixt the twoe kings of Englande, the father and the sonne and there cleved to the sonne the Queene his mother, and both his bretherne Geffrey and Richarde, and the Earle of Chester, and William Patryk with his three sonnes, and the Earle of

¹C Tusedaye
²C commandment
³C avenge
⁴Ll – Rhes
⁵C – brother to Owen

Mellent, [145v] Bernard de Seritate, Camerarius de Tankarvilla, Valeran de Hibera, Gocelyn Crispyn, Gilbert de Regulariis, Symon de Monteforti, Raff de Say, Hughe de Sant Mara and the Frenche Kinge and the Earle of Flanders gave succours to the yonge kinge, and he toke Hughe Lacy and Hughe Beauchampe in the castell of Vernoyll. Yet the elder Kinge was not discouraged but hyred[1] Almaines and Brabanders to his souldiers and Rhes Prince of Southwales sent to him Howell his sonne with a fayre companie of men to serve him. And the Kinge was very gladde and sent the Lorde Rhes great thankes, and the Kinge overthrewe his enimyes dyverse tymes and toke Radulf de Fulgeriis and the Earle of Chester prisoners. But William Patryk and Hastulph de Hillario escaped and the Earle of Leycester and Hughe de Nova Castello (as they began a sturre in Englande) were taken at Bury by the elder Kinges souldiers and emprisoned. [146] And in[2] this meane tyme Ierwerth ap Owen brought his power against Caerlhyon, and they of the towne fought with him, but he overthrewe them, and toke many prisoners, and wonne the towne, and layed siedge to the castell which was yelded him furthwith, in exchange for his prisoners. And his sonne Howell brought all Gwent Iskoed to his subjection, savinge the castell, and toke pledges of the inhabitantes of the countrey. Also at this tyme David, sonne to Owen Gwynedh, Prince of Northwales, made warre against his brother Maelgwn, which kept the Ile of Mone, or Anglesey, and brought his people over Menai (for so is named the arme of the sea that separateth hit frome the maine lande) and chaced his brother out of the Ile into Irelande, and brought all the Ile to his subjection. Also he chaced all his bretherne and cosins out of Northwales, and toke all their landes to him self, and toke his brother Maelgwn, as he came from Irelande, and kept [146v] hym in close prison, and Conan his brother dyed.

In the yere 1175 Howell, sonne to Ierwerth ap Owen of Caerlhyon, toke his uncle Owen Penkarn prisoner, and put out his eies, and gelded him, lest he shulde beget children which shulde enherit Caerlhyon and Gwent. But God provided punishement, for upon the Saturday folowinge came their a great army of Normaines and Englishmen before the towne, and wonne hit, with the castell, maugre Howell and his father, who was not pryvey to his sonnes lewde deede. And this yere the elder Kinge came to Englande, and William Kinge of Scottes and Roger de Molbraye were taken prisoners at Alnewyke by the barrons of the north, as they came to destroye Englande, in the quarell of the yonge

---

[1]C – but hyred   [2]C – in

Kinge. And the elder Kinge put them in saffe kepinge, with the Earle of
Lycester, and reaceved Hughe Bygod Earle of Norfolke to his [147]
peace, and returned to Normandy with a great army of Welshmen,
which were sent him from David Prince of Northwales, to whome the
Kinge gave his sister Emma in mariage. And the Kinge sent the
Welshmen over the ryver Sene, to cutte awaye the vyttailles which
came to his enimyes campe. Wherfore the French Kinge came to talke,
and shortely they concluded a peace, so that all the bretherne desired the
father forgevenes. And this tyme dyd David prince of Northwales
(beinge bolde of the Kinges affinitie) emprison his owne brother
Rodricke in boltes, because he desired parte of his fatheres landes. And
the yere folowinge came bothe the Kinges to Englande, and the Scottes[1]
Kinge was sette at libertie and he became lyedgeman unto Kinge
Henrie, and swore to him with all the lordes of Scottelande spirituall and
temperall and delyvered the Kinge the townes of Rockesburgh and
Berwicke, and the castell of Maydens. And shortely after dyed Roger
[147v] Earle of Cornewall base sonne to Henrye the First, and the Kinge
seased his landes in Englande, Wales and Normandy to himself, for John
his youngest sonne, save a small portion which he leaft his doughters.
And aboute the same tyme dyed Richarde Earle of Glocester, and
Philippe his sonne was created in his steede. Also William Earle of
Arundell dyed shortly after at Waverley, and was buryed at Wyndham,
wherof he was patrone. And this yere dyd Rhes Prince of Southwales
come to the Kinges courte at Glocester and brought with him suche
lordes of Southwales as had offended the Kinge, to do the Kinge
homage, which pleased the Kinge wonderfull well. And thees were they
that came with Rhes: Cadwalhon ap Madock of Melyenyth his cosine
germaine, Enyon Clut of Elvael, Enyon ap Rhes of Werthrynyon
(which twoe had maryed twoe of his doughters), Morgan ap [148]
Caradock ap Iestyn of Glamorgan, Griffith ap Ivor ap Meuryg of
Saynhenyd, Seysilht ap Dyvynwal, of the Hyer Gwent (which three had
maryed his sisters) and Ierwerth ap Owen of Caerlhyon. And the kinge
receaved them all to his peace, and restored to Ierwerth ap Owen
Caerlhyon againe and they returned home with great joye. And[2] shortly
after William de Bruse Lord of Breknoke desired Seisylht ap Dyvynwal,
and Geffrey his sonne, and a great number of the worshipfullest men of
Gwent lande to a feast to the castell of Abergevenny (which he had
receaved of them by composition), [and] they mistrustinge him not,
came thither. But he, like a traytor and murtherer, had a great number

[1]C Scottishe   [2]C But

of armed men[1] within the castell, which fell upon this lorde and the rest and without mercy slewe them all. And furthwith went to Seisylhts house (beinge not farre thence) and toke his wief, and slewe Cadwalader his sonne before his mother and destroyed the house. And this was a lamentable daye to all the lande of Gwent [148v] and a lesson to trust the treason of the Normaines and Englishmen, which the Welshemen colde never doe afterwarde.

And in Northwales Rodryk brake his brothers prison, and escaped, and came to Anglesey, and all the countrey receaved him for their lorde, because they abhorred the ingratitude of there prince, which unnaturally disherited all his bretherne and cosines, upon hope of ayde of his brother in lawe, the Kinge. And likewise Rodryke [was][2] receaved as lorde and prince in all the countrey above Conway and Prince David fledde thrughe the ryver of Conway and there remained for a tyme. And this yere dyed Cadelh, sonne to Griffith ap Rhes, and brother to the Lorde Rhes, after longe siknes and was buried honorably at Ystradflur. The next yere dyed David Bishop of Menevia, and Perys[3]★ was made bishope in his place. And this yere the Lorde Rhes Prince of Southwales[4]★ made a great feast at Christmas in his castell of Abertivi, [149] whiche feast he caused to be proclaymed thrughe all Britaine longe before. And thither came many strangers, which were worthely receaved, and honorably enterteined, so that no man departed miscontented. And amonge dedes of armes, and other showes, Rhes caused all the poetes of Wales (which they calle bardh, and in the plural number beyrdh) to come thither, and caused chairs to be sette in his hall, where they shulde dispute togeather in diverse artes and sciences, and great rewardes, and riche giftes were appointed for the overcomers and at the ende they of Northwales wanne the price. And amonge the musicions Rhes his owne housholde men were counted best. And this tyme was their a lawe made in Englande for the murther of priestes bishoppes and religiouse men, wherby hit was made fellonye.[5] For before that tyme the temporall powers entermedled not with any suche [149v] matter, and the punishment was onely excommunication. And shortly after Enyon Clut and Morgan ap Meredith were both slaine by treason of the Normaines that enhabited the marches.

And the Lorde Rhes dyd builde the castell of Rhayader Gwy, which is to saye, the fall of Wy, for the ryver Wy falleth there[6] over a great and

[1]C – men
[2]Ll – was
[3]C Pyrs

[4]Ll Northwales; corrected from C Southwales
[5]C fellome
[6]Ll – there

highe rocke. And the sonnes of Conan ap Owen Gwynedh made warre against the lorde Rhes, and Cadwalhon, brother unto Owen Gwynedh★ and uncle to David and Rodryke, which fledde to the Kinge for succours, and as he was conveyed home by the Kinges men, to enjoye his patrymonye, was cruelly murthered by the waye, and those, whome he hoped to be his helpe and frendes, he founde traytours and buychers.[1] And about this tyme William kinge of Sicilia [150] maryed Johan doughter to Kinge Henrye the elder. And the Kinge of Englande bought therldome of Mouch in France of Hughe de Brume, earle thereof, for 6000[li] of silver[2]★ And this yere beinge 1179 were the bones of noble Kinge Arthure and Gwenhwyvar his wief founde in the Ile of Avalhon (that is to saye, the Ile of Aples) without the Abbey of Glastonburye 15 fote within the earth in a holowe elder[3] tree, and over the bones was a stone, and a crosse of leadde, with the[4] writinge turned towardes the stone wherin were graven thees woordes:

Hic iacet sepultus inclytus Rex Arthurus in insula Avalonia.

The bones were of a mervelouse biggenesse, and in the scule were 10 woundes, of which one was great and seamed to bee his deathes wounde. [150v] And the queenes heare was to the sight fayre, and yelowe, but as soone as hit was touched hit fill to ashes. This grave was founde by meanes of a bardh, or poet, which the Kinge hearde at Penbroke declare in a songe the worthye actes of that noble Prince, and the place of his buryall. Therefore let William Parvus and Polydor Virgill, with their complices, stoppe their lyinge mouthes, and desist to obscure and darken the gliteringe fame and noble renown of so invincible and victoriouse a prince, with the envyouse tetraction and vile sclannder of their vituperouse and venomouse tonges, thinkinge they may cover with the clowde of oblivion, and burye in the pytte of darkenes, those noble actes and princely deedes, by their wilfull ignnorance and dogged envye, whereof the trumpette of fame hathe [151] sounded not onely in Britaine but thrughe all Europa. But remittinge the discoveringe and blasinge of their cankered mindes towardes the honour of Britaine to suche as can[5] better painte them in their owne colors, I will returne to my matter. Kinge Henrie the elder forsoke his wief for certeine consideraciouns, and kept her in prison

[1]C butchers
[2]C – of Hughe . . . silver
[3]Ll older
[4]C – the
[5]Ll came

many yeres. And aboute this tyme Randulph de Poer with a great number of gentillmen was slaine by certeine yonge men of Gwentlande to revenge their Lordes deathe.

And the yere 1183 was Henrye Duke of Saxonie banished his countrey and came to Kinge Henrie, his father in lawe, for succors. And this yere dyed Henrie the yonge Kinge and was buried at Rome. The yere ensuinge [151v] the Duke of Saxonie came unto Englande, and his wief was brought to bedde of a sonne, which was[1] named William. And William de Manndevill Earle of Essex went to Flanders with an army, to succor the Earle against the Earle of Henande, or Henegowe. And shortly after John the Kinges yongest sonne was dobbed knight, and toke his journey to Irelande. And Hughe de Lacy, Lorde of Midya, was slaine by a sicke man, and John returned home from Irelande at Christmas. And this yere the sonne was eclipsed upon May Daye.[2] And Howell ap Ieaf Lorde of Arwystli dyed, and was buryed at Ystradflur. And the yere 1186 dyed Geffrey Duke of Britaine the Kinges thyrde sonne, leavinge behinde him a doughter, and his wief [152] great with childe of a sonne which was[3] named Arthure.

And this tyme was Cadwalader, the sonne of the Lorde Rhes, slayne pryvely in Westwales and buried in the Ty Gwynne. The next yere Owen Vychan the sonne of Madocke ap Meredith was slaine in the castell of Carrek Gova harde by Oswaldestre in the night tyme, by the twoe sonnes of Owen Kevelyog, Gwenwynwyn and Caswalhon. And shortly after Lhewelyn, sonne to Cadwalhon that was murthered by the Englishmen, was taken by his owne bretherne, and his eies put out. And this yere Maelgwn sonne to the Lorde Rhes brought his power against Tenby, and by plaine force wonne the towne, and spoyled hit, and brenned hit to asshes. This Lorde [152v] was fayre and comelye of person, honest and juste of condiciouns, beloved of his frendes, and feared of his foes, against whom (especially the Fleminges) he atcheved diverse victories. In the yere 1189 Henrie the secunde surnamed Curtmantell, Kinge of all Britaine, Duke of Gascoyne, Gwyne and Normandy, passed out of this transitorie lief, and was buryed at Fonttenyarde, and after him was Richarde his sonne crowned in his steed. And he receaved homage of William Kinge of Scottes, and delivered him againe the castell of Maydens, or Edenburgh, Rokesburgh, and Berwike, which Kinge Henrie had longe kept. And this yere the Lorde Rhes, gathered all his streingth and wonne the

[1]Ll – was
[2]C manye Dayes
[3]Ll – was; C was *later added above line*

castelles of Seyncler, Abercorran and Llanstephant, and brought all the whole countrey to his subjection, and toke Maelgwn his sonne [153] and kept him prisoner, in whome remained all the hope of Southwales. And the yere ensuinge, Rhes dyd builde the castell of Kydwyly, and Gwenlhian his doughter dyed, the fayrest and goodliest woman in all Wales. Aboute this tyme Kinge Richarde made the Bishop of Durham earle of Northumberlande for a 1000^{li} and afterwarde he saide in jeste that he had made a yonge earle of an olde bishoppe. And shortly after Kinge Richarde toke[1] his journey to the Holy Lande, to make warre[2] againste the enymyes of Christes fayeth. And the Bishop of Ely, the Kinges Chauncelor and Vicegerent, made a great diche about the towne of London. And Griffith Maelor or Griffith Bromfelde, Lorde of that parte of Powis, dyed, a noble [153v] man, and a wise, and that in liberalitie passed all the lordes and noble men of his tyme. He had by his wief (doughter to Owen Gwynedh Prince of NorthWales) a sonne called Madok, which succeded his father in [that][3] parte of Powis called Powys Vadock. And aboute this tyme dyverse noble men of Englande dyed at Acon, as Henry Earle of Leycester, the Earle of Ferrers, Ranulphe de Fevergres, Ranulphe de Alta Ripa, and at home William Marshall, Geffre Fitzpeter, Hughe Bardulf and William Briwer were the nobles that bare most rule in Englande in the Kinges absence. And Rhes Prince of Southwales wonne the castell of Dynevwr, and Owen his sonne dyed at Ystradflur. [154] And aboute this tyme Kinge Richearde wanne the Kingedome of Cyprus, and gave hit to Guido[4] Kinge of Jerusalem, upon condicioun he shulde release to Richarde his claime of Jerusalem, which he dyd. And the Kinge maryed at Cyprus Beregaria doughter to the Kinge of Navarra. And shortly after Maelgwn, the sonne of the Lorde Rhes, escaped out of prison, where his father had kept him for a longe tyme. And the Lorde Rhes gote the castell of Lhanhayaden and the countrey aboute. And Griffith ap Cadwgan dyed.

And Kinge Richarde, after he had atcheved, with his nobles, the Earle of Leycester, Bartholomewe Mortimer, [154v] Radulph de Malo Leone, Andrew de Chevegny, Gerarde[5] de Furnevale, Roger de Lacy, William de Stagno, Hughe de Nevella, William de Porcell and Henry Duthe his standardberer, many worthy deedes of armes against the infidelles, in his returninge home throughe Austrych was taken prisoner, by Lupolde, the Duke therof, and presented him to Henrye the Emperour, who kept him

[1] Ll to
[2] C – warre
[3] Ll his

[4] C Gwido
[5] C – Andrew . . . Gerarde

prisoner untill suche tyme as he had payed 20,000¹ marks for his ransom, layinge to his charge that he had spoyled the Ile of Sicilie in his vyage towardes the Holy Lande. And the same yere Rodryke, the sonne of Owen Gwynedh (by the helpe of Gothicke Kinge of Man) entred the Ile of Mone and brought hit to his subjection. [155] But before the ende of the yere, the sonnes of his brother Conan chaced him out of the Ile and gote hit themselves. And at this tyme Maelgwn, the sonne of Rhes Prince of Southwales, layed siedge to the castell of Ystradmeuryg and wonne hit. Also Howell (surnamed Says, that is to saye, Saxon, or Englishe, because he had served in Englande), sonne to the saide Prince Rhes, gote the castell of Wyst upon the sodeine, and toke Philippe de Gwys and his wief, and his twoe sonnes prysoners therin. And seinge he had more castelles then he coulde well defende, determined to rase the castell of Llanhayaden. And the Fleminges understandinge that, gathered all their streingth, and came thyther the daye appointed to [155v] rase the castell, and sette fierclye upon the men of Howell and Maelgwn, and slewe many of them, and put the rest to flight. But they gathered a greater power shortly after, and came thyther againe, and rased the castell to the grounde, without any lette or staye. And upon this, Anaraud, the sonne also of the Prince Rhes, moved with filthy ambition and covetousenes of landes, toke his twoe bretherne, Howell and Madocke, prisoners (under the color of frendship) and put out both their eies.

And the yere 1184 Kinge Richarde came into Englande,★ and beinge at dyner in his litle hall of Westminster, heringe howe the Frenche Kinge dyd besiedge Vernoyll, he swore he wolde never turne his face till he had fought with him, yf he durste² abide, and caused the walle to be broken before him [156] and so passed to Normandy and receaved his brother John to mercye and raysed the siedge. For the Frenche Kinge fledde as sone as he herde of Kinge Richardes comminge. This yere Maelgwn, sonne to Prince Rhes, gave his brother Anaraud the castell of Ystradmeurig for his prisoners, which he sette at libertie. And Rhes himself dyd reedifie againe the castell of Rhayader Gwy. But his owne sonnes layed wayte for him, and toke their father prisoner, fearinge lest he woulde avenge their cruell and unnaturall deedes. Parte by the meanes of Howell his sonne, which was blinde, he escaped out of Maelgwn his sonns prison, and toke the castell of Dynevwr, which Maelgwn kept, and destroyed hit. And the sonnes of Cadwalhon ap Madocke, of Melyenydh, wonne the castell of Rhayader Gwy [156v] and fortified hit for themselfes.

¹C 200,000   ²C dyd

And at this tyme, Llewelyn, sonne to Ierwerth Drwyndwn (or
Edwarde with the broken nose) which was eldest sonne to Owen
Gwynedh Prince of Northwales, remembringe his right and title to his
enheritance of Northwales (althoughe his father had bene disherited by
his brother David), called togeather all his frendes by his mother, which
was Marred, doughter to Madok ap Meredith Prince of Powis, and also
made a[1] confederacye with his cosines germaines the sonnes of Conan ap
Owen Gwynedh, chalenged the rule of Northwales, and entred the
countrey, whiche yelded to him, and toke him for their Lorde. And so
without bloodshed he receaved all Northwales into[2] his subjection,
except 3 castelles which his uncle David kept by force of Englishmen, in
whome was all his trust, because of his wief Emma, aunte to the Kinge
of Englande, and thus David lost his lande, and Llewelyn began to rule
the yere of our Lorde 1184.*

[157] Lhewelyn the sonne of Ierwerth eldest son to
Owen Gwynedh

After Lhewelyn, sonne of Ierwerth, had taken in his handes the rule
of Northwales, as right enheritor therof, Roger Mortymer came with a
great power to Melyenydh, and built the castell of Kymaron, and
brought the countrey to his subjection and chaced awaye the twoe
sonnes of Cadwalhon ap Madok Lordes of the countrey. And at the
same tyme Rhes and Meredith, sonnes to Prince Rhes (beinge twoe
lustie gentilmen), gathered together a number of wilde heades of the
countrey and came to Dynevor, and gote the castell from their fathers
garrison. And afterwarde they went to Cantref Bychan, and the whole
countrey receaved them gently, and delyvered the castell to their
handes. And their father beinge therwith sore displeased layed pryvey
wayt for them and by treason of their owne men (which were afrayed
any further to offende their lorde and prince) they were taken and
brought to their father [157v] who kept them in saffe prison.

The yere ensuinge ther was a combate appointed betwixt the Frenche
kinge and fyve knightes with him, against Kinge Richarde and fyve
other, which shulde ende all the contraversies. Which fight Kinge
Richarde was gladde of, but the Frenche Kinge, like a snayle, drewe in
his hornes and forsoke the battaill. And in Wales the Prince Rhes
gathered a great army, and layed siedge to the towne and castell of

[1] C in   [2] C to

Caermardhyn, and in shorte tyme wonne them bothe, and spoyled and
destroyed them, and returned with a great butty and leadde his saide
armye to the Marches, before the castell of Clun, which after a longe
siedge and many a fierse assaulte, he gote and brenned hit. And from
thence he went to the castell of Radnor, and likewise wonne hit, to the
defence wherof came Roger Mortymer and Hughe de Saye, with a great
armye of Normaines [158] and Englishmen well armed, and tryed
souldyers. And Rhes, which had wonne the castell, determined not to
kepe his men within the walles, but boldely like a worthye prince, and
couragiouse lyon,★ came out into the playne beside the towne, and gave
them battaill, where his men (althoughe for the most parte unarmed, and
not accustomed to the battaill) declared that they had come of Britons
bloodde (whose title the noble Romaine Emperors dyd so muche desire,
as a token of manhood and worthynes), chosinge rather to dye with
honor and in the defence of their countrey, than to lyve with shame,
dyd so worthely behave themselves that their enimyes forsoke the felde,
with great losse of their men. And Rhes pursued them tyll the benefite
of the night shadowed them with her darkenes, and furthwith he layed
siedge to the castell of Payn in Elvel, and gote hit. And thither came
William de Bruse the owner therof, and made peace with Rhes, of
whom he receaved the same castell againe. [158v] And not longe after
the Archebishop of Canterburie (whom Kinge Richarde had substituted
his Leeftenant in England) came with an huge power towarde Wales and
layed siedge to the castell of Gwenwynwyn at the Poole.[1] But the
garrison [defended][2]★ the holde so manfully, that he loste many of his
men and coulde do no good. Therfore he sent for myners, and sette
them on worke to undermyne the walles, which when the garrison
understoode, and knowinge how their enimyes were much stronger
then they, were content to geve up the castell, so the[y] might departe
with their armor freely. Which offer the Archbishop toke and suffred
them to passe quietely, and fortified the castell againe strongely to the
Kinges use, sette therin a garrison, for the defence therof, and returned
to England. And furthwith Gwenwynwyn layed siedge to hit againe,
and shortely after receaved hit upon the same condicouns, that his men
had geven [hit][3] up, and kept hit to his owne use.

And the next yere after was there a great and terrible plage [159]
thrughe all the Ile of Britaine and France, of the which dyed a great
number of nobles beside the commen people. And this yere the 4th daie

[1] C Pole   [3] Ll – hit
[2] Ll – defended; *supplied from HC*

of Maii[1]* Rhes sonne to Griffith ap Rhes ap Tewdur Prince of
Southwales departed out of this lief, thonely ancre, hope and staye of all
that parte of Wales. As he that brought them out of thraldom and
bondage of stranngers and sette them at libertie, and had defended them
dyverse tymes in the felde manfully, had daunted the pryde and corage
of their cruell enimyes, which he dyd either chase out of the lande, or
compelled by force to lyve quietly at home. Woo to that cruell desteine,
that spoyled the miserable lande of her defence and sheelde, which as he
descended of noble and princely bloodde so he passed all other in
commendable qualities and laudable vertues of the minde. He was the
overthower of the mightie, and setter up [of][2] the meeke, the over-
turner of holdes, the separator of troopes, the scatterer [159v] of his foes,
amonge whome he appeared like a wilde boare amonge whelpes, or a
lyon, that for angre beateth his tayle to the grounde. Alas for the honor
of the felde, the sheelde of his knightes, the defence of the lande, the
beautie of armes, the arme of streingth, the hand of liberalitie, the eie of
gentillnes. In this prince were comprehended the magnanimitie of
Hercules, the worthinesse of Hector, the manhodde of Achilles, the
discretion of Nestor, the quickenesse of Tideus, the streingth of Samson,
the beautie of Parys, the eloquence of Ulisses, the wisedom of Solomon,
and the fiersenes of Ajax. Woo ones againe unto that tempestiouse fate
and to cruell Atropos, which without discretion cutteth the thredde of
all mens lyves, and bereved us of this paragon of nobilitie, before his
tyme. The poore commyns shall lake their defender, the hungrie their
foode, the thurstie their drinke, the naked clothinge and all men shall
[160] want great rewardes and liberall giftes. The eare shall misse the
plesannt talke and sugred woordes. The eies shall not see the beautifull
face and noble behavior of their Lorde and Prince. And thus the Welsh
Cronicler maketh a great discurse in the praise of this prince, which I
will passe over, both for lacke of feat wordes, to English his and for
tedyousenes of the thinge[3] hit self. And where amonge a great number
of Welshe songes made in his prayse, one made certeine Latine verses as
the tyme dyd serve (which was in the middell of the reigne of
barbarousenes) as hereafter foloweth.

> Nobile Cambrensis cecidit diadema decoris;[4]
> Hoc est, Rhesus obit, Cambria tota gemit.
> Rhesus obit; non fama perit, sed gloria transit:
> Cambrensis transit gloria, Rhesus obit.

[1]C 4th of Maij   [3]Ll Kinge
[2]Ll – of   [4]Ll doceris

Rhesus obit, decus orbis abit, laus quaeque[1] tepescit;
  In gemitu viuit Cambria, Rhesus obit.
Semper Rhesus abit, populus quem totus[2] amauit.
  Lugent corda, tacent corpora, Rhesus obit.
Rhesus obit, vexilla cadunt; regalia signa
  Hic iam nulla levat dextera,[3] Rhesus obit.
[160v] Rhesus obit, ferrugo tegit galeam, tegit ensem;
  Arma rubigo tegit, Cambria, Rhesus obit.
Rhesus abest, inimicus adest, Rhesus quia non est.
  Iam tibi nil prodest, Cambria, Rhesus abest.
Rhesus obit, populi plorant, gaudent inimici;
  Anglia stat, cecidit Cambria, Rhesus obit.
Ora rigant elegi cersis[4] mea fletibus isti,
  Cor ferit omne ducis dira sagitta necis.
Omnis lingua canit Rheso preconia, nescit
  Laudes insignis lingua tacere ducis.
Ploratu plenae vitae laxantur habenae.
  Meta datur mori, laus sine fine ducis.
Non moritur, sed subtrahitur,[5] quia semper habetur
  Ipsius egregium nomen in orbe novum.
Camber, Locrinus tibi, Rhese, et Rex Albanactus[6]
  Nominis et laudis inferioris erant.
Caesar et Arthurus, leo fortis uterque sub armis,
  Vel par vel similis Rhesus utrique fuit.
Rhesus Alexandro, volendo par fuit alter,[7]
  Mundum substerni gliscit uterque sibi.
Occasus solis tritus Rhesi fuit armis,
  Sensit Alexandri ortus ubique manum.[8]
Laus canitur cineri;[9] sancto cantetur[10] ab omni
  Caeli laus Regi debita spiritui.
Penna madet lachrimis, quae[11] scribit thema doloris,
  Ne careat forma litera cesset ea.

[161] And after his buryall, with great solemnitie, at Saincte Davyes, thees verses were graven upon his sepulcre:

[1] *Pen20* quoque
[2] *Pen20* populo quem viuus
[3] Ll dextra; *Pen20* dextera
[4] Ll cersis; C certis; *Pen20* cunctis
[5] *Pen20* subtraitur
[6] C Camber, Locrinus, tibi Rhesus, et
  Albanactus; *Pen20* Camber, Locrinus
  Reso rex Albaque nactus

[7] *Pen20* Rhesus Alexander in velle pari fuit
  alter
[8] *Pen20* solis in orbe manum
[9] Ll cui; *Pen20* cineri
[10] C cantor; *Pen20* cantetur
[11] *Pen20* quod

Grande decus tenet iste locus, si cernitur ortus;
  Si quis sit finis[1] queritur, ecce cinis:
Laudis amator, honoris odor, dulcedinis auctor,
Rhesus in hoc tumulo conditur exiguo;
Caesaries quasi congeries solis radiorum,
  Principis et facies vertitur[2] in cineres.
Hic tegitur, sed detegitur quia fama perennis,
  Non sinit illustrem voce latere ducem.
Colligitur tumba cinis hac, sed transvolat ultra
  Nobilitas claudi nescia fine[3] brevi.
Wallia iam viduata dolet ruitura dolore,
  Principis interitu nulli pietate secundi.

This prince had many sonnes, and doughters, as Griffith, who
succeded his father, Cadwalhon, Maelgwn, Owen, Howell Says,[4]
Anaraud, Meredith and Rhes. And of his doughters one called
Gwenlhian was maryed to Edneved Vachan, and was grandfather to
Owen Tudur, and the rest were maryed to other lordes in the countrey.
And after the death [161v] of Rhes, Griffith his sonne conveyed all the
countrey into his subjection, and enjoyed hit in peace, till Maelgwyn his
brother, which his father had disherited, made a leage with Gwenwynwyn, sonne to Owen Kevelyoc, Prince of Powys, and bothe together
levyed a number of men and came sodenly upon Griffith at Aberystwyth, and slewe a great number of his men and toke him prisoner,
and recovered all the countrey of Caerdygan, with the castelles. And
Maelgwn sende his brother to be emprisoned with Gwenwynwyn, and
he for despite delyvered him to Englishmen, and Gwenwynwyn
recovered all Arwystli to himself.

And aboute that tyme there was great warre in Northwales, for David
sonne to Owen, late prince, came with a great army, as well Englishmen
as Welshmen, thinkinge to recover the lande againe. But Lhewelyn his
nevew, then in posession and right enheritor, came boldlye and mete
him and gave him battaill and, [162] puttinge his people to flight, toke
him prisoner, and kept him saffe and afterwarde enjoyed the countrey
quietly. Towarde the ende of this yere dyed Owen Kevelyoc Lorde of
the Higher Powys and left his lande to Gwenwynwyn his sonne, after
whome that parte of Powys was named Powys Wenwynwyn, in
difference of the other, Powys Vadocke, which was the Lorde of

---

[1] C fit finis; *Pen20* sit finis   [3] *Pen20* fune
[2] Ll veritur; *Pen20* vertitur   [4] C – Owen . . . Says

Bromfelde. There dyed also Owen sonne to Griffith Maelor of Bromfilde, and Owen of Brythtyr, sonne to Howell ap Ieaf, and Maelgwn (sonne to Cadwalhon ap Madocke Lorde of Melyenydh). And at this tyme Trehayarn Vychan (a man of great power in the countrey of Breknoke), as he came to speake with William Bruse Lorde therof, to Llancors, was sodenly taken and, by the Lordes commaundent,[1] tyed to a horse tayle and drawen thrughe the towne of Aberhodni, or Breknoke, to the galowes [162v] and there beheaded, the body hanged up by the feete 3 dayes. This cruell deed, upon no just cause, caused his brother, his weif and his children to flee the lande. And the yere ensuinge Maelgwn the sonne of Prince Rhes, after he had emprisoned his elder brother, gote his castelles of Abertivi and Ystradmeuryg and the youngest sonne of Prince Rhes wonne the castell of Dynevwr from the Normaines.

And this somer Gwenwynwyn entendinge to extende the lymites[2] of Wales to their olde meres, gathered a great army and layed siedge first to the castell of Payne, in Elvel, which was [of] William de Bruse and made proclamation that as soone as he had wonne the castell he wolde brenne all the whole countrey to Sevarne without mercie. And because they lacked engines and myners they laye three weekes at that castell and the murtherers sent for succours to Englande, wherupon Geffrey, Lorde Chief Justice of Englande, [163] gathered a great power, and joyninge with him all the Lordes marchers came to reise the siedge. And first fearinge the fortune of the[3] battaill sent to Gwenwynwyn to have a treatie and peace concluded but he, and suche as were with him, wolde in no wise condescende to peace and made answere they wolde at that journey revenge their olde wronges. Wherupon the Englishe lordes dyd first enlarge Griffith sonne to Rhes Prince of Southwales, whom they knewe [to be an] enymy[4] to Gwenwynwyn, and he gathered a great power, and joyned with the Englishe lordes, and so they came towardes the castell. And Gwenwynwyn mette them stoutlye, and there beganne a cruell battaill with muche slaughter one either partie. But at the last the victorie fill to the Englishmen and Gwenwynwyn lost a great number of his men, amonge which were Annaraud sonne to Enyon, Owen ap Cadwalhon, Rhyryd[5] ap Iestyn, and Roberte ap Howell; and Meredith ap Conan [163v] was taken prysoner, and many moe. Mathias Parisiensis sayeth this battaill was fought before the castell of Maude and that, of the Welshmen, there were slayne 3700. And after this victorie the Englishe

[1]C comaundement
[2]Ll lymities
[3]Ll – the

[4]Ll knewe enymy; to be an *supplied from* HC
[5]C Richard

lordes returned home with muche honor. And furthwith Griffith sonne
to Prince Rhes recovered by force and goodwill of the people all his
lande, savinge twoe castelles, Abertivi and Ystradmeurig, which his
brother Maelgwn, by the succours of Gwenwynwyn, wrongefully had
taken from him. And his brother Maelgwn, fearinge his displeasure, toke
a solempne othe before noble and religiouse men, which were aboute to
make peace betwixt them, that, yf his brother Griffith wolde geve him
pledges for thassurance of his owne person, he wolde delyver him by a
daye the castell of Abertivi. And Griffith dyd soe, but assonne as
Maelgwn gote the [164] pledges he fortified the castell, and manned hit
to his owne use, and sende the pledges to be kept in prison, to
Gwenwynwyn, who hated Griffith to the deathe. But shortly after by
Goddes helpe they brake the prison and escaped home.

In the yere 1199 Maelgwn sonne to Prince Rhes layed siedge to the
castell of Dynerth and gote hit, and slewe all the garrison, which his
brother Griffith had leaft to defende hit. And at the same tyme Griffith
wonne the castell of Kylgeran, and fortified hit. And this yere Kinge
Richarde, as he dyd vewe the castell of Chaleus in the countie of
Lemovyll,[1] was striken with a quarell, and sore wounded wherof he
dyed the 9 of Aprill. And left by testament John, his brother, enheritor
of all his landes, havinge no respecte to his brother Geffreys sonne
Arthure, Duke of Britaine, which was his right heire. [164v] And this
John, surnamed Without Lande, was crowned Kinge of Englande with
great tryhumphe. And the Frenche Kinge furthwith made warre againste
him to whom Arthur Duke of Britaine cleved, thinkinge therby to
obteine the crowne of Englande. Also the Kinge of Scottes by means of
Roger[2] Bygod* came to Yorke and sware upon fidelitie to the Kinge of
Englande.

The yere folowinge dyed Griffith sonne to Conan ap Owen
Gwynedh, a noble man, and was buryed in a monks coull at the Abbey
of Conwy, and so were all the nobles (for the most parte) of that tyme
buryed. For they were made beleve, by the Popes champyons, that that
strange weede was a sure defence betwixt their soules and hell, howe
soever they dyed. And all this baggage and superstition receaved they
with monkes, and friers, fewe yeres before that, oute of Englande. [165]
For the first abbey, or friershouse, that wee[3] reede of in Wales (sith the
destruction of the noble house of Bangor, which savered not of Romish
dregges) was the Ty Gwyn built the yere 1146. And after they swarmed

---

[1]C Lenovyl   [3]Ll was
[2]C Hughe

like bees throughe all the countrey, for then the clergie had forgoten the lesson they had receaved of the noble clercke Ambrosius Telesinus, who writinge in the yere 540 when the right Christen fayeth (whiche Joseph of[1] Arimathia taught at the Ile of Avalon) reigned in this lande, before the proude and bloodthursty monke Augustyn infected hit with his Romish doctryne) in a certeine ode hath thees woordes:

> Gwae'r offeriad byd
> Nys angreiffia gwyd
> ag ny pregetha;
> Gwae ny cheydw i gaill
> Ag ef yn vygaill
> Ag nys areilia;
> Gwae ny cheidw i dhevaid
> Rag bleidhie Ruveniaid
> A'i ffon glwppa.*

[165v] Which maye bee this Englyshed welny woorde for woorde:

> Woe bee to that priest yborne
> that will not cleanly weede his corne
> and preache his charge amonge;
> Woe bee to the sheppard I saye
> that will not watche his folde alway;[2]
> And woe to him that will not kepe
> From Romish woolfes his seely sheepe
> with his clubbe so stronge.[3]

And because no man shulde doubte of them, I have sette them here as they were written by him, that therby[4] hit may bee proved howe the Britons, the first inhabitauntes of this Realme, dyd abhorre the Romishe doctryne taught in that tyme, which I am sure is nothinge amended nowe. And that maye be to us a myrror to see our owne folly, wherby we degenerat from our forefathers as well in religyon, as in other thinges.

But to the matter.[5] This yere Maelwyn ap Rhes seinge he coulde not[6] well kepe Abertivi [166], of very despite to his brother and hate to his owne countrey, he solde hit to the Englishmen for a small some of

---

[1] Ll ab
[2] C + And biulde hit verye stronge
[3] C – And woe . . . so stronge
[4] C were bye
[5] C – But . . . matter
[6] Ll – not

money, which was the key and locke of all Wales. And the same yere
Madocke, sonne to Gruffith Bromfelde, dyd builde the Abbey of
Lhaneguester, called in Englishe commenly Val Crucis. This yere Kinge
John made peace with the Frenche kinge, and with Arthure Duke of
Britaine his nevewe, and maryed Isabell doughter and heire unto the
Earle of Engelisme, which was before assured to Hughe de Brune[1]
Vicount of Carce, wherfore the sayed Hughe forsoke Kinge John and
became his enimye. And the yere 1201 Lhewelyn ap Ierwerth, Prince of
Northwales, beinge a lusty yonge man, banished his cosine Meredith,
sonne to Conan ap Owen Gwynedh (suspected of treason), out of the
lande, and seased the cantref of Lhyn, and Evryonyth (which were
Conans) into his owne handes. [166v] And that tyme were monkes
placed at the newe house in Ystradflur. And shortly after Meredith the
sonne of Prince Rhes was slaine at Carnwylhyon by treason. And his
elder brother Griffith seased upon his castell in Lhanymdhifri and his
landes. This Griffith was a wise and discreat gentillman, and one that was
like to have brought all Southwales to good order, and obedience. But
cruell fortune, which had frowned upon that counntre, suffred him not
longe to governe his lande after his fathers steppes, whom, as he
succeded in rule, so he dyd in all martiall prowesse, and nobilitie of
minde. This prince dyed upon St. James Daye ensuinge, and was buryed
at Ystradflur, with great solemnitie. He left behinde him a sonne called
Rhes, as right enheritor of Southwales, whose mother was Mawde,
[167] doughter to William de Bruse. And this yere dyed Arthure Duke
of Britaine at Rome, not without suspicioun of poyson ministred by his
uncles meanes, who caused his sister Elynor to be conveyed to England,
and to be kept in prison myserably in the castell of Bristowe, as longe as
she lyved. Also the Frenche Kinge gote all Normandy (savinge Roan,[2]
and twoe castelles) by the treason of the Normaines, who hated[3] John to
the death. The next yere after that certeine lordes of Wales gote the
castell of Gwerthrynyon which was Sir Roger Mortymers, and made hit
plaine with the grounde.

    And Lhewelyn ap Ierwerth Prince of Northwales, callinge to
memorye his estate and title, and howe all the princes of Wales,[4] by the
ordinnance of Rodrike the Great and after by the lawes of Howell Dha,
ought [167v] of right to acknowledge the Prince or Kinge of Aberfrawe
and Northwales as their liedge lorde, and holde their landes of him and
of non other, and howe of late yeres, by neglygennce of his predecessors

[1] C Brime   [3] C hatethe
[2] C Roone   [4] C – of Wales

they did not use their accustomed duetie, but some helde of the Kinge
of Inglande, and other ruled as supreme powers within their owne
countreys, therfore he called a parliamente of all the lordes in Wales,
which for the most parte appeared before him, and swore to bee his
liedge men. But Gwenwynwyn Lorde of Powis wolde not come thither
nor take the othe of alledgyanc, which disobedience the Prince declared
to all his lordes, and they thought hit was meete that Gwenwynwyn
shulde be constrayned, by force, to do his dutie orels to lose his lande.
Yet one of his lordes named Elisse ap Madock wolde not agree to hurte
Gwenwynwyn [168] in any case, but departed awaye sodenly. And
Lhewelyn came with an army to Powys. Yet by the meanes of certeine
learned men they were made frendes, and Gwenwynwyn became
Lhewelyns liedge man, and confirmed that both by othe and writinge.
Then[1] Lhewelyn remembringe howe Elisse ap Madock had served him,
seased upon all his landes. And Elisse fledde the countrey, but afterwarde
yelded himself to the Princes mercye, who gave him the castell of
Crogen and 7 towneshippes withall. And here I thinke hit not unmeete
to declare the cause why the Englishmen use to call the Welshmen
Crogens, as a woorde of reproche and despyte. But yf they knewe the
beginninge, they shulde finde hit contrary, for in the vyage that Kinge
Henrie the Secunde [168v] made against the Welshmen, to the
mountaines of Berwyn, as he laye at Oswadstre, a number of his men
that were sent to trye the passages, as they wolde have passed Offas diche
at the castell of Crogen, at which place there was, and is at this daye, a
narrowe way thrughe the sayde diche, for that diche appeareth yet to
this daye very depe, thrughe all that countrey, and beareth his olde
name, thees men, I saye, as they wolde have passed this strait, were
mette withall, and a great number of them slaine, as hit appeareth by
their graves at this daye, of which the straite beareth the name. Therfore
the Englishemen afterwarde, not forgeatinge this slaughter, used to cast
the Welshmen in the teethe in all their troubles with the name of
Crogen, as that therby they loke for no favour, but rather vengement, at
their handes, and so in processe of tyme grewe to be taken in [169] an
other signification.

Nowe when Lhewelyn had sette all those parties in good order, he
returned to Northwales, and by the way fortefied the castell of Bala in
Penlhyn. And at this tyme Rhes sonne to Griffith ap Rhes (by right
Prince of Southwales) gote the castell of Lhanymdhyfri[2] upon
Michelmas Daye. This yere lost Kinge John all Normandy with

Angyow, Mayn, and Potiers. And Hugh Gurnay, Robert Fitzwater and
Bayer de Quinti, which had a great parte of thees countreys under their
rule, delyvered all up to the Frenche Kinge, at the first somon, yet
Roger Lacy kept his castelles as longe as he had any hope of succors.
Aboute this tyme there was in Englande one called Symon de Thurnay,[1]
a great divine and philosopher, who dyverse tymes made his advant that
he knewe all that was to be knowen, [169v] and sodenly he fill to suche
ignorannce that he colde nether rede nor understande his pater noster.

    The yere next ensuinge the forsaide Rhes ap Griffith ap Rhes gote
the castell of Lhangadawc and fortified hit to his owne use. But shortly
after Maelgwn his uncle with his frende Gwenwynwyn came with a
stronge power before the castell of Lhanymdhyfry and wonne hit, and
frome thence they removed to Lhangadawc and likwise gote hit, and
suffred the garrison to departe. And from thence the forsaide Maelgwn
sonne to Prince Rhes went to Dynerth and fynished the castell which he
had began there. And this yere David sonne to Owen Gwynedh, after
Prince Lhewelyn (his nevewe) had sete him at libertie, fledde to
Englande and gote an army to restore him to his anncyent estate in
Northwales [but all in vaine], for his nevewe* mette him in the Marches
and overthrewe him, and he returned to Englande and for very sorowe
dyed shortlye after. The next yere to this [170] was Howell, sonne to the
Prince Rhes (beinge blinde), slaine by his brother Maelgwns men at
Kemais, and buryed by his brother Griffith at Ystradflur. And as this
Maelgwn bare all the rule of Southwales, his brother Griffiths sonnes,
Rhes and his bretherne, wonne from him the chief defence of all his
countrey, the castelles of Dynevwr and Llanymdhifri. And William
Marshall, Earle of Penbroke, layed siedge to the castell of Kylgeran and
wonne hit, and shortly after Maelgwn ap Rhes hyred an Yrishman to
kyll[2] Kedyvor ap Gruffith, and Maelgwn toke his foure sonnes and put
them to death. Thees were towarde gentilmen and came of a noble
stocke, for their mother Susanna was doughter to Howell, by a doughter
of Madock ap Meredith Prince of Powis. The yere 1205 dyd Maelgwn
builde a castell at Aberenyawn, and there came such a number of fish to
Aberystwydh as the like was never seene before. [170v] The 2e and 3e
yere after, the Frenche Kinge gote many townes and castells in Gwyen.
And there fill a great debate in Englande betwene the Kinge and the
clergie about the election of the Archebishop of Canterburye, in
somuche that the yere 1208 the Pope denniced[3] all Englande accursed,

and no service was used in any churche within Englande. And this yere
the Kinge dyd banishe William de Bruse, with his wief, the lande, for
displeasure he bare to his sonne. And the Kinge seased their landes to his
owne handes and they fledde all together to Irelande, and there
remained for a while. This yonge man was of great power in the
Marches of Wales but extreme cruell and unjuste. And the same yere
Gwenwynwyn came to Shrewsburye to speak with the Kinges Counsaill
and their he was detained [171] prisoner. And Prince Lhewelyn
conquered all his countrey, with his townes and castelles, and kept them
to his owne use. And when Maelgwn ap Rhes understoode that, and
howe Lhewelyn made his viage to Southwales, he overthrewe his
castells of Aberystwydh, Ystradmeurig and Dynerth, which he before
fortified, dispairinge to withstande the Prince. But the prince kept on his
journey to Aberystwydh, and builde the castell againe, and fortified hit
and seased to his owne use the cantref of Penwedyg, and the lande
betwixt Dyvy and Aeron, and gave hit to his nevewes the sonnes of
Griffith ap Rhes, and so returned home with great joy. And this tyme
Rhes Vychan, sonne to Prince Rhes, layed siedge to the castell of
Llangadawg, and wonne hit, not remembring his promise and leage with
his brothers sonnes Griffith ap Rhes, and howe [171v] worthely they
had served him in his necessities. Therefore, as soone as they herde this,
both Rhes and Owen came before the saide castell, and wonne hit by
assaulte, and slewe, or toke prisoners all the garrison and brenned the
castell to the earth.

The yere 1210 Kinge John made a vyage to Irelande with an army of
great power, and wanne the countery of Connacht, and toke Cathol
their prince prisoner. Also he spoyled Hughe de Lacy Lorde of Mydy of
his castelles and landes, and toke William de Bruse the yonger, and
Mawde de Sant Valeryke his mother, and brought them both to
England with him and caused them cruelly to bee famyshed to deathe in
the castell of Wyndsor.

And this yere the Earle of Chester reedified the castell of Dyganwy
(which stoode upon the sea shore east of the ryver of Conwy) whiche
Prince Lhewelyn had before destroyede. Also he fortified the castell of
Trefynnon [172] or Saynt Wenefredes, and Prince Lhewelyn entred the
Earles landes and destroyed a great parte therof, and returned home with
a great spoyle. Also Rhes Vychan, sonne to Prince Rhes, fearinge Prince
Lhewelyn, which defended his nevewes the sonnes of Griffith in their
right, went to the Kinge for succours, which he receaved with a good
will, and by their meanes he layed siedge to Lhanymdhifri, and when
the garrison sawe no hope of succours they gave hit up, upon

condicioun they might departe, bagge and baggage, horses and all, and so they dyd. Likewise, Gwenwynwyn which the Kinge helde in prison, was sette at libertie, and the kinge fearinge the Princes streingth,[1] sent an army with him, by whose meanes he recovered all his countrey againe in shorte space. And when Maelgwn herde this, he likewise came to the Kinges courte and became the Kinges man. [172v] And returninge home with a great number of Normaines and[2] Englishmen, joyned to them all the power he colde make in Wales. And contrarye to the othe he had made to his nevewes Rhes and Owen, began to spoyle the countrey, and comminge to Cantref Penwedig camped at Kilkennyn, and lay there all night consultinge upon his vyage. And his nevewes heringe this, havinge but a small power not above 300 of chosen men, came and lodged harde by unknowinge to their enymyes, and when they understoode by their spies that all was quiet in Maelgwns campe, and howe they mistrusted nothinge, thees 2 lordes prosecuted thenterprice, which they had taken in hande, boldely. And peceably entringe the campe came where they thought Maelgwn laye, or they were espied, and their they [173] gave alarum and slewe a great number before they awoke. And the rest heringe the noyse and halfe amased by meanes of the darkenes escaped awaye, thinkinge some great power had bene there, and Maelgwns men defended them manfully, untill suche tyme he had goten away upon his feete by benefite of the night. And his nevewe Conan ap Howell and his cheef counsailler Griffith ap Cadwgan were both taken, and Enyawn ap Caradawc with a great number slaine. And aboute this tyme Gilbert Earle of Glocester fortified the castell of Buelht, where a litle before he had lost many of his men. And this yere Maud de Bruse wief to Griffith ap Rhes dyed and was buryed in the monks coulle in Ystradflur by her husbande.

The next yere ensuinge Kinge John had many complaintes made unto him by the Marchers[3] upon [173v] the Prince Llewelyn, howe he entred their countrey and spoyled, and brenned all as they went, and slewe there men. Wherfore the Kinge gathered a great army thrughe all England, and also[4] called to him suche lords and princes of Wales as helde of him, as Howell the sonne of Griffith ap Conan ap Owen Gwynedh, which Lhewelyn had banished, Madock, sonne to Griffith Maelor, lorde of Bromfelde, Chirke and Yale, Meredith ap Rotperte, Lorde of Kedewen, Gwenwynwyn, Prince of Powis, Maelgwn and Rhes Vychan, sonnes to the Prince Rhes, and Princes of Southwales,

[1] power
[2] Ll – and
[3] Ll marches
[4] C – also

and with this great armye entred Northwales by Chester, mindinge to destroye all that bare lief[1] within that countrey. And the Prince heringe all this preparation against him, as well of his owne countrey men as others, commaunded all suche as inhabited the inland or midle countrey which is nowe[2] parte of Denbighe and Flintshires to remove all their [174] goodes and cattells to Snowdon hilles for a tyme. And so the Kinge came alonge the seashore to Rudlan, and so passed furth[3] over the Ryver Clwyd, and came to the castell of Teganwy, and there remained awhile. But Llewelyn cut of his vittayles behinde him, so that he colde have none from Englande, and there coulde not a man scatter from the army but he was slaine. And many[4] skirmishes fought, where North-wales men, both for the advantage of the straites and knowledge of the places, had the overhand. At the laste they were gladde to taste horseflesh for pure neede. And when the Kinge sawe no remedy, he returned home in a great rage leavinge the countrey full of dead bodyes and caused suche pledges as he had to be hanged. And in August next ensuinge he returned againe with a greatter army and the [174v] beforenamed lordes with him, and entred Wales at Blackemonasterie or Oswester,* of which was lorde John, sonne to William Fitzalan. And this tyme the Kinge passed the ryver of Conwy, and encamped there by the ryver side. And sent parte of his army to brenne Bangor, with gwydes[5] of the countrey, and so they dyd, and toke Rotperte the Bishoppe prisoner, which was after ransomed for 200 haukes. And the Prince seeigne all Englande and Wales against him, and a great parte of the[6] lande wonne, thought hit best to entret with the Kinge and therupon sent Johan his wief, and the Kinges doughter (for the Kinge had begotten her upon Agatha, doughter to Roberte Ferrers, Earle of Derby) to her father, for to make a peace. And she founde the[7] meanes, that upon[8] pledges geven for safconduit, the Prince came to the Kinge, and made peace with him and dyd him homage. [175] And besydes that, gave him pledges and promised the Kinge 20000 head of cattell and 40 horses towardes his great charges. And also he graunted the Inland to the Kinge forever.* And therupon the Kinge returned to Englande with great tryhumphe, after he had brought all Wales under his subjection savinge Rhes and Owen sonnes to Griffith ap Rhes.

Therfore he gave strayt commaundment[9] to Fulke Vycont of Caerdyff[10] (called Warden of the Marches, a cruell tyrant and

[1] Ll – lief
[2] Ll no
[3] C – furth
[4] C – army . . . many
[5] C gwyds

[6] C his
[7] C a
[8] Ll – upon
[9] C comaundement
[10] C Cardiff

welbeloved of the Kinge) to take an army with him, and joyninge with
Maelgwn and Rhes, to compell the forsaide sonnes of Griffith to obey
the Kinge, and so he dyd. And came all together to the cantref of
Penwedige and the yonge lordes seinge no remedy, sent to Fulke for
peace and saffeconduite to passe to the court, which he graunnted them
all, and they gave the Kinge all their landes [175v] betwixt Aeron and
Dyvi and the Kinge[1] receaved them gently. And after they had done
him homage, they returnned home againe. And Fulke before his
departure[2] fortified the castell of Aberystwydh and manned hit to the
Kinges behoof. And furthwith Maelgwn, as he was very unconstant, and
Rhes Vychan repented of the peace they had made with the Kinge, and
layed siedge to his castell at Aberystwyth, and gote hit, and destroyed it.[3]
Which thinge, when their nevewes Rhes and Owen sawe, that there
uncles had broken the Kinges peace, they made a rode into Maelgwns
countrey, and slewe a great number of his men and returned with a
riche butty.

   And the next yere Prince Lhewelyn, not beinge able to abyde the
displeasures which the garrisons that the Kinge left in his newe[4] castelles
in Northwales dyd to his people, called to him Gwenwynwyn from
[176] Powis, Maelgwn ap Rhes from Southwales, Madocke ap Griffith
Maelor from Bromfelde, Meredith ap Rotpert from Kedewen and
opened to them this miserable case, howe they which were wont to
have a prince of their owne[5] nation, nowe (by their owne wilfullnes)
were subjected to a stranger, and declared unto them howe that, yf they
wolde agree amonge themselves, they might defende their auncient
estate still. Which they all promised to doe and swore fealtie to Prince
Llewelyn, and furthwith gathered an armye and wonne all the castelles
the Kinge had builte[6]* in Northwales, save Rudlan and Dyganwy, and
comminge to Powis layed siedge to the castell which Robert Vypont
had made at Mathraval. And when the Kinge herde this he leveyd an
army and came thither, and reised the siedge, and after caused the castell
to be rased, and returned home. [176v] And beinge at Nothingham and
heringe howe the Prince of Wales destroyed all the Marches, he caused
3 children which were pledges to bee hanged, Howell the sonne of
Cadwalhon, Madocke ap Maelgwn and Meurig Barrech. Also Robert
Vypont did hange at Shrewsburie Rhes ap Maelgwn, not beinge yet 7
yeres of age, and so cruelly martyred the innocentes to revenge the
offences of others.[7] In the meane while that the Kinge remained at

[1] Ll – Kinge
[2] C he departed
[3] Ll – it
[4] C nevews

[5] Ll – owne
[6] C – the Kinge . . . builte
[7] Ll other

Nothingham he receaved a letter from the Princesse of Northwales (his doughter) howe his nobles had conspired with the Frenche Kinge against him, and for proffe therof Robert Fitzwater, Eustace Vesty and Stephen Randell were secretly[1] fledde to France. And the Frenche Kinge prepared an army to come to Englande, under the colour that the Kinge was a rebell from the churche, because he wolde not condescende to the Bishoppe of Romes requestes.

[177] The yere 1213 Innocens Pope of Rome dyd release Prince Lhewelyn, Gwenwynwyn and Maelgwn of the othes they had made to Kinge John, and willed them, under the paynes of cursinge, to annoy, and trouble him all that they colde, as the enimye of Christes Churche. And furthwith Llewelyn recovered all the inlande countrey, which to that tyme was in the Kinges handes. And Kinge John heringe howe the Frenche kinge was in Fflandres, and had a great navy at Dam, thinkinge to bringe the Earldome to his subjection, sent William de Longa Spata Earle of Salisburie and Dawnmartyn,[2] Earle Boleyn, and Hughe de Nova Villa, or Nevill, thither with a great navy, which overthrewe the Frenchmen and returned home with a great spoyle. And shortly after the Kinge graunted the Pope his request and had absolution, and sayled to Rochell, where the Earle of those Marches and [177v] Geffrey de Landanano[3] were reconcyled to him.

The yere folowinge King John made peace with the Frenche Kinge for 5 yeres. And Rhes sonne to Griffith ap Rhes seinge he coulde have no parte of his fathers landes, which was[4] heire to Prince Rhes, but that his uncles kept all the countreys by force, he made his complainte to the Kinge. And the Kinge pittyenge his estate, sent to Fulke Vycount of Caerdyffe (and Warden of the Marches) and to the Steewarde of Herforde, commaundinge them to take all Ystradtywi[5] from Rhes Vychan (which other call Rhes[6] Grug) except he wolde let his nevewes enioye the castell of Lhanymdhyfri, with the territorie belonginge therto. And they sent to Rhes to knowe his mynde, and he answered stoutly they shulde not have foote of landes of him. Therfore Fulke gathered a great army [178] [and] mette with yonge Rhes at Talhwynelgam[7] where he loked for him with a number of men that he had goten in Breknoke. And thence they marched in three battailles towardes Dynevwr, of which yonge Rhes leade the first, Fulke the secunde, and Owen brother to Rhes the thyrde. And Rhes Vychan

[1]Ll – and Stephen Rudell were secretly
[2]C Damartyn
[3]C Landanamo
[4]Ll – was
[5]C Ystradtivy
[6]C- Rhes
[7]C Talhwynelgain

came boldly and mette with them,[1] and gave them battaill, wher at the ende he was put to flight, with the losse of a great number of his men. And he went streit, and manned the castell of Dynevwr and brenned the towne of Lhandeilaw Vawr and kept himselfe in the wilde and rough places. And his enimyes layed siedge to the castell of Dynevwr and at the first assault they wonne the first warde and the garrison toke the kepe for their defence, which they defended manfully. And they without made engins to cast in great stones and [178v] beganne to undermyne the walles, so that the capteine fill to suche a composition that, yf he were not succoured by the next daye at noone, he wolde delyver up the castel upon condicioun all his men might departe with their armour and weapons. And so they dyd, for they had no succours and afterwarde they brought the Cantref Mawre to their subjection. And Rhes Vychan removed his wief and children[2] to his brother Maelgwns countrey and leaft the castell of Lhanymdhifri well fortified and manned. And yonge Rhes, after the departure of Fulke, came with an armye of Welshmen and Normaines to Lhanymdhifri, and before they were encamped the capteine delyvered up the castell, the garrison departinge with their lyves. And shortly after Rhes Vychan was taken at Caermardhyn and committed to the Kinges prison. [179] And Prince Llewelyn layed siedge to the castelles of Dyganwy and Rudlan and wonne them both and so[3] the Kinge had no holde, nor castell within his lande.

In the yere 1215 dyd Kinge John with the Earles of Chester and Derby take the crosse. But the rebellion of his barrons stayed his jorney, for they required of him certeine auncient lawes and customes to be kept, which he denyed to doe. Therfore they made a confederacye with Lhewelyn Prince of Wales that he shulde sturre upon his parte, and they wolde upon theirs, and gathered an army, appointinge Robert Fitzwater their capteine and came to Bedforde, where William Beauchampe receaved them into the castell. And from thens they went to London, where they were joyfully receaved. And the Kinge gathered his power, with William Marshall Earle of Penbroke, and layed siedge [179v] to the castell of Rochester, which was manfully defended three monethes by William de Albinneto, but at the last taken by force, and with the saide William, William de Lancaster, William de Emmefforde, Thomas de Moletun, Quync Gyfforde, Odynell Bobi [and] Odnell de Albineto, which the Kinge sent to the castell of Corff,[4] to be emprisoned sure. And the Pope cursed all such as made warre against Kinge John.

[1] C – and . . . them
[2] C childerne
[3] Ll – so
[4] C Corfe

Yet upon the other side, Prince Lhewelyn levyed an army and came to Shrewburye, which towne and castell were delyvered to him without any lette, and remained there a while. In the meane tyme Gyles de Bruse, Bishop of Herforde and chief of this conspiracie, sonne to William de Bruse, sent his brother Reynalde to Breknoke, and all the people receaved him as their lorde, and gote all his castelles without gainesaynge of any manne, first Abergevenny, then furthwith [180] Penkelhy, Castell Gwyn (or White Castell), Grosmunde and the Ile of Kynvryk.* And when the Byshop came thither himself, they delyvered him the castelles of Aberhodni, Hay, Buelht and Blaenlhifni and he[1] promised Castell Paen and Clun, with all Elvel, to Walter Vychan ap Eynon Clud. Likewise yn the same tyme yonge Rhes (sonnne to Griffith ap Rhes) and Maelgwn his uncle were made frendes and went both to Dyved and recovered all the west lande savinge Kemais to them selves, which they all destroyed, and brent.[2] And they overthrewe the castell of Arberth and Maynclochawg, and after that Maelgwn and Owen,[3] brother to Rhes, went to Northwales to Prince Lhewelyn and dyd him homage. And yonge Rhes gathered a great power and came to Kydwyli and brought[4] hit to his subjection and Karnwylhyon also, and rased the [180v] castell, and likewise the castell of Lhychwr. And from thence he leadde his army to the castell of Hughe de Myles, at Talybonedh,* and gote hit by force and slewe a great number of the garrison, and the daye after he toke his jorney to Sayntgennyd, but the garrison brent the towne and departed. Therfore he layed siedge to the castell of Ystymlhwynarth,* and the daye folowinge gote hit, and brenned hit and the towne also. And he gote all the castelles of Glamorgan* within three dayes after and returned home with victorie and tryhumphe. And at this tyme was Rhes Vychan (or Rhes Grug, uncle to yonge Rhes, and sonne to Prince Rhes) sette at libertie by the Kinge, leavinge his sonne and 2 other pledges for him. And this yere were twoe abbotts consecrated bishoppes, Ierwerth of Saynt Davyes and Cadwgan of Bangor. [181] And Gyles Bishop of Herforde, by the Popes comaundement, made peace with Kinge John. And at his returne he dyed at Glocester and Reynalde (his brother) enjoyed all his patrimonie and this Reynalde maryed the doughter of Prince Lhewelyn.

And shortly after the saide Prince came with a great army to Caermardhyn and layed siedge to the castell, and the 5th daye hit was yelded to him, which he rased to the grounde. And so he dyd with the

[1] Ll – he   [3] C – Owen
[2] C – which . . . they brent   [4] C gat

castelles of Lhanystephant, Saynt Clare, and Thalbocharne.★ And frome
thence he went to Caerdygan and gote the Newe Castell in Emlyn and
subdued Kemays, and gote the castell of Trefdraeth (called in Englishe
Newporte) and rased hit to the grounde. And the garrison of Abertyvi
delyvered him the castell upon Saynt Stephens Daye, [181v] and the
daye after he had the castell of Kylgerran. And from thence Prince
Lhewelyn returned to Northwales with great honor and tryhumphe and
thees were the lordes that awayted upon the Prince: Howell ap Griffith
ap Kynan, Lhewelyn ap Meredith ap Conon, Gwenwynwyn and
Meredith ap Rotpert, Maelgwn and Rhes Vychan, sonnes to the Prince
Rhes, and Rhes and Owen sonnes to Griffith ap Rhes and the power of
Madocke ap Griffith Maelor. And all this wynter was the fayrest wether
that ever was sene.

   And the yere folowinge the Prince went to Aberdyvi to make an
agreament betwixt Maelgwn and Rhes Vychan, sonnes to Prince Rhes,
and their nevewes, yonge Rhes and his brother Owen, and there he
devyded Southwales betwixt them [182] after this maner: Maelgwn had
3 cantreffs of Dyved, Gwarthaf, Kemays and Emlyn and Penlhwynawg,★
and the castell of Kylgeran, and in¹ Ystradtywy he had the castell of
Lhanymdhyfri and twoe comotes Hirvryn and Malhaen, and
Maenawrvydhey, and in Caerdygan 2 comots, Gwynionydh and
Mabwynyawn. And to yonge Rhes and Owen his brother came the
castell of Abertyvi and the castell of Nant yr aryan, or Silverdale, and
300 towneshippes of Caerdygan withal. And Rhes Vychan (otherwise
called Rhes Gryg) had the castell of Dynevwr and the Cantref Mawr and
the Cantref Bychan (except Hyrvryn and Mydhvey) and the comotes of
Kydwyli and Karnwylhyon. And this division accomplished, the Prince
returned home, and herde by the way howe Gwenwynwyn (contrary
[182v] to his othe and bondes in writinge) hade forsaken the Prince and
become againe the Kinges man, which greved the Prince very muche.
And therfore he sent unto him bishoppes and abbottes, to move him to
remember his othe and promise, and his pledges geven to the prince,
and to shewe him his owne hande therupon, to see yf he wolde come
againe and to promise him the Princes favor. But he wolde in no case
heere of reconciliation. Wherfore the Prince entred Powis with fyer and
sworde and subdued the countrey to himself. And Gwenwynwyn fledde
to the Earle of Chester for succoures, and there remained for a while.

   And this yere Lewis sonne to the Frenche Kinge, beinge called by the
barrons of Englande, landed at Tanet and so came to London, and

¹Ll – in

receaved to his handes all the holdes by the waye and there receaved
homage of the barrons. [183] And from thence went towardes
Wynchester, where Kinge John was, and by the waye gote the castelles
of Rygat, Guyldforde,[1] and Fernod,[2] and Winchester with the castell
were delyured him. And Kinge John fledde to the Marches to Herforde
and sende to Reynalde Bruse, and to the Prince for frendship. But they
wolde not here him. Therfore he destroyed the castelles of Radnor and
Hay, and came alonge to Oswester, which beinge John Fitzaleyns he
brenned to the earth. And from thence he went north warde and
prepared a great army and had with him thees noble men: William de
Albermarle, [the] Earle of Glocester, Philippe de Albineto, John
Marshall, Ffalcasius a stranger and a notable★ good souldier (to whome
the Kinge gave in maryage the doughter of the Earle Ryvers, with the
castell of Bedforde), William Earle of [183v] Salysburie the Kinges
brother, William Briwer, Walter Bec. Also he appointed governors of
the north, Hughe Bayllol and Phillippe Halcotts. And he made Roberte
de Veteri Ponte, Geffrey Lucy and Bryan de Lyst governors of the citie
of Yorke. And upon the other parte, Lewys comminge frome
Winchester toke the castell of Odyham and came to London with a
great tryhumphe, where Geffrey Maundeville Earle of Essex was slaine
by misfortune, runninge at the tylte. And the lordes that mainteined the
quarrell were thees: William Earle Warren, William Earle of Arundell,
William Earle of Salisburie, which forsoke the Kinge at the ende,
William Marshall the yonger, William de Maundeville, Robert Fitzwater, William Huntyngfelde, all southern men, and Robert de Rosse,
Peter de Bruse, and Richard Percy, northern men. And all this while
Hughe [184] Burghe kept the castell of Dover worthely, to the behofe
of the Kinge. And as Kinge John was makinge preparation at Newerke
he fill sicke and dyed, and lyeth buried at Worcester.

   After the deathe of Kinge John, Rondell Earle of Chester, William
Marshall Earle of Penbrok, William Earle Ferrers, Philiippe de Albineto
and John Marshall crowned Henry his sonne Kinge of England at
Glocester. And in the meane while Lewis besiedged the castell of Dover
in vayne, and returninge[3] to London the towre was delyvered him. And
afterwarde he gote the castelles of Hertforde and Berkamsted, and uppon
that ther was a truse concluded betwixt both Princes for a while and
Lewys returned to France. And this yere dyed Howell ap Griffith ap
Conan and lyeth buried at Conwey.

[1] C Gwylford   [3] C returned
[2] C Ffernam

The yere 1217 many of the nobles of England forsoke [184v] Lewis, whome they had called,★ and contrarye to the[ir] othe came to Kinge Henry as: William de Albineto Lorde of Bealwer besides Notyngham, which was prisoned in Corffe, and William Earle Warrene, William de Albineto Earle of Arundell, William Longa Spata Earle of Salusburie, William Marshall the yonger, and William de Cantilupo. And Lewis shortlye after landed at Dover with a great army, and layed siedge to the castell, but all in vayne. And from thens he came before the castell of Wyndsor, and colde not get hit, and toke[1] his jorney to Lyncolne and thyther came the armye of Kinge Henrie. And there was a great cruell battaill fought, and Lewis put to flight, and a great number of his nobles taken as: Saier Earle of Winchester, Henry de Bohume[2] Earle of Hertforde, Gilberte de Gante[3] Earle of Lyncolne, [185] Robert Fitzwater, Richarde Montfytchet, Gilbert de Clare, William Mombray,[4] William Beauchampe, William Mandit, Aymer Harcourt, Roger de Crescy, William de Colvyll, William de Rosse, Robert Roppeley. And there were slaine Symon de Vescy, Hughe de Roc, Reynalde Crescy Constable of Chester, Geraulde de Farnevause and many other. Also Hughe de Burghe Capteine of Dover, Henry de Tubervill, and Richarde Swarde gave the Frenche Kinges[5] navy (wherof Eustace, a monke, was capteine) an overthrowe.

In this meane tyme Reynalde de Bruse dyd agree with the Kinge, unknowinge[6] to the Prince and contrarye to his promise, wherfore yonge Rhes and Owen (his sisters sonnes) seinge he, in whome they trusted most, deceaved them, they rose againste him and wonne all Buelht from him, saving the castell. And when the Prince herde of this agreement he was sore offended withall, and came with an armye to Breknoke, and layed siedge [185v] to the towne of Aberhodni, and the burgesses of the towne came to the Prince and by the meanes of yonge Rhes the Prince toke 100 markes and 5 pledges of them and raysed his siedge, and toke his jorney over the Blacke Mountaines (where he lost muche of his cariages) towards Gwyr. And as he encamped[7] at Lhangruc, Reynald Bruse came to him, with six knightes in his companie, and desired his father in lawe of his[8] pardon for his offence and he receaved him gently, and gave him the castell of Sainthennyd,★ and Reynalde committed hit to the custodie of Rhes Vychan. And after the Prince had sette all thinges in good order in that countrey he

[1]Ll to   [5]C – Kinges
[2]C Bohum   [6]C unknowen
[3]C Gaunte   [7]C camped
[4]C Monbray   [8]Ll – his

marched to Dyved, and beinge at Kevyn Kynwarchan,[1]* the Fleminges
sent to him, to desire peace. But the Prince wolde not graunt them their
request. And yonge Rhes was the first that passed the Ryver [186]
Cledhay to fight with them of the towne. And beholde, Ierwerth
Bishop of St. Davyes, with all his clergie came to the Prince to desire
peace to the Flemynges, which after longe debatinge was thus
concluded. First that all the inhabitantes of Rosse and the lande of
Penbroke shulde become the Princes subjectes, and ever from thence
furthe take him for their liedge lorde. Secundaryly, that they shulde paie
him 1000 markes, towards his charges, before Michelmas next ensuinge.
Thirdely that, for the performmance of thees,[2] they shulde delyver
furthwith to the Prince twentie pledges, of the best in all the countrey,
which they dyd. And the Prince, after he had brought all Wales to his
subjection, returned to Northwales with much honor. And shortly after
this yere ther was a peace concluded betwixt the Kinge and Lewis the
Frenche [186v] Kinges sonne, and the Kinge promised the barrons all
their requestes and Lewis retured towardes France. And shortly after
William Marshall Earle of Penbroke gote the towne of Caerlhyon and
made warre[3] against the Welshmen (whom contrary to their promise the
[barons][4] left out of the conclusion of peace*). Therefore Rhes Vychan
rased the castell of Sainthenyd and all[5] the castelles he had in his custodie
in that countrey. And banished all the Englishmen that dwelled there,
with their wives and children, for ever and devided the countrey to the
Welshmen, which have kept hit unto this daye.

The yere ensuinge Prince Lhewelyn put his garrisons in the castells of
Caermardhin and Abertyvi. And yonge Rhes, by the Princes consent,
went to the Kinge and dyd him homage for his landes. And at this tyme
William Earle of Arundell, Rondell Earle of Chester, and William
Ferrers,* Earle of Derby, and Bryan Lisle toke their [187] vyage towarde
the Holy Lande. In the yere folowinge Rhes Grug sonne to Prince Rhes
maried the doughter of the Earle of Clare. And John de Bruse maried
Marvred the doughter to Prince Lhewelyn, and William Marshall the
elder dyed and left after him 5 sonnes, and 5 doughters, which doughters
were thus maryed: Maude to Hughe Bygod, the secunde to John
Warrenne de Monte Camisii,* Isabell to Gilbert de Clare, Sibill to
William Earle of Derby, Eve to William de Bruse, betwixt which 5 all
his great inheritannce was after devyded, for all his sonnes dyed without
issue and were every one after an other Earles of Penbroke.

[1]C Kynvarchan
[2]C this
[3]C warres
[4]C they; barons *supplied from HC*
[5]C- all

The yere[1] 1220 Lhewelyn Prince of Wales lead an army to Penbroke against the Flemings, which contrary to their othe and leage had taken the castell of Abertivi,* which castell the Prince wonne [187v] and destroyed the garrison with fier and sworde, and rased the castell. And from thence he went to Wystlande,[2]* and rased the castell and brenned the towne. Also he caused all Haverforde to be brenned to the castell gates and destroyed all Rosse and Daugledhau and they which kept the castell sent to him for truse tyll Maii, which was concluded upon condiciouns, and so he returned home. Also this yere certeine lordes of Wales besiedged the castell of Grosmont, which was Reynaldes de Bruse. Therfore the Kinge came with an army to the Marches, and reysed the siedge, and came as farre as Montgomery, and built a newe castell there. And as William de Albineto Earle of Arundell, Henry de Bohume Earle of Herforde, and Sayerns de Quincy Earle of Winchester were commyinge home frome the Holy Lande they dyede by the waye.
[188] The yere folowinge fill their a great discention betwixte Prince Lhewelyn and Griffith his sonne, for this Griffith enjoyed the cantref of Meryoneth without his fathers consent, and therfore his father sent for[3] him [to come][4] to him. But he wolde not come. Therfore the Prince sware he wolde be revenged upon him and his complices for that dishonor and came with a great army to Meryonedh, and his sonne feared him not, but gote his people in the felde ready to abide the battaill, and as they were in fight[5] there was a peace concluded. And Griffith yelded to his father, and cryed him mercy, and his father forgave him his offence, and toke Meryonydh and Dydwy* from his sonne, and builte a castell their. And this tyme yonge Rhes forsoke Prince Lhewelyn (because Abertivi was not delyvered him as the promise was at the devydinge of Southwales), and went to William Marshall Earle of Penbroke. [188v] Therfore Lhewelyn came to Aberystwydh and seased the castell, and all the territorie to his own use. And yonge Rhes heringe this went to the Kinge, to complaine upon the Prince. And the Kinge sent for the Prince to Shrewsburie and made him and Rhes frendes, and the Prince promised to doe with Rhes for Abertivi as he dyd with Maelgwn for Caermardhyn. And this wynter John de Brewes, by the consent of the Prince Lhewelyn, fortified the castell of Sainthenyd. And Isabell the Kinges mother maryed the sonne of Hughe de Brune Earle of Marche, without makinge of the Kinge pryvey therto.

[1]C + folowinge
[2]C Whitelande
[3]Ll – sent for
[4]to come *supplied from HC*
[5]C – they . . . fight

And William de Fortibus Earle of Albermarle made an insurrection in Lyncolneshire, which was sone appeased, and the Kinge seased into his handes certeine honors and castelles that diverse men kept in their handes wthout juste cause [189] as: Falcasius de Breaut kept the Earledomes of Northampton, Oxforde, Bedforde and Buckingham, with the castelles and holdes; Peter de Malo Lacu the castelles of Corffe and Shyrburen,[1] with Somersetshire and Dorsetteshire and the liberties and forestes; Philippe de Marke the castelles of Peke and Nottingham, and Notinghamshire and Derbyshire. Gegelarde de Siconia kept Wyndsor and Odhiam, which for the most parte[2] the Kinge receaved to his hande. And Hubert de Burghe was created Earle of Kent and Chief Justice of England, and maryed the Kinge of Scottes sister. The yere after yonge Rhes, sonne to Griffith ap Rhes, departed out of this worlde beinge a lustie gentilman and endowed with many notable vertues and was buryed at Ystradflur. And Prince Lhewelyn gave parte of his landes to his brother Owen and parte to his uncle Maelgwn.

[189v] The yere after Christes incarnation 1223, came William Marshall from Irelande and landed at St Davys with a great army. And shortly after layed siedge to Abertivi and gote hit and from thence marched to Caermardhyn and also gote hit. Which newes, when the prince herde, he was sore offended and sent Griffith his sonne with a power of men to staye the Earle for passinge further and Griffith went to Kydwyli and, understandinge that the burgeses of the towne ment to betraye him, he brenned the towne, churches and all to the earth. And William Marshall passed the Ryver Towy at Caermardhyn, and Griffith mette with him and gave him battaill, which was very doutfull,[3] and endured tyll night. And then either partie withdrewe themselves and the ryver betwixt them.[4] And after they had layen so certaine dayes Griffith, for lake of vittayles for his army, [190] which were aboute 9000[5] men,★ returned bake. And the Earle went to Kylgeran, and begane to builde their a very stronge castell and streight he receaved letters from the Kinge to come speake with him, which he dyd by sea, and left his army to continue the worke he had begonne. And the Kinge and the Archebishopp beinge at Ludlowe, sent for the Prince, and wolde fayne have agreede them. But hit wolde not bee, and so they departed. And the Earle wolde have passed to Penbroke by lande with the streingth of the Earle of Derby and Henry Pygot Lorde of Evas. But the Prince sende[6] his sonne to kepe the passage at Carnwylhyon and he himselfe

[1] C Shirburne
[2] C partes
[3] C doubtefull
[4] Ll – them
[5] C 4000
[6] C sent

came as farre as Mabudryd and, when he understoode that[1] the Earle
returned backe to Englande, he also returned to Northwales. And
certeine of the barrons, mislikinge the rule of Hubert de Burgh,
conspired [190v] against the Kinge and him as: Rondell Earle of
Chester, William de Fortibus Earle of Albermarle, Johnes Constable of
Chester, Falcasius de Breant, Hughe de Veteri Ponte, Bryan Lysle,[2]
Patrike de Malo Lacu, Philippe Marke, William Lorde de Cantilupo.
But the matter was appeased, and the Kinge gote the castell of Bedforde
by longe siedge, wherin was William de Breant brother to Falcasius.
And this tyme dyed William de Longa Spata Earle of Salusbury. And the
yere folowinge Sarancus de Malo Leone delyvered Rochell to the
Frenche Kinge. And Falcasius was banished Englande and came to suche
povertie that he begged from dore to dore. The yere 1226 dyd Rhes
Vychan, sonne to Rhes Gruc, take his father prisoner and wolde not
sette him at libertie till he had delyvered to him the castell [191] of
Lhanymdhifri. And this tyme dyed Meredith Archedeacon of
Caerdygan, sonne to Prince Rhes, and was buryed by his father at
Saincte Davyes. The yere folowinge Kinge Henrye came with a great
army to Wales as farre as Keri, and encamped there. And upon the other
side* Prince Lhewelyn called to him all the power of Wales,[3] and
encamped not farre of. And there were diverse great skirmishes and
cheefly upon one daye the most parte of bothe armyes were in the felde,
and a great number slaine of the Kinges men. And William de Bruse,
sonne to Reynalde, was taken prisoner, which paied for his ransome the
countrey of Buelht and a great some of money. And there was a peace
concluded and the Prince came to the Kinge, and dyd honor him, but
not as[4] his Kinge and lorde, and every parte[5] returned home.

    And shortly after there fill a contencioun betwixt the Kinge and
Richarde Earle of Cornwall, [191v] his brother. And thees lordes helde
with Richarde: Randell Earle of Chester, William Marshall Earle of
Penbroke, Gilberte Earle of Glocester, William Earle of Warren, Henrye
Earle of Herforde, William Earle Ferrers, and William Earle of
Warwike. But this debate was sone finished and the Kinge and his
brother were[6] made frendes. And the yere[7] 1230 Henry made a journey
to Fraunce to conquer againe that which his father lost, but he returned
backe without doinge any good. And this tyme dyed Lhewelyn sonne to
Maelgwn in Northwales, and was buryed at Conwey. And Prince

[1] Ll – that
[2] C Liste
[3] Ll – of Wales
[4] C – as

[5] C either parties
[6] C – were
[7] C + folowinge

Lhewelyn caused William Bruse to be hanged in Northwales, because he founde him suspiciously in his wives chamber (Kinge Henryes sister). Gilberte of Clare Earle of Glocester dyed and his wyf[1] maryed Richarde [192] of Cornewall and the Kinge gave the gardinage[2] of his sonne to the Earle of Kent. And Maelgwn sonne to Prince Rhes dyed, and was buryed at Ystradflur, and yonge Maelgwn his sonne enherited his landes. The yere ensuinge dyed William Marshall Earle of Penbroke, and Richarde his brother enjoyed his enheritannce.[3]

And the Kinge leade a great army to Wales, and after he had remained in the Marches a while, he returned to Englande, and left Huberte de Burghe (Earle of Kent) with his army to defende the Marches. And he, by spies, understoode where certeine Welshmen entred the Marches to spoyle, and sette upon them by Montgomery and[4] slewe a great number of them. And the Prince beinge therwith sore offended gathered an army, and [192v] to revenge his men entred the Marches with fier and sworde, and slewe all that withstoode him, and brenned the castelles with the garrisons without mercye. And first the castell of Montgomery, for the Earle withdrewe himselfe for feare. Then the castelles of Radnor, Aberhodni, Rhayader Gwy★ and so he went thrughe Gwentlande to Caerlhyon and after longe fyght[5] and losse of many of his men, gote the towne and left nothinge but ashes and likewise he dyd with the castelles of Neth and Kydwyli. Therfore the Kinge caused the Prince to be denounced accursed, and came to Herforde with a myghty army, and sent a great number of his nobles with the most parte of his armye to Wales, havinge their guide a freer of Cummer.★ And there [193] they mette with a number of Welshmen, which at the first encounter fledde and the Englishmen folowed to the straytes where the embushmentes[6] laye, which fill upon them, and slewe a great number of the best souldiers, and the rest escaped with fleeinge. Therfore the Kinge wolde have brenned the house of Cumner, but the prayor[7] payed 300 markes. And the Kinge returned to Englande after he builde the castell of Maude. And this meane while Maelgwn, the sonne of Maelgwn ap Rhes, layed siedge to Abertivi, and gote the towne and destroyed hit to the castell gates, and slewe all the inhabitantes. And shortly after he returned with his cosine Owen, sonne to Griffith ap Rhes, and certeine of the Princes capteines, and brake downe the bridge upon the [193v] Ryver Tivi, and layed siedge to the castell, and with engines and mynes[8]

[1] Ll – wyf
[2] C Gwyardinge
[3] C inherited his lands
[4] Ll – and

[5] C siedge
[6] C – embushment
[7] C prior
[8] C meanes

cast downe the castell and wonne hit, and returned home with much honor. The next yere to this Prince Lhewelyn entred Englande and returned with a riche spoyle of goodes, cattayll,[1]* and men. Therfore the Kinge seassed a subsedye to subdue the Welshmen. And Huberte de Burghe was accused upon certeine articles and committed to prison. And Rondell Earle of Chester dyed and John his sisters sonne (by the brother of the Scottes Kinge) was Earle of Chester after him, and he maryed the doughter of Prince Lhewelyn and an other of his nevewes had the Earledome of Lyncolne. And Effrayn Byshoppe of Lhanelwy* dyed, also John de Bruse was drawen by [194] his owne horse tayle tyll he dyed miserably. And the somer folowinge, Richarde Earle of Cornewall fortified the castell of Maisyved or Radnor, which the Prince had lately destroyed.

And shortly aftere[2] Prince Lhewelyn came with an army to Breknoke and brenned all the townes[3] and castelles in the countrey, and laye a moneth at[4] the castell of Breknoke, and went without hit, and brent the towne and went homewarde with a great butty. And by the waye he brenned the towne of Colunwy or Clun, and receaved all the countrey called the Valley of Tyveidiawc,* but he could not gette the castell. And of this countrey was lorde, John Ffitzalan. And after he overthrewe the Redde Castell in Powis and brenned the towne of Oswaldstre, and so came home. And upon this, Richarde Marchall, Earle of Penbroke fille at debate with [194v] the Kinge, and Huberte de Burghe* brake out of the castell of[5] Devises and came bothe to Wales and joyned with the Prince against the Kinge, and the Earle, with Owen ap Griffith ap Rhes, came to Mynw,[6] or St. Davies, and killed and spoyled all the kinges servauntes and frendes within the towne. And after came Maelgwn and Rhes Gruc, with the power of the Prince, and joyned with them, and they wonne all thees castelles: Caerdyf,[7] Abergyvenny, Penkelhi, Blaenlhifni, Bwlch y Dinas, and rased them all save Caerdyf.[8] And the Kinge gathered a wonderfull great army as well Flemings, Normaines, and Gascoynes, as Englishmen, and entred Wales, thinkinge to destroye the whole countrey, and encamped at Grosmont, and the Earle with the power of Wales encamped harde by. [195] And as the Kinges men wolde have entred further they were mette with all, and lost 500 horse wherupon the Kinge had advise to returne home, and so he dyd. And the Earle, with the power aforsaide, laye[9] before Caermardhyn three

[1]C chattells
[2]C + the
[3]C towne
[4]C in
[5]C- the . . . of

[6]C Myniw
[7]C Cardiff
[8]C Cardiff
[9]C laide

monethes, but hit was so manfully defended that they colde not come by hit. And at the last, there came in[1] the Kinges shippes, and manned and vittailled the towne of newe, wherfore they raysed the siedge and departed. And shortly after Rhes Gruc, sonne to the Lorde or Prince Rhes, dyed at Lhandeylawe Vawr, and was buryed honorably besides his father at Saincte Davies. And Maelgwn Vychan sonne to Maelgwn ap Rhes fynished the castell of Trefilan which his father had begonne.

The yere after mans salvation 1234 Richarde Earle of Penbroke, by the counsaill of Geffrey de Maristo, went with an army to Irelande, wherfore he was slayne in fyght by treason of his owne men and his brother Gilbert enherited his landes. [195v] In that tyme the Kinge sent the Archebishop of Canterburie, with the Bishoppes of Rochester and Chester, to entreate with Prince Lhewelyn for to make peace with the Kinge, but they returned without doinge of any good. And John Monumetensis, whome the Kinge had made Warden of the Marches entred Wales, and came backe in post leavinge his men for the most parte slayne and taken behinde him. And this [year] Prince Lhewelyn sette Griffith his sonne at libertie, which he had kept in prison six yeres for his disobedience. And at this tyme dyed Robert Fitzwater, who, as Mathias Parisenses sayeth, had a stone aboute his necke of such vertue that he coulde not dye as longe as hit was was there. Also Roger de Somery dyed and Cadwalhon ap Maelgwn of Melyenydh. The yere after dyed Owen sonne to Griffith ap Rhes, beinge a noble gentillman and very wellbeloved, and was buryed by [196] his brother Rhes at Ystradflur. And Kinge Henry maryed the secunde doughter of the Earle of Province called Elynor, and Frederike the Emperor maryed Isabella sister to Kinge Henry. And the yere after Madoc sonne to Griffith Maelor Lorde of the Lower[2] Powis, or Bromfelde, Chirke and Yale, a man very juste and mercifull, dyed and was buryed honorably at the Abbey of Lhanegwester, or Valcrucis, which he had builte, and he left behinde him a sonne named Griffith to enherit his landes.[3] Also Owen ap Meredith ap Rotperte of Kedewen departed out of this worlde. And the same yere Gilberte Earle of Penbroke by treason gote the castell of Morgan ap Howell, called Marchen, and fortified hit very stronge for feare of the Prince. And the Earles[4] of Cornewall and Penbroke toke the crosse. And the next springe dyed [196v] Johan, doughter of[5] Kinge John, Princesse of Wales, and was buryed upon the sea shore in the house of Aber,* as her pleasure was. And furthwith the Prince dyd

builde a house of barefote freers over her grave. And John Scotte, Earle
of Chester, dyed without yssue. Therfore the Kinge seased that
Earldome to his owne handes.

In the yere 1238 Lhewelyn Prince of Wales called all the lordes and
barrons of Wales before him to Ystradflur, and there every [one][1] of
them swore to be fayethfull subjectes, and dyd homage to David,
Lhewelyns sonne. And the saide David toke from his brother Griffith
Arwystli, Keri, Keveiliawc,[2]★ Mowdhwy, and Mochnant, and
Caerenyon, and lette him onely enjoye the cantref[3] of Lhyn. This
Griffith [197] was the elder brother and a lustie gentillman, but yet basse
borne. The somer folowinge the Earle of Cornwall and William de
Longa Spata, the yonger, toke their vyage towardes the Holy Lande.
And Symon de Monteforti fledde from Fraunce to Englande, and the
Kinge gave him the Steewardship of Englande, with the Earledome of
Leycester. This tyme dyd David (sonne to Prince Lhewelyn) take his
brother Griffith, beinge in saffe conducte of the Bishop of Bangor,
contrarye to his othe, and upon whose promise he was content to speake
with his brother, and emprisoned him in the castell of Criketh.[4] The
yere after Christes incarnation 1240 Lhewelyn ap Ierwerth the moste
valyannte and noble prince, which brought all [197v] Wales to his
subjection, and had so often put his enymyes to flight, and defended his
countrey, and augmented the meares therof further then they had been
many yeres before, passed out of this transitorie liefe, and was honorably
buryed at the Abbey of Conwey, after he had governed Wales well and
worthely 56 yers.★ This Prince left behinde him one sonne called
Davidh begotten upon his wief Johan, doughter to Kinge Johan[5] of
Englande, by whome also he had a doughter called Gladus, maryed to
Sir Raffe Mortymer. Also he had an other sone called Griffith whom his
brother wronngfully kept in close prison as longe as he lyved as shall be
herafter declared.

[198] Davidh the sonne of Lhewelyn

Davidh, to whom all the barons in Wales had made an othe of
fidelitie, toke the government of Wales after his father. And the moneth
folowinge came to the Kinge to Glocester, and dyd him homage for the
Princedome of Wales. And likewise all the barrons of Wales dyd the

---

[1]Ll – [one] *supplied from HC*   [4]C Criccieth
[2]C Kedewen   [5]C John
[3]C cantrefs

Kinge homage for their landes and furthwith the Englishmen beganne to trouble the Welshmen, after their accustomed use.★ And[1] Gilbert Marshall came[2] with an army★ and fortified the castell of Abertivi. And the Earle Warren dyed. The yere ensuinge the Kinge came with a great armye to Wales and many noble men yelded to him, because they hated David betrayer of his brother and accursed of the Pope. And the Kinge fortified the castell of the [198v] Deserte[3] in Flintshire★ and receaved pledges of the Prince. And the Kinge gave to Griffith, sonne to Gwenwynwyn, Lorde of Powis, his enheritance and to the sonnes of Meredith ap Conan their landes in Meryonydh. And the Prince accompanied the Kinge to London, and delyvered him Griffith his brother to be kept in the towre of London prisoner. And shortly after Gilbert Marshall Earle of Penbroke was slayne by misfortune fightinge at the turney at Herforde. The Bishopp of Bangor came to the courte to sue for the delyverance of Griffith (sonne to Prince Lhewelyn), but the Kinge knowinge him to be a man of great corage wolde in no wise graunte him libertie.

The yere after Kinge Henry went to Fraunce with an army to succor Hughe de Brunne, [199] his father in lawe, and to recover some of that which his father had lost. But all in vayne, for the people favored the Frenche Kinge, and there he lost a great number of his men, amongst which was Gilbert de Clare. And this tyme Maelgwn Vychan fortified the castell of Garthgrugun and John de Mynoe the castell of Buelht, and Roger Mortymer the castell of Melyenydh. And the somer folowinge the Kinge began to trouble the Welshmen very sore and to take their landes by force without[4] juste title or rightfull cause This yere dyed Hughe de Albineto Earle of Arundell, therfore his landes were devyded betwixt his foure sisters. And to the eldest, which had maryed John Fitzalan Lorde of Oswaldstre and Clunne, came the Earldome of Arundell in which house hit remaineth at this daye.★ [199v] In the yere 1244 dyed Rhes Mechilh sonne to Rhes Gruc of Southwales. And Prince Davidh sente to Rome to commplaine to the Pope howe the Kinge of Englande commpelled him unjustly to hold his landes of him. Therfore the Pope sent to the Abbote of Albercom[5] commyssion to enquire of this matter.

At[6] this tyme as Griffith sonne to Prince Lhewelyn wolde have escaped out of the towre, commynge throughe a wyndowe, he fill downe and brake his necke. And Prince David gathered all his streingth

[1] C + sent   [4] C + any
[2] C – came   [5] C Abercome
[3] C Dessert   [6] C And

to be avenged of the wronges which the Earles of Clare and Herforde, with John de Monmouth and Roger Muhand and other Marchers, dyd to his people. And all the lordes in Wales obeyd him save Griffith sonne to Gwenwynwyn and [200] Morgan ap Howell, which twoe were compelled to obey also. And the Prince entred the landes of the[1] Marche and spoyled and destroyed a great parte therof, and the said Earles and his men fought dyverse tymes, and sometymes the one and sometymes the other had the victorie. This yere dyed a noble man called Meredith ap Rotperte, and was buryed at Istradflur. The yere ensuinnge the Marchers and the Welshmen mette not farre from Montgomerye, where was a cruell fight and 300 of the Welshmen slayne, and a great number of the Englishmen, amonge whom[2] there was slayne a noble knyghte called Herbert[3] Fitzmathewe. And shortly after the Kinge gathered an huge armye of Englishmen and Gascoynes, and entred Northwales entendinge to destroye the countrey. But the Prince mette with his people in a [200v] strayte, and fought with them, and put them to flighte where the Kinge lost a great number of his most worthye souldyers and nobilitie, and the most parte of all his Gascoyns. Therfore seinge he coulde do no good he sent for the Irishmen, which landed at the Ile of Mone, or Anglesey, and spoyled a great parte therof, tyll the inhabitantes of the Ile gathered[4] together and mette with them, with their spoyle, and chaced them to their shippes. And the Kinge manned and vittayled his castelles, and returned to Englande.

This yere dyed Walter Marshall Earle of Penbroke and Anselme (his brother) without issue and their landes came to their fyve sisters. Likewise manye nobles dyed without issue male [201] at this tyme as: the Earle of Arundell, the Earle of Chester, the Earle of Essex, the Earle of Huntingdon and dyverse other. And in the beginninge of the next yere, beinge 1246, David Prince of Wales, after he had gotten the love of his subiectes, and atchived manny notable victories against the Kinge and the Lords Marchers, passed out of this lief, and was buryed at Conwey by his father, after he had ruled Wales fully fyve yeres, leavinge no issue of his bodye to reigne after him, to the great discommforte of the whole lande.[5]

[1]Ll – the
[2]Ll – whom
[3]C – Herbert
[4]C + them
[5]C lands

[201v] Lhewelyn and Owen sonnes to Griffith

When all the lordes and barrons[1] of Wales understoode of the death of
the Prince, they came togeather and called for Lhewelyn and Owen
Goch, the sonnes of Griffith, sonne to Prince Lhewelyn, and brother to
David, as next inheritors (for they estemed not Roger Mortymer sonne
to Gladus, sister to David, and righte enheritor by the order of lawe) and
dyd them homage, devydinge the Principalitie betwixte them twoe.
And at this tyme the Kinge, heringe the death of the Prince, sent one
Nicholas de Myles as Justice of Southwales, to Caermardhyn, and with
him in commission Meredith ap Rhes Gruc and Meredith ap Owen ap
Griffith, to disherite Maelgwn Vychan of all his landes. Wherfore the
said [202] Maelgwn fledde to the Princes to Northwales for succours.
And the Kinge came thither, with a great armye, against the Princes, and
this Maelgwn and Howell ap Meredith (whome the Earle of Clare had
by force spoyled of all his landes in Glamorgan), and after the Kinge had
remained a while in the[2] countrey, and coulde do no good, he returned
backe. This tyme dyed Raffe de Mortymer, which had maryed Gladus
Dhu doughter to Prince Lhewelyn and sister to David, and Sir Roger
Mortymer, his sonne, enjoyed his enheritance which also shulde of right
[have] bene Prince of Wales. The yere ensuinge dyed Howell ap
Ednyved Bishop of Lhanelwy at Oxforde[3] and Anselme was Bishop of
Saincte Davyes. [202v] And the 20 daye of February was there a great
earthquake. And Haralde, Kinge of Man, came to the courte and dyd
homage to Kinge Henry, and he dubbed him Knight. This yere the
Kings half bretherne[4] came to Englande, Guido de Lyzium, William de
Valenti (which maryed the doughtor and heire of Warreyn de
Monthensilo).[5] The thirde brother Anselme was a priest, and a sister
named Ales, whiche was maryed to John Earle of Warren. The somer
folowinge Rhes Vychan sonne to Rhes Mechylh gote his castell of
Carrec Kynnen which his mother had delyvered to the Englishmen.
And the Kinge graunted to the abbottes of Conwey and Ystradflur the
body of Griffith ap Llewelyn [203] and they conveyed hit to Conwey
where he was honorably buryed. And William Ferrers[6] Earle of Derby
and his wief (beinge either of them above an hundred yeres of age[7])
dyed. And William de Longa Spata Earle of Salusburie was slayne in the
Holy Lande, leavinge one onely doughter after him maryed to Henrie

[1]C barrons and lords
[2]Ll – the
[3]C Oxenford
[4]C brethren
[5]C Montethensilo
[6]C Ferers
[7]C old

Lacy Earle of Lyncolne. Within a while after dyed Gladus doughter to
Prince Lhewelyn, and wief to Sir Raffe Mortymer,[1] in the castell of
Wyndsor.★ And Henry Hastinges dyed. This yere next was so drye that
there fill no rayne from the ii of March to the assumption of our Lady.
And William sonne to Gurwared★ (which the Kinge had appointed
Steewarde of the landes which he [203v] had taken from Maelgwn
Vychan) dyed. Shortly after Edward, the sonne of Kinge Henrie, maryed
Elynor doughter to Alfonce Kinge of Castell.

And the yere 1254 there sprange a great debate betwene the princes
of Wales, for as Lucane sayeth, Omnis potestas impatiens consortis
erit.[2]★ So Owen coulde not be content with half the principalitie, but
gote his yonger brother Davyd to him and together leveyd a great
power to disherite Lhewelyn, who puttinge his truste in God and in his
owne manhod and his men mette with them in the felde,★ and after
longe fight gave them an overthrowe, and toke them bothe prisoners
and kept them saffe, and seased all their landes into his owne handes,
[204] and enjoyed alone the principalitie of Wales. This tyme dyed
Thomas Walys Bishop of Saincte Davyes. The[3] yere ensuinge came
Prince Edward Earle of Chester to Wales, and fortified and manned his
castelles there, and returned[4] quietly. But shortly after came all the lordes
of Wales to Prince Lhewelyn, and made their complaintes to him, with
wepinge eies, howe cruelly they were handled by Edwarde, and other of
the nobles[5] of Englande, and their landes taken frome them by force,
and yf they dyd offende they were punished, but where they were
wronged they founde no remedy. Therfore they protested before God
and him that they wolde rather dye in the felde in defence of their right,
then to be made [204v] slaves to strangers. And the Prince, pytyinge his
estate and theirs also, determined with them utterly to refuse the rule of
the Englishmen, and rather to dye in libertie than to lyve in shame and
opprobye. And gathered all his power, and first recovered againe all the
Inlande of Northwales and afterwards all Meryonydh and suche landes as
Edwarde had usurped in Caerdigan, which he gave to Meredith sonne
to Owen ap Griffith. And Buelht he gave to Meredith ap Rhes and
chaced away Rhes Vychan and so honorably devyded all that he wonne
amonge his barrons and kept nothinge to himself but the perpetuall fame
of his liberalitie, and he recovered Gwerthrynyon from Sir Roger
Mortymer. [205] And this tyme Richarde de Karm[6]★ was made Bishop
of St. Davies. The somer folowinge Prince Lhewelyn made warre

[1]C + Knight   [4]C + home
[2]Ll exit   [5]C others the nobles
[3]C This   [6]C Karne

against Griffith ap Gwenwynwyn, who served the Kinge, and wonne all Powys from him, save the castell of Poole, and a little of Caerenyon, and the lande by Sevarne side.

And this tyme, Rhes Vychan ap Rhes Mechylh had obteined of the Kinge a great army (wherof one Stephen Baucon was capteine) to recover his lands and came[1] to Caermardhyn by sea and from[2] thence marched towardes Dynevwr, and layed siedge to the castell. But the Princes power came with his cosines to reyse the siedge and their was fought a blooddy battaill[3] as ever was fought in Wales of so many men, and the Englishmen were put to flight and lost of their men above 2000 [205v] souldiers. And from thence this army entred Dyved and brenned all the countrey and destroyed the castelles of Abercorran, Lhanystephant, Maenclochawg and Arberth, and returned home with muche spoyle. And forthwith, not beinge able[4] to abide the wronges that Geffrey Langely (lieftenant to the Earle of Chester) dyd to them, the Prince entred the Earles landes, and destroyed all to[5] the gates of Chester, one either side the water. And Edwarde the Earle fledde to his uncle, then chosen Kinge of Romaines, for succours and returninge[6] back with an army durst not fight with the Prince, which had 10000 armed men, every one sworne to suffer death (yf neede required) in the[7] defence of their countrey. Yet Griffith ap Madok Maelor commenly surnamed Lorde of the Pallays of Brenne★ (which is a castell standinge upon a [206] very highe rocke of situation impregnable in the Lordeship of Chirke), this Griffith Lorde of Bromfelde and Chirke and all those countreys forsoke the Prince, and served the Earle with all his power, which Earle was counted a cruell and unjuste manne, havinge no regarde to right, promise or othe.

And the next yere Prince Lhewelyn seased to his handes Kemais and made peace betwixt Rhes Gruc★ and Rhes Vychan, his brothers sonne, and gote the castell of Neweporte and all Rosse savinge Havyrforde. And destroinnge the countrey as they went, came to Glamorgan, and rased the castell of Lhankynuth.[8]★ And returninge to Northwales, the Prince mette with Edwarde Earle of Chester (to whom his father had geven Gascoyn and Irelande) and caused him to retyre. And the Prince destroyed the landes of Griffithe [206v] Lorde of Bromfelde. Wherfore the Kinges of Englande and Almaine wrote to him gently to retyer backe, but he wolde not. And devidinge his armye into twoe battailles

[1] C went
[2] Ll – from
[3] C as bloody a battaill
[4] C – able
[5] C – to
[6] C returned
[7] C – the
[8] C Llankymwth

there were 15000 foote men and 500 horse[1] well appointed (yea and
more as Mathias Parisiensis sayeth) in every battaill. And Edwarde sent
for the Irishemen, to come to his succours, but the Prince preventinge
that made ready his shippes, and mette with them upon the seas, and
overcame them, and sent them home with great losse. Wherfore the
Kinge, in a great rage with his sonne, gathered all the strength of
Englande from Saint Michaelles Mount to Twyed and came to
Northwales as farre as Dyganwy but the Prince caused all the vittayles
[207] to be removed over the Ryver Conwey and kept all the straytes
and passages so narrowly that the Kinge was compelled to retyer to
Englande with great losse.

    And Prince Lhewelyn, callinge[2] to him all the power of Southwales,
came to the Marches, where first Griffith Lorde of Bromfelde yelded to
him (because the Kinge coulde not defende his landes) and seased to his
handes all the landes in Powys, and banished the Lorde Griffith ap
Gwenwynwyn, and wonne the castelles of Gilbert de Clare, Earle of
Glocester, where also he gave the Englishmen an overthrowe and slewe
a great number of the worthiest souldiers, and suche as the Kinge loved
well.[3] Wherfore the Kinge called his streingth to him, and sent to
Gascoyn and Irelande for succours and came to Wales [207v] in harvest
tyme, and destroyed all the corne where he went. And not marchinge
ferre beyonde Chester he returned backe without doinge any notable
acte, for God (as Parisiensis sayth) defended the poore people that put
their whole confidence in him. And James Audeley (whose doughter
Griffith Lorde of Bromfelde had maryed) brought a great number of
horsemen from Almaine to serve against the Welshmen, which with
their great horses and unaccustomed kinde of fight overthrewe the
Welshmen at the first encounter. Wherfore shortley after, myndinge to
revenge that displeasure, they made a rode into the said Lorde Audeleys
landes, and the Almaines pursued them, which fledde to the straytes, and
then returned, so fiercely that the Almaines colde not well retier, but
were all for the most parte slayne. [208] And this tyme was there in
England great skarsitie of beeffes and horses, wherof they were wont to
have many thousandes yerly out of Wales, and all the Marches was made
as a desolate and deserte place. This yere dyed Maelgwn Vichan, and
was buryed at Ystradflur. And the next springe all the nobles of Wales
came to geather and swore either[4] to other to defende their countrey to
the deathe, and never to forsake one[5] an other, and that upon paines of

[1] C horsemen
[2] C called
[3] C – and suche . . . well

[4] C one
[5] Ll – on

cursinge. But shortly after Meredith ap Rhes of Southwales, regardinge
not his othe, served the Kinge. And the Kinge called a parliament for a
subsedy to conquere Wales, when he had so many losses, and of late all
the countrey of Penbroke brenned and spoyled, where [208v] the
Welshmen had founde salte plentifully, which they lacked. And there in
Parliament William de Valentia accused the Earles of Leycester and
Glocester, as the workers of all this mischief, and[1] the Parliament brake
without the graunte of any[2] subsedye.

And shortly after there was a parliament holden at Oxforde, where
the Kinge and Edwarde his sonne were sworne solempnely to obey the
lawes and statutes of the realme. But the Kinges bretherne Guy and
William, with Henry sonne to the Kinge of Almaine and John Earle
Warren, forsoke the othe and departed away. And there the lords of
Wales offred to be tryed by the lawe for any offences they had
committed against the King unjustly. [209] But Edwarde wolde not[3]
here of hit, but sent one Patrike de Saus* as lieftenant for the Kinge to
Caermardhin, and with him Mredith ap Rhes. And this Patrike desired
to speake (upon peace) with the Princes counsaill. And the Prince,
meaninge good fayeth, sent his brother David, which he hade sette at
libertie, and Meredith ap Owen and Rhes ap Rhes to entreat with them
to Emlyn. But Patrike, meaninge to entrappe them, layde an embushment of armed men by the way, and as they shulde have mette, thees
men fill upon the Welshmen and slewe a great number of them. But the
lordes, which escaped, reysed the countrey furthwith, and folowed
Patrike and slewe him, and the most parte of all his men. And after this
the Prince, desirous of peace, offred the Kinge 4000 markes, and to his
sonne 300 [209v] and to the Queene[4]* 200 to have peace. But the
Kinge answered: what is this to oure losses, and refused hit.

And the yere ensuyinge dyed Mathias Parisiensis, monke of St Albans,
which wrote the Cronicles and acts from the conquest of[5] William
Duke of Normandy to this yere, whose noble worke I wolde desire to
reade as doubte of the credite of my Welshe author. The same yere was
the Kinge absolved of his othe by the Pope, or to speake hit plainely,
had licence to forswere himself. And the yere 1260 dyd diverse of the
barrons agree to put those statutes in execution which they were sworne
to at Oxforde. And chief of them were Symon de Monteforti Earle of
Leycester, Richarde de Clare Earle of Glocester [210] Humfrey de
Bohune Earle of Herforde, and many moe. And upon the other parte

[1]C + so
[2]C any graunte of
[3]Ll – not

[4]Ll Guyen; C Gwyen; Queene *supplied
    from HC*
[5]C – the . . . of

dyverse lordes (not esteminge their othe and promise)[1] mainteined the Kinges cause. And Prince Lhewelyn destroyed the landes of Sir Roger Mortymer, because he (contrarye to his othe) mainteined the Kinges quarrell, and toke from him all Buelht, savinge the castell which the Princes men gote by night, withoute bloodshed and therin muche munytion. And so after the Prince had passed throughe all Southwales he returned to his house at Aber, betwixt Conwey and Bangor. Also Edwarde the Kinges sonne, which likewise had sworne, toke[2] the castelles of Hay, Breknoke and Huntingdon and committed them to the custodie of Sir Roger Mortymer. And Robert Ferrers Earle of Derby, true to nether parte, spoyled the citie of Worcester, and was taken [210v] and committed to prison. And Edwarde, which was the first, moved the barrons to see a redresse, made warre against them, and spoyled the citie of Glocester.* The yere folowinge dyed Owen ap Meredith Lorde of Kedewen. And shortly after dyed the Earle of Glocester. And this somer dyd certeine of the Princes men take (upon the sodeine) the castell of Sir Roger Mortymer in Melyenydh and slewe the garrison, and toke Howell ap Meurig the capteine,[3] with his wief and childrene, and furthwith sent to the Princes lieftenant and he came and destroyed hit. And Sir Roger Mortymer heringe this came with a great strength of lordes, and knightes to Melyenydh, where the Prince came also. And Sir Roger kept himself within the walles of [211] the broken castell, and sent to the Prince for licence to departe without hurte. And the Prince seinge his enimye within his dannger[4] toke compassion upon him, because he was his cosine, and suffred him to departe with his people[5] without hurte. And the Prince receaved homage of the inhabitantes. And from thence the Prince went to Breknoke at the request of the people, which swore fidelitie unto him, and so he returned to Northwales. And then Symond Montforde gote Glocester, Worcester and Brugge. And as the Kinge wolde have passed by water from the towre to[6] Wyndesore, the Londyners cryed out upon him, and used irreverent woordes towards him, and standinge upon the bridge caste stones at his barge, so that he[7] was compelled to return to the towre againe. And there was a peace concluded betwixt the Earle and the Kinge, [211v] who swore to performe the statutes of Oxforde, and that all strangers shulde avoyde the realme, but suche as the Kinges fayethfull subjectes thought meete to tarye. Also that noble men and

[1]C – and promise
[2]C to
[3]C – the capteine
[4]C danger
[5]C – with his people
[6]Ll of
[7]Ll – that he

wise of the realme shulde have the rule, under the Kinge, with many other. But Edwarde manned his castelles, and fortified them.

And Prince Lhewelyn beinge confederate[1] with the barrons destroyed the Earldome of Chester, and rased twoe of Edwardes castells, Dygannwy and Deserte, and thyther came Edwarde without doinge any thinge. This yere John Estrange the yonger, beinge Constable of Montgomery, came with a great number of Marchers by night throughe Kery to Kedewen, which when the countrey men understoode they gathered together, and sette upon them, and slewe 200 of his men. And he escaped with the reste backe againe. [212] And shortly after the Marchers and the Welshmen mette beside Clun,[2] and there the Englishmen had the victori, and a great number of the Welshmen slayne. And at the tyme David the Princes brother (which he had sett at libertie) forsoke him, and succoured his foes with all his powere. And Griffith ap Gwenwynwyn gote the castell of Molde and rased hit.

And the yere ensuinge the Kinges and their sonnes,* neglectinge their manyfolde othes and promises,[3] gathered a great army with succors of Scottelande, which John Comyn, John Ballyoll[4] Lorde of Gallowey, and Roberte Bruse Lorde of Anandale and John Walleys, brought with them and first wonne by force Northhampton, where the schollers of Oxforde, which the barrons had removed thither, defended the walles stoutly [212v] for a while. In that towne were taken Symon Montforte the yonger, Peter Monford,[5] William Ferrers, Baldwyn Wake, Adam Newemarket, Roger Bertram, Symon Fitzsymons (which was the first man that barre enseigne against the Kinge), Beringary Watervyle,[6] Lango Gubion, Thomas Mansell, Roger Boterilan,[7] Nicholas Wake, Robert Mentron, Philippe Dribri and Grinbalde Pancefote, all knightes and men of worship, which the Kinge committed to saffe custody. In the meane while the barrons beinge at London went to besiedge Rochester, which Earle Warrenne kept and after they had wonne the bridge and the gate, where Roger Leyburne was sore wounded, they herde of the Kinges comminge to London, and returned thither. But the Kinge passed by Kyngeston and toke the castell. [213] And frome thence he went to Tynbridge and gote hit, which was also the Earle of Glocesters, and from thence he came to Wynchelsey,[8] and so to Lewys, to which place the barrons came, and there was fought a cruell battaill, wherof the victorie fill to the barrons. And there were taken bothe the

---

[1] C confederated
[2] C Clunne
[3] C – and promises
[4] C Bailloll

[5] Ll – Peter Monford
[6] C Watervill
[7] C Botenilnam
[8] C Winchester

Kinges, Edwarde the Kings sonne, Humfrey de Bohune Earle of Herforde, John Fitzalen Earle of Arundell, John Comyn, Roberte Bruse, William Bardalf, Roberte Totenhall, Roger Sonery, Henry Percy, and Philippe Basset. But William de Valence Earle of Penbroke, John Warren Earle of Surrey, Gwy de Lyzymaco,[1] Foulke Fitzwarren Lorde of Whittington, Henrie Bygod and William Wilton fledde at the beginninge, and saved themselves. And the Earle kept the Kinge of Romaines in the towre of London, and Edwarde [213v] and Henrie the Kinges sonnes in the castell of Dover. And Kinge Henry he ledde with him thrughe the lande. And certeine lordes Marchers as Roger Mortymer, James Audeley, Roger Leyburne, Haymo Estrange, Roger Clifforde, Hughe Turbevyle, gathered a newe army against the Earle of Leycester and his complices. But the Prince of Wales came with his power, and toke the castells of Haye and Ludlowe, and joyninge with the Earle came to meete with them but they sent to the Earle, and agreed with him. In the meane while Edwarde which was in the castell of Herforde escaped, under the color of exercisinge himself in ridinge, as the Earle[2] had geven him leave. And also[3] the Earle of Glocester forsoke the barrons and served the Kinge. Therfore the Earle and the Prince destroyed all Glamorgan, and [214] the castell of Monmuth, which was the Earles of Clare. And in the meane while the Kinges sonne and the Earle of Glocester went with a great army to Kyllingworth, where they toke the Earle of Oxforde, as he wolde have entred in. And the Earle of Leycester, heringe that, came thitherwarde, and encamped at Everham, where he was compassed aboute[4] with three campes of Edwardes, the Earle of Glocester, and Sir Roger Mortymer, and beganne to dispayre of the victorie, and made proclamacioun that suche as wolde dye in the quarell of justice, and for the defence of the lawes of theire[5] countrey to abyde, and the rest to departe quietlye. And callinge for a priest confessed himself, and his sonne Henry willed him to be of good cheere, and conforted him not to dispayre and he answered [214v] that he dispayred not, but was readye to dye in[6] Goddes cause, and for justice sake. And upon that both the armyes joyned and the Earles men fought manfully, but at the last were overthrowen, and the Earle slayen and afterwarde cruely dismembred, and his hed and membres sent to the wief of Sir Roger Mortymer to Wygmor. There were also slayne: Henry his eldest sonne, Hughe Spenser Justice of Englande, Peter Monteforte, William de Mandevyll, Raffe Bassett, Walter Crepinge,

William de Eboraco, Roberte Sregod, Thomas Hostle, John Beauchampe and Roger Roule all worthy men, and a great number of the
meane people especially of the Welshmen that were with him. And this
yere dyed Meredith ap Owen defender[1] [215] of Southwales* and was
buried at Ystradflur. And Gwy and Symonde de Monteforte escaped
over the sea, where after Gwy slewe Henrye sonne to the Kinge of
Romaines as he herde masse at Viterby not ferre from Rome. And this
yere 1266 one Adam Gurdon, beinge disherited for defendinge the
Earles quarell, kept the highe way betwixt Alton and Farnham, and
robbed all that passed by. And when Edwarde the Kinges sonne herde
therof, he thought to trye what a[2] man this Gurdon was, and he rydde
that way, smally accumpained, and Gurdon byd him stande[3] and paye
his ransome ere he passed. The other sayed he was not in his dette, but
he offred to trye who shulde paye other and together they went alone,
and either [215v] founde other valyante and stronge, and the Earle spake
and tolde him who he was, and Gurdon threwe away his weapon, and
cryed[4] him mercy, and he pardoned him and estemed him well ever
after.

The yere ensuinge Kinge Henry leade a great army towardes Wales.
And by meanes of Octobonus, the Popes legate, there was an accorde
made betwixt the Kinge and the Prince at the castell of Montgomery,
upon Calixtus Day, for which peace the Prince gave the Kinge 30,000
markes, and the Kinge graunted the Prince a Charter, to receave from
thence furth homage and fealtie of all the nobilitie and barrons of Wales.
And all the forsayed barrons shulde ever after holde of the Prince, as
their liedge lorde, and he to bee called and [written][5] from thence furth
Prince of Wales. [216] And in witnesse of this the Kinge put his seale
and hande to the saide Charter, which was likewise confirmed by the
auctorytie[6] of the Pope. And the yere after this dyed Grono sonne to
Ednyved Vychan, a noble man and chief of the Princes counsaill. Also in
the yere 1270 dyed Griffith Lorde of Bromfelde, and was buryed at Val
Crucis,* which by his wief, doughter to James Audely, had 4 sonnes:
Madoke Vychan* to whome came Bromfelde by devision,[7] and the
Kinge gave the wardeship of him to John Earle Warren, who built the
Holte castell, and garded the lande to his owne use; the secunde sonne
Lhewelyn had to his parte Chirke and Nanheudwy, whose wardeship
was geven to Sir Roger Mortymer, which kept the lande to him and his

[1]C – defender
[2]C – a
[3]C stay
[4]C asked

[5]Ll – written
[6]C aucthoritie
[7]C dyvision

heires; [216v] the thirde sonne Griffith Varvgwyn¹ had Jale and
Glyndyfrdwy,² this was grandfather to Owen Glyndwr; and the fourthe
sonne had Kynllayth.

And at this place leaveth myne author, and writeth no further of the
ende of this Prince, but leaveth him at the hiest and most honorable
staye that any Prince of Wales was in of many yeres before, beinge
abashed peradventure, or rather ashamed to declare the utter fall and
ruine of his countrey, wherunto there owne pride and discorde hathe
leade them, as hit doth evidently appeare to him that searchethe out
their histories. But I entendinge to fynishe that worke which I have
taken in hande, and promised to accomplish at the beginninge of this
boke, have sought out in other cronicles, [217] written in the Latyne
tonge, especially in the cronicle of Nicholas Treuet³ (which wrote from
the beginninge of the reigne of Stephen to the coronation of Edwarde
the Secunde) and suche other, as muche as I colde finde touchinge my
matter, which is as here after foloweth.

The yere of our Lorde 1270 John Earle Warren slewe Alen le Souch,
Lorde Chief Justice, in Westminster Hall. The yere after Edmonde Earle
of Lancaster maryed the doughter of William Albemarle Earle of
Holdernesse, which by her mother (doughter to Baldwyn Ryvers) was
enheritor of Devonshire and the Ile of Wight, but she dyed before her
parentes. And the yere folowinge Edwarde with his brother Edmunde
went to the Holy Lande, where at Acon he was in daunger to be slayne
by a villaine (under [217v] the color of delyveringe of a letter) which
gave him fyve woundes with a knife. And the yere 1272 dyed Henry
Kinge of Englande. And Edwarde his sonne, comminge from the Holy
Lande 2 yeres after, was crowned at Westmyster Kinge of Englande. To
which coronation the Prince of Wales refused to come, althoughe he
was sent for, layinge for his excuse that he had offended many noble
men of Englande, and therfore wolde not come in their daunger
without he had for pledges the Kinges brother, with the Earle of
Glocester, and Roberte Burnell, Chief Justice of Englande. Wherewith
the Kinge was sore offended, but dissimmlinge his displeasure for the
tyme, came shortly after to Chester, willinge the prince to come thither
to doe him homage, which, when the Prince detracted, the Kinge
gathered an army to compell him therto. [218] And the yere folowinge
the Countesse of Leycester, wief to Symonde Monteforte (which
remained at a nonry in Montargis in Fraunce) sent her doughter to

¹C Varwn gwynne   ³C Trevet
²Ll Glynofrdwy

Wales, to marye the Prince, as hit was agreed betwixt them in her
fathers tyme. And with her came her brother Aymeryke[1] and a fayre
companie, and fearinge the cost[2] of Englande, they[3] kept their course to
the Iles of Sylle,[4] where by chaunce they mette with 4 shippes of
Bristowe,★ which sette upon them, and toke them, and brought them to
the Kinge, who entertained the lady honorably, and committed her
brother to be kept prisoner in the castell of Shyrborn, and frome thence
removed him to the castell of Corffe.

And the Kinge prepared 2 armyes, of which he ledde one himself to
Northwales, as farre as Rudlan [218v] and fortified the castell. And the
other he sent with Paganus de Camurciis, a worthye souldier, to
Westwales, who brenned and destroyed a great parte of the countrey.
And this yere hit rayned bloodde in dyverse parties of[5] Wales. The yere
ensuinge the lordes of Southwales came to the Kinges peace and dyd
him homage, and delyvered the castelles of[6] Ystradtywy unto the Kinges
lieftenante, Paganus de Cammurciis. And the Prince understandinge this
and seinge that his owne people had forsaken him, sent to the Kinge for
peace, which was[7] agreed upon thees conditiouns.★ Ffirst that all those
which the Prince kept prisoners of the Kings frendes, and for his cause,
shulde be sette at libertie. Secundaryly that the Prince [219] shulde paye
to the Kinge, for his favor and good will, 50000 markes, to be payed at
the Kinges pleasure. Thirdely that 4 cantreds shulde remaine to the
Kinge and his heires forever, which cantredes I thinke were thees:
Cantref Rosse, where the Kinges castell of Dyganwy stoode, Cantref
Ryvonyog, where Denbighe is, Cantref Tegengel, where Rudlan
standeth and Cantref Dyffryn Clwyd, where Ruthyn is. And also that
the Lords Marchers shulde quietly enjoye all the landes they had
conquered within[8] Wales, and that the prince shulde paye yerly for the
Ile of Mone, or Anglesey, 1000 markes which payment shulde beginne
at Michaelmas then next ensuinge. And that also he shulde paye 5000
markes out of hande. Fourthly that yf the Prince dyed without issue, the
Ile shulde [219v] remaine to the Kinge and his heires, and that the
Prince shulde come to Englande every Christemas to doe the Kinge
homage for his landes.[9] And that all the barrons in Wales shulde holde
their landes of the Kinge, savinge fyve in Snowdowne, which shulde
acknowelege the Prince to be their lorde. Fifthly that he shulde for his

[1] C Americk
[2] C coastes
[3] Ll the
[4] C Ile of Sylley
[5] Ll in

[6] Ll in
[7] Ll – was
[8] C in
[9] C – for . . . lands

lief enjoye the name of Prince, and none of his heirs after him. And that[1] after his death the foresaide fyve barrons shulde holde of the Kinge and of none other. And for the performannce of thees articles he shulde delyver the Kinge 10 hostages of the best in Wales without emprisoninge, disheritinge, or tyme of delyverannce determined.* And also the Kinge to chose 20 within Northwales, which [220] shulde take their othes with the[2] Prince to performe all those articles. And yf the Prince shulde swarve from any of them and beinge therof admonished wolde not amende and redresse, they shulde forsake him, and become his enimyes. Also the Prince was bounde to lette his bretherne enjoye their landes in Wales, of the which David had longe served the Kinge. And the Kinge had made him knight, contrarye to the maner of Wales, and had geven him in maryage the doughter of the Earle of Derby, whose first husbande was lately deceassed, and nowe[3] the Kinge gave him Denbigh in Northwales and 1000 poundes landes therwith. His other brother Rodericke was lately fledde to Englande out of prison, and the thirde, Owen, was delyvered at this composition. [220v] And at this tyme the Kinge buildede a castell at Aberystwyth and returned home to Englande with muche honor. And the people graunted him the twentith parte of their goodes towards his charges in this warre. And the yere folowinge the maryage was celebrated at Worcester betwixt Elynor doughter to Symon Montfort and the Prince, where were present both the Kinge and the Queene, and the most parte of the nobilitie of Englande.

And the yere after Roger Mortymer sette up, at Kyllingworth, a rounde table for an hundred knightes, to be exercised in the feates of armes and thither resorted many knightes from diverse countreys. And the Kinge of Scottes dyd his homage to Kinge Edwarde and obteined the Kinges letters that his [221] succors in the last warres of Wales were not done by the name of service, but of good will. And this tyme there was a statute made at Glocester called Quo Warrante, wherby every man was bounde to shewe wherby he held his landes, and the firste that was called was the Earle Warren, who drawinge out an olde sworde sayde,* by this warrant myne anncestors wonne their lands, and by this I doe and will holde myne. And all the barrons applyed to his answere and the Quo Warrante was no more talked of.

Not longe after David, Lorde of Denbigh, was made frende with his brother the Prince, upon condicioun he shulde never after serve the

[1]C – that   [3]C – nowe
[2]C their

Kinge of Englande as he had before, but become his utter enimy to the[1] death. And furthwith David toke the castell of Hawarden, and therin Roger Clifforde (a noble knight), and slewe [221v] all that resisted, and after spoyled all the countrey, and with his brother layed siedge to the castell of Rudlan. And the Kinge heringe this, hasted thither with a great army to raise the siedge. And the Prince retyred backe with his armye. And the same tyme Rhes the sonne of Maelgwn, and Griffith the sonne of Meredith ap Owen, and other noble men of Southwales, toke the castell of Aberystwyth, and dyverse other castelles, alongest[2] that countrey, and spoyled all the Kinges people that enhabited there aboutes. Therfore the Kinge sent the Archbishop of Caunterburye to talke with the Prince and his bretherne, whiche returned without doinge any good and by the Kinges commanndement deninced them and all their complices accursed. [222] And furthwith the Kinge sent his army by see to the Ile of Mone or Anglesey, which they wonne, and slewe such as resisted, for the cheffest men served the Kinge, as ther othe was. So they came over against Bangor, where the arme of the sea (called Menay whiche devideth the Ile from the mayne lande) is narrowest, and the place called Bonp y don[3]★ and their made a bridge of boates and plankes over the watter, where before Julius Agricola dyd the like when he subdued the Ile[4] to the Romaines, and not betwixt Man and Britanie, as Polydor Virgill shamefully affyrmeth. This bridge accomplished, that 60 men might well passe over in a front, William Latymer, with a great number of the best souldiors, and Lucas Thany[5] Steewarde of Gascoyne, with his Gascoynes [222v] and Hispaniardes (wherof a great number were come to serve the Kinge), passed over the bridge, and there sawe no sturre of enymyes. But as sone as the sea beganne to flowe, downe came the Welshmen from the hilles, and sette upon them fierslye, and either slewe or chaced them to the sea to drowne themselves. For the water was so highe that they colde not atteine the bridge, savinge William Latymer alone whose horse caryed him to the bridge, and so he escaped. In the meane tyme was the Earle of Glocester and Sir Roger Mortymer with an army in Southwales and their fought with the Princes frends (for many served the Kinge) at Lhandeylo Vawr, and gave them an overthrowe but he [223] lost there yonge William de Valence, the Kinges cosine germaine. And all this while the Prince destroyed the countrey of Caerdigan, and all the landes of Rhes ap Meredith who served the Kinge in all thees warres. And

[1] C – the
[2] C alonge
[3] C Bonpe y donne
[4] Ll – when he subdued the Ile
[5] C Tamy

afterwarde the Prince separated himself from his army with a fewe, and came to Buelht, thinkinge to remaine there quietly for a while. And by channce as he came by the water Wy, there were Roger Mortymer★ and John Giffarde, with a great number of souldiors, and either partie were abashed of other,[1] and Mortymers men were of that countrey, for he was lorde therof. And the Prince departed★ from his men, and went to the valley with his Esquier[2]★ alone, [223v] to talke with certeine lords of the countrey. And some of his men seinge their enimyes came downe from the hill, and kept the bridge called Pont Orewyn,★ and defended the passage manfully, tyll one declared to the Englishmen where a forde was a little beneth, and they sent a number of their men with Helyas Walwyn that way, which sodenly fell upon them that defended the bridge, in their backes, and put them to flight. The Princes Esquier[3] tolde the Prince (as he stoode secreatly abydinge the comminge of suche as promised to meete him, in a litle grove), that he herde a great noyse and crye at the bridge, and the Prince asked whether his [224] men had not taken the bridge, and he saide, yes, then I passe not, and all the power of Englande were upon the other side. But beholde the horsemen about the grove, and he wolde have escaped to his men, and they purused him so harde that one Adam Franketon★ ranne him throwe[4] with a staffe, beinge unarmed, and knewe him not, and his men[5] beinge but a fewe stode and fought boldlye, ever lookinge for their Prince, tyll the Englishmen by force of archers mixt with the horsemen wonne the hill and put them to flight. And as they returned Franketon went to spoyle him whome he had slayne. And when he sawe his face he knewe him [224v] very well, and stroke of his hed, and sent hit to the Kinge at the Abbey of Conwey, which receaved hit with great joye, and caused hit to be sette upon London Bridge. And this was the ende of Lhewelyn, betrayed by the men of Buelht, whiche was the last Prince of Britons bloode, which without interuption bare dominion and rule in Wales. So that the rule and government of the Britons ever continued in some place of Britaine from the first comminge of Brute, which was the yere before Christes incarnacioun 1136, to the yere after Christe 1282 by the space of 2418 yeres.

And the Kinge brought all the countrey to his subjection [225] save the castell of Ber, which he at the last wanne by famyn, grauntinge the garrison their pardons. And shortly after the countrey menne themselves brought to him David, and he kept him in Rudlan castell, and after put

[1] Ll others
[2] C Esquiers
[3] C Esquiers
[4] C thrugh
[5] Ll – men

him to cruell death at Shreusburye.[1] And the Kinge builded twoe stronge holdes in Northwales, Conwy and Caernarvon, where his sonne Edwarde was borne, and was the first [of] strange bloode that was called Prince of Wales, althoughe a cronicler that wrote at Rome nameth his father Prince of Wales, and that is as true as Man is Mona, which he also boldely and blindly affirmeth in his mappe of Englande. Likewise Rhes Vychan heringe this yelded himself to the Earle [225v] of Herforde, and he sent him to the towre of London by the Kings commaundement, to be imprisoned there. And so the Kinge passed[2] thrughe all Wales and brought the whole countrey in subjection to the crowne of Englande to this daye.*

Yet shortly after Rhes ap Meredith made an insurrection in Southwales, the Kinge beinge then one the other side the sea. And Edwarde Earle of Cornewall came with an army against him and put him to flight, and wonne his castell of Drosolan[3] where he loste a noble man, Lorde de Monte Camysii* and rased the castell, and returned home againe. [226] Also in the yere 1293 the Welshmen arose againste the Kinge in diverse places at ones, for the Southwales men chose for their capteine Maelgwn Vychan, and destroyed all Penbrokeshire, and Caerdygan, and returned home with riche spoyles. Also they of Glamorgan and there aboutes, takinge one named Morgan for their lorde, and drove the Earle of Glocester out of the countrey, and recovered againe that which his auncestors by force and great wronge had taken from the said Morgans predecessors. And besides all this Madocke sonne to Prince Lhewelyn* gathered a great power, and fill upon the towne of Caernarvon and slewe a great [226v] number of Englishmen, which were come thither to the fayre, and spoyled the whole towne. Therfore the Kinge called backe his brother Edmunde and Henrye Lacy Earle of Lyncolne and Lorde of Denbighe, whiche had an army ready to passe to Gascoyne, and they went streighte to Northwales, and not farre from Denbighe Madocke mette with them, and gave them battaill, and put them to flighte killinge a great number of their men. Then the Kinge went thither himself, and passed the Ryver Conwey where his army[4] lacked vittailles, for Madockes men kept all the wayes. And at the last[5]* thearle of Warwike [227] (havinge a spye where a great number of them laye in a playne betwixt twoe woodes), came thither by night, and because they were wonte to receave the horsemen ever upon their longe speares, he mixte ever crosse bowes and

longe bowes with the horsemen, and so sette upon them and slewe a
great number. And at this tyme the Kinge built the castell and towne of
Beaumarys in the Ile of Anglesey. And so puttinge all thinges in a
quiettenesse returned home. But afterwarde this Madocke gathered a
number of men and came as farre as Oswestree and the people yelded to
him. [227v] And there he overthrewe the power of the Lordes
Marchers, wherof the Lorde Estrange[1] was capteine, not farre from
Knockinge, and spoyled their countreys miserably. And shortly after he
gave them an other overthrowe, and then they gathered a greatter
powere and gave him battaill upon the hille called Kevyn Digolh, not
farre from Caurs,★ as he was comminge towardes Shrewisburye. And
there after longe fight he was taken and his men put to flighte, and he
sent to the Towre, to perpetuall prison.★ After this there was nothinge
done in Wales worthy memory, but that is to bee redde in the Englishe
Cronicle.[2]

Finis★

---

[1]C Strange   [2]C Chronicles

NOTES

The references are to the folio numbers of the manuscript or their versos, shown thus [2] or [2v] in the text.

folio

1v **5 yeres:** C has '8' but in the margin has a later correction to '5'; *HC* follows the text of C with 'eight'; N 5 yeres.

2 **Because . . . :** in C this is preceded by a 3–4 line space to indicate the interjection by the author, which in Ll begins a new folio. *HC* has rearranged Llwyd's introductory section by setting the Description at the very beginning of the work and as a consequence has rewritten this long opening sentence.

2v **Henander:** the handwriting in C is unclear, but *HC*'s rendering as 'Henegaw' tends to confirm that reading of it in C also. The name occurs again on f. 151 as 'the Earle of Henande, or Henegowe', *HC* 'Henald or Henagow', N Henander.

3v **martiall:** C 'materiall' is an example of miscopying in C corrected in a later hand, usually that of John Dee; *HC* 'martiall prowess' could indicate a different source copy or, as is more likely, an attempt to improve on Llwyd; N martiall.

3v **to utter thinges:** the omission of this phrase in *HC* as well as in the original (uncorrected) text of C must have a bearing on the nature of *HC*'s source.

4 **erroures confuted at large:** the work was published after Llwyd's death, as *Historiae Brytannicae Defensio* (London, 1573), above, pp. 3, 13–14. For Vergil: *Polydore Vergil's English History*, i, ed. H. Ellis, Camden Soc., xxxvi (London, 1846).

5 **dednitions:** thus also in C whereas *HC* has the more likely and probably corrected form 'derivations'.

5v **the countrey one this side . . . Mers . . . one this side . . .**

Shropshire: Llwyd was probably resident in England when he wrote this in 1559: he was still a member of the Arundel household and represented East Grinstead in the Parliament of that year. *HC* has adapted the phrasing to read 'the countrie betweene it and England . . . Y Mars' and 'Englandward, beyond these old meeres a great waie as in . . . Shropshire', and has thereby obscured part of the significance of Llwyd's words. Llwyd refers again to the use of the Welsh language in Shropshire and Herefordshire on f. 23v.

6   **66^{li}:** both MSS use the conventional contraction 'li'; *HC* has '200 pound'.

7   **the Lande of the Mone:** C 'ye Mone', *HC* 'the land of the Mon'; one of many such minor errors attributable to copyists, though in instances such as this where both MSS agree broadly, lack of revision by Llwyd himself might have been contributory.

7   **Yf this . . . reade:** in C these words are later insertions, partly in the margin, partly above the line, so that the phrase was probably missed by the copyist. The identical omission in *HC* has an obvious bearing on considerations of his MS source.

7–7v   **Tacitus . . . wanne the ile:** for Agricola's crossing Cornelii Taciti, *De Vita Agricolae*, ed. R. M. Ogilvie (Oxford, 1967), 104–5; Smith, *Llywelyn ap Gruffudd*, 538–9; below, note f. 222.

7v   **Nowe whether is hit:** this strange syntax occurs in C, N and also remarkably in *HC*.

7v   **well:** C corrected above the line to 'Now' in a later hand, probably John Dee's; *HC* also has 'Now' so that C may well reflect a correction by Dee after seeing *HC*.

8v   **frutefullnes of grasse:** a later correction in C to 'fertilitie of the grounde' as in *HC* and possibly for the same reason as in the preceding note.

8v   **Caersegonce:** also in *HC,* one of several instances where 'c' is misread for 't'.

8v   **and Menai:** C has a later alteration to 'the river Menai', again by Dee and possibly after seeing *HC* 'the sea and Maenai'.

8v **southwest:** Ll has incorrectly 'southeast', here corrected from C, *HC* 'southwest'.

9v **Ganioc:** *HC* agrees with C 'Gannoc', but the reference in both MSS to 'Edwarde the first' who annexed Creuddyn to Caernarfonshire does not appear in *HC*.

9v **Gologion . . . Rythyn:** in C 'Rythyn' is altered in a later hand to 'Dogvulyn'. *HC* has 'Coleigion, Lhannerch and Dogueilyn'.

11 **in right order . . . placed hit here:** a line drawn through in a different ink, and in another hand in right-hand margin 'nota Mathravall'; in C this reference is underlined; *HC* replaces 'the woorke' with 'historie folowing' (see also note f. 13 below).

11 **three partes:** omitted in C but inserted in margin by Dee; the phrase is missing in *HC* which suggests that Dee had access to another MS of Llwyd's work.

11v **Cantref Rayader:** Ll omits 'Cantref', here inserted from C; *HC*, 'Cantref Rayader' as in C.

12v **and Comote Haverne; Cantref Kynan hathe:** these words appear to be a miscopied insertion. The sentence would make sense as 'Cantref Kedewen, hathe comote Kynan, Comote Kevelioc and Mawddwy'. 'Haverne' seems to anticipate the next (third) part of Mathrafal 'betwixt Wy and Sevarne'. 'Haverne' has no real existence as a commote, and appears as such only here and in Gruffudd Hiraethog's list NLW, Peniarth MS 163, Part ii, ff. 57–60 (1543); see above, p. 14 and n.54 for the correspondence between Llwyd's list and that of Gruffudd Hiraethog; also, *HW*, I, 281–6.

13 **thyrde:** the correction of 'thyrde' to 'secunde' in the MS, reinforced by a note in right hand-margin (both in the same hand as the text) is mistaken and corrected 'thyrde' is given in the text. A previous reference to Mathrafal (f. 11) has to do with the three kingdoms formed by Rhodri Mawr, whereas here the reference is to the three parts of Powys or Mathrafal: Powys Fadog, Powys Wenwynwyn and 'the lande betwixt Wy and Sevarne'; C correctly retains the original 'third' as does *HC*.

14 **to women:** Ll in the right hand-margin in another hand 'nota howe the iii wymen had Northwales'. Whereas both Ll and C agree on the reference which follows to Stradwen as daughter to 'Addeawn ap Kynan ap Endaf', *HC* makes her daughter to 'Caduan ap Conan ap Endaf'. This is as it appears in the triad itself (*TYP*, App. V, Triad 5, 258); *HC* was possibly able to correct Llwyd by referring to the printed text which had been published *c.* 1567 (*TYP*, xl). The existence of MS copies of the triads *c.* 1500 is discussed in *TYP*, xlii, where reference is made (n.1) to a copy possibly in the hand of Gutun Owain. Llwyd's declared source was, however, the 'Britishe Cronicle'; his own words are: 'here I thinke hit good to let the reader underestande what the Britishe Cronicle saithe of Northwales, which affirmeth that three tymes hit came by enheritannce to women.' No such reference occurs in any of the known versions of *Brut y Tywysogyon* or of *Brenhinedd y Saesson*, which tends to reinforce the view that Llwyd's 'Britishe Cronicle', 'British booke', 'Welsh booke' or 'Welsh historie' was some other compilation of historical events. Llwyd's own description of his source, that it 'dothe aswell entreate of the warres be-twixt every of thees three princes [of Gwynedd, Powys and Deheubarth] as betwixt them and the Saxons, Northmannes and the Fleminges' (f. 6) is too inexplicit to be of much help in resolving this important issue. For the role of women see also note f. 16v and above, pp. 19, 26.

14 **Ystoreth:** *HC* Yscroeth, see n.8v above, for misreading of 'c', 't'.

14v **Guildas woordes whiche saieth:** for Buylke (Bolg) and the position of Man *in umbilico maris inter Hibernam et Britanniam*, see Nennius, *British History and the Welsh Annals*, ed. J. Morris (London and Chichester, 1980), 59, 60 (§ 8, 9).

15 **Edyrn:** C 'Edwyn', in left-hand margin, 'Edyrn' in Dee's hand.

15v **In this tyme:** initial 't' of 'this' seems to have been deleted; in C 'this' is deleted and 'his' in margin in the same hand. It may be noted here also that *HC* has 'wiseman' for 'prophecier'.

15v **thyther [from] Afrike:** 'from' is omitted also in C but added in Dee's hand in the margin; N has 'out of'.

16 **Ethelfryd . . . Cantie:** the strange omission in C of any reference to this northern ruler is repeated in *HC* where a marginal note refers

forward to a later insertion by Powel into Llwyd's text, at the end of the reign of Cynan Dindaethwy, relating to Brochfael Ysgythrog. Ll in the left-hand margin in a different hand has 'nota who was father to Cadvan'. For a discussion of Æthelberht's relations with the Christians of the West, and of the identities of the Welsh leaders opposed to Æthelfrith and Æthelberht, see *HW*, I, 172–8, 180–2; and on Brochfael Ysgythrog *TYP*, 319. Forms in text have been extended from MS 'Ethelfryd Rex North' Ethelbert Cantie'.

16v   **Esilht . . . Cadwalader:** neither MS gives Esyllt's full lineage, C omitting Rhodri Molwynog and Ll Idwal Iwrch, though Ll deletes 'Ydwal', inserting 'Rodri Malwynog' above it. A marginal note, 'the sonne of Idwall the Roo', presumably refers to Rhodri Molwynog though it is misplaced. Another immediately above it should probably read 'not[a] Esilht verch Cynan'. The account of the death of Cynan [Dindaethwy] and the succession of his daughter Esyllt [*s.a.* 817, f. 30] does not repeat her lineage but gives that of her husband Mervryn Frych at some length to display his noble descent from the lords of Powys. Neither does it make any further reference to her role as the third woman to rule North Wales (see note f. 14), strangely since hers is the only one of the three instances to be recorded in the early genealogies (*HW*, I, 323–4, nn.12, 15; *TYP*, 260 n.5; P. C. Bartrum, *Early Welsh Genealogical Tracts* (Cardiff, 1966), 9 *et passim*).

19   **Debelenos:** thus also in C, but *HC* 'Montgomerys'; N Belesmos.

20   **Croneth:** i.e. 'Gro Nedd', a corruption of 'Gorfynydd'; see *HW*, I, 275 n.264.

21   **Cantref Cochywthees:** this reflects the confusion resulting from the traditional reputation of Morgannwg as a land of seven cantrefs. The various MS lists differ as between, for instance, the name 'Cantref Gwent' and 'Cantref Gwent Uwchcoed' and that of the first of the three cantrefs of Gwent; the placing of the commotes Ewyas and Erging; and more particularly the name and location of the third cantref in Gwent – which would have been the seventh of the ancient divisions of Morgannwg. *HW*, I, 275 discusses the confusion but does not refer to the customary naming of this last cantref as 'Cantref Coch' (or 'Cantref Cochion'). The framework for Llwyd's Description is probably the list of cantrefs and commotes in NLW, Peniarth MS 163, ff. 57–60,

transcribed by Gruffudd Hiraethog in 1543, above p. 14 and n.54 and note f. 12v. It ends 'Cantrev Cochion yw y seithved Cantrev o Vorganwg, a hwnw a vesurwyd, o Vynwy hyd yn Mhont Caerloew; neu cantrev Coch yn y Ddena, hyd Caerloew' (Cantref Cochion is the seventh Cantref of Glamorgan measured from Monmouth to Gloucester Bridge; or Cantref Coch in the Dean, as far as Gloucester). The manuscripts of Llwyd's work provide examples of scribal misunderstanding compounding error. *HC* has silently changed this to 'Cantref Coch was the seauenth Cantred of Morganwc'.

21   *olim* **Strygil:** MS reads 'Olyn Strygil'; in C 'Olyn' has been deleted and '*olim*' placed above it in another hand which does not appear to be Dee's; *HC*'s misreading as 'Glyn' reflects his misunderstanding of the intention here; N 'Olyn'.

24–24v   **And this shalbe a sufficient description . . . frome the first inhabiting therof to this daye:** *HC* gives no explanation for replacing this entire passage with 'This shall suffice for the description of the countrie, and therefore let us now proceed to the Brytish copie'. It may have been at least partly due to the possibility of confusion with regard to Llwyd's purpose between 'to this daye' and his earlier 'to Lhewelyn sonne of Gruffith ap Lhewelyn' (f. 2). Llwyd's meaning, however, seems clear enough from his practice in the Description, and less frequently in the historical account, of referring to the situation as it was in his day, for example, the Welsh language in the Marches (f. 5v and note); the division into shires (ff. 8v, 11v *et seq.*).

26v   **the same yere beinge 721:** this is ambiguous, but must relate to the year of Adelard's battle against Rhodri, that is the first battle at Heil or Heilyn in all versions of *BT*, but not named by Llwyd. See *BS*, 9.2n. On the two other battles mentioned, Garthmaelog and Pencoed (*Pen20* Penkwn), see *Pen20Tr*, 2.5n. Whereas therefore by this evidence Llwyd's source could have been either *Pen20* or *RBH*, his preceding account of the reign of Ivor owes nothing to the *Pen20* or *RBH* versions. It is nearer to, but clearly not derived from, the more extensive account in *BS*, including, for example, the identification of Ivor as Ine King of Wessex, *BS*, 1.8n., though (f. 25v) he gives the 'Englishe Cronicle' (C 'chronicles') as his authority. Llwyd's chronology up to and including the succession of Rhodri Molwynog in 720 has no basis in *BT*, though Rhodri's death is recorded by him as in *BT s.a.* 754.

29v **And the yere 787 . . . or Dyvet:** *HC* follows C in omitting this reference. Llwyd's dating is again at variance with *BT*. The date generally given for the death of this Maredudd is 796 (*HW*, I, 262) as in *BS*, but 786 in *Pen20* which also records erroneously his death in the battle of Rhuddlan (*Pen20Tr,* 4–5n.; on the dating, see ibid., lxvi, 3.1–3n.). There is also obvious misdating by Llwyd of the immediately preceding references to the first Danish incursions into England (not mentioned in *BT*) and Ireland, and to the battle of Rhuddlan. *HC* makes some adjustment to these dates but retains Llwyd's incorrect linking of two events given separately in *BT* and specifically two years apart in *Pen20* and *BS*, namely the battle of Rhuddlan and the death of Caradog, king of Gwynedd. This is a strange echo of *Pen20*'s error in respect of the death of Maredudd, and the link thus made by Llwyd and recounted in *HC* has been claimed to be responsible for the popular 'traditional' tale of Caradog's death. Lloyd quotes the authority of Harleian MS 3859 to trace this Caradog's pedigree back to Cunedda through the Cuneglasus of Gildas, and surmises that he was the eighth-century ruler of the three cantrefs of Arfon, Llŷn and Arllechwedd before they were combined under Merfyn Frych in one kingdom with Anglesey (*HW*, I, 133, 201 n.31; 237 and nn.47, 48; also *Y Cymmrodor*, XL, 140–1 n.2); for Caradog ap Gwyn ap Gollwyn see also Bartrum, *Early Welsh Genealogical Tracts*, 97, 104–5.

31v–32 **the seven Kingdomes:** C has no marginal numbering and omits Hampshire, Wiltshire and Dorset in the description of Wessex, representing a whole line missed in the MS; the omission is repeated in *HC*, which nevertheless follows Ll in its marginal numbering; N is like C here.

32v **Beurnrhed**: the name also occurs two sentences later, but in C and *HC* the first reference is written as 'Berthred'; in the second occurrence C has 'Bewrnrched' and *HC* 'Burchred'; N has Bernrhed.

32v **battaill of Ketill . . . dyed Mervryn Vrych:** these two events are recorded separately in this way in the main *Brut* versions. *HC*, however, links them with the phrase 'wherein, as some doo write, Mervyn Vrych . . . was slaine' thus possibly providing a precedent for the *Gwentian Brut*'s 'pure invention' (*HW*, I, 324 n.16). *HC* gives no indication that this phrase is Powel's own interpolation nor that he had changed the preceding annal, the death of Idwallon, to 841, thereby making incorrect his date for both these events.

33 **at the Ile of Tenet . . . firste tyme they wyntred in England:** this is omitted in C so that text reads 'and remained that winter at Wintred in England'. *HC* has obviously adapted this so as to read 'and remained that winter *and* wintred in England'.

33 **Kyngen slayne . . . owne men:** *Pen20Tr* and *BS* 'slain', *RBH* 'strangled'; *BS* alone refers to 'own men'; *Pen20Tr* that he was killed by 'Pagans' and *RBH* 'gentiles'. *BS* has misinterpreted the Latin original *a gentilibus* or *a gentibus* possibly reading *a gente*. See *Pen20Tr*, 4.16–17n.; *HW*, I, 322 and n.9. *HC*'s enlarged account 'This yeare 854 Kongen King of Powys died at Rome, being slaine or choaked (as some saie) by his owne men' compresses the two references to Cyngen and both versions of the manner of his death.

34 **bearinge wronge:** C 'learninge false' occurs also in *HC* which thus repeats what is obviously a misreading of 'bearinge' (but is corrected in *HC*, 1811) and is another instance where *HC*'s MS copy bore a close resemblance to C when compared with Ll; N 'bearinge wronge'.

35 **In whose place . . . 7 monothes:** omitted from *HC*; a whole MS line in this section is missing in C.

35 **battaill of Gweythen:** *Pen20Tr* s.a. 862 and *RBH* s.a. 860 'Cadweithen was expelled'; *BS* 'the battle of Gweithen' has misinterpreted the personal name. A later reference by Llwyd to 'the battaill of Catgwethen' (f. 37) also resembles *BS* 'battle of Gweithen' (*Pen20Tr* and *RBH* s.a. 882 'died Cadweithen'). In both these instances a version of *BS* seems to have been Llwyd's source. *HC* follows Llwyd in the first reference but omits the second (*s.a.* 882). For the *BT* versions see *RBH*, 9.5–6, 28nn.

35 **the said Danes:** in the MS 'said' is added in the margin; it seems to be a later addition and does not appear in C nor *HC*; N 'the said Danes'.

35v **towne of Alclyd:** C, N (and *HC*) agree. It is probably a misreading of *BS twr* 'tower' (*Pen20*, *RBH caer* 'fortress').

36 **Gwyriad his brother . . . his sonne:** 'brother' in *BT* versions but one MS copy of *AC* has *Rotri et filius eius Guriat* (see *Pen20Tr,* 5.16n.). Also the BBB version of *BS* has 'son'. See *BS*, 25, n.2.

36v **in Westsex:** in C this marks the end of f. 41v; f. 42, containing the following verses, has been added, probably by John Dee:

Tri mab oedd y Rodri mewn tremyn y kaid:
Cadell Anarawd Merddyn;
Rhanny y wnaed rhwn a vy yn vn
Rhoddiad holl Gymry rhyddyn.

Rhoddiad y gavad er gwell dun yvyill,
Dinevwr y Gadell,
Y mab hynaf vy stavell,
Penna oedd ef pwy wnay well.

Three sonnes had Rodry, thus named:
First Cadell, Anarawd, and Merddyn;
All Wales (one kingdom once called)
Betwixt them three have parted byn.

Dynevwr great, a gyft full wyde,
To Cadell then was geven free,
Who was the eldest strongly tryde
And bare the price of all the three.

A note in the margin alongside the English translation reads: 'Morice Kyphin did thus trans[late] them 1578 Feb. 12 after my cosen Thomas Griffith had geven me . . .' (above, p.4) The verso is blank and the folios thenceforward, from f. 43, have been renumbered. Dee's interest is demonstrated also by the numerous genealogical notes added by him on the preceding ff. 41–41v. N does not have these verses. Llwyd's first reference to Rhodri's division of Wales (ff. 5v–6) does not name any of the sons, but gives North Wales to the eldest and Mathrafal to the third (f. 11). Here (ff. 36–36v) he names Anarawd, the eldest, as ruler of North Wales and makes Cadell the second son; he inherits South Wales and gains Powys 'by force from his brethren'. For *HC*'s elaboration on 'Y Tair Talaith', and a reference to conflicting versions of the apportionment, see Williams, 'Ysgolheictod hanesyddol', 220; *HW*, I, 326–7, n.27.

37 **battaill of Catgwethen:** see note f. 35 'battaill of Gweythen'.

234234234234 N234234 NOTES

37v Black Normanes: *HC* reads 'black nation'; *Pen20* has 'y Normaniaid duon', trans. *Pen20Tr*, 'Black Norsemen'.

38 other, I meane . . . Vandals: the phrase omitted in C has been left out in *HC* also and the sense 'reconstructed'. Both MSS have left out a verb such as 'came' before 'the Vandals' and this has been inserted in N and also in *HC* and is inserted in the text.

38v mansions: this is the word in Ll, C, and N and has obviously been miscopied. *HC* replaces it with 'and invaded the countrie'.

38v Budingtone: Ll has missed the section between the two references to Budington and the text is supplied from C. *HC* follows the fuller and more correct reading in C, which is included also in N.

40 Epitaph as here foloweth: the epitaph is missing in Ll. That it was the clear intention to include it is shown by the words 'a certayne clerke made his Epitaph as here foloweth' (as in C and N) and the blank two-thirds of a page which follows. The epitaph is taken from MS C, f. 46v. The text is corrupt and shows some verbal differences from that given in N and *HC*. There is a much more accurate text in *Asser's Life of Alfred*, ed. Stevenson, 95, and in the text of the chronicle of Henry of Huntingdon, *HH*, 298. The text given in MS C is preceded by the words 'Sint tibi Christus honorem'; the meaning of the words is unclear and they have been omitted.

41v hungar: it seems as if the copyist writing 'Hungar' took this to be a person's name; C has lower case initial, 'hungar', the form given in the text.

42v Gwayth . . . Newe Citie: *RBH* gives 922 and *BS* 919 as the date of this battle, which Llwyd associates, probably through *HH*, with *ASCh* ('Mercian Chronicle') Brecananmere (*s.a.* 916). Leland, *Itinerary in Wales*, 104, has 'Breknoc Mere . . . in Walshce Llin Seuathan' but it was identified by Camden as Llangorse Lake. *HW* agrees with this, adding 'but the exact position of the "llys" is not easily determined' (*HW*, I, 331, n.41). Recent excavations of a 'crannog' in the lake suggest that the site had been built in the tenth century, and could have contained a small timber-built seasonally occupied hunting lodge (E. Campbell and A. Lane, 'Llangorse: a tenth century royal crannog in Wales', *Antiquity*, 63 (1989), 675–81).

43 **her Epitaph was this**: the text of the epitaph is corrupt and obvious errors have been corrected from the text in *HH*, 308.

44 **to winne his frendeship:** Ll has 'duringe his frendeship', here corrected from *HC*.

44v **Then dyd Aulaf . . . Reynalde . . . Christen fayeth:** the copyist of C was misled by the two occurrences of 'fayeth' at the end of a line and omitted this entire reference. *HC* follows C and omits also the earlier reference to the conversion of the people of the five cities and replaces it with the conversion of Olaf (Aulaf), though not of Ragnald (Reynalde).

45 **contrarye . . . Wherupon Edmunde:** the omission in C is another instance of miscopying between occurrences of the same word, 'Edmunde' in this case. *HC* also omits the reference.

46 **Rem:** *HC* gives 'Run' as the second son.

47v **972 . . . sonnes of Gwyn:** C, N and *HC* have the more correct date 961, the date in *BT,* except *RBH*, 963; C, *HC* have 'Edwyn' for 'Gwyn'.

51 **But to the historie:** this is not given in *HC* which has at this point the title 'Meredyth the sonne of Owen ap Howel Dha' followed by 'This Meredyth ap Owen, hauing slain Cadwalhon, obtained the rule and gouernment of Northwales', and then continues as in Ll.

52 **Llannylltut:** Ll reads 'Llanystud', *HC* 'Llanrystud', but *Pen20* reads 'Llanylltud', and the text has been amended accordingly.

52 **Glwmaen:** *BT* initial G as in *Ll*, which is very close to *Pen20*, BS *Glwmayn*; *Pen20Tr*, 10.7n. argues the correct form to be *RBH Gluniairn*, 'Iron Knee'; C, *HC* have Elwmaen.

52v **And Meredith:** in *HC* this is preceded by the title 'Edwal ap Meyric the sonne of Meredyth', followed by 'This Edwal being in possession of the principalitie of Northwales, studied to keepe and defend his people from iniuries and wrongs. But Meredyth' and continues as in Ll.

54 **Anachorate a holye man:** 'an anchorite' followed by a gloss
would seem to have been the intention. Remarkably *HC* has
'Anachoret' but omits the gloss.

59v **I saide Knotte will rewarde thee:** the erroneous 'wee rewarde
thee' in Ll deepens the obscurity of unpunctuated direct speech; C 'will
rewarde' reads more easily and text has been corrected to 'will'.

60v **sette one . . . thy selfe:** this proverb, strangely miscopied in Ll
('thy eagge'), is similar to that in *RBH* and identical with *Pen20Tr* 'urge
on thy dog but go not with him'; see *RBH*, 21.38–23.1n. The proverb
is quoted in William Salesbury, *Oll Synnwyr pen Kembero Ygyd*, ed. J. G.
Evans (Bangor and London, 1902) [unpaginated]: 'Annoc dy gi, ac na
ret canto.'

64 **tooke all the Normaines . . . tythed them:** this account of Earl
Godwin's cruel treachery towards Alfred son to Ethelred and his Norman
companion, though more brief, is broadly similar to that in *BS* (*s.a.* 1043)
which has as its source a Latin version of a Saxon, not a Welsh chronicle
(*BS*, xiii–xiv). One striking resemblance lies in Llwyd's phrase 'tythed
them' and *BS degymmv y meibion*, translated as 'decimated'. The account
itself is fairly commonplace in medieval annals and chronicles.

65 **to be revenged . . . Wales:** it would appear that in C, where this
entire line is omitted, a copyist sought to make sense of the passage by
deleting 'who' and inserting 'and Griffith' in its place; *HC* follows
closely the version in C; N retains the line.

69 **slaine by his owne brother:** apart from the omission of 'slaine' in
Ll, both MSS agree on this reading. *Pen20Tr s.a.* 1061 and *RBH s.a.*
1063 have 'by his own men' and, on the omission in *BS*, see *BS*,
73.11–12n. A comment in the margin of Ll reads 'not men'. The words
'by his owne brother' are followed by 'Mariarig Scotus', an intrusive
reference to Marianus Scotus that is difficult to explain; it is possible that
a reference, made perhaps in a marginal note, to Scotus's 'Universal
Chronicle' as an authority was erroneously incorporated into the text. It
is omitted from the present text. Though not named by Llwyd as an
authority for the 'Cronica Walliae', there is a reference to 'Mariani Scoti
Chronica' in his *Commentarioli . . . Fragmentum*, p. 31b. For Scotus,
Gransden, *Historical Writing in England*, 145–6.

71 **571:** C '171' seems to be a copying error as both MSS agree on '271 yeres' later in the sentence. *HC*'s dates are respectively 544 and 171. The date 544 in the margin in C is in Dee's hand and was probably inserted by him after seeing *HC*.

77v **this tyme was Caerdiff buylt:** according to Llwyd's own chronology 'this tyme' was the year 1080; the annal recording the building of Cardiff castle occurs only in *BS* and in Peniarth MS 213, an incomplete and composite copy in the hand of John Jones Gellilyfdy made up of *Pen20Tr* and *RBH* versions (MS D in *Pen20Tr*, l-li) which 'probably shows the influence of *BS*' (ibid., 17. 30–1n.). Llwyd's account agrees elsewhere with *BS* and Peniarth 213 where they differ from *Pen20Tr* and *RBH*: see, for example, Rhys ap Tewdwr's victory in 1088 'at Llechryd', Ll, f. 78v (*Pen20* Llech y Kreu, *RBH* Llychcrei), compares with Peniarth 213 Llechyd and *BS* y Llechryt – the latter unlikely to be correct according to *Pen20Tr*, 18.11n. Instances where Ll and Peniarth 213 agree but differ from *BS* and *BT* include Ll, f. 47, 'Anaraud the sonne of Gwiriad', Peniarth 213 'anarawd vab gwiriad'; Ll, f. 181, 'and Thalbocharne', Peniarth 213 'a thalbocharo' (*BS* Talacharn, *BT* Talycharn); Ll, 176v, Peniarth 213 Meurig Barrech (*Pen20* Bartech, *RBH*, *BS* Barach). Llwyd also omits the name *Hirmawr* (present in *BT*, *BS*) as does Peniarth 213 and BBB. He could not possibly have seen Peniarth 213, but John Jones could have copied from a source combining both *Pen20* and *RBH* versions (*Pen20Tr*, li).

80v–85v **And thees Normaines . . . And William Rufus:** between these two points C, from the start of f. 89, has misplaced a number of folios: beginning ff. 89–91 with the appointment of Gerald as steward of Dyfed (Ll, 84–85b), then from f. 92 reverting to the section (Ll, 80v–84) beginning 'And these Normaines' followed by the section (Ll, 84) 'And the yere ensuing William Rufus returninge from Normandy . . .', thus duplicating almost the whole of the reference up to 'And William Rufus after . . .' on f. 97v in C. The two references to William Rufus may explain the confusion of folios in this last instance but does not, of course, explain the earlier misplacing. Folios in C are renumbered in this erroneous sequence throughout, and a blank verso to f. 91 probably reflects the effect of this.

81 **Londres or London . . . nameth him:** the tale of the conquest of Glamorgan by Robert Fitzhamon and his twelve knights does not occur

in any version of the *Brut*. However, one isolated reference to a knight called London is made in the context of an attack by Gruffudd ap Rhys on a castle in Gower: 'William of London through fear of him [Gruffudd] left the castle' (*Pen20Tr,* also *BS s.a.* 1113, *recte* 1116); cf. Ll, 104v *s.a.* 1116. This was more than twenty years after the events in Llwyd's tale (ff. 79v–80) and nothing in this reference connects William of London either with Fitzhamon and his knights or with his castle of Ogmore, or indeed with that of Oystermouth (see *HW*, II, 440, 441 n.153; Nicholl, *The Normans in Glamorgan, Gower and Kidweli*, 77–8). Llwyd's account differs materially from the versions prevalent in south Wales in the fifteenth and sixteenth centuries and it has none of the many 'explanations' of place-names which feature so prominently in those texts. (See Rice Merrick, *Morganiae Archaiographia,* 19; G. J. Williams, *Traddodiad Llenyddol Morgannwg,* 186–9, with a reference to Llwyd's account ibid., 188 n.119.) It is also very different from the briefer version in Leland, *Itinerary in Wales*, 38. See also above, pp. 25–6. Llwyd's tale is woven tightly into the text following the *Brut* reference to the defeat of Llywelyn ap Cadifor ap Collwyn and his brothers (of whom Llwyd says later that Einon was one) and echoes the *Brut* account of the death of Rhys ap Tewdwr, slain by the French inhabiting Brycheiniog, with whom fell the 'Kingdom of the Britons' (*Pen20, RBH, BS s.a.* 1093). Although it must remain open to question whether Llwyd's 'Welsh booke' was his source for the entire tale or for the name 'London' only, the textual evidence suggests strongly that the balance of probability lies with the former.

83 **Kelhy Tarvawc:** C 'Kelhy tarvawc', *HC* 'Celli Tarvawc', *Pen20,* Kelli Taruawc, *BS* Kelli Carnawc (with *Carnant* above, later hand), an example in the MSS of *BT* of confusing 'c' and 't' (see notes ff. 8v, 14, above). *HW*, II, 406 n.30 follows *RBH* 'Carnant', probably the more correct form (see *Pen20Tr*, 20.10n.; *BS*, 89.3n.). In this instance, however, Llwyd's account seems to have been based on *Pen20*.

85 **Griffith and Cadwgan sawe, they:** C 'ap' is obviously incorrect, probably a misreading of the ampersand; the erroneous reference to Griffith *ap* Cadwgan made necessary the following singular pronoun 'he'.

85 **to lande . . . by channce:** C (f. 90v) omits this whole line, and 'they' has been inserted above after 'thinkinge' in an attempt to make sense of the result; the passage when repeated in f. 96v is correctly copied; N retains the line.

86   **Richard his sonne:** Ll Roger, the name that appears in *AC* and *BT* rather than the correct 'Richard', is a mistaken extension of the abbreviation 'R', now corrected in text. See *HW*, II, 463 n.3 and *Pen20Tr*, 22.28n.; *HC* has 'Richard'.

86v   **Tekingill:** *Pen20 Blidense*, *RBH* 'Blif', *BS* 'Blydense'. *Pen20Tr*, 23.18n.: 'No remains of a castle have been found at Blyth, but Tickhill, since it belonged to the honour of Blyth, was sometimes called "castellum *Blidense*". The castle meant here is that of Tickhill.' Llwyd makes no reference to the variant form of the name nor does he identify any source for it. There is an obvious suggestion of confusion with an anglicized form of Tegeingl.

88   **Cardigan:** Ll Caerdyd; *HC* Caerdhyd, an error for *Pen20*, *RBH* Keredygyawn; text here corrected to 'Cardigan'.

92   **Bishop of Glocester:** occurs only in *BS*, 109; *RBH*, 59 'sheriff', *Pen20Tr* 'chief justice' (see *HW*, II, 427 n. 90). *HC*, bishop of Hereford.

92v   **thees foure . . . castell of Rydcors:** 'castell' only in *BS* 'Kastell Ryt Coruonec', *Pen20* 'ryd Corruonet'; *RBH* 'Ryt Cornuec'. Llwyd's identification of this ford with Rhyd-y-gors, taken up by *HC*, is unlikely to be correct as 'these four' were ranged against Owain ap Cadwgan in Powys while the castle of Rhyd-y-gors stood on the Tywi a mile south of Carmarthen (*HW*, II, 401). For a suggested location of the ford within the parish of Llanfihangel Genau'r Glyn, see *Pen20Tr*, 30.4–5n.

96   **26 adaye:** also N. *BT* versions (*s.a.* 1106, 1107) differ: *BS* 'four and twenty [pence]; *Pen20Tr* 'two shillings of silver'; *RBH* 'twenty-four pence'; Ll and N are thus more accurate than C '20 dayes' (*HC* 'twenty daies').

106v–107   **theeffe and murtherer:** C has 'murtherer' only. *Pen20Tr* 'accursed petty thief'; *RBH* 'petty thief' (*s.a.* 1116); *HC* 'murtherer'.

109   **Owen was begotten . . . Edwyn:** the preceding list of Owain ap Cadwgan's six brothers is given as it appears in all three versions of *BT*; the seventh, Owain begotten on Iwerydd daughter of Edwin, appears only in *BS* and is probably a misunderstanding of a reference immediately after this in *Pen20Tr* and *RBH* to 'Iwerydd mother of

Owain and Uchdryd sons of Edwin' (see *BS*, 135.33–4n.). The *BS* version seems therefore to have been Llwyd's source in this instance. In referring to the sixth son Maredudd, 'by Evron daughter to Hoedlyw', C omits 'daughter to', and renders the name of Iwerydd as 'Iwerth'. This faulty version was obviously the source for *HC* 'Evrvron Hoedliw' and 'Inerth'.

109v **and half Penlhyn . . . to Enyon:** the additional phrase in C 'and the other halfe of Penlhyn' occurs in *Pen20Tr* and *RBH*. Curiously it is missing in *BS*. The phrase would have occupied a complete MS line in Ll and its omission is more likely to be the result of a copying error rather than a different *BT* source. *HC* again follows C in this. Both Ll and C have 'to Enyon' but *Pen20Tr*, *RBH* 'to Cadwgan's son', *BS* 'Cadwgan's sons' (see *BS*, 137.11n.).

111v **the yere ensuinge:** *Pen20Tr* and *BS* refer to 'a year of peace' immediately before this entry *s.a.* 1119 corrected to 1122, Llwyd's probable date. It does not occur in *RBH* which might strengthen a supposition that it was Llwyd's source for this section. For the chronological implications of this difference in the *BT* versions see *Pen20Tr*, 49.1n.

112 **cold not come by hit:** *Pen20Tr* and *RBH s.a.* 1121 'and when he came to seek a portion of Powys he obtained none' which is missing in *BS*. C omits this particular reference, as does *HC*. *Pen20Tr* and *RBH* (though again not *BS*) also confirm Llwyd's account a few lines later of bringing the 'chiefmen and the catteill to Lhyn' by Owain and Cadwallon, sons to Gruffudd ap Cynan.

115v **Madocke ap Idnerth:** Ll reads 'Madocke and Idnerth', here corrected from C, where, however, the scribe would appear to have missed out the preceding line 'with . . . Mredith' and linked the first 'Mredith' with 'and Rys' in the following line. The general account of the attack on Ceredigion differs slightly in *RBH* from both *Pen20Tr* and *BS* (*s.a.* 1135); see *BS*, 145.23–4n.). Llwyd follows the *RBH* version.

115v **Fitzorc:** this form occurs only in *Pen20*; *orc* may be an error for *oit* as in *RBH* and *BS* and the reference is probably to William fitz Odo. See *Pen20Tr*, 51.36n.; *HW*, II, 473 n.46.

116 **perinrie:** quite plainly thus in MSS Ll, N and clearly a scribal error; neither does C 'prince' seem to fit the context. *HC* has 'the pride of the nobles'.

116v **well learned:** *HC* continues the sentence with no change of type (i.e. as though it was part of Ll's text) 'and Elen the wife of Hova ap Ithel Velyn of Yal. He reformed the disordered behavior of the Welsh minstrels, by a verie good Statute which is extant to this daie'. There follows, indented and in the smaller type used for *HC*'s additions, a brief description of the three kinds of minstrels and of the Statute. See above, pp. 30–1.

118 **Raffe Bishop of Orkeneys:** this reference in Llwyd's account of the battle of 'Almerton' (Northallerton, 'the battle of the standard') in 1138 tallies with the 'Radulfum episcopum Orcadum' in Sir Henry Saville's printed version of Henry of Huntingdon's Chronicle (in *Rerum Anglicarum Scriptores*, 1596), and with the identical reference in *Henrici Huntendunensis Historia Anglorum*, ed. T. Arnold (Rolls Series, 1879), 262, which correspond to the reading in *HH*, 712–13. *The Chronicle of Henry of Huntingdon,* ed. T. Forrester (London, 1853) preferred Roger Wendover's 'Bishop of Durham' even though the two MSS consulted gave *Orcadum*. In Llwyd's time, of course, Henry of Huntingdon's work was available only in manuscript. A copy listed in the 1609 catalogue of the Lumley library bears the signatures of Lumley and Arundel only, but it could, of course, have been seen by Llwyd (see Jayne and Johnson, *Lumley Library*, no. 1184). In any case it seems significant that Llwyd accepted without question Henry of Huntingdon's version. Trevet, *NT*, 8–9, gives a different account. For Llwyd's use of Huntingdon, above, pp. 39–42.

119–119v **And afterwarde . . . at libertie:** text differs from *HC* in its account of events between the battles of Lincoln and Winchester.

120 **Caernaunvonshire:** this eccentric spelling does not seem to be miscopied as the central *n* is confirmed in the margin.

122 **dyed Rhun:** the eulogy follows closely that of *Pen20* and *RBH s.a.* 1145, 1144, *recte* 1146, whereas *BS* has a single short sentence. Later, f. 127, the sequence of the attacks by Rhys and Maredudd, sons of Gruffudd ap Rhys, on Ystrad Cyngen, Aberafan and Cyfeiliog also follows the text in *Pen20* and *RBH s.a.* 1152 and not as it appears in *BS*.

124v **builde . . . Oswaldestre:** underlined in the text and written in the left-hand margin to give further emphasis to the underlined words 'Oswestry castle'; and the reference to the building of a castle in Iâl a few lines earlier is similarly noted in the margin by the words '1149 Owen Gwynedd built the castle of Yale'. Both marginal entries are in a later hand. For the castle, Tomen y Rhodwydd, *HW*, II, 492 n.23.

126 **he fill . . . companyons:** due to a scribal error C omits the lines between the two references to 'companyons'; *HC*'s version reads 'they fierslie set on him and his companie'; N retains the line.

128v **Mortimer:** William, count of Boulogne and Mortain; cf. f. 135v.

129v **[ground]:** C 'grounde' but a blank space in Ll. Llwyd's account of this ambush at the 'woode called Coed Penarlage' (Hawarden Wood) follows closely that of *Pen20Tr* (*s.a.* 1156). The brief references by Paris and Trevet (*HistAng,* II, 57; *NT*, 43) lack most of the details, though *NT* does mention a house for the Templars (Ll, 130). However, William of Newburgh, *Historia Regum Anglicarum,* ed. H. C. Hamilton (London 1856), 95–6, or idem in *Chronicles of Stephen, Henry II and Richard I,* ed. R. Howlett, 2 vols (Rolls Series, 1884–5), i, 106–9, not only speaks of the difficulty of the ground and the ambush by the Welsh but adds other details given later by Llwyd, such as the death of Fitz John and de Courcy and the danger to the king himself (Ll, f. 134v). In the same passage Newburgh also links this battle with the duel fought between Robert de Mountfort and Henry, earl of Essex in 1163; *NT*, 53, *pro fuga praelii contra Gualenses* is a less precise link even than Ll's 'battaill fought against the Welshmen in the Marches, where the Kinge was present' and Paris does not connect the duel with a battle in Wales (Ll, 134v, *NT*, 53; *CM*, II, 221; *HistAng*, 321). *HC* 'silently' relocates the battle at Coed Eulo, then adds his own gloss which seems to link the duel with another similar ambush 'in a strait at Counsylth not far from Flynt', and brings forward into this gloss Llwyd's later reference (f. 134v) to the death of Fitz John and de Courcy and his claim that 'the Kinge fledde himself, as sayeth any Frenche Cronicle'. A marginal note in Ll on the same folio, 'see and loke Ffabian etc' is a reminder that Fabyan's very brief account does mention the founding of an abbey at Basingwerk (R. Fabyan, The *New Chronicles of England and France* ed. H. Ellis (London, 1811, 273). The battle of 'Cunsylht' (Coleshill) described by Llwyd (f. 125v, an account reproduced in *HC*) was, of course, fought in 1150 between

Owain Gwynedd and Madog ap Maredudd of Powys (aided by Ranulf earl of Chester) and did not involve the king of England. See also *HW*, II, 494 for this battle.

129v **to a place . . . Kilowen:** this entry occurs only in *RBH*. See *Pen20Tr*, 59.25–6n. and *HW*, II, 498 on this mistaken attempt by *RBH* to explain the place-name; for further discussion of this conflict of 1257 see J. G. Edwards, 'Henry II and the fight at Coleshill', *WHR*, 3 (1966–7), 251–63.

129v **Bryn y Pina:** *RBH* 'Tal Llwyn Pina', *Pen20* 'Tal Llwyn Pynna', *BS* 'Tal Llwyn Pennant'. Llwyd (not Powel, as *HW*, II, 498 n.53) identified this *BT* location as Bryn y Pin above Kinmel, 'a spot which fits in well with the geography of the campaign' (*HW*, ibid.).

132 **Kevyn yr Eskayr Main:** *Pen20* 'Kevyn Restyr Mein', *RBH* 'Kevyn Restyr', *BS* 'Kyven Rychtir'. However, MSS B, D of *Pen20* (Mostyn 143 and Peniarth 213) *Yr Escair Main*; (see *Pen20Tr*, 61.24n.) which suggests that Llwyd followed a similar version of *Pen20*. *HC* on the other hand has 'Kefn Rester', which is the incomplete *RBH* form.

135 **sonnes of Wynyawn:** also 'the sonne of Wynnyon' (f. 18v) 'the sonne of Elviw' for Mabelfyw and 'the sonne of Uchdrud' for Mabudrud (f. 19v). Though the Welsh forms may 'explain themselves as of dynastic origin' (*HW*, I, 267), translating them seems to display overenthusiasm by Llwyd to provide English equivalents. The plural forms, which appear also as 'sonnes of Uchdryd' or 'Uchtryd' (ff. 19v, 121) are more difficult to explain. References to the sons of Uchdryd (ab Edwin) occur with some frequency in relation to conflicts in Powys in the early years of the twelfth century (for example, *BS*, 113, Ll, f. 95) and these may have been in Llwyd's mind. *BS* alone refers to the place-name as 'Mabuchtryt' (for example, *BS*, 148 *s.a.* 1144), rather than the customary Mabudrud. Llwyd does occasionally use the Welsh forms Mabwynyawn, ff. 18, 182; Mabudryd, f. 190. The only reasonably firm conclusion seems to be that these provide additional evidence of Llwyd's relative lack of acquaintanceship with south Wales.

136v **vawarde:** an archaic form for 'vanguard' (*Shorter Oxford English Dictionary*). *HC* 'ward' follows C 'warde' and seems to miss the point of Llwyd's account in which a small group of the Welsh force is confronted unexpectedly by the advance guard of the king's army in which were placed the 'pyked [picked] men of all the army'. Here again *HC* 'piked men' seems to be a misunderstanding.

139   three monethes . . . Prestatyn: all three versions of *BT* have 'three months', but C (and *HC*) 'two months'. The reference to Prestatyn in both MSS appears in *RBH*, *BS* *s.a.* 1167 but not in *Pen20*; see *Pen20Tr*, 65.4–5n. The following reference to the destruction of the castle at Prestatyn, which brought Tegeingl under Owen's subjection, occurs only in C (followed again by *HC* and inserted in this text) and does not occur in any of the *BT* versions (but see *HW*, II, 520).

141–142   named Madocke . . . the language they founde there: for Llwyd's version of the Madog story and Powel's additions to it see Williams, 'Ysgolheictod hanesyddol', 122 n.48; 222 n.71, also above, p. 25.

142   Earle of Strigill: *BS* jarll Amhwydic (Shrewsbury); *RBH* Strifug (Stristig, Tristig); *Pen20* Richard yarll vab Gilbert Strangysboy (MSS B, D add iarll Ymwythic); *AC* comes de Striguil. See *Pen20Tr*, 65.34n.; *HW*, II, 537–8 and n.4.

142v   7 pledges: all *BT* versions give this number of hostages, but the reference is omitted in C (and *HC*).

142v   payed . . . 300 horses . . . 14 pledges: *Pen20Tr* and *RBH* 'promised', *BS* 'submitted to his will for'; Ll seems to have mis-understood an original such as *BS* since later Rhys's 'promise' is fulfilled in Pembroke by the offer of 86 horses (see note ff. 143–143v below); *Pen20Tr* and *BS* 'fourteen hostages', *RBH* 'twenty-four hostages'.

143   Arwystly and Elvael: thus in *BS*, but (more correctly) 'Ystlwyf and Efelffre' in *RBH* and *Pen20Tr*. See *BS*, 173.32n. It is perhaps noteworthy also that *BS* gives no date for the king's arrival in Pembroke and neither does Ll, whereas *Pen20Tr* and *RBH* have 'the eleventh day from the Calends of October'.

143–143v   7 calendes . . . brought to Penbroke: *Pen20Tr* 'the seventh day from the Calends of October', *RBH* 'twelfth day . . .', *BS* no date. *BS*, 175.5–6n. argues that *Pen20* is correct. C's omission of a specific date, which could arguably reflect a later copyist's awareness of the *BT* differences, is followed by *HC*. Rhys's selection of 86 horses would have been from the 300 originally promised (see note f. 142v above). *Pen20Tr* and *BS* agree that they were brought to Pembroke, but *RBH* 'Whitland'.

148v **Perys:** C Pyrs, *HC* Piers, for Peter de Leia, consecrated in November 1176.

148v **prince of Southwales:** Ll Northwales: an obvious error rendered correctly in C and amended in text.

149v **Cadwalhon, brother unto Owen Gwynedh:** the account which follows, repeated in *HC,* appears to relate to Cadwaladr ap Gruffuth brother of Owain Gwynedd and Cadwallon ap Madog of Maelienydd, a kinsman of the Lord Rhys; see *HW*, II, 567, n.164.

150 **And the Kinge of Englande . . . silver:** in Ll these four lines are bracketed with a note in the margin, in the same hand as the MS, 'note this to be rased'. C has a virtually identical note, again in the MS hand. This is a unique instance of identical marginal notes in the two MSS and could possibly represent a note inserted originally by Llwyd himself.

155v–156v **1184 Kinge Richarde came into Englande . . . Llewelyn began to rule the yere of our Lorde 1184:** all versions of *BT* agree on the commonly accepted date of 1194 for both these events, i.e. the return of Richard I to England and the beginning of Llewelyn ap Iorwerth's rule in Gwynedd. The date of 1184, which occurs in both Ll and C (corrected to 1194 in *HC*), is at variance also with the contemporary chronology of both MSS, such as the death of Henry II in 1189 and of his third son Geoffrey, duke of Brittany, in 1186. This makes the agreement of both MSS all the more unexpected (note f. 158v below). These are isolated errors of dating, and Llwyd has the accepted chronology thenceforward. Surprisingly, however, although he gives the correct date, 1240, for the death of Llywelyn ap Iorwerth, he seems to repeat this initial error in stating that he reigned for 56 years (see note f. 197v below).

158 **and couragiouse lyon:** taken directly from *BT*, probably *RBH*

megys llew dyfal (like a fierce lion) rather than *Pen20 megys llew o rymus law* (like a lion with a strong hand). *HC* omits this description.

158v **garrison [defended]:** there is a verb lacking in C also, another surprising example of a common scribal error, as is 'so the[y] might departe' a few lines later; N, *HC* have 'defended' and 'they' and the corrections are made in the text.

159 **4th daie of Maii:** *Pen20Tr* and *BS* have 'the fourth day from the calends of May'. See *BS*, 193.29n.; *HW*, II, 582 n.37. The eulogy follows most closely that of *Pen20* rather than *RBH* which does not have the Latin elegiac verses and epitaph. Llwyd's transcript of the verses and epitaph is almost identical with that in *Pen20* (*Pen20Tr*, 77–8) and variant forms are given. A few of the differences are manifestly scribal errors, but others, such as the use of the form *Resus* throughout (*Pen20 Rhesus*), *populus quem totus* (*Pen20 populo quem viuus*), *volendo par fuit* (*Pen20 in velle pari*), and the final line of the epitaph *Principis interitu nulli pietate secundi*, which does not occur in *Pen20*, together may suggest a different source copy. Texts of the prose eulogy and poem other than those in *Pen20* were certainly circulating during the fourteenth century. Thomas Jones, 'Molawd a marwnad yr Arglwydd Rhys: fersiynau ychwanegol', *BBCS*, 24 (1970–2), 276–81, drew attention to a text in *Polychronicon Ranulphi Higden*, ed. C. Babington, 9 vols (Rolls Series, 1865–86), viii, 158ff. which gives part of the prose eulogy that appears in Latin in the 'Cronica de Wallia' ('"Cronica de Wallia" and other documents from Exeter Cathedral Library MS 3514', ed. T. Jones, *BBCS*, 12 (1946–8), 31) and seventeen lines from the verse tribute. The texts were also used, though not in an identical manner, in the chronicle of Hailes Abbey, a Cistercian house in co. Gloucester, in Bodley MS Laud Misc. 529. Not one of the known texts includes the last line in Llwyd's text and he was evidently drawing upon a source other than any one of those that may be recognized at present. Much of the prose eulogy and the whole of the Latin elegiac verses are omitted from *HC*, but Powel refers to the 'worthie commendation' of the prince that appears in 'the Britishe booke' and which was included in Higden's *Polychronicon* and Richard Grafton's *Life of Richard I*.

164v **Roger Bygod:** C, *HC* have Hugh Bygod, but Roger is correct.

165 **Gwae'r offeriad byd . . . ffon glwppa:** this Welsh version of

the verse appears in C, f. 173v but not in Ll. That it was intended to be inserted later is suggested by the sufficient space left at the end of Ll, f. 165. In C also it seems probable that the Welsh words were added later by another scribe. In 1551, some years before Llwyd wrote his 'Cronica Walliae', William Salesbury quoted the same verse on the title page (verso) of his Welsh translation of the epistles and gospels, *Kynniver Llith a Ban,* ed. J. Fisher (Cardiff, 1931); and in 1567 Richard Davies also quoted it in the Preface to his Welsh translation of the New Testament, *Rhagymadroddion 1547–1659,* ed. G. H. Hughes (Cardiff, 1951), 32.

169v   **in Northwales . . . for his nevewe:** there is a phrase missing here in both MSS. *HC* has 'but all in vaine', the source of the insertion in text (see note f. 158v above).

174v   **Blackemonasterie or Oswester:** the name *Album Monasterium* ('Blanchemonasterie') was given to both Whitchurch and Oswestry (see *HW,* II, 635 n.118; Phillimore, *OP,* III, 233). The error here is common to both MSS but it is difficult to ascribe it to Llwyd, who would surely have been familiar with this area. *HC* has the correct form 'Blanchmonasterie'.

175   **the Inland . . . forever:** for Llywelyn's submission in 1211, *Pen20Tr,* 85; *RBH,* 190–3; *HW,* II, 635–6; J. Beverley Smith, 'Magna Carta and the charters of the Welsh princes', *EHR,* 99 (1984), 344–62.

176   **the Kinge had builte:** N and all three versions of *BT s.a.* 1211 include this phrase, omitted in C (and also *HC*). It is thus another instance where *HC* follows C when it differs from Ll and is at variance even with the *BT* sources.

180   **the Ile of Kynvryk:** *HC* also has 'Ile of Cynuric' for *Pen20* 'Ynys Kynwric', *RBH* 'Ynys Gynwreic', *BS* 'Ynys Gynwric', that is, Skenfrith; see *Pen20Tr,* 90.17n.

180v   **castell of Hughe de Myles, at Talybonedh:** *Pen20Tr s.a.* 1215 'the castle of Hugh de Meules at Tal-y-bont', *RBH* and *BS* 'Hugh's Castle'. This is Llandeilo Tal-y-bont, the site, until its recent removal to the Museum of Welsh Life, St Fagans, of the ancient parish church, on the east bank of the river Llwchwr near Pontarddulais. A castle mound is visible there and a nearby farmhouse still carries the name Castell Du (*An Inventory of the Ancient Monuments in Glamorgan: the Early Castles* (London, RCAHMW, 1991), 64–6).

180v **Sayntgennyd . . . Ystymlhwynarth:** *Pen20*, *RBH* 'Seinhenyd . . . Ystumllwynarth', *BS* 'Ystumllwyniarth yn Sain Henydd'. For the identification of 'Seinhenydd' as Swansea see C. A. Seyler, 'Seinhenyd, Ystumllwynarth and Ynysgynwraid', *ArchCamb*, CI (1950–1), 23–4; *Glamorgan County History*, III, ed. T. B. Pugh (Cardiff, 1971), 220–3.

180v **castelles of Glamorgan:** *Pen20* 'Morgannwg', *RBH* 'Gower' (Gwyr), *BS* 'Gower and Morgannwg'. It seems clear that the *Pen20* version was Llwyd's source for the passage to which he refers in this and the preceding two notes. *HC* in this last instance has adopted the more correct 'Gwyrland'.

181 **and Thalbocharne:** *Pen20* 'a Thalycharne', that is, Laugharne.

182 **Penlhwynawg:** *Pen20* 'Pennlunyawc', that is, Peuliniog.

183 **a notable:** preceded at the end of the previous line by 'a noble' deleted. The correction is not made in C, and so remains 'a noble' as it does in *HC*.

184v **Lewis . . . called:** thus also C; *HC* adds 'in before' but gives no source.

185v **Lhangruc . . . Sainthennyd:** 'Llangiwc' is obviously intended and appears in all *BT* versions. Llwyd also mirrors the mistranslation in *Pen20* where the sense requires that Reginald de Braose surrendered Seinhenydd to Llywelyn as in *RBH* and *BS* (*Pen20Tr*, 95.29–30n.). For 'Seinhenydd' see note f. 180v above.

185v **Kevyn Kynwarchan:** *Pen20* f. 241b 'Ceuyn Kynwarchan', that is, Cefn Cynfarchan (*HW*, II, 652 n.210).

186v **their promise . . . peace:** C's apparent correction to 'they left', although probably inspired by the preceding 'their promise', makes no real sense. *HC* 'the barons' is more likely in the context, and Ll may well reflect a copyist's omission of 'barons', corrected in text.

186v **William Ferrers:** *Pen20Tr s.a.* 1218 'earl Ferrars', *RBH* and *BS* 'earl Marshal'. See *Pen20Tr*, 96.30n. Llwyd adds the earl of Arundel to the names given in the *BT* versions.

187 **the secunde . . . Monte Camisii:** the second daughter is not named; *HC* has Ioane.

187 **Abertivi:** thus in *Pen20*, but *RBH* and *BS* 'Arberth', more correctly on this occasion. See *Pen20Tr*, 97.35n.

187v **Wystlande:** *Pen20Tr*, *RBH* and *BS* 'Wizo's castle' translates the Welsh *Pen20* Castell y Wys, *BS* Castell Gwys, *RBH* Castell Gwis. Again the *Pen20* version seems to have been Llwyd's original.

188 **toke Meryonydh and Dydwy:** Meirionnydd and Ardudwy; the castle was Castell y Bere in Meirionnydd.

190 **aboute 9000 men:** no figure is given in any of the *BT* accounts. In this instance *HC* has the figure of 9000 (as opposed to C, 4000) and gives as his authority 'M. Paris 423'; the figure of 9000 is given by Paris as the number of Welshmen slain (*CM*, III, 76).

191 **upon the other side:** *s.a.* 1228 *BS* 'on the other side,' *RBH* 'from the other side of the wood', *Pen20Tr* 'and there'. Here Llwyd's version seems to be nearer *BS*.

192v **Rhayader Gwy:** *BS* and *RBH* 'a'r Gelli' (Hay); but *Pen20Tr*, 'ar Hay' (retraced by later hand) with *adr* added by later hand to give 'a Rhayadr'. *Pen20* is clearly therefore the (faulty) source of Llwyd's version. Llwyd himself may have added Gwy in an attempt to give precise identification to the place-name (see also, for example, Ll, f. 26v 'Garth Maelawg'; 'Mynydh Carno'; f. 48v 'Caerlhion upon Uyske'; f. 134v 'Pencadayr'; f. 194v 'Mynw' for similar erroneous identifications).

192v **freer of Cummer:** Llwyd fails to identify Cummer as Cwm-hir; not in *BT*, but taken from Paris *CM*, III, 203; see *HW*, II, 676.

193v **cattayll:** C's version 'chattells' provides an example of contemporary interchangeability in the emphasis of the meaning.

193v **Effrayn Byshoppe of Lhanelwy:** Bishop Abraham of St Asaph, died 4 February 1233.

194 **Tyveidiawc:** *Pen20* 'Dyffryn Teueidyat', the valley of the Teme, or Tempsiter (J. E. Lloyd, 'Border notes', *BBCS*, 11 (1941–4), 53–4).

194v **Huberte de Burghe:** Ll has 'Herberte', corrected in text from *HC* 'Huberte'.

196v **buryed . . . in the house of Aber:** *Pen20* places Joan's death at Aber and her burial 'in a consecrated enclosure which was on the shore bank'. *Pen20Tr,* 104.28n. correctly takes this to be 'on the shore of Anglesey', where the Franciscan friary of Llan-faes was founded by Llywelyn in Joan's honour. For the site and Joan's coffin and lid (in Beaumaris church), *An Inventory of the Ancient Monuments in Anglesey* (London, RCAHMW, 1937), 5, 66–7.

196v **Keveiliawc:** it appears thus in all *BT* versions; one can but surmise that a copyist's error explains C's 'Kedewen'. *HC* follows Ll with 'Cyuelioc'.

197v **governed . . . 56 yers:** an error for 46 years. See note f. 156v.

198 **after their accustomed use:** *Pen20Tr s.a.* 1240 'remembered their old custom', but not in *RBH* and *BS*. See *Pen20Tr,* 105.20–1n.

198 **And Gilbert . . . came with an army:** *BS* 'Walter Marshal came', *Pen20Tr* and *RBH* 'the English sent Walter Marshal'. Llwyd 'Gilbert Marshall' (followed by *HC*) is wrong, as Gilbert, then earl of Pembroke, sent his brother Walter to occupy Cardigan. See, for instance, *HW*, II, 695; *DWB,* 617.

198–198v **castell of the Deserte in Flintshire:** *Pen20Tr s.a.* 1241 'a castle at Diserth in Tegeingl'; cf. Ll, 211v: 'Edwardes castells Dygannwy and Deserte'; *Pen20, RBH, BS* name Degannwy and Carreg Faelan (*s.a.* 1241). *Pen20* is clearly the source for the first entry; the second may well have been influenced by *NT*, 253 *castra Dissard et Gannock*. It is strange that in neither instance does Llwyd offer an explanation for his use of the form 'Desert'. On Diserth and Desertum see *HW*, I, 213 and n.103; R. A. Brown, H. M. Colvin and A. J. Taylor, *The History of the King's*

Works, II (London, 1963), 644–5; and for Castell-y-garreg and Carreg Faelan, see *Pen20Tr*, 105.32–3n.; *HW*, II, 699 and n. 35.

199 **Earldome of Arundell . . . at this daye:** one of many references by Llwyd to the earldom of Arundel, reflecting his close connection with the earldom under the house of Fitzalan. Whereas frequently such references are omitted in *HC*, in this instance some additional details are given.

203 **Wyndsor:** occurs only in *Pen20 s.a.* 1251. MS D of the *Pen20* version adds of Gwladys that 'she was the wife to Ralf de Mortimer' and *BS* 'the wedded wife of Sir Randulf Mortimer'. See *Pen20Tr*, 109.2n.; *RBH*, 243.27n.

203 **William sonne to Gurwared:** the reference to his death at this time is incorrect and occurs only in *Pen20*; see *Pen20Tr*, 109.16n. *HC* omits the entire reference; and in C (f. 203) a note in the margin, 'all this is left out in Doctor Powel his history' is probably by Dee, as is a similar marginal comment shortly afterwards, 'D Powel hath it not', concerning the reference to the death of 'Thomas Walys bishop of Saincte Davyes'.

203v **Omnis . . . erit:** the quotation is from Lucan, *Bellum Civile*, I, 93.

203v **mette . . . in the felde:** *RBH* and *BS* name Bryn Derwin as the battlefield, also Owain Goch as the only brother captured. Llwyd thus follows *Pen20* in these two respects (*Pen20Tr*, 110.6–7n.). His date of 1254, however, is given only in *BS*; *RBH* and *Pen20* have 1255. See *Pen20Tr*, 108.36–8n. on the chronology.

205 **Richarde de Karm:** *Pen20* f. 273a *'richyard de Kaerrin'*, *RBH* and *BS* 'Rys'. Thus a version of *Pen20* was clearly Llwyd's source though the copyist of Ll as of C failed to identify Carew. *HC* omits the reference; a note in the margin of C, 'not D.P.' is again by Dee.

206 **Pallays of Brenne:** *HC* has Dinas Bran.

206 **betwixt Rhes Gruc:** in C inserted above the line in a different, precise hand, probably Dee's, 'Meredith ap', and in the same hand, vertically along the left-hand margin, 'Blwyddyn wedi hynny i Kymerth

Lin ap Griffith dir Kemmais ac i gwnaeth heddwch rhwng Meredith ap
Ris a Ris i nai ef. That is to say, the yere following, Lin ap Griff seased
Kemais and made peace betwixt Mredith ap Rice and Rice his nevew.
lib. Brit'. Presumably, the marginal note was to explain the correction to
the text. The wording does not in fact match exactly any of the printed
BT versions; *Pen20 s.a.* 1258 *recte* 1257 comes nearest.

206 **Lhankynuth:** nearer *Pen20* 'Llankynnwch' than *RBH*
'LlannGenev' or *BS* Llann Gynnen (*recte* Llan Gyneu). It is identified as
Llangynwyd in *Pen20Tr*, 111.22–3n.; see also *HW*, II, 721, n.29; Smith,
Llywelyn ap Gruffudd, 102.

209 **Patrike de Saus:** *Pen20* and *RBH s.a.* 1259 'Padrig Dysaws'; *BS*
'Padric Dwysoc' is a misreading of the same form (*BS*, 245.2n.). *BT*
forms for Chaworth are Dysaws, de Sawns, de Chawns. Llwyd follows
Pen20 and *RBH* in placing the parley in Emlyn, describing 'Padric
Dysaws' as the king's seneschal in Carmarthen. *HC* has 'Patrike de
Canton', with Matthew Paris as his authority.

209v **the Queene:** Ll and C have 'Guyen' and the text is corrected
from *HC* 'the Queene'. For Llywelyn's proposals, as given in a chancery
document, offering king, queen and the Lord Edward a sum of money
each, sums different from those cited by Llwyd, Smith, *Llywelyn ap
Gruffudd*, 122–3.

210 **And Edwarde . . . Glocester:** miscopying has left the meaning
unclear.

212 **the Kinges and their sonnes:** the author refers to Henry III and
his brother Richard of Cornwall, King of the Romans, and their sons,
the Lord Edward and Henry of Almain, all four of whom were later
captured at Lewes, the capture of the first three being mentioned on the
next folio. Llwyd refers, f. 206v, to letters written by 'the Kinges of
Englande and Almaine' to Llywelyn ap Gruffudd in 1257.

214v–215 **defender of Southwales:** Maredudd's description as
'defender of all Deheubarth' occurs only in *Pen20 s.a.* 1265.

216 **Griffith . . . Val Crucis:** the account (not derived from *BT*
texts) of the division of Gruffudd ap Madog's territories reflects Llwyd's

interest in Northern Powys (Powys Fadog), due to his attachment to the Fitzalans, lords of Oswestry and Clun, who, by obtaining the lordships of Chirk and Bromfield and Yale, secured an extensive part of Powys Fadog. *HC* omits.

216 **Madocke Vychan:** Correctly, Madog ap Gruffudd (d. 1277) whose *sons* Gruffudd and Llywelyn were given in wardship to Warenne and Mortimer and died in 1282.

218 **shippes of Bristowe:** all versions of *BT* give 'merchants of Haverford' as the captors; but that they were in fact sailors from Bristol is argued in *HW*, II, 757 n.211, and more recently in Smith, *Llywelyn ap Gruffudd*, 396 n.21. Llwyd's account of this whole affair follows closely that of Nicholas Trevet (*NT*, 294, as outlined by Smith, ibid.) and tends to confirm Llwyd's claim that Trevet was one of his main sources after 1270 when his own copy of the 'Britishe Cronicle' came to an end.

218v **upon thees conditiouns:** summaries of the terms of the treaty of Aberconwy given in English chronicles, including Trevet (*NT*, 297–8) on whose text Llwyd has depended, are noticed, along with the record sources, in Smith, *Llywelyn ap Gruffudd*, 438–45. For the treaty, J. G. Edwards, *Littere Wallie* (Cardiff, 1940), 118–22.

219v **without emprisoninge . . . determined:** from Trevet (*NT* 297), following the text of the treaty as in *Littere Wallie*, 121.

221 **Earl Warren . . . olde sword sayde:** the story of the Earl Warenne's bold declaration, from Guisborough, *Chronicle*, 216, is examined in D. W. Sutherland, *Quo Warranto Proceedings in the Reign of Edward I, 1278–1294* (Oxford, 1963), 82 n.2; M. T. Clanchy, *From Memory to Written Record: England 1066–1307* (London, 1979), 21–8. Contrary to Llwyd's intimation, the *quo warranto* proceedings were certainly not terminated by the declaration attributed to Warenne.

222 **Bonp y don:** it is easy to assume that this most unlikely-sounding name represents a copyist's error. This is possibly why *HC* revised it to 'Moel y don', a location, probably known to him, in Anglesey near to Bangor, and near also the traditional site of Agricola's crossing; cf. above, note ff. 7–7v. It is nevertheless worth noting that C agrees with Ll's rendering of the name and that *HW*, II, 762 n.235 queries Powel's

authority for his version: also that none of the English or Welsh chronicles gives the crossing-place a name. Much more recently Smith, *Llywelyn ap Gruffudd*, 538–42, questions *HC's* account and suggests that a crossing of the straits between Bangor and Llan-faes rather than Moel y Don would have been far more likely. As to Llwyd's form of the name, *Bon y Dom* occurs in *Historia Gruffud Vab Kenan* as the name of a castle in Anglesey. Thomas Pennant associates this with the location of Moel y Don ferry, referring to the account in *Historia Gruffudd vab Kenan* that the castle was called in olden times *Castell Aeloedd* (Avloed) *Frenin* and adding 'but by the country folk *Bon y Dom*'. Leland, *Itinerary in Wales*, 129, however, refers to '*Porth Bon* (finis) *y don* (. . . a waue)'. See *Historia Gruffud vab Kenan*, ed. D. S. Evans (Cardiff, 1977), 2.22n.; also *HW*, I, 8 n.18.

223 **Roger Mortymer:** both MSS agree on 'Roger' but *HC* has 'Edmund', and 'Edmund Mortymers men' later in the same sentence; Trevet has *Edmundus de Mortuo-mari* (*NT*, 305); and *Flores Historiarum*, ed. H. R. Luard (Rolls Series, 1890), 57, names Edmund in this context, but mistakenly for Roger. *HC* quotes both Trevet and 'Matthew Westminster' as his authorities. For a discussion of the respective roles of Edmund and Roger Mortimer, see Smith, *Llywelyn ap Gruffudd*, 551–2, 558–9, 564–6.

223 **And the Prince departed:** in C this marks the beginning of f. 217v, which bears a note, in a different, finer script along the length of the left-hand margin, in the upper half, in three vertical lines: *Spiritus Grono ap Ednyvet apparuit super mortem Principis et ita affatur*; in the lower half, in two vertical lines: 'Dowed i wyr Gwynedd galon galed, mae mifi yw Gronw gwir vab Ednyved. Pe biasswn byw gidam llyw nis lleddessid kyn howssed, dros vod gwaed ar frwydd ag orwydd mewn llydded'; f. 218 (inserted in MS with a blank verso) has this verse:

> Tell thou the men of Gwynedd rude
> harde harted and unpure
> That I am Gronoo, right sonne to
> Ednyvet Vychan sure.
> Yf my Carckas had life enioyed
> and with my Prince and Powre,
> his death shuld not so easily
> made hym thrugh force to cowre,
> Till Horse most wery might be sene
> And speare with Bloodd had coloured bene.

Part of the Welsh text, from NLW MS 872D, is given in Rhidian Griffiths, *1282: A Collection of Documents* (Aberystwyth, 1986), 25.

223 **his Esquier:** C 'his esquiers'. The English chroniclers differ: Guisborough, *Chronicle*, 220 *cum solo armigero*; *NT*, 305 *cum paucis*; but in the Hagnaby chronicle (BL Cotton Vespasian, Bxi, f. 28), after the battle, no one remained *nisi dominus Leulinus et armiger eius* (Smith, *Llywelyn ap Gruffudd*, 564). On the *BT* account 'with but a few men' see *Pen20Tr*, 120.36n.

223v **Pont Orewyn:** probably an English chronicler's attempt to render *Pont Irfon*, though it is strange that neither Llwyd nor Powel identified it as such. For a detailed account of the events surrounding the death of Llywelyn ap Gruffudd, and especially of the remarkable resemblance to Guisborough's account of the battle of Stirling Bridge, 1297, see Llinos Beverley Smith, 'The death of Llywelyn ap Gruffydd: the narratives reconsidered', *WHR* (1982–3), 200–13; Smith, *Llywelyn ap Gruffudd*, 550–67.

224 **Adam Franketon:** for Stephen de Frankton as a person possibly responsible for the prince's death, Llinos Smith, 'Death of Llywelyn ap Gruffydd', 202–3, 211–12 and the sources cited.

225v **crowne of Englande . . . daye:** C has a note in the left-hand margin in Dee's hand 'Here D Powel left of'. *HC* omits the preceding reference to the birth of King Edward's son and Llwyd's attack on Polydore Vergil but adds the line 'Thus endeth the Historie of the Brytish Princes' before continuing his own account as far as the reign of Elizabeth I. The first section up to the revolt of 1294–5 nevertheless incorporates Llwyd's account, though this is unacknowledged (see above, pp. 18–19).

225v **Lorde de Monte Camysii:** Trevet (*NT*, 315) is one of several chroniclers who record the death of Sir William de Monte Canisio (Montchensy, Munchanesy) for whom see Arnold Taylor, *Studies in Castles and Castle-Building* (London, 1985), 217–18. Both the continuation of the Welsh chronicle in *Pen20* and *BS* record the death at Dryslwyn of John Peulard (wrongly known as 'John Pennardd') whom Taylor identifies as John de Bevillard (ibid., 209–17). The absence of any reference to John Peulard indicates that Llwyd had not seen the continuation in the Peniarth 20 MS.

226 **Madocke sonne to Prince Lhewelyn:** *HC* 'being of the kindred of the last Lhywelyn'; *NT*, 333 *de genere Lewelini*; Guisborough, *Chronicle*, 251, *de sanguine principis Leulini*. There may have been a tradition to account for these identifications. This Madog was, in fact, the son of Llywelyn ap Maredudd, the last vassal lord of Meirionnydd, who was slain in battle in 1263, and was a fifth cousin to Llywelyn ap Gruffudd (see *Pen20Tr*, 122.7n.; *DWB*, 608; Smith, *Llywelyn ap Gruffudd*, 583).

226v **and at the last:** the deletion in C of *at* must represent a later attempt to make sense of the phrase after the copyist's omission of 'the last'.

227v **the hille called Kevyn Digolh, not farre from Caurs . . . :** Cefn Digoll, or Mynydd Digoll, a long ridge of high moorland to the east of Welshpool, in the lordship of Caus, referred to also as Hir Fynydd or Hir Fryn. Modern maps show it as Long Mountain. The name 'Cefn Digoll' occurs in medieval Welsh literature, notably in the prose tale *Breudwyt Ronabwy*, ed. M. Richards (Cardiff, 1948), 9, and in the poet Cynddelw's *englynion* to Owain Cyfeiliog (*Gwaith Cynddelw Brydydd Mawr*, ed. N. A. Jones and A. P. Owen, I (Cardiff, 1991), no. 17). See also Phillimore in *OP*, IV, 666; T. Pennant, *A Tour in Wales*, ed. J. Rhys, 3 vols (Caernarfon, 1883), iii, 196–7. For Cefn Digoll in relation to the defeat of Madog ap Llywelyn at Maes Moedog in Caereinion, for which Trevet is an important source, J. G. Edwards, 'The battle of Maes Madog and the Welsh campaign of 1294–5', *EHR*, 39 (1924), 1–12; idem, 'The site of the battle of "Meismeidoc", 1295', *EHR*, 46 (1931), 262–5; R. F. Walker, 'The Hagnaby chronicle and the battle of Maes Moydog', *WHR*, 8 (1976–7), 125–38. Llwyd refers earlier (f. 23v) to 'Carrs' (Caus) as one of several locations in the Marches where Welsh was spoken in his day. His map 'Cambriae typus' (1568) shows 'Cours' as being SE of Welshpool and immediately east of a small mountain range running N–S.

227v **to perpetuall prison:** thus in Trevet *s.a.* 1295, *NT*, 338: *Circa festum vero S. Laurentii, Madocus, qui se principem Walliae fecerat, captus et Londonias adductus, perpetuae custodiae mancipatur. Pen20Tr*, 'Madoc and his son were seized'; *BS*, 'Morgan and Madog . . . were hanged and quartered'. *HC* follows Llwyd but adds: 'There be some which affirme, that Madoc was not taken, but rather after manie aduentures and sundrie conflicts, when the Welshmen were brought into an issue of great extremitie, the said Madoc came in, and submitted himselfe to the king's peace, and was receiued upon condition, that he should pursue Morgan [ap Maredudd] till he had taken him and brought him to the king's prison: which was done . . .', terms of submission not authenticated in record evidence. Llwyd's statement that Madog endured 'perpetuall prison' is confirmed by references, including BL Add. MS 7965, f. 69, to his confinement in the Tower of London.

227v   **Finis:** in C f. 221 this is followed by a note in the hand of Sir Robert Cotton, 'At London 17 July 1559 by Humffrey Lloyd'; ff. 222–4 are blank; ff. 225–7 have various genealogical notes in which the name Llwyd occurs with some frequency; and f. 227, right-hand margin, 'This much was written out of the Brytishe bok wher the History of Humfrey lloid is in Welsh written'.

INDEX

INDEX 289

Wales, south (Southwales) 28–9, 31, 33, 67, 70, 72, 75, 76, 77–82, 84, 86, 92, 96, 97, 99, 100, 101, 102, 103, 104, 110, 111, 112, 113, 114, 117, 118, 121, 122, 123, 124, 125, 126, 127, 140, 141, 142, 150, 151, 153, 157, 158, 160, 161, 163, 164, 166, 168, 169, 170, 172, 176, 186, 187, 188, 189, 190, 192, 196, 209, 212, 213, 214, 217, 219, 221, 223; *see also* Deheubarth, Dinefwr

Wales, west (Westwales) 86, 87, 88, 102, 105, 114, 122, 127, 128–9, 134, 159, 165, 175, 200, 219; *see also* Dyfed

Walkelin Meminot (Walkelyn) 151

Walker, bishop of Durham, *see* Walcher

Wallace, John, *see* Walleys, John

Walleys, John 215

Wallingford (Wallingeforde) 106, 108, 153, 158

Walsingham, Thomas 56

Walter, bishop *recte* sheriff of Gloucester 135

Walter, son of Miles of Gloucester, earl of Hereford 159

Walter ap Llywarch, *see* Gwallter

Walter fitz Richard (Walter ap Rikart) 163

Walter Fychan ab Einion Clud, *see* Gwallter Fychan

Walter of Guisborough 45, 56–7, 58, 59

Waltheof (Waltelf), Earl 121, 122

Walwern, *see* Castell Dafolwern

Walwyn, Helyas 222

Walwyn's Castle, *see* Castell Gwalchmai

Waleys, Thomas le, bishop of St David's 210

Wake, Baldwin 215

Wake, Nicholas 215

Warebirith, *see* Weardbyrig

Warenne, Alys, countess 209

Warenne, Earl, *see* Warenne, William, Earl (d. 1148)

Warenne, Countess 164

Warenne, John 199

Warenne, John, Earl (d. 1304) 57, 209, 213, 215, 216, 217, 218, 220

Warenne, William, Earl *recte* John (d. 1304) 73

Warenne, William, Earl (d. 1148) 152, 164

Warenne, William, Earl (d. 1240) 197, 198, 202, 207

Warham (Warrham) 91, 139, 151

Warwick (Werigewic) 96

Warwick, Henry Beaumont, earl of (d. 1119) 142

Warwick, William, *recte* Thomas earl of (d. 1242) 202

Warwick, William Beauchamp, earl of (d. 1298) 59, 223–4

Warwickshire (Warnvycheshire) 88

Waterford 169

Watervill (Watervyle), Beringary 215

Watchet (Wered, Weshport) 96, 103

Watling Street (Watlyngstreete) 108

Waverley 172

Weald, the (Andredesleig) 93

Weauldyne, *see* Maldon

Weardbyrig (Warebirith) 96

Wearmouth (Wyrynindham) 84

Welsh (language; British, Cambraec) 2, 5–6, 7, 8, 15, 16, 25, 63, 64–5, 66, 67, 68, 69, 74, 75, 77, 78, 81, 82, 94, 99, 117

Welshe Mers, *see* Wales, March of

Welshpool (Poole) 73, 81, 138, 179, 211; *see also* Red Castle

Wendover, Roger of 35, 43–4, 46, 47, 51

Wered, *see* Watchet

Weregewic, *see* Warwick

Weshport, *see* Watchet

Wessex (West Sexe, Westsex) 37, 83, 84, 86, 87, 88, 91, 92, 98, 108, 109, 119

West Angles 87

West Saxons 87, 106, 108

Westchester 159

Westminster 57, 119, 120, 130, 177, 218

Whilar, river, *see* Chwiler

Whitam, *see* Witham

White Castle (Castell Gwyn, Whit Castell) 80, 195

Whitland (White House, Tŷ Gwyn) 156, 169, 175, 184

Whitney 82

Whittington 24, 73, 82, 216

Wight (Wighte, Wycht, Wyghte), Isle of 63, 88, 106, 115, 150, 218

Wiglaf (Wylaf), king of Mercia 87

Wigmore (Wygmor) 159, 216

Wild (Weilde) Merlin, *see* Merlin Silvestris

Wilfred, bishop of St David's 124

Wilfrid (Wilfride), St 85

William I, king of England (William Bastarde) 37, 46, 47, 65, 117, 119, 120, 121, 122, 124, 213

William II, king of England (William Rufus) 124, 125, 126, 127, 128–9, 130

William, count of Boulogne and Mortain, William, earl of Mortimer 159, 164